*Koestler*

*By the same author*

Scotland the Brave
Spectrum, *ed. with Ian Gilmour*
The Foster Gang, *with Henry John May*
Embarkation for Cythera
The Kerry Kyle

# *Koestler*

A BIOGRAPHY

Iain Hamilton

SECKER & WARBURG
LONDON

First published in England 1982 by
Martin Secker & Warburg Limited
54 Poland Street, London W1V 3DF



ISBN: 0-436-19101-6

Printed in Great Britain

*For Jean*

# *Contents*

## CONTENTS

# *Acknowledgements*

ACKNOWLEDGEMENTS AND THANKS are due to the following (or to their executors), who are not, of course, to be held responsible for any of the sins of omission and commission that may be found in the text:

Rolf Albonico, Julian Amery, Kingsley Amis, Martin D'Arcy, SJ, Raymond Aron, David Astor, Edward Atiyah, Aaron G. Auerbach, Sir Alfred Ayer, Angelica Balabanoff, Jacques Barzun, Marston Bates, Simone de Beauvoir, Menachem Begin, Daniel Bell, John Beloff, Ludwig von Bertalanffy, Benjamin S. Blum, Charles Bohlen, François Bondy, Philip Bonsal, Franz Borkenau, Elizabeth Bowen, Frank Bowles, Harvey Breit, George P. Brett, Irving Brown, Grete Buber-Neumann, E. E. Bullen, James Burnham, Frank Barron, Sir Cyril Burt, Sir Herbert Butterfield, Albert Camus, Charles Cape, Maurice Carr, Sir Peter Chalmers-Mitchell, Vernon I. Cheadlc, Norris B. Chipman, Schalom Ben-Chorin, Colin Clark, John Cohen, Jonathan Cole, Cyril Connolly, Robert Conquest, Patrick Cosgrave, Richard Crossman, Ely Culbertson, Preston S. Cutler, Lord Dacre, Saul David, Moishe Dayan, David S. Devor, Lovat Dickson, Jacques Doré, Stillman Drake, Tom Driberg, Peggy Duff, Sir Arthur Eddington, Ferol Egan, T. S. Eliot, Imogene E. Ellis, L. Elmhirst, D. J. Enright, A. S. Epstein, Alvin C. Eurich, Henry Fairlie, Duncan Fairn, Stanley Firman, Ruth Fischer, Jill Foot, Michael Foot, Peyton Ford, E. M. Forster, Viktor E. Frankl, Richard Friedenthal, Roland Grant, Lord Gardiner, Sir Ian Gilmour, Bt, David Golan, Victor Gollancz, A. L. Goodhart, Celia Goodman, Mark Graubard, John Grigg, J. P. Guilford, David Ben-Gurion, Hamish Hamilton, Esther Hammer, John Hampden, Harry Hansen, Sir Alister Hardy, Irving B. Harris, Anthony Hartley, Rhea Hartley, F. A. Hayek, Bruno Heilig, Louis Heren, C. R. Hewitt, Ernest R. Hilgard, Christopher Hollis, Henner Mueller-Holtz, Sidney Hook, Peter Howard, Langston Hughes, Sir Edward Hulton, Hubert H. Humphrey, Aldous Huxley, Sir Julian Huxley, James J. Jenkins, Roy Jenkins, C. E. M. Joad, R. D. Jones, Michael Josselson, Robert P. Joyce, Carl G. Jung, R. O. Kapp, E. Lowell Kelly, George F. Kennan, Arnold Kettle, H. B. D. Kettlewell, Seymour S. Kety, Pearl Kluger, G. F. Kneller, Arthur Koestler,

Cynthia Koestler, Teddy Kollek, Alexandre Koyré, Irving Kristol, Herbert Kupferberg, R. Clyde Larkin, Melvin J. Lasky, Gerald Leach, Timothy Leary, F. R. Leavis, Laurie Lee, P. Leoni, Saul Levitas, Charles M. Lichenstein, Jack Lindsay, Emanuel Litvinoff, Lord Longford, Konrad Lorenz, Sir Bernard Lovell, Jay Lovestone, Sir Robert Lusty, Malcolm MacDonald, Paul D. Maclean, H. W. Magoun, André Malraux, Thomas Mann, Oscar A. Mareni, Kingsley Martin, James B. McConnell, Sir Peter Medawar, Ved Mehta, Peter Mendelssohn, Karl E. Meyer, George Mikes, John A. Miles Jr, Robert Morris, Leonard Mosley, Raymond Mortimer, Malcolm Muggeridge, Raymond E. Murphy, Nicolas Nabokov, Richard M. Nixon, George Orwell, John Osborne, Wilder Penfield, H. A. Pestalozzi, A. D. Peters, Sir Arthur Peterson, Rodney Phillips, Sir George Pickering, Père Piprot, Michael Polanyi, Sir Karl Popper, Karl Pribram, J. B. Priestley, Jean Queval, Goronwy Rees, S. Reich, Robert Reinold, Joseph B. Rhine, Martin Richmond, Paul Roazen, Denis de Rougemont, Earl Russell, Esther Polianowsky Salaman, Giorgio de Santillana, William Sargant, Arthur J. Schlesinger Jr, G. Scholem, Cecil Scott, Moishe Sharret, Edward Shils, Lord Sieff, Ignazio Silone, Derek Sington, B. F. Skinner, D. W. Smithers, J. R. Smythies, Lord Snow, T. M. Sonneborn, Paul-Henri Spaak, Manès Sperber, Helene Steinemann, John Strachey, N. S. Sutherland, Julia Tardy-Marcus, Kenneth V. Thimann, J. M. Thoday, Hugh Thomas, James C. Thomson Jr, W. H. Thorpe, Baruch Tomaschoff, Stephen Toulmin, Philip Toynbee, C. Truesdell, Harry S. Truman, Donald Tyerman, José Verges, E. F. Vollenweider, John Wain, Mary Warnock, J. B. Watson, Paul Weiss, Alexander Weissberg-Cybulski, Chaim Weizmann, Dame Rebecca West, Jerome B. Wiesner, Renée Winegarten, L. Hollingsworth Wood, Michael Yudkin, and Christian Zevros;

and also to: *L'Action*, *Atlantic Monthly*, British Broadcasting Corporation, *Cambridge Review*, *Chicago Sun-Times*, *Chicago Tribune*, *Christian Science Monitor*, *Colliers Magazine*, *Combat*, *Commentary*, *Commonwealth Review*, *Country Life*, *Droit et Liberté*, *The Economist*, *Encounter*, *Evening Standard*, *Figaro Littéraire*, Hansard, *Hibberts Journal*, *Horizon*, *Hudson Review*, *The Humanist*, *L'Humanité*, *Illustrated London News*, *Jerusalem Post*, *Jewish Chronicle*, *Life*, *Manchester Guardian*, *National Review*, *La Nouvelle Critique*, *Neue Zürcher Zeitung*, *New Leader*, *New Republic*, *New Scientist*, *New Society*, *New Statesman and Nation*, *New York Herald Tribune*, *New York Review of Books*, *New York Sunday Times*, *New York Times*, *New York Times Book Review*, *New York Times Magazine*, *New York World Telegram*, *L'Observateur*, *Observer*, *Opera Mundi*, *Palestine Post*, *Partisan Review*, *Picture Post*, *San Francisco Chronicle*, *Saturday Review*, *The Spectator*, *The Statesman of Calcutta*, *Sunday Times*, *Time*, *Time and Tide*, *The Times*, *The Times Literary Supplement*, *The Times of India*, *Tribune*, *Die Welt*, and the *Yale Daily News*.

* *

Finally and less formally: the extraordinary variety of circumstances which conspired to delay the completion and publication of this book is now so much water under the bridge, but it would be impossible for me to fail to express my gratitude for the exemplary support of my publisher, Tom Rosenthal, the wisdom of my editors, David Farrer and Peter Grose, the efficiency of Alison Samuel and Eve Ford – and, above all, the forbearance of my wife, Jean Campbell Hamilton, who had to put up with more than the usual typing and retyping and photocopying in the face of abnormal stress and strain.

# *Preface*

I WAS PLEASED BY the suggestion that I might write a biography of Arthur Koestler. For many years I had admired his work (the greater part of it, at any rate) and welcomed its considerable influence both on political thought and on the intelligent layman's understanding of the history and philosophy of science.

Our paths had crossed many times over a period of twenty-five years, but we had met only twice – once at a luncheon party to celebrate his move to the publishing house of which I was then Editorial Director, and some years later, after the publication of *The Ghost in the Machine* (which I had reviewed), at a cocktail party. The latter was a typical enough London literary occasion. The rooms of the large apartment in which it was held boomed with the clash of competing egos and crackled with malicious gossip. Authors and critics, academics, editors and publishers were busy promoting themselves in the usual fashion. But even here, islanded somehow in the stupendous din, the conversation of this rather short and oddly diffident, and typical (as he is accustomed to describe himself) 'Central-European member of the educated middle classes' had the stimulating quality of the best of his writing. Every now and then his expression, normally reserved to the point of severity, would lighten, and he would permit himself a smile. That smile, with something perhaps of mischief in it, immediately wiped twenty or thirty years off his age. He seemed to move about the crowded rooms as if in an envelope of calm. It was an odd illusion, generated (I conjectured) by his powerful but strangely enigmatic personality.

Koestler the man certainly impressed me, and intrigued me, no less than his books had done. That was all very well; but how could one write a biography – meaning by this something of more substance and depth than a magazine 'profile', however extended – of someone very much alive and as active as ever, if not more so? Given the subject's cooperation, I was assured, it might be possible; and Koestler apparently was willing to cooperate. But what form would our cooperation take? I had many misgivings. These arose not at all from any preconceptions of Koestler's attitude, or his estimate of himself and his achievements, but rather from the experience, gained during my own time as a publisher, of 'biographies' of live celebrities which for the most part amounted to little more than exercises in public relations at worst or weekend journalism at best. No harm in that, of course, when the subject is a footballer, an actress, a superannuated politician, a retired financier, or something of the sort. But I knew that I had neither the wish nor indeed the competence to do a hagiographical PR job on Koestler. I knew very well that this was not what my publisher had in mind. And it would have surprised me greatly if this was what Koestler wanted.

In short, I came to the conclusion after a few days of brooding that I could take on this job only if I had adequate and original source material – and a (more or less) free hand. I could not see Koestler agreeing to this.

But here I was mistaken. Not long after the idea had been put up to me, Koestler gave me luncheon. It was an excellent luncheon, and so was the conversation, which ranged far and wide over politics, history, literature, philosophy – and entertaining gossip about friends and acquaintances we had in common. It was quite clear to me that Koestler – most courteously, of course – was sounding me out, sizing me up, reassuring himself about my suitability. In the end he said that I could indeed have the 'free hand' which I required. I could feel free to write about him, he suggested with a smile, as if he were already dead. That, of course, was an impossibility. Koestler himself might have looked with equanimity on my 'pre-empting of *The Times*' obituary' (his jocular phrase), but a great many others involved in the story would undoubtedly have taken exception. Still, it was a generous and encouraging gesture.

More seriously, he agreed to give me access to some of his papers (not *all*, of course, but more than enough for my purpose) and also to subject himself to some tape-recording sessions (a form of interviewing which he dislikes intensely, but which in the event he and I endured cheerfully).

I am indebted to him for his generosity.

The documentation which Koestler made available to me was supplemented unexpectedly almost a year after that meeting by the invaluable collection of letters written by his second wife, Mamaine Paget, to her twin sister, Celia, between 1944 and 1954, a crucial and in some ways traumatic decade in Koestler's life. Mamaine was devoted to Koestler (as he, in a different manner, to her), and although they were to part after ten years of life together, they remained close friends until her untimely death (which was probably the severest of the many blows he has had to endure). Mamaine seems to have been a highly intelligent, cultivated (and attractive) woman of great sensibility, deeply interested in all aspects of Koestler's multifarious activities, and always ready to subordinate her own interests to those of her husband. Her letters to her twin, dashed off at speed, throw an affectionate and revealing (though occasionally far from rosy) light upon her admired and difficult husband during the hectic years when the pressures on him sometimes brought him close to a breakdown.

I am indebted to Celia Goodman not only for making those letters available to me but also for her generous help in annotating and glossing them, and for correcting the occasional howler in early drafts.

This account of Koestler's life and work makes no pretence, of course, of being a 'definitive' biography. In so far as it is possible (and that is not very far) to encompass definitively the life of even the simplest of human beings – and Koestler is anything but simple – between the covers of a book, that is something that can only be attempted some years after death has drawn its definitive line. So much is obvious. What may not be quite so obvious, however – and this is something that both Koestler and I are in agreement in wishing to emphasise strongly – is that this book is in no sense an 'official' or an 'approved' biography. In all my dealings with Koestler he consistently and scrupulously refrained not only from any attempt to influence my opinions and critical comments on his character and work, but also from discussing those private aspects of his life incorporated in my narrative.

And so the book reflects my personal opinion of the man and his achievements, not Koestler's estimate of himself (whatever that might be).

A final and important point. The book is mainly, though not by any means exclusively, concerned with the middle years of Koestler's life and work – from 1940, that is, to 1970. This period of thirty years divides itself neatly into two equal parts. The first comprises the political years when *Darkness at Noon* and *The Yogi and the Commissar* were of incalculable value in the enlightenment of intellectuals in North America, Western Europe, and beyond, bemused by the Soviet myth and the Allies' wartime propagation of Stalin as kindly, pipe-smoking Uncle Joe – a truly herculean task which Koestler worked at tirelessly until, as he wrote in 1955, '. . . Cassandra has gone hoarse, and is due for a vocational change'. He had for many years, in fact, wished to return to his earlier, scientific, interests. In that year he resolved to do so. And so the second part of the period on which I concentrate saw the publication of *The Sleepwalkers*, *The Act of Creation*, *The Ghost in the Machine* (a trilogy in which he explored in depth and developed in copious detail various themes which he had sketched, not altogether satisfactorily, in the earlier *Insight and Outlook*), and *Beyond Reductionism: New Perspectives in the Life Sciences*, the edited transcript of an interdisciplinary symposium which he had organised.

For me, at least, the works of those thirty years are his lasting achievement, the novels and political writings and activities on the one hand, and the scientific works on the other, being the obverse and reverse of the same coin.

The first thirty-five years of his life I have sketched briefly, because he has covered them himself in the four autobiographical works,* on which I have drawn heavily. Hardly any other documentation exists for that period in his life; most of his papers were lost during the collapse of France in 1940; and the few communications I have received from those who knew him before World War II are of little interest.

From 1970 onwards Koestler's work showed an inclination towards certain preoccupations – with, for example, extra-sensory perception, psychopharmacology, parapsychology and a kind of mysticism – which happen to be of little interest to me. In *Janus: A Summing-Up*, Koestler returned to a hypothesis which he first advanced in *The Ghost in the Machine*. Drawing largely upon the researches and conclusions of the distinguished neurophysiologist, Dr Paul

* *Scum of the Earth*, *Dialogue with Death*, *Arrow in the Blue* and *The Invisible Writing*.

Maclean, at the National Institute of Mental Health, Bethesda, Maryland, he suggested that Man is neither the more or less satisfactory end-product of the Darwinian evolutionary process of random mutations reinforced by natural selection nor a Special Creation by 'God or whatever means The Good', but rather an appalling and disastrous aberration, a biological freak, an accident.

In a review of *Janus* I described Koestler's diagnosis of our condition and the remedy he prescribes:

> '... the huge neo-cortex of the human brain, the reasoning part of which can physically be likened to an infinitely complex computer, is imperfectly co-ordinated with the two other parts which we have inherited from primitive mammals and still more primitive reptiles. From this flaw in this biological freak, appearing suddenly on the scene (for the "missing link" is still missing), comes man's aggressiveness, unique in the animal creation, and the fearsome predicament of humanity which is now intensifying at an exponential rate thanks to the recent advances in science and technology. The reader will find this summed up in *Janus*. He will also find the remedy proposed by Koestler in *The Ghost in the Machine*. Since a biological malfunction needs a biological corrective, the remedy must obviously be found in the biological laboratories in the form of some substance which will reconcile our matchless reasoning powers with our primitive instincts ... I think that he is wrong in this – and I think also that in suggesting such a "remedy" he is acting against his own true nature. What is missing here (although not in essence from all the most moving parts of his work) is God ... My reading of Koestler's works has convinced me that he is *au fond* a deeply religious man. He has never admitted this, confessing only to several experiences of the quasi-mystical Freudian "oceanic" feeling ...'

Right or wrong, that is my opinion, and I regard his later excursions into synchronicity, ESP, and other paranormal hypotheses as the consequence of his (as I see it) refusal to come to terms with that part of his nature which I discern in the best of his works. There is an interesting passage in his present wife Cynthia's frank contribution to *Astride the Two Cultures**, the *Festschrift* celebrating her husband's seventieth birthday:

> 'During the time of Pope John, Arthur was attracted to Roman Catholicism. I remember one evening his brother-in-law, Arthur Goodman, who was a Catholic, expressing doubts about his religion. Arthur made such a moving dissertation about the beauty of symbolism in the Catholic faith that his brother-in-law, whose doubts were real, was quite overwhelmed. Arthur was equally vehement about not taking that symbolism literally.
>
> 'On the other hand, as he says, with his head in the clouds, he likes to keep his feet planted firmly on the ground. Mysticism *per se* is not enough for him; indeed it disgusts him ...'

Be that as it may, my (no doubt unfortunate) lack of interest in the so-called 'Psi-factor' in such alleged paranormal phenomena as psychokinesis and the

* Ed. Harold Harris, London, Hutchinson, 1975.

like, effectively disqualifies me from dealing in detail with his later works. Even if I had the competence to find my way through those murky and tangled thickets, I should refrain from doing so. As I write in my final chapter: '. . . I hope that I may be forgiven if the last part of my biographical account is offered in summary form. That there is a book to be written about Koestler's researches and speculations in this field I have no doubt. But I am not the man to write it: and I say this not merely because of my prejudices (and ignorance, too, I suppose), but also because of my respect for and admiration of this "representative European intellectual's" achievements in those other fields in which I am rather more at home.'

# PART ONE

# *1905–1940*

# CHAPTER I

# *1905–1926*

ARTHUR KOESTLER WAS BORN in Budapest on 5th September 1905. His mother stemmed from one of the old Jewish families of Prague, proud of their descent from eminent rabbinical scholars but long assimilated entirely to Germanic culture and, by the end of the nineteenth century, people of some social standing in imperial Vienna. For her, as for many others like her in the lands of the easy-going Hapsburg Empire, Judaism was a matter of no great consequence: a complex of traditions to be honoured nominally, of course, but one which set her apart in no discomfiting way from those of the family's wide circle of friends in the city who did not happen to be Jewish. She was an attractive and much sought-after young woman.

Life changed abruptly for her, however, when her father, financially ruined and disgraced, was packed off by the family to America, never to be seen again. She left her beloved Vienna to live with her married sister in Budapest. There, at the age of twenty-seven, she married Henrik Koestler, a successful business-man, two years her senior, who had begun his career as a draper's errand-boy at the age of fourteen. By the time he married, at twenty-nine, Henrik had travelled throughout Germany and England, established business contacts with manufacturers in those countries, and opened a firm of his own. Eight years later their son, Arthur, was born into comfortable bourgeois circumstances.

Koestler's earliest memories group themselves around three dominant themes: guilt, fear, and loneliness. Between the ages of three and twelve he was given into the charge of a long succession of German, French, and English governesses, all of whom he recalls with distaste. Worse still was the parlourmaid Bertha, a bony, horse-faced woman with an inexplicable grudge against life. She was devoted to Mrs Koestler, but she tyrannised Arthur. And so Koestler's reminiscences of childhood are almost invariably unhappy. Some of them – like his memory of a tonsillectomy performed without anaesthesia – are charged with terror. Worst of all was a succession of lurid and harrowing scenes between his parents who, for a considerable period, were all but entirely estranged.

While the conflict between Koestler's parents was at its height, the First

World War broke out, ruining his father's business. The family left the spacious apartment in Budapest and moved to a boarding-house in Vienna. From then on they never had a permanent home, moving between the two cities and staying in a succession of furnished lodgings.

No doubt the boy's loneliness and unhappiness had accelerated his intellectual, while retarding his emotional, development. He learnt avidly, read greedily, developed an early passion for mathematics, physics, and the construction of mechanical toys. In his early teens he was fluent in German, French and English, as well as Hungarian. His elementary education over, he decided that he wished to study physics and engineering. His parents agreed and so he had his secondary education in a *Realschule*, that is, one which specialised in science and modern languages as opposed to the *Gymnasium*, which prepared for a career in the Humanities, with emphasis on Latin and Greek.

The heroes of his boyhood were Darwin and Spencer; Kepler, Newton and Mach; Edison, Hertz and Marconi. But, obsessed by the mysteries of infinity and eternity, he was profoundly unsatisfied with the materialistic attitude which in those days still informed the teaching of science.

The last two years of his secondary education Koestler received at a small boarding school in Baden, near Vienna. He was unpopular with his fellow-seniors and suffered accordingly (although he had the consolation of being initiated into the delights of sexual experience by a generous maid, Matthilda).

In his 'Portrait of the Author at Sixteen' Koestler paints himself newly emerged from a tormented childhood as an exasperating and pathetic figure – very short, slim, his hair plastered down with water and brilliantine, and with a constant smirk on his rather handsome, though infantile, face which looked impudent but in fact masked boundless timidity and insecurity.

> 'The conviction that whatever I did was wrong, a pain to others and a disgrace to myself, had laid a permanent foundation of anxiety and guilt . . . In addition, there was a circumstance which for some time tortured me more than anything else at sixteen. I was the shortest boy but one in the class, and that one happened to be a dwarf . . . I refused to go to dancing classes for fear that I would be forced to dance with taller partners . . . The examples of Napoleon, Beethoven and other undersized great men comforted me, but not much. Nor did they serve as a warning against the short man's traditional vanity, aggressiveness, and lust for power . . . Such, then, was the anatomy of the accursed shyness which I carried throughout my youth as a leper carries his bell . . . and most of the time I felt that I was living in a portable prison of my own devising, surrounded by cold stares of bewilderment and rejection.'

* *

It was thanks to the advice of his mother's respectable and trustworthy friend, Herr Finanzrat Dr Benedikt, who had urged her that her son, on entering his university career, should apply for membership of the 'Unitas' fraternity, that Koestler found an escape-route from the torments that had plagued him during his lonely childhood and awkward adolescence.

What Dr Benedikt had omitted to tell Mrs Koestler was that 'Unitas' was one of twelve Zionist duelling fraternities in the University of Vienna – one of the Jewish *Burschenschaften* or student Korps, modelled more or less on the pre-Napoleonic *Landsmannschaften* of the German states – in which those who were (or were considered by their Christian compatriots to be) Jewish could prove themselves the equal of 'pure' Aryans in sabre-fencing, ritual drinking, roaring the medieval student-songs of Germany, wenching and brawling. Whether Benedikt refrained deliberately, or simply because he was in a hurry to get away, one can only guess. Had he explained this, it would have come as a surprise; for young Koestler had never heard of Zionism. For that matter, neither he nor his parents had had any personal experience of anti-semitism. Yet Mrs Koestler was a native of the city which was then, and had been for many years, the headquarters of the political Zionist movement and in which, among German-Austrians especially, anti-semitism was already becoming virulent; while her husband was a native of the city, Budapest, in which the movement's founder, Theodor Herzl, had himself been born. This gives some indication of the extent to which Koestler's parents had been assimilated to the German, and also in his father's case, the Hungarian cultural tradition. Neither had the slightest vestige of the ghetto mentality.

Koestler was stimulated and excited by the strange surroundings and rituals, but above all by the experience, quite new to him, of being accepted into a friendly and fraternal community.

Hahn, the fencing master, asked him what he thought of Zionism.

> 'I answered truthfully that I had never thought about it and hardly knew what the word meant. It meant in substance . . . that the Jews had been persecuted during some twenty centuries and that there was no reason to expect they would not be persecuted in the twenty-first. To argue with anti-semites was all the more hopeless as the Jews were in fact a sick race. They were a nation without a country, which was like being a man without a shadow; and they were socially top-heavy, with a disproportionately great number of lawyers, merchants, intellectuals, and with no farmers or peasants – which was like a pyramid standing on its top. The only cure was: return to the earth. If Jews wanted to be like other people, they must have a country like other people . . .'

So, painlessly and promptly, Koestler was converted to Zionism.

Two years after joining 'Unitas', Koestler had become its president and also chairman of the convention of all twelve Zionist *Burschenschaften* in Austria, at the age of nineteen, the youngest ever to have occupied that position in the thirty years of their existence. He had good reason to be pleased with himself. But very soon many questions forced themselves into his mind and dispelled his complacent self-satisfaction.

On a fine morning in the spring of 1924, sitting on a bench in the *Volksgarten* with a pile of books beside him, Koestler became vividly aware for the first time of his deeply divided personality. He opened a pamphlet which described the latest Arab riots in Jerusalem. He read of children being put to the sword as in the days of Herod, of Jewish pioneers being killed after having been blinded and castrated, of the refusal of the British mandatory administration to allow the Jews to arm in self-defence. As he read, a wave of moral indignation rose within him and he felt himself seethe and choke with impotent anger.

When the wave of fury had subsided he picked up the next book in the pile beside him – an introduction to Albert Einstein's theory of relativity.

> 'A phrase suddenly struck me and has remained in my memory ever since. It said that the theory of General Relativity led the human imagination "across the peaks of glaciers never before explored by any human being". This cliché had an unexpectedly strong effect. I saw Einstein's world-shaking formula – Energy equals Mass multiplied by the square of the velocity of light – hovering in a kind of rarefied haze over the glaciers, and this image carried a sensation of infinite tranquillity and peace. The martyred infants and castrated pioneers of the Holy Land shrank to microscopic insignificance . . . This change in perspective was accompanied by an equally pronounced physiological change. The sensation of choking with indignation was succeeded by the relaxed quietude and self-dissolving stillness of the "oceanic feeling".'

From that moment and for a long time to come Koestler was to experience the disturbing alternation of those mutually exclusive states of mind: stumbling, as he puts it, 'along my zig-zag path, pulled in opposite directions by political fanaticism and contemplative detachment . . .'

In 1924, however, Koestler was in no mood of philosophical resignation; and although he was frequently, especially at critical moments in his life, to experience the 'oceanic feeling', it was to action rather than contemplation that he then felt himself called. The Zionist activities into which his membership of 'Unitas' had plunged him had first made him conscious of his 'Jewishness' and then led him to reject it. Judaism did not attract him, having been brought up in a completely assimilated environment. Through the Zionist movement, he had come for the first time into contact with Polish and Russian Jews who had been brought up in the Talmudic schools and whose *lingua materna* was Yiddish. He disliked this mediaeval language from the first moment he heard it. He was no less repelled by the ghetto mentality which it reflected. The more he found out about Judaism the more distressed he became – and the more fervently Zionist. The Jewish State was the only cure for a sickness which he could not name or define . . . When the Jewish State was established, the cure would be automatic and all would be well.

But the cautious policy of official Zionism depressed him, consisting as it did mainly in appeals for money for the Jewish National Fund, the Jewish Reconstruction Fund, the Hadassah Hospital, the Hebrew University, the Bezalel Art School – and money for the salaries of the multitude engaged in the collecting of money.

New inspiration came with the emergence of Vladimir Jabotinsky, the flamboyant writer and activist from Odessa. Jabotinsky's aim when he founded his own movement the 'Zionist Activists' in 1924 (later called the 'League of Activists'), was to bypass the official Zionist bureaucracy in Vienna and concentrate on the *Burschenschaften* which, in the shrewd opinion of his advisers, were a reservoir of youthful energy frustrated by the dreary fund-raising tasks imposed on them.

Koestler and three of his companions founded the Austrian branch and drew up a detailed programme which embodied Jabotinsky's convictions that the aim of Zionism should be the speedy creation of a Jewish majority in Palestine; mass immigration to be facilitated by an international loan; and the establishment of a Jewish state, industrialised and armed, on both sides of the Jordan.

In 1924, when Zionism as a world-force was weak and the Arab birth-rate in Palestine far exceeded the annual immigration of Jews, such an aggressive policy must have seemed wildly irresponsible and unrealistic to the leaders of the official movement and its bureaucracy. There was no foretelling then, of course, the terrible events which were to lead, after Jabotinsky's death, to the acceptance of his militant triumphalism and so, by the harsh logic of events, to Israeli expansionism.

In his inaugural speech to the Knesset in June 1977, Menachem Begin quoted Jabotinsky's saying that 'The people of Israel and the land of Israel are one', and added for good measure a defiant declaration that:

> 'the Jewish people has an historic, eternal, and inalienable right to the land of Israel, the land of our forefathers.'

That was precisely what the young Koestler believed in 1924, as a militant Revisionist. Years later, during the terrorist campaign against the British mandatory power led by Menachem Begin and the Irgun Zvai Leumi in clandestine association with the official militia, Haganah (and later still, during the first Arab-Israeli war), he was to revise radically his Revisionist opinions, and then to reject the romantic extremism of Jabotinsky.

But,

> 'In 1924, when I became involved in Zionist politics, everything seemed simple and clear; we, the opposition, were in the right and the others were in the wrong.'

Although Zionism had rescued Koestler from the lonely torments of adolescent introspection he was not without other troubles. He rapidly became bored by the technicalities of steam-boilers, electric generators, steel processing, and the like. After his third semester he rarely went to lectures, scraping through examinations by shutting himself up for a week or so beforehand and cramming night and day. While his evenings were spent in political activity (and the associated pleasures of *Wein, Weib und Gesang*), he spent his days in a remote corner of the University library absorbing the psychological theories of Freud (and the schismatic schools of Adler, Jung, and Steckel) and at the same time attempting to keep abreast of the revolutionary developments in theoretical physics – studies wholly unrelated to his technological curriculum.

In the late autumn of 1925 Koestler's father, during a lean period, pulled himself together and found enough money for a trip to England, where he hoped to re-establish contact with English textile manufacturers. He took his wife with him for moral support, and their son was left by himself in the shabbily respectable boarding-house which had been their home for the past three years.

Not long after his parents' departure, Koestler solved one of his problems by completely abandoning his studies.

> 'One night in October I came home late after a long discussion on free will and determinism with a Russian student named Orochov. He had stubbornly defended the determinist position, while I maintained that, within certain limits, man has freedom of decision and ultimate mastery of his fate. We had drunk no alcohol, only pints of weak tea, but I went away feeling drunk and elated . . . I got home, and in a state of manic exaltation, lit a match and slowly burnt my Matriculation Book. This document, in Austria called *Index*, was the student's sacred passport . . . The burning of my *Index* was a literal burning of my bridges and the end of my prospective career as a respectable citizen . . .'

The euphoria which followed this drastic decision was very soon dispelled by the onset of guilt and remorse. So intense was this pressure of guilt that for months he could not bring himself to get out of bed until the middle of the afternoon.

His parents, who were still in England, knew nothing of this, and Koestler exacerbated his feeling of guilt by writing lying letters to sustain them in the belief that in a few months' time he would be earning a salary and supporting them. He had no plans except 'to lead his own life', whatever that was to be. He had no idea of becoming a writer: the few poems and stories he had written were bad and he knew it. And although he took Zionist politics seriously, the thought of emigrating to Palestine did not enter his head during the early phase of his psychological crisis.

The track that a man's life followed, his friend Orochov maintained, was wholly determined by outside forces. One was born on to a certain track, as a train is put on its run according to the timetable, and, once on the track, free will had gone. If one accepted that condition, Koestler told his friends who were attempting to argue him back to reason and routine, running on rails became a habit one could no longer break. The answer was to jump off the track before the habit was formed. His prudent friends were unimpressed by the arguments Koestler used to justify his existentialist protest against rationalism, his leap into the darkness of absolute uncertainty, his deliberate self-derailment – the more so because he made no attempt to explain to them the quasi-mystical experience which had prompted it. They said that to throw away a safe profession at the last minute was to act like a complete fool.

To which Koestler's reply was that he *wanted* to act like a fool.

As the weeks went past, however, and the initial flash of illumination faded away, the need to escape from the limbo of inaction and the burden of remorse and guilt became pressing and the idea of emigrating to Palestine as a '*Khaluts*' or pioneer – that is, an agricultural worker without capital – gradually took shape. It was not easy to put into practice. Most of the immigration certificates for '*Khalutism*' were distributed by the Zionist Organisation to left-wing Socialist groups. The newly founded Revisionist Party had as yet received no certificates. But after a crash-course in Hebrew and some wire-pulling, he was put on the waiting-list by the head of the Organisation's office in Vienna, and in the middle of March 1926 his certificate arrived.

He wrote a lengthy prevaricating letter to his parents, declaring that he was going to spend a year in Palestine as an assistant engineer. Such practical experience, he explained, would make it easier for him to get a good job in Austria. In fact he was bound for a collective settlement, *Kvutsa Heftsebā* – *Kvutsa*, signifying 'settlement', is more or less synonymous with the now more usual *Kibbutz* – in the Valley of Yesreel, now the most fertile plain in Israel but in 1926 still for the most part stony desert, infested with malaria, typhus and marauding Bedouin tribesmen. He knew nothing of agriculture. His motivation owed nothing to Judaism or Socialism. He was escaping. That was enough.

On 1st April the entire *Burschenschaft* turned out in ceremonial order and sang the Zionist Anthem on the platform as the train carried Koestler off into uncertainty.

# CHAPTER II

# *1926–1929*

THE ORIENTAL ATMOSPHERE OF Haifa, where he spent a day or two with the leader of the local branch of the Revisionist Party, Dr Abram Weinshall, before leaving for the settlement, stimulated Koestler's romantic imagination.

The harsh reality of Heftsebā, a rather dismal and slumlike oasis in the wilderness, consisting of wooden huts, surrounded by dreary vegetable plots, was another matter.

Nor did he receive the welcome he must have expected. The pioneers were at their evening meal when he arrived – all exhausted, eating their bread and soup in silence. A plateful of soup was passed down to him, but no one asked him who he was or what he wanted.

Eventually he explained that he had come with the intention of joining the settlement for a year or two, after which he would find a job in Tel Aviv or go into politics. This was not well received. The pioneers of Heftsebā – almost all of them former lawyers, architects and academics from Vienna and Prague – had dedicated their lives to hard labour and an extreme form of primitive communism. Koestler's attitude struck them as frivolous. His membership of the Revisionist Party also told against him, for those idealistic socialists regarded Jabotinsky as a militaristic Fascist.

On his very first evening, Koestler had been weighed in the balance and found wanting. Out of kindness, however, he was not turned away at once, but told that he could stay on probation. Five weeks after he arrived he was told that the Members' Assembly had decided that he was not well equipped for *Kvutsa* life.

A succession of ill-paid jobs in Haifa followed – when he was often on the verge of starvation – until by chance he ran into Dr von Weisl, a companion of 'Unitas' days, now Middle East correspondent of the Ullstein newspapers. The encounter led indirectly to his being sent to Berlin, on the initiative of Jabotinsky, to run the newly established headquarters of the international Revisionist movement.

The four months Koestler spent in Berlin with the grandiloquent title of

World Executive Secretary of the Revisionist Party were among the dreariest he remembers. His work consisted in explaining the decisions of the central committee to the various branches, answering their queries, and spurring them to greater activity. It was a dull business and the pay was meagre. Surviving on next to nothing in Palestine involved a good deal of discomfort, but at least it had been an adventure. Drudging as an office worker in Berlin on a hundred marks a month was not. His furnished room near the Alexander Platz cost him sixty marks a month. That left him with just over one mark a day, enough for a hot meal.

Once again, in September 1927, just before his twenty-second birthday, Weisl came to his rescue. Weisl's employers, the powerful Ullstein group of newspapers, were sending him to the Far East on an assignment that seemed likely to keep him away from Jerusalem for at least a year. A temporary replacement had to be found. He suggested Koestler. Here at last was the chance of starting on a stable professional career.

The House of Ullstein published four daily newspapers in Berlin alone as well as a dozen weekly and monthly periodicals, and its news service had subscribers all across Europe from Scandinavia to the Balkans. In the twenties it exercised real political influence and was regarded as the embodiment of everything progressive and cosmopolitan in the Weimar Republic. For every staff vacancy there were many well qualified candidates; and it must have seemed unlikely, even to the kindly Weisl, that Koestler would be appointed. But the unlikely happened; and at the end of September, almost exactly two years after the burning of his Matriculation Book (and his bridges), Koestler arrived in Jerusalem as the Middle Eastern correspondent of the House of Ullstein. He had already picked up the basic tricks of the trade from Weisl and found little difficulty in churning out the wordy political articles and *feuilletons* expected of him. His employers were pleased and soon raised his monthly retainer from two hundred marks to seven hundred, on top of which he earned another three hundred or so from his articles. Although he now had to provide for his parents (living in a furnished room in Budapest, his father's English expedition having come to nothing), he was able to lead a comfortable existence.

His social position, however, was awkward, although he had the formidable name of Ullstein behind him. As a member of the Revisionist opposition he was boycotted by the Zionist bureaucracy and ostracised by 'official' Jewish society. As a Zionist, he was barred from social contact with the Arabs. And, of course, he was ineligible for membership of the British clubs.

Not that this worried him greatly. Much of his time was spent in travels throughout the Middle East, from Cairo to Baghdad, collecting material for his articles. For almost two years he wrote on an average three long pieces a week for the newspapers and magazines owned or serviced by the Ullsteins. In addition to covering and commenting on political developments in the area he wrote innumerable light articles in a whimsical vein about anything that occurred to him – the brothels of Beirut, Bedouin costumes, the Queen of Sheba, the Hebrew theatre.

His youthful appearance sometimes introduced an element of farce into more serious occasions. Not long after he had settled down to the job, he was sent to Iraq to cover one of the recurrent government crises. On his arrival in Baghdad he applied for an interview with King Feisal, the friend of T. E. Lawrence and hero of the Arab revolt.

> 'I was received by Tahsin Bey, the King's adjutant, in a resplendent white uniform; he had been advised of my arrival which, as befitting the representative of the biggest Continental newspaper chain, had also been announced in the local press. Tahsin Bey received me kindly; but whenever I broached the subject of politics, or the audience with His Majesty, he side-tracked the conversation and with a friendly smile inquired what young boys were taught in European schools. After the ritual number of cups of sweet and bitter coffee, and a painfully dragging conversation, he rose and concluded the talk with the question:
>
> "And when can we now expect the visit of your papa?"
>
> 'He obviously thought that the representative of Ullstein's must be a middle-aged worthy who had sent his son ahead on a courtesy visit. For once, however, I proved equal to the occasion by declaring with a courteous bow:
>
> '"Mon père, c'est moi."'

An inauspicious beginning. The King, a sad figure by this time, received the strange young man who was his own father and spoke freely about the disunity of the Arab world.

In spite of such experiences Koestler grew bored. By the early summer of 1929 he had had more than enough of the Middle East, and especially of Jerusalem.

In June he went to Berlin on leave, determined not to return to Jerusalem. Dr Magnus, Ullstein's director of personnel, listened to him sympathetically and sent him to Paris to fill a vacancy in the bureau of the Ullstein News Service.

## CHAPTER III

# *1929–1932*

UNDER THE SPELL OF Jabotinsky, Koestler had hoped, and failed, to find fulfilment in his work for the most intransigent wing of the Zionist movement. The realities of Palestine had ground away the edge of his political idealism and now, in his disillusionment, he put Zionism behind him to start a new chapter in his life. The dilemma between action and contemplation which had plagued him in Vienna was (he mistakenly thought) resolved.

In the period of intellectual stagnation that lay ahead he was indeed to find success as a journalist and as a lover of women – and to find fulfilment in neither. He was still, in short, at the age of twenty-four, a green romantic, an emotional adolescent. He was nearly as unbalanced, naïve, unsure of himself and ready to fly off at a tangent as he had been at sixteen.

In Palestinc, Koestler had been his own master for the most part, finding his own subjects and writing about them as he pleased, and under no obligation to keep office hours. Life in Paris was very different. The bureau chief, Dr Leo Stahl, a strait-laced Bavarian Jew who had won the Iron Cross in the trenches, was a strict disciplinarian, and the atmosphere in the Ullstein office – an apartment in the elegant Madeleine district – was more like that of a boys' school or a military barracks than of a newspaper office.

The regular staff consisted of Stahl, his two assistants, Koestler and an easy-going Saarlander named Brix, and a vivacious young secretary, Bébé, the daughter of an Austrian army officer. When he presented himself at the office on his first day, Koestler was welcomed by an inscription on the flowery wallpaper behind Bébé's desk:

> 'Today arrives the prodigy from the Wailing Wall, now all will be well.'

He quickly returned the compliment by falling in love with Bébé and getting into her bed. It was good while it lasted, which was not for long. Still,

> 'My happiest memories of Paris are the few months when we lived, loved, and laughed together.'

But even if Koestler had been emotionally much more mature than in fact he was, it is unlikely that his work would have allowed him to develop a lasting relationship with Bébé or any other woman. During his fourteen months with the Ullstein bureau in Paris, his nose was kept hard up against the grindstone of office routine.

He was rescued by the revival of his interest in scientific developments. It was in this, rather than in politics or the endless pursuit of the ideal woman, that his intense romanticism found its most satisfying expression.

When the Prince de Broglie was awarded the Nobel Prize for Physics in 1929 for his work on the nature of light, Koestler called on him before he himself received the official news of the award.

> 'He was as happy as a schoolboy, made no effort to conceal it . . . One or two journalists had already telephoned and asked him idiotic questions about sun-spots and death-rays, so he was much relieved to discover that I had been a student of science and took a passionate interest in physics. We talked for about three or four hours . . .'

His article appeared a few days later in the *Vossische Zeitung.* Dr Franz Ullstein, the senior partner in the firm, read it and decided that Koestler had a special knack for popularising scientific subjects. Thereafter he regarded Koestler as his special protégé and in September 1930 recalled him to Berlin and appointed him successor to Professor Joel as science editor of the *Vossische Zeitung* – and science adviser to all the other publications of the Ullstein Trust. He made his mark effortlessly in this, and a year later his success was rewarded when, in addition to his scientific work, he was appointed foreign editor of the *Berliner Zeitung am Mittag.* His income was now almost twenty-four thousand marks a year, not far from the maximum that a German journalist could earn.

One of his first science articles in the *Vossische Zeitung* discussed the possibilities of harnessing the power locked in the atom:

> 'If our reading of these phenomena is correct, then we are on the eve of a new era in the history of man, and the technological progress of the last hundred years, which has so radically changed the face of the earth, will be regarded by the future historian as a mere fumbling prelude to the performances of an utopian society . . . It is characteristic that the signs of the coming new technological age should appear in these times of social and political confusion, of a chaotic malaise . . .'

The confusion and chaos had put an end to the period of Koestler's political latency.

He had arrived in Berlin from Paris on 14th September 1930, the day of the Reichstag elections in which the National Socialists had increased their vote by 80 per cent and the Communists by 40 per cent, crushing the parties of the Centre and increasing the pressure on the hapless Social Democrats. The showdown was approaching.

'Though the Ullsteins were Jews, they tried to Aryanise the firm by degrees, in an indirect way. The victims of the purge were, as far as I can remember, all Jews; the newly hired members of the staff all Aryans . . .

'The building in the Kochstrasse became a place of fear and insecurity which again reflected the fear and uncertainty of the country in general . . .'

* *

In spite of his success as a scientific journalist, which he enjoyed, Koestler was far from happy; and it was the desire to escape from his personal dilemma, no less than his reading of the political writing on the wall, that edged him into the absolutist arms of the Communist Party, which had a readymade answer for everything. He immersed himself in Communism's sacred texts and sought out party members to act as his gurus during his approach to conversion.

In Palestine he had sought and failed to find the Promised Land. Perhaps it was to be discovered in the vast country of the Five Year Plan and collectivised agriculture to which millions of the downtrodden elsewhere (not to mention the comfortably off intellectuals plagued by guilt precisely because they were not downtrodden) looked as longingly as Christians, Jews and Muslims ever looked to their holy shrines. Utopia was being built there in steel and concrete while the liberal democracies were lurching into violent chaos.

In the Soviet Union the shining future of the brotherhood of man was manifesting itself in the present while the West was floundering hopelessly in the quicksands of the past, menaced yet again by the evil spirits of conflicting nationalisms. After the elections of September 1930 Koestler had seen the liberal middle class of Germany betray its convictions and throw all its principles overboard. Active resistance against the National Socialists seemed only possible by throwing in one's lot either with the Socialists or the Communists, and Koestler despised the compromising, opportunistic, soft-centred Socialists who a decade before had stifled the German revolution and (as he saw it) made an unholy mess of their Republic. He was ready to be converted by his gurus.

In 1930 Communism was indeed a powerful myth. The Soviet reality was, of course, very different, but that was not yet widely known. It was true that certain foreign technicians working in Russia had been tried on strange charges of industrial sabotage, and condemned; but, however superficially unsatisfactory the evidence brought against them, was it not all too likely that they had indeed been agents of capitalist powers anxious to impede the onward march of Socialism? It was easy to write off anti-Communist propaganda as a tissue of hysterical falsehood. No prominent Soviet politican had been tried in public. No member of the opposition to Stalin had been executed. It was true that Trotsky, the leader of the opposition to Stalin, had been exiled, but surely there must have been good and compelling reasons for it; and, in any case, exile was a mild enough punishment for one endangering the progress of a glorious revolution. Dazzled by the statistics of the Soviet Union's economic expansion, and ignorant of the fact that the brutal implementation of the Five Year Plan and the collectivisation of the peasantry were already creating human suffering on an unprecedented scale, Koestler (like so many other intellectuals thirsting as never before for certainty) was in no mood to question the quasi-religious myth and its magnetic attraction.

So, before the end of 1930, he discovered the infallible antidote to despair. Secure at last within an intellectually closed system (and protected by the dialectical correctness of its casuistry from such corrosive doubts as would otherwise have been raised by the German Communists' readiness to make common cause whenever convenient with Hitler's streetfighters against the despised Social Democrats), his feet were firmly set on the road that would soon lead to membership of the Party. Wherever he looked, in whatever field of social, economic, or cultural activity, the Communist movement appeared to him as the logical extension of the progressive humanistic liberalism and *avant-gardisme* which had once been represented by the Ullsteins: the continuation and fulfilment of the great Judeo-Christian tradition; the new, fresh branch on the tree of European progress.

Many months were to pass, however, before he felt ready to take the final step and move out of the cosiness of fellow-travelling into the more arduous role of Party member. In the meantime he had no difficulty in throwing himself enthusiastically into his new job as science editor, roaming through the realms of physics and fantasy. The more he became engrossed politically in historical materialism and the schema of a world governed by the class struggles of Economic Man, the more romantic became his approach to science, itself in the throes of a revolutionary crisis which was shaking all familiar assumptions and replacing traditional concepts of reality by a new picture of the world. His life as a scientific journalist was immensely varied and exciting. Many of his articles, forecasting future developments in science and technology, were so far in advance of their time (and so imbued with romantic enthusiasm) that they drew angry protests from academics demanding his dismissal. His political gurus, on the other hand, seemed to be satisfied with his submission to the social and political aspects of Marxist-Leninist-Stalinist orthodoxy.

> 'When I ask myself with the melancholy wisdom that comes after the event how I could have lived for years in this mental trance, I find some comfort in the thought that mediaeval scholasticism and Aristotelian exegesis lasted for a much longer period, and completely befuddled the best brains of that time.'

* *

Koestler's small, red motor-car (which he called 'Mausi') spent most of December 1931 in a garage undergoing extensive and expensive repairs to the engine. In the early afternoon of Saturday the 30th he collected it and drove to the apartment of his friend, Dr Alfred Apfel, a famous lawyer, Communist sympathiser, and gambler who gave a poker party every week. A heavy and jovial Johnsonian character, Apfel was renowned for his wit and for his skill at cards. Amid such jolliness and the coining of brilliant aphorisms, he generally had little difficulty in fleecing his opponents. Koestler, who was addicted to poker, but was not much good at it, was well used to losing. At this session, however, for some reason he bet more heavily than usual and as a result lost the equivalent of several months' salary.

From the poker game he went on in a mood of dejection to a party at which he got drunk. The temperature outside was well below zero. There was no anti-freeze in the radiator of his car. In the morning he found that the engine-block had burst, a thick icicle protruding from one of the cylinder-heads.

> 'On seeing my dismay, a girl who had been at the party, and who had always got on my nerves, offered me the hospitality of her nearby flat; this again leading to the consequences which were to be expected. I woke up . . . with a super-hangover mixed with self-reproach, anxiety, and guilt, next to a person whom I disliked, financially broke, and with a bust-up car.'

Back in his own flat, nursing his hangover, Koestler had the feeling that this sequence of minor misadventures might be expressing a symbolic warning, as if some mute power were tugging at his sleeve and indicating cryptically that the time had come to remake his life.

The time had come, he decided, for decisive action. So he sat down, wrote a letter of application for membership of the Communist Party, and sent it, together with a *curriculum vitae* and a declaration of his readiness to serve the cause in whatever capacity the Party decided, to the Central Committee.

A week or so after sending off his letter of application, Koestler received a reply typed on a sheet of plain paper:

> 'With reference to your esteemed of Dec. 31, we shall be glad if you will meet a representative of our firm, Herr Schneller, at the offices of the Schneidemühl paper-mill next Monday at 3 p.m.'

Excited by this conspiratorial response, Koestler presented himself punctually at the mill. Half an hour later a thin, bony man, with a pinched face and an awkward smile, turned up and invited him to the café across the street. He seemed ill at ease and at first Koestler took him for some underling in the Party bureaucracy. But this was in fact Ernst Schneller, well-known as a Communist deputy in the Reichstag and a member of the Central Committee of the Party; less well-known as head of its Agitprop department; and not at all well-known as boss of one of the Comintern's espionage networks serving the interests of the Soviet Union.

> 'He did not ask many questions, but enquired in some detail about the exact position I held at Ullstein's. I told him of my desire to throw up my job and to work for the Party only, as a propagandist or, preferably, as a tractor-driver in the Soviet Union . . . Schneller, however, explained to me patiently that the first duty of every Communist was to work for the Revolution in his own country; to be admitted to the Soviet Union, where the Revolution had already triumphed, was a rare privilege, reserved for veterans of the movement. It would be equally wrong to quit my job; I could be much more useful to the Party by carrying on with it and keeping mum about my political convictions. Useful in what way? I asked . . . Schneller said there were many ways by which

I could influence the policy of the paper through small touches . . . he could delegate somebody less busy than himself, who would be at my disposal at practically any time for my political guidance. Besides, through this mutual friend, I could hand on to the Party any political information of special interest that came my way. The Party would probably be forced underground quite soon, and, if that happened, people like myself, in respectable positions, untainted by suspicion, would be even more valuable in the life-and-death struggle against Fascism and imperialistic aggression. . . . We agreed to meet in a week's time, when he would introduce me to my future political guide. "Who is that going to be?" I asked. "A comrade called Edgar," said Schneller.

'After saying good-bye to him, it suddenly occurred to me that nothing had been said about my formal admission to the Party. . . . I ran after Schneller and put the question to him. He smiled his awkward smile and said: "If you insist, we will make you a Party member, but on condition that your membership remains secret . . . Tell me what cover-name you choose," said Schneller, "and I'll bring along your Party card the next time."

'My mind, for a moment, was blank. Then a name occurred to me, and I said: "Ivan Steinberg" . . . Ivan sounded Russian and nice . . .

'I met Schneller again one week later at the same place. Instead of Edgar, he had brought a girl along, whom he introduced as Comrade Paula, a collaborator of Edgar's . . .

'This second meeting with Schneller was the last one . . . I wrote down Paula's telephone number and arranged to meet her two days later at my flat. Then Schneller produced my Party card, with "Ivan Steinberg" written on it, and we shook hands awkwardly . . .

'At the appointed hour, Paula and Edgar appeared at my flat in Neu Westend. They had come by taxi, and Paula had brought her typewriter. Edgar was a smooth and smiling, blond young man of about thirty. He suggested that I should tell him any bits of political information or confidential gossip that I had picked up in the House of Ullstein. After a minute or two, he asked whether I had any objection to Paula taking down what I said on her typewriter; it would "save work". I had no objection.

'During the next few weeks, my only Party activities consisted in dictating, once or twice a week, reports to Paula. Sometimes Edgar dropped in too and listened with his smooth, slightly ironical smile, while pacing up and down the room . . .

'Though I accepted the necessity for conspiratorial vigilance, I felt increasingly frustrated . . . I had offered to sacrifice my job and lead the humble life, driving a tractor in the Russian steppes; that was a petty-bourgeois romanticism. I pressed Edgar to let me join a cell where nobody knew me except under my cover name; he said I might be found out and thereby lose my usefulness to the Party. I asked him what else I could do. He said he would think about it. But weeks passed and nothing happened.'

In his capacity as foreign editor of the *Berliner Zeitung am Mittag* Koestler had access to virtually all the confidential political information that arrived in this important nerve-centre of the Ullstein Trust. He passed this on weekly to his *apparat* contacts.

His assistant was the son of a retired ambassador who regularly entertained senior members of the General Staff and the foreign service. Koestler recruited him to the service of the cause and charged him to keep his ears open and report anything of interest that he heard at home. The flow of information from this source considerably increased the value of Koestler's reports. In addition to this activity, Koestler and another Party-member, Alfred Kantorowicz, organised a caucus of fellow-travellers among the Ullstein staff – a dozen or so of whom met weekly at Koestler's flat to exchange information and discuss ways and means of countering the growing pro-Nazi tendencies within the organisation.

It was by such means that the innumerable Comintern *apparats* were at the time fishing for the hearts and minds of liberals in similar study-groups and discussion-circles formed in universities, newspaper offices, government agencies and industrial enterprises throughout the democracies.

Koestler's group, however, was not a particularly successful one. In his own words:

> 'With the constant dismissals at Ullstein's, and the shadow of Hitler lying across the country like a monster-shaped cloud, our motley little crowd of intellectuals was too scared to be capable of any clear thought . . . The Liberals in Germany – and elsewhere – have rarely understood that there are situations in which caution amounts to suicide.'

Their cowardice and helplessness made him glad and proud to be a communist.

Within two or three months his undercover work for the Comintern came to an abrupt end. His assistant was gradually overcome by remorse, and one morning, after a sleepless night, presented him with an ultimatum: either Koestler would allow him to hand to the managing director the letter of confession he had written or he would shoot himself. Koestler, who declined to read the young man's letter, tried to argue him out of his quixotic and absurd demand: they had not broken the law; they had neither stolen military secrets nor sold political documents. Such arguments failed to impress the young man standing in front of Koestler's desk, his eyes red and swollen, and with black stubble on his pallid face. He was obdurate. To be a Marxist or Socialist was one thing. But to pass on information to agents of a foreign power, whether or not he and Koestler were spies in the strictly technical sense, was treason.

In the end Koestler gave the letter back to the boy and told him to hand it in and go to hell. A few days later the Ullsteins dismissed Koestler quietly, without mentioning his assistant's confession, and gave him a lump sum in compensation for the remaining term of his five-year contract. His usefulness to the Comintern *apparat* ended, Schneller and Edgar dropped him without ceremony.*

* Schneller was to die in jail, Paula to be executed in Ravensbruck, and Edgar, whose real name was Fritz Burde, having become head of the Red Army Intelligence Service in Scandinavia, was recalled by the GPU to Moscow after the arrest and execution of Mikhail Nikolaevich Tukhachevski during the Great Purge. There, with many thousands of others in Soviet military intelligence, he was done to death as a 'German Spy'.

Koestler sent most of his generous pay-off to his parents in Budapest, gave up his flat in the expensive district of Neu-Westend, and moved to the apartment house on Bonner Platz known as the Red Block because most of the tenants were writers and artists of Marxist views. He joined the local Communist cell and so began at last to lead the full life of an ordinary Party member, toeing the line laid down from on high, perfecting his mastery of Marxist jargon, learning to avoid any original form of expression or turn of phrase, drilling himself in the discipline of instant, unquestioning obedience to *diktats* which, before his conversion, he would have taken to be the utterances of lunatics, and learning to read sound Marxist sense into manifest nonsense.

Outside the Party cell which had become his universe he had few friends and social contacts, and most of them were either Communists or fellow-travellers. Two of them were later to play an important part in his life: the physicist Alexander Weissberg, a member of the Austrian Communist Party, and his wife Eva, a painter and ceramics designer. Koestler had known Eva, a dark, strikingly beautiful girl, since his childhood. She and Weissberg were soon to emigrate to the Soviet Union* where an important research job awaited him at the Ukrainian Institute for Physics and Technology.

Koestler had given up the idea of serving the cause as a tractor-driver; but he was still anxious to get to Russia. The Party was favourably disposed, on the understanding that he would travel in the guise of a bourgeois liberal reporter and write a series of articles on the Five Year Plan, in the course of which he would carefully document the overcoming of his anti-Communist prejudices. He signed a contract with a literary agency which undertook to syndicate his articles to some twenty European newspapers of a more or less liberal character. Months passed, however, without any sign of his visa.

The poet, Johannes R. Becher, president of the League of Proletarian Revolutionary Writers of Germany, came to his aid and procured for him an official invitation from MORP, the International Organisation of Revolutionary Writers (a Comintern 'front'), and an advance of three thousand roubles from the Russian Publishing Trust. Over and above the syndicated articles he was to write a book-length account of the conversion of a liberal, to be entitled *Russia Through Bourgeois Eyes*.

By the end of July 1932 the arrangements were complete. He felt the same sense of exhilaration at having burnt his bridges as he had known six and a half years before, leaving Vienna for Palestine. But this time there was no crowd on the platform to cheer him on his way, only Lotte, the latest of his Helenas, stood by the window of his compartment.

> 'As the train moved out of the Bahnhof am Zoo, she made a mocking curtsey; I never saw her again. When I turned away from the window, I felt, for a moment, a very lonely voyager. Then I became immersed in a pamphlet on the increase of steel production under the Five Year Plan.'

* And where in due course they were to suffer torments at the hands of the GPU during the Great Purge. Much of the background material for *Darkness at Noon* was supplied by Eva from her own experience.

# CHAPTER IV

# *1932–1933*

SINCE KOESTLER'S IDEA OF the USSR had been formed by the rosy compound of Soviet propaganda and wishful thinking, he fully expected that at the frontier he would (as the slogan had it) 'change trains for the twenty-first century' and enter a paradisial super-America vibrant with activity, efficiency, and enthusiasm. The reality was different.

As the train crawled across the Ukrainian steppe towards Kharkov, he saw at every station hordes of ragged peasants offering ikons, linen, and other household treasures in exchange for bread, the women holding up to the compartment windows their stick-limbed, pot-bellied, starving infants. The great famine of 1932–33, the product of the forced collectivisation of farming and the ruthless implementation of the industrial Five Year Plan (designed primarily to increase the Soviet Union's military strength at whatever cost), was already raging. But Koestler knew nothing of this, and perhaps the Russians on the train who told him that those wretches were anti-social *kulaks* who had brought their misfortune upon themselves by resisting collectivisation actually believed this explanation themselves.

Koestler's faith, at any rate, permitted him to accept it.

He spent his first fortnight on Soviet soil in Kharkov, then capital of the Ukraine, where he stayed with Alex and Eva Weissberg in their small – but, by Russian standards, luxurious – apartment attached to the Ukrainian Institute for Physics and Technology where they were employed.

During his last four months in Berlin he had acquired Russian by the same 'pressure-cooker' method by which he learnt modern Hebrew before setting out for Palestine. It was ungrammatical but fluent and he had no difficulty in getting about on his own. His 'inner censor' was kept hard at work, for Kharkov seemed to him much more like a vast, sprawling semi-oriental village than the mighty Manhattan he had expected. The only public conveyances were old electric streetcars which ran at infrequent intervals, crammed inside and covered outside with passengers clinging to every available handhold. On his first journey pickpockets relieved him of his wallet, fountain pen, and cigarettes.

Most of the stores were all but empty and the only goods readily available seemed to be postage-stamps, contraceptives, and fly-paper. In the market, people with anything to sell or barter squatted in the dust with their goods spread out before them – a handful of nails, a tattered quilt, a pot of sour milk, a painted Easter egg, a small piece of dried-up goat's cheese, hemp slippers, soles and heels torn off from boots. Such were the commodities being offered in exchange for some black bread or a packet of coarse tobacco.

The wretched creatures crowding the market square were, he was told, *kulaks* who had been expropriated. In fact, they were ordinary peasants driven by hunger out of the countryside and into the city. Entire villages had been abandoned, whole districts depopulated. Millions of starving men, women, and children were on the move, dragging themselves from town to town in search of food, dying in the streets.

Officially, however, the famine did not exist, merely certain *trudnesty* (difficulties) 'on the collectivisation front'.

After a fortnight in Kharkov, Koestler visited various industrial centres to collect material for a series of articles on the Five Year Plan. He had then intended to visit the coal mines of the Donetz basin, but for some reason the necessary permit was withheld. Nor was he allowed to visit the collective farms in the Ukraine manned by half a million ethnic Germans, descendants of colonists invited to settle there by Catherine the Great. No reason was given for this refusal (and years were to pass before he learned that these communities were among those most devastated by the famine).

Still, he had enough material for six long articles, and on his return to Moscow he took them for preliminary censorship to the headquarters of his sponsor in MORP (the International Organisation of Revolutionary Writers). The experts of MORP thought them too romantic on the one hand and too mechanistically critical on the other. Koestler dutifully revised them in the light of their criticism and then took them to be officially censored at the Press Department of NARKOMINDYEL (the People's Commissariat for Foreign Affairs). The head of the department, Constantin Umansky*, received him affably, passed the articles, and laughed when Koestler told him of his experiences at MORP.

> 'You are officially a bourgeois correspondent,' he said, advising Koestler to steer clear of MORP, 'so you had better stick to us here in the NARKOMINDYEL and keep away from those Communist zealots. We'll look after you – but keep your mouth shut about your Party membership and Comintern connections.'

It was not to be quite as simple as that for Koestler during his travels. He carried with him two particularly important documents. One was a 'strong' letter signed by the head of AGITPROP EKKI (the Department of Agitation and Propaganda of the Executive Committee of the Communist International) which informed whomsoever it might concern that Comrade Koestler, a delegate of the Revolutionary Writer's League of Germany, was travelling under the sponsorship of the Comintern. The other was a letter from NARKOMINDYEL

* Later Soviet Ambassador to Mexico.

identifying him as a bourgeois foreign correspondent working for several important and influential newspapers. The latter entitled him to stay in Intourist hotels; to travel in the 'soft class' on trains; and to buy his food at INSNAB, the stores reserved for the diplomatic corps and foreign technical advisers and journalists.

He had been advised never to show this bourgeois, NARKOMINDYEL documentation at the Party offices and factories that he visited, nor to travelling companions, for fear that it might arouse distrust and suspicion. On the other hand it would be foolish to display his Comintern documentation from AGITPROP EKKI to hotel managers, railways officials, and store managers, for that would deprive him of the preferential treatment for bourgeois tourists who had to be humoured for propaganda reasons.

So Koestler set out from Moscow on his long journey to the Caucasus and Soviet Central Asia with one set of documents in his right-hand pocket and the other in his left-hand pocket. He never pulled out the wrong set, thanks to the simple memorising device that the Comintern, the organising agency of world revolution, was 'on the left'.

From Ordkhonikidse Koestler crossed the Caucasus by car to Tiflis, the capital of Georgia. The hair-raising drive up to the 7,500 foot high Kasbeck Pass and down to the vineyards induced in him a holiday mood, and during the two weeks he spent in Tiflis he developed an affection for the stubborn, hard-drinking and irrepressible Georgian people, in spite of the intense anti-Russian feeling he could sense wherever he went.

After a couple of days in the Intourist hotel he accepted the invitation of a newly acquired friend, Oragvilidze, the Georgian Minister of Education, and moved into the tiny three-roomed house which Oragvilidze shared with his mother. The Minister, a well-read and thoughtful young man, had studied in both Berlin and Moscow, and his conversation had none of the heavy, jargon-laden and cautious orthodoxy to which Koestler had become accustomed in his dealings with high Party officials and which he had himself, willingly but painfully, learned to imitate. There were no visits to factories in Tiflis for Koestler – not even a cursory study of Plan-fulfilment figures.

One evening Oragvilidze took him for dinner at a garden restaurant in the hilly outskirts of Tiflis. There were candles on the table, and a gypsy orchestra. Koestler had not dreamt that such places still existed in the Soviet Union. Had he been aware of the full extent of the suffering caused elsewhere over vast areas of the Union by the *trudnesty* 'on the collectivisation front', the impression made by the heroic procession of *zakushka*, *shaslik*, *shushkebab*, *lulakebab*, that passed across the table would no doubt have been of a different order – until the third or fourth bottle had gone, at any rate.

* *

After three weeks in Baku, where he had an unhappy love-affair, he crossed the Caspian Sea, and it was in a sullen and dejected mood that he began his journey from the nondescript Russian garrison town of Krasnovodsk into the sullen and dejected wastes of Turkestan.

His depression as the train crawled slowly through the desiccated landscape was intensified by a feeling of *déjà-vu*, for during his years in the Middle East he had become all too familiar with the atmosphere of decline and desolation lying on lands which had once been rich and fertile and were now largely desert.

At Ashkhabad, the capital of Turkmenistan, where there was no hotel, the GPU found a cell-like room for him in the *dom sovietov*, the Town Soviet's hostel for visiting officials. He stretched out on the iron bed and abandoned himself completely to misery and guilt. On the other side of the corridor there was a blocked and overflowing latrine, and its stench poisoned the air. He felt forsaken by God in a godforsaken country. What on earth, he asked himself as he lay on the uncomfortable bed, enveloped in gloom, staring at the stains of crushed bedbugs on the wall, was he doing in Ashkhabad?

Disappointment also awaited him in Samarkand and Bokhara, the first crumbling into squalor and the second being modernised more ruthlessly than any other Asian town he had seen. Much of the Old City was being razed to the ground. The famous collection of codices and manuscripts built up during the years when Bokhara was the centre of Muslim scholarship was dispersed, many of its treasures pilfered or burnt. The Citadel had been transformed into a college, the Emir's harem into a lunatic asylum.

Each morning Koestler was roused by the blare of loudspeakers exhorting the faithful to empty their bowels, do ten minutes of physical exercise, eat their breakfast and get to work. 'Within four years,' the chairman of the town-planning committee told him, 'Bokhara will have become a European town.'

From Bokhara, Koestler went on to Tashkent, and then, after a week on a state farm in Kazakstan, he returned to Kharkov. There he spent the last weeks of 1932 and the first three months of 1933 working up his travel notes into a book which he entitled *Von Weissen Nächten und Roten Tagen* (White Nights and Red Days).*

* *

On 30th January 1933, Adolf Hitler became Chancellor of the Reich. Koestler was at the Weissbergs' Kharkov apartment when news came of the burning of the Reichstag (28th February).

The National Socialists' victory was finally confirmed by the March election in which they received 44 per cent of the vote, the Social Democrats dropping to 18 per cent and the Communists to 12 per cent. Legislation was pushed through the Reichstag enabling Hitler to govern by decree. Communist deputies were arrested or excluded. The Republic died quietly; the Third Reich came into being with Hitler as its *Führer*, and the process of *Gleichschaltung* – that 'coordination' by which all the machinery of the state was geared to Hitler's will – was set in motion. Any doubts about the seriousness of his anti-semitism were dispelled in April, when Jews were by decree excluded from government service, the universities and the professions, and forbidden to marry 'Aryans'.

* A heavily cut version was published in the German language in 1933 by the Ukrainian State Publishing Company for National Minorities. 'White Nights' is an allusion to his experiences during the Graf Zeppelin expedition to the Soviet Arctic, which he had reported for the Ullstein chain.

Koestler had become one of Europe's many political exiles, but many weeks were to pass before he became fully conscious of the transformation and its implications. As he continued to write *White Nights and Red Days*, his main problem was neither the future of Europe nor his own but simply of how to go on working in an unheated room during that disastrous winter of famine, industrial dislocation and bitter cold. He had food enough, being billeted in the Intourist hotel for the privileged, the Regina, but Kharkov's electricity supply had broken down and the temperature in his room rarely rose above freezing point.

The Ukrainian capital lived in a permanent blackout, paralysed by hunger, darkness, and frost. The streetcars ran only twice a day, in the morning and evening, to get the half-starved workers to and from the factories. In offices people worked by the light of kerosene lamps, huddled in quilts and surrounded by clouds of condensed breath. The chambermaid who worked on Koestler's floor in the Regina fainted one morning from hunger and later told him that she had not eaten for three days, her three-day ration of four pounds of black bread having been withheld by the Cooperative bureaucracy because she had only just arrived from the country – although there, as she told Koestler, many people were now dying of starvation.

No news of such sufferings appeared in the Kharkov newspaper which Koestler read each morning. Instead, he learnt about the 'fulfilment' and 'over-fulfilment' of plans, competitions between 'shock-brigades' in factories, the opening of giant new industrial plants in the Urals, the statistics-studded texts always accompanied by photographs of young people laughing and holding up banners, or some picturesque Asian elder 'happily' learning the Cyrillic alphabet. There was never a word about famine, economic disorder, epidemics of typhus, the virtual depopulation of great areas of the countryside. Even the fact that there was no electricity in Kharkov was never mentioned in the Kharkov newspaper.

This gave Koestler a feeling of dreamlike unreality, as if the paper was concerned with some different and distant country which had no point of contact with the daily struggle for sheer existence around him. But, still secure in his faith, he remained a convinced Communist. And so he not only accepted the famine as inevitable, but also the necessity of the ban on foreign travel, foreign newspapers and books, and the dissemination of what he knew very well to be a grotesquely distorted picture of life in the non-Communist world as well as in the Soviet Union.

He was sustained also by his conviction – shared, he thinks, by every other Communist pilgrim encountering in those days the shock of Soviet reality – that conditions in Russia were what they were not because of any flaw in the Communist system but rather because of the backwardness of the Russian people. In Western Europe the Revolution would, of course, take an entirely different form.

Thus fortified, Koestler got on with his book and finished it during April, sending copies off to the State publishing trusts in Moscow, Kharkov, Tiflis, and Erevan with whom he had signed contracts for editions in Russian, Ukrainian, German, Georgian and Armenian.

What was his next move to be? That would depend on the reaction of the literary bureaucrats, and especially those who would be responsible for the Russian-language edition, for that would be the one which really mattered. He went to Moscow while waiting for their decision, and there he met many leading Russian Communists in and out of favour, among them Nikolai Ivanovitch Bukharin, who had been expelled from the Politburo in 1929 because of his 'right-wing' views but who still exerted considerable influence from the wings, and Karl Radek, formerly in disgrace as a Trotskyist but now readmitted to membership of the Party and serving the cause as a member of the editorial board of *Izvestia*.

Those two made an especially deep impression on him.

Late in July Koestler learned to his disappointment that his book would not be published in the Russian language because, according to the senior bureaucrat who told him of the publishing trust's decision, it was written in a 'too frivolous and lighthearted style'.

Shortly afterwards, Paul Dietrich, his immediate superior in the German section of the Comintern, informed him that the Party had decided against his staying in the Soviet Union. He would, it was considered, be more usefully employed in Paris, where the German Communist leaders and intellectuals who had escaped arrest were gathering. Koestler was surprised by the relief with which he received this news: until that time he had refused to admit to himself that he found life in Russia desperately depressing. He was still a faithful Communist of course. It was different in the Soviet Union only because of the backwardness of the Russians. *Wir Werden es besser machen* (we shall do it better), he told himself, concealing his pleasure at the prospect of putting his second Promised Land behind him.

He returned to Kharkov and, while he waited for his exit permit, stayed with the Weissbergs for a week or two. Once again he enjoyed the evening games of poker with the absent-minded Professor Shubnikov and other scientists from the Ukrainian Institute for Physics and Technology (all of whom five years later, during the Great Purge, were to testify that Weissberg was a Gestapo spy, and then obligingly to confess that they had themselves been in the pay of the Germans).

'Whatever happens, Arthur,' said Weissberg, seeing Koestler off at the station, 'hold the banner of the Soviet Union high.'

# CHAPTER V

# *1933–1936*

VIRTUALLY PENNILESS THOUGH HE was (for the roubles he had earned in Russia were not convertible), and with no idea of what the future might hold, Koestler was still overjoyed to be back in Europe. He spent three or four days in Vienna, renewing old acquaintances.

Before leaving Moscow he had invested most of his remaining roubles in a small diamond. In Vienna he sold it for a sum which covered the cost of a return ticket to Budapest and left enough for a week's living expenses.

His intention had been to spend no more than a week in Budapest visiting his spendthrift father and selling a few travel articles about the Turanian Basin in Central Asia – by tradition the cradle of the Magyars – and so ensuring that he would not arrive penniless in Paris. But a stroke of luck kept him there, and on holiday from politics for three months.

One day in Moscow, a few weeks before his departure, he had been sitting alone in a mood of depression on the terrace of the Café Metropole.

> 'I began to write the play then and there, on the paper-napkins of the Café Metropole. It was, of course, an unforgiveable heresy: "escapism" is almost the deadliest sin for a Communist, and I felt rather like a schoolboy drawing obscene pictures on the blackboard all set for a solemn lesson in History. I finished the play in three weeks, the last act on the train that took me out of Russia. I called it *Bar du Soleil.* It was a play without literary pretensions, a flight from the pressures of reality, and I described it accordingly as "An Escapade in Four Acts".'

Soon after his arrival in Budapest he gave the typescript of the play to a friend, Andor Németh. Two days later Németh brought him the news that the director of Budapest's leading modern repertory theatre, the Belvárosi Szinház, had bought it for a considerable advance. They decided that Németh should translate the play into Hungarian (Koestler had written it in German) and that they should appear on the bill as co-authors. Németh's mistress, Juci, calculated that the advance would keep him and Koestler for three months.

During this time they would collaborate on another play and other projects, among them detective stories for pulp magazines, and make (so they thought) a lot of money.

Apart from the advance on *Bar du Soleil*, their collaboration had no success. The play was never produced, and a second play on which they worked together was never finished. But Koestler, whose holiday mood persisted, enjoyed himself. In the evenings they went to one or other of the cafés where the various literary cliques gathered, listened to the latest jokes and discussed every subject under the sun except politics. Within a few days Koestler had made the acquaintance of many prominent Hungarian writers, among them Frederick Karinthy, the novelist, Attila Jossef, the poet, and Paul Ignotus, critic and essayist. He found the hothouse atmosphere of literary Budapest strangely fascinating.

Early in September, not long after his twenty-eighth birthday, having decided that the time had come to end his escapist interlude, he took the train for Paris and started work at the office of the 'World Committee for the Relief of the Victims of German Fascism', the cover-name of the headquarters of Willy Muenzenberg, the Comintern propaganda chief in Western Europe.

The 'World Committee for the Relief of the Victims of German Fascism', which Muenzenberg had established in Paris after Hitler's accession to power, was a brilliantly successful example of a Communist-controlled 'front'. Camouflaged as a philanthropic organisation, it had branches throughout Europe and North America, on the executive committee of which sat, as Koestler says, 'highly respectable people, from English duchesses to American columnists and French savants, who had never heard the name of Muenzenberg and thought that the Comintern was a bogey invented by Dr Goebbels'. Care was taken to ensure that no Communists – apart from such acceptably eccentric celebrities as J. B. S. Haldane and Henri Barbusse – were associated with the organisation, and its supporters never suspected that the Paris secretariat was one of the Comintern's most important outposts.

> 'The success with which the Communist line,' as Ruth Fischer wrote, 'was propagated among Social Democrats and Liberals during those years, the publication of *Ce Soir* in Paris, and *P.M.* in New York, the thousands of painters and writers and doctors and lawyers and debutantes chanting a diluted version of the Stalinist line – all this had its root in Willy Muenzenberg's International Workers' Aid.*'

Koestler's role in the campaign was the important one of following the 'Muenzenberg Trust's' propaganda in the British parliament and press, charting the currents of British public opinion, and drawing the appropriate tactical conclusions. He also edited the daily bulletins issued to the British and French Press.

Then Koestler was assigned to another job. A vast and growing quantity of documents, pamphlets, newspaper clippings, and other material had been assembled, and Muenzenberg decided to make them the basis of an 'Anti-Fascist

* *Stalin and German Communism*, Harvard, 1948.

Archive', later to be known as the 'Free German Library'. Koestler was sent to work in the archive. It was an unobtrusive job which he liked well enough, but it was also a manifest demotion. Early in 1934 he resigned.

* *

Once again he was almost penniless. He tried to interest publishers in his book about the Soviet Union, but without success. His play was turned down by all the theatre managements he approached. He could not get a job on a newspaper because his French, though fluent, was far from perfect. What was he to do?

His cousin Theodore from Budapest unexpectedly turned up in Paris where he had established a French publishing house. He commissioned Koestler to write a popular *Encyclopaedia of Sexual Knowledge*. Koestler finished the book in eight weeks and received for the copyright the outright fee of forty pounds – to which his cousin generously added an *ex gratia* payment of twenty pounds when the *Encyclopaedia* became an international best-seller. Koestler knew very well that he was being outrageously exploited, but in spite of this he was to collaborate in the production of two further sex books for his cousin.*

Not long after he had finished the *Encyclopaedia*, Muenzenberg asked him to write a fund-raising pamphlet about a home for German refugee children which was running out of money. A firm believer in Marx's tenet, 'No revolutionary theory without revolutionary practice', Koestler went off to the house in Maisons-Laffitte, called La Poponnière, which housed thirty young Germans, the children of Communists, between the ages of two and sixteen. He intended to spend only two or three days there, but two months were to pass before he left it. He incorporated his experiences there in a novel which won a prize but was never published, *The Adventures in Exile of Comrade Cheepy Bird and his Friends*.

In Paris the Association of German Writers in Exile met every week. Members gave readings from their works which were then followed by a discussion. The Association was officially non-political, apart from its opposition to the National Socialist regime; but in fact it was run as a 'front' by a caucus of Communists, including Anna Seghers, Ergon Erwin Kisch, Gustav Regler, and Bodo Uhse – all established writers.

When Koestler had finished his novel, the Association invited him to read extracts from it at one of their meetings. The reading itself seemed successful enough, but on the following evening the Communist caucus met to condemn the book as frivolous and decadent, based on the unholy methods of bourgeois individual psychology instead of sacred Soviet Realism.

It was even suggested that the heresies were serious enough to call for measures beyond the competence of the caucus. Koestler retorted angrily, thus putting himself still more in the wrong. The disciplinary action by 'other organs of the Party' did not materialise. No penance was called for. It might have been easier for him if it had been. As it was, feeling himself despised by the Party and no longer having any friends outside it, he fell into despair.

One night in his dreary hotel room on the Boulevard de Belleville, after a few weeks of living on the charity of a friendly pair of social workers who had a small

* Under the pseudonym of Dr Costler, see pages 34 and 50.

flat in the same hotel, he decided that the misery of his existence had become unbearable. He stuck paper over the gaps in the door and window-frame and dragged his mattress across the floor to the gas-tap. He turned on the gas and lay down. Just then a book fell from the shelf above and hit him full in the face. The sharp blow sobered him up and he decided to go on living.

As Koestler was recovering, Peter Maros, the friend who, in Berlin, had encouraged him to clear the last hurdle of doubt and submit to the demands of Communist dogma, sought him out and asked him to take charge of the publications department of the newly formed 'Institute for the Study of Fascism'. This was, of course, a Communist enterprise, but it differed in many ways from those of the 'Muenzenberg Trust'. Maros saw it as a quasi-academic research institute, aimed at a study of social phenomena somewhat beyond the limits laid down by the Party line and its changing slogans. To succeed, therefore, it had to be untainted by anything that could be recognised as leftist propaganda.

All that Koestler received in return for the effort he put into what turned out to be a full-time job, and one which completely absorbed him for nine months, was his Metro fares and a mid-day meal. In spite of this (or, perhaps, because of it), he was happy at the Institute – even when penury obliged him to move out of the cheap Belleville hotel and into a hayloft in the grounds of a colony of cranks at Meudon-Val Fleuri, between Paris and Versailles. His health improved; his depression lifted; he was contented. At last (he felt) he was leading a true Communist life of poverty, dedication, and obedience.

For six months or so all went well. The eight members of the Institute's staff all got on well together, without jealousies or intrigues. Koestler produced a bi-monthly bulletin and a series of pamphlets, and provided several anti-Fascist authors with research-material for their books. He wrote a number of articles for the Paris evening newspaper *L'Intransigeant* and organised the supply of documentary material to various cultural organisations and trades unions. He was happy in the belief that he was doing something useful for the Party – and taking no Party money in return. But the day of the 'People's Front' was not yet. The efforts of Maros and Koestler were sabotaged by 'Jan', a Moscow-trained *apparatchik* who in a short while succeeded in destroying Maros's brainchild.

* *

Koestler's private life was more settled now than it had been for some time. Earlier in the year he had found another Helena in the person of Dorothy, Peter Maros's sister-in-law, and at the beginning of August had left the hayloft in the cranks' commune at Val Fleuri and moved into her room in a small hotel on the Ile St Louis. Dorothy had a part-time job and an allowance from her mother, the widow of a Berlin banker, of five pounds a month. Koestler wrote occasional articles for Leopold Schwarzschild's liberal weekly, *Das Neue Tagebuch*. They lived frugally, but were happy together; and Koestler, withdrawn for the moment from political activity, was free to start work on the historical novel which had been taking shape in his imagination around the shadowy figure of Spartacus, the Thracian gladiator who had led the servile revolt against Rome in 73 BC.

The name of Spartacus was well known to German Communists, because Rosa Luxemburg and Karl Liebknecht had called the revolutionary movement, which they founded in 1917 and out of which the German Communist Party had grown, the *Spartakus-Bund*. In fact, as Koestler discovered when he began his research, Spartacus had been the inspiration of many revolutionary groups in Europe from the eighteenth century to the twentieth. The more he delved into the historical background, the more fascinating became the many questions unanswered by the meagre sources. What manner of man was this who, following his escape with a small band of fellow-gladiators from a training-school in Capua, had gathered round him an army of seventy thousand slaves which had come close to conquering Rome? What were the aims of his revolution? How had he been able for two years to dominate southern Italy? Why had his revolution crumbled suddenly into bloody defeat?

> 'From the moment when I had joined the Communist Party three and a half years earlier, I had been submerged in the stream of Revolution. Now I was coming up for air, looking at the stream, wondering where it was leading, and trying to find out about the nature of the forces that made it move. At first, my imagination had been caught by the picturesque and romantic aspects of the Slave War: the circus gladiators who were its leaders, their camp in the crater of Vesuvius, and by the fact that the Slave Army came within an ace of conquering Rome and thus altering the whole course of history. But soon my interest shifted from the picturesque façade to the historical and moral lessons of the first great proletarian revolution.'

Koestler's days were now spent in the Bibliothèque Nationale, digging deep into Roman history during the last years of the Republic, amassing notes to lend a sharp verisimilitude to the framework within which his Spartacus destroyed his Utopia and brought about his own downfall by his reluctance to liquidate dissidents and establish total despotism.

It seemed to him that there were many parallels between Rome of antiquity and Europe of the present – the collapse of traditional values, a rapidly accelerating transformation of the economic system, large-scale unemployment, social unrest, the ruin of the peasants, a declining birth-rate and a spectacular increase in divorces and abortions, corruption in administration, and decadence among the rulers.

Into his imagined antiquity he projected those uncertainties, doubts, and questions about modernity which his Communist faith had not allowed to enter his conscious mind:

> 'It was not I who asked these questions, it was the material in which I was working . . . Up to now, I had been critical of the Soviet leadership and the Comintern bureaucracy, but not of the basic teaching of Communism, which I regarded as historically correct, and as self-evident as the axioms of Euclid. Now, the more engrossed I became in my subject, the more questionable became the very foundations of the doctrine, the more cracks appeared in the wall around the "closed system", and the more fresh air blew in.'

But much was to happen before he realised that the walls had crumbled into dust and that he was no longer cocooned in a closed system of doctrine and dogma.

When Muenzenberg asked him in December to go to the Saar and edit a weekly propaganda sheet, he took on the job without demur.

* *

The Saarland, with its coal-mines and its 600,000 German-speaking inhabitants, had been claimed for France by Clemenceau after the First World War. But the Peace Conference had decreed that for fifteen years it would be administered by the League of Nations, at the end of which period a plebiscite would settle the matter.

The date of the plebiscite had been fixed for 13th January 1935, and when Koestler arrived in Saarbrücken in the middle of the preceding month, the propaganda battle between the 'German Front' and the 'People's Front' was at its peak. The former consisted of the various groups which favoured absorption in the Third Reich, the latter – comprising Communists, Socialists, and Liberals – called for the maintenance of the *status quo*. The third alternative to be placed before the Saarlanders in January – incorporation into the French republic – had no chance whatsoever.

Koestler's task, of course, was to support the 'People's Front'. It was not a particularly easy one. Until June the Communists had vehemently denounced the Socialists' and Liberals' demand for the maintenance of the *status quo* and campaigned mystifyingly for *Eine Rote Saar in Soviet-Deutschland* – 'A Red Saar in Soviet-Germany'. To vote for the *status quo* would be to act as an agent of French imperialism. The fact that Germany was National Socialist, not Communist, was a detail of little importance. The official line was that the German Communist Party had merely carried out a strategic retreat in 1933, and, indeed, that Hitler's apparent victory was beneficial because it had rescued the masses from the influence of the 'Social Fascists' and so accelerated the speed of Germany's march towards proletarian revolution.

Early in June, however, the Communist line was changed abruptly and the Comintern's official weekly laid it down that

> 'The interests of the workers and the toiling population demand a decision which shall provide the greatest possibility for the development and extension of the anti-Fascist class struggle. Under the present conditions, and in spite of the hostility of the Communists to the capitalist regime, this possibility is offered by the *status quo*. . . . For the time being the Communists decide for the *status quo* in order the better and more rapidly to develop the revolutionary forces . . .'

The first issue of Koestler's paper, *Die Saar-Ente*, was also the last. He never learned why the Party did not keep it going until the referendum. Perhaps some realist decided that it was pointless to waste any more of the Party funds. In the event 90 per cent of the Saarlanders voted for a return to Germany. The Communists might as well have stuck to their original line. By collaborating with the National Socialists to demoralise and destroy the forces of moderation in Germany, the Communists had destroyed themselves. The proletariat had thrown in their lot with Hitler and the Saarlanders gladly did likewise.

Before returning to Paris, Koestler renewed his acquaintance with a number of leading Party officials whom he had not seen for some time, among them Paul Dietrich of the German section of the Comintern, and 'Edgar', who had been his first contact with the Berlin *apparat.* He also met Grete Buber-Neumann, Muenzenberg's sister-in-law and the wife of Heinz Neumann, who had engineered the Communist revolt in Canton in 1929. They all struck him as curiously grey and haggard in appearance, and markedly reserved in manner, but he had no idea at the time that they had more on their mind than the Saar's forthcoming referendum.

During the first three weeks of December, following the assassination of Sergei Kirov, the Leningrad Party boss, one hundred and four people were executed in Russia without trial. Grigori Evseevich Zinoviev, the first President of the Comintern, Lev Borisovich Kamenev, president of the Moscow Soviet, and several other old Bolsheviks had been arrested, tried, and convicted of being 'politically and morally responsible' for Kirov's death. (After two more trials, the second of which opened the nightmarish series of 'show trials' in 1936, they were executed.) Many thousands of smaller fry were already being deported to Siberian labour camps. The Great Purge was beginning, and perhaps Dietrich, 'Edgar', Grete Buber-Neumann and the other prominent officials who had foregathered in Saarbrucken had some premonition of the wave of terror that would eventually drown not thousands but millions.

* *

Koestler, quite unaware of the ominous significance of Kirov's death and its immediate consequences, returned to Paris and his study of the Spartacus of antiquity whose scruples had doomed him to defeat. His ignorance of the means by which the Spartacus of modernity was preparing to consolidate his absolute power concealed from him the irony implicit in the task to which he had turned his hand.

* *

At this stage, Dorothy's brother, Ernie, who had been practising medicine in Switzerland, decided to emigrate to the Volga-German Republic in the Soviet Union where he had been offered a job as hospital surgeon. The lease of his flat in Westbühl, a suburb of Zurich, had six months to run and he offered it to Koestler and Dorothy rent-free. Koestler's cousin Theodore (the sex-book publisher), having decided to introduce a more literary element into his list, had agreed to pay Koestler five pounds monthly against all rights in *The Gladiators*. With Dorothy's regular monthly allowance from her mother, they were sure of ten pounds a month. They reckoned that they could survive on that in Zurich (although the monthly income would be lower than that of an unemployed Swiss worker living on relief), and there they would have peace and quiet. Koestler could work on *The Gladiators* undisturbed and (since the Party forbade them to make any contact with Swiss Communists) without political distractions. So they packed their few belongings and moved from their hotel room in Paris to the pleasant three-room apartment in Zurich.

In March, a dilemma presented itself. Dorothy's German passport expired and could not, so she thought (as a Jew, a Communist, and a refugee from the National Socialist dictatorship), be renewed. There was nothing for it but marriage, an institution which both she and Koestler regarded with contempt in spite of the fact that the Socialist Fatherland had long since replaced sexual libertinism with the rigorous and puritanical 'new proletarian morality'.

Arrangements were made, the date fixed, friends informed. And then, a day or two before the wedding was due to take place, Dorothy came into Koestler's study, with what he recalls as an expression of deep gloom, to tell him that she had received a letter from the German Consulate saying that her passport could, after all, be renewed. Koestler was delighted.

> '"Wonderful," I said. "Now we can call the whole thing off, and live happily ever after." Dorothy looked at me pensively from under her tousled hair. "But I have written to everybody that we are getting married," she said. "If we call it off, what will people say?" So we went to the Humms to borrow their wedding rings for the ceremony. Neither of us breathed a word about this new turn of events. To save our self-respect, the marriage had to remain a reluctant passport affair.'

Would Koestler and Dorothy have lived 'happily ever after' if their relationship had not received the stamp of official recognition? Probably not. At the age of thirty Koestler was no readier than he had been at twenty-five to settle down with one woman, with or without benefit of marriage contract. He was still in search of the ideal Helena, who, by definition, could never be an actual and present partner. And so, after a few months of marriage, he and Dorothy agreed to separate. There was no quarrelling, no bitterness, and they remained friends.

Their separation, however, signalled the end of a period of peace almost unique in Koestler's early adult life. With Dorothy had gone the five pounds a month which she had received from her mother. The lease of the apartment was running out. *The Gladiators* was far from completion, and Koestler's publishing cousin had lost interest in it. Theodore arrived in Zurich to break the news that he and his brother Frederic had decided that if Koestler was to continue receiving his five pounds a month he would have to produce another sex book – *Sexual Anomalies and Perversions* this time – instead.

Koestler agreed, reluctantly moved to Budapest and got to work on the sex book. In spite (or because) of his frustration, Koestler succeeded in dictating the two hundred and fifty thousand words of *Sexual Anomalies and Perversions* at top speed. He also, between the summers of 1935 and 1936, translated S. Fowler-Wright's novel *Prelude in Prague* into German; wrote a chapter on Paris for a continental guide-book published in English; two film treatments (neither of which was sold); rewrote a play as a short story for a literary competition (which it failed to win); contributed articles and book reviews regularly to *Das Neue Tagebuch*; put together a synopsis for another projected sex-book; and drafted half of a propaganda novel, *The Good Soldier Schweik Goes to War Again* which had been commissioned by Willy Muenzenberg and which was never to be completed.

Koestler estimates that in the course of that year he turned out half a million words.

But the inward-looking, over-heated life of bohemian Budapest, with all its scandals and delights, could not for long provide adequate compensation for the strain of the frenzied work by which Koestler was earning his living. He decided to return to Paris.

# CHAPTER VI

# *1936–1938*

THE SUCCESS OF HITLER'S bold gamble in occupying the Rhineland in March 1936 brought it home at last to Stalin that now that Hitler's 'last territorial demand' in the West had been so easily satisfied, it was only a matter of time before he would turn to the East.

And so, the Comintern was instructed to redouble its Popular Front efforts in the West. Overnight yesterday's 'Social Fascists' became today's comrades in the struggle to halt National Socialism and Fascism, and protect the Soviet Union.

The year 1936 brought a new cause to be exploited. Spain had descended into chaos under a Popular Front government and, on 13th July, General Francisco Franco led an Army mutiny in Morocco. Within two days it had spread to the mainland. Spain was at once in the grip of a deadly civil war. Franco's forces were supported by Italy and Germany, the Popular Front by the Soviet Union and Mexico and by the many foreign volunteers, Communist for the most part, who formed the International Brigade. Overnight the country became a symbol.

A fortnight after Franco had raised the standard of revolt, Koestler went to see Willy Muenzenberg, who in his capacity as head of the Comintern's West-European AGITPROP Department was now in charge of the propaganda campaign in favour of the Spanish Loyalists. Koestler wanted to join the Spanish Republican Army but Muenzenberg, whose help he sought, did not approve:

> 'He measured human actions by their propaganda value, and saw no point in journalists wasting their time in the trenches.'

He had a better idea. Koestler had a Hungarian passport and a press card from *Pester Lloyd*, a Budapest newspaper. Why shouldn't he go to General Franco's headquarters in Seville and collect information about German and Italian intervention? Koestler agreed.

> 'The *Pester Lloyd* would be a good cover, but there were several snags. The *Pester Lloyd* would, of course, never agree to sending me to Spain, and if Franco's intelligence department were to check on my credentials, the game

would be up . . . Secondly, other foreign correspondents might find it strange that a small Hungarian paper was sending a special war correspondent to Spain instead of relying, as usual, on agency reports. It was therefore necessary to get an additional assignment from some other newspaper which would make the journey more plausible . . . In the end Otto [Katz] suggested, *faute de mieux*, the London *News Chronicle* . . . Otto had friends on the paper's staff who could get me an accreditation without difficulty and delay. We then worked out a cover story on the following lines. I would travel as a correspondent of the *Pester Lloyd*, and would only mention the *News Chronicle* if this became unavoidable . . . I would confidentially admit that, though my sympathies were the same as the god-fearing *Pester Lloyd*'s, I had been forced for financial reasons to accept a second assignment from a London newspaper whose editors were unfortunately prejudiced against General Franco; but they had given me a free hand to report the facts objectively, and thus a chance to influence British Liberal opinion in favour of Franco.'

It was a very thin cover indeed. Even if the Nationalist authorities in Seville did not penetrate it, there was some risk that one of the German correspondents at Franco's headquarters might recognise Koestler. But Koestler, buoyed up once more by a bridge-burning mood, was not alarmed. He collected his letter of accreditation from the *News Chronicle*'s Paris Office, left for England, and on 22nd August embarked at Southampton in the *Almanzora*, bound for Lisbon.

His story was accepted there without question by the honorary Hungarian consul, a jovial Danish business man whose wife was a pro-Franco Portuguese aristocrat. They introduced him to the Catholic leader Gil Robles and to General Franco's brother, Nicolas, who was operating in Lisbon under the *nom-de-guerre* of Fernandez d'Avila. They were no less helpful, and thirty-six hours after disembarking in Lisbon Koestler left for Seville armed with a safe-conduct signed by Nicolas Franco and a personal letter of recommendation from Gil Robles to General Queipo de Llano, commander of the Seville garrison.

All went well during his first day in Seville. In the streets there was ample evidence of Nazi intervention in the shape of German airmen wearing the white overalls of the Spanish Air Force but with a swastika between the wings embroidered on their blouses. A friendly and indiscreet Englishman who had volunteered for the Nationalist air force obligingly supplied him with details of the types, markings, and approximate numbers of German aircraft already delivered to the insurgents. Captain Bolín, head of the press department at the Nationalist headquarters, accepted his credentials and arranged an exclusive interview with General Queipo de Llano, who, believing that Koestler was in sympathy with the rebels, spoke unguardedly about foreign aid.

On the second day, however, he ran into trouble at the Hotel Christina, where all German officers were billeted. As he entered the lounge he noticed four uniformed German air force officers sitting at a table in the company of a fifth man in plain clothes who shortly got up and walked past Koestler. They recognised each other instantly, as old colleagues from Ullstein's in Berlin.

Herr Strindberg, son of the great Rupert Strindberg, was clearly acting as a war correspondent for Ullstein's who were now a Nazi Trust. He knew of course that Koestler was a Communist. The latter bluffed his way out of the dilemma, picking a quarrel, storming out of the hotel, hurrying to General Queipo's headquarters where he said that he had been recalled by his newspaper and obtained, with no difficulty, his exit-permit. As soon as he had collected his case and his passport, he hired a car to Gibraltar. An hour after he had crossed the frontier a warrant for his arrest was issued in Seville on the instructions of Captain Bolín, who was heard to swear that he would shoot Koestler like a mad dog when he got hold of him.

In the safety of Gibraltar Koestler filed a story for the *News Chronicle* recounting his exploits and discoveries during his brief stay in Seville, and describing his successful fooling of Bolín and Queipo. It appeared on the front page and was picked up by many other newspapers. On his way back to France from Gibraltar he stopped for a day in London and called at the *News Chronicle* office in Bouverie Street, where he was warmly welcomed by the foreign editor, Norman Cliff.

* *

Koestler was now admitted to Muenzenberg's inner circle and appointed liaison officer between the Paris headquarters of the Comintern-controlled 'Spanish Relief Committee' and its London offshoot, 'The Commission of Inquiry into Alleged Breaches of the Non-Intervention Agreement in Spain', which proceeded to hold a public show trial on the lines of the Reichstag Counter-Trial.

When the hearings of the 'Commission of Inquiry' in London had ended, Koestler was sent to Madrid on a special assignment on behalf of the Spanish Government as well as the Comintern. His task was to search the papers left behind by right-wing politicians who had fled Madrid at the beginning of the war in the expectation of finding documents to prove that Germany had taken a direct hand in preparing the insurrection. He spent three or four weeks in the city, collecting material, experiencing the horrors of bombing in a city with scarcely any anti-aircraft defences, and observing among his fellow-foreigners that strange 'mixture of passion and farce . . . of vanity and sacrifice, of the grotesque and the sublime' that was the consequence of the 'last twitch of Europe's dying conscience' galvanised by the Comintern's international propaganda campaign.

As he was nearing the end of his task, during the first week of November, Largo Caballero's government gave up Madrid for lost and fled to Valencia. A day or two later Koestler, with two large suitcases full of documents, followed in the company of three members of the air force squadron formed by André Malraux with whom the Communist Party in Madrid had put him in touch. It was a hair-raising journey because the Anarchists, furious at what they considered the Government's desertion, had armed patrols out on the road to Valencia stopping cars coming from Madrid, requisitioning them, and arresting the passengers. Fortunately Koestler was carrying, in addition to his Foreign

Ministry and Communist Party safe-conducts, a paper which one of the French airmen had obtained from the Anarchists, so he got through safely to Valencia and eventually back to Paris, where he undertook the writing of a book under the instructions of Muenzenberg who urged him to fill it with atrocity propaganda.

Such scruples as Koestler had at the inclusion of 'black propaganda' stories and photographs supplied by the Comintern were dispelled by the no less unscrupulous nature of the Nationalists' propaganda. At the beginning of January 1937 the German version of his book was published by Muenzenberg's Editions de Carrefour under the title of *Menschenopfer Unerhört*. A week or so later, when the French translation, *L'Espagne ensanglantée*, was at the printers, Koestler was ordered to return to Spain for the third time. This time he went as correspondent for the loyalist *Agence Espagne*, as well as for the London *News Chronicle*.

On 27th January, after a party with W. H. Auden and others, he left for Malaga, accompanied by a Norwegian journalist, Gerda Grepp. On the following day they arrived, to find half the city in ruins, the population obviously demoralised, and the Loyalist troops in a state of total disarray, as they awaited the final stage of General Queipo de Llano's offensive. Within a day or two it became all too clear that Malaga was about to fall to the Nationalists without a struggle.

Koestler spent that night with Sir Peter Chalmers-Mitchell, a long established British resident of Malaga. In the morning he decided to stay on and thereby gratuitously placed himself in a position of great danger. He knew that the Nationalists were exacting at least an eye for an eye and a tooth for a tooth in retribution for the appalling atrocities committed by the Loyalists in the weeks before and immediately after the rebellion. But he chose to stay behind in Malaga with the elderly Englishman.

Why?

> 'I thought that if we remained inconspicuous during the first few days, until things calmed down and the British Consul came back to Malaga, he would somehow manage to get us both across the nearby frontier to Gibraltar. Never before had a foreign journalist witnessed what happened when the insurgents took over a town; from the point of view of the newly founded *Agence Espagne*, this project seemed worth the risk. Besides, in view of General Queipo's repeated [broadcast] threats of a "terrible retribution against the Anarchist stronghold" [which Malaga in fact was], we both had the irrational and rather silly conviction that the presence of two "neutral observers" would have a restraining influence on the behaviour of the insurgents when they entered the town.'

Koestler was fortunate. The Nationalist who had threatened to shoot him like a mad dog, Captain Luis Bolín, refrained from doing so when he and his men burst into Sir Peter's house and recognised Koestler.

Koestler spent four days in Malaga jail, from where he was transferred on 13th February to the Central Prison of Seville. There he was to remain most of the time in solitary confinement, and in constant fear of execution as a spy, until 14th May, when he was exchanged for a Nationalist hostage held by the Government.

Sir Peter had been freed and allowed to go to Gibraltar, thanks to the intervention of the commander of a British destroyer which had arrived at Malaga. Before leaving, he sent the news of Koestler's arrest to the *News Chronicle* over the ship's radio. This set in motion the public campaign which saved him. The organiser of the campaign and the driving force behind it was Dorothy, the wife from whom he had parted.

> 'The day when the news of my arrest had appeared in the French papers Dorothy had peremptorily asked the Party to be sent to London for the purpose of initiating a public protest. The Party was sceptical, and thought that in view of the unsavoury facts that might come out, the less said about me the better. But by-passing all obstacles, Dorothy went to England, a country where she had never been before, to mobilise public opinion for her husband, of whom nobody had ever heard before. Her task was all the more difficult as even my official employers, the *News Chronicle*, knew next to nothing about me. I had only met two members of its staff personally: Norman Cliff and Willy Forrest. I had never met the editor, and all in all the paper had published perhaps half a dozen despatches by me. Though the *Chronicle* did everything in their power to help Dorothy, they were naturally handicapped by these facts. Yet Dorothy, whom I knew as a shy and inhibited young woman, suddenly revealed the qualities of a fighting Amazon. She was tireless and ingenious, tactful and dogged. She spent sixteen hours a day collecting signatures from politicians and men of letters, lobbying in the House of Commons, interviewing Dukes and Archbishops, engineering petitions and protest-resolutions. Her tongue-tied manner achieved more in England than eloquence could have done; her sincerity was instantaneously convincing; the fact that she spoke as the distressed wife of a husband in prison was more effective than any political argument. There were many who helped, but it was Dorothy who saved my life.'

Her efforts had resulted in telegrams and letters of protest being addressed to General Franco by organisations of all kinds and by hundreds of individuals, among them fifty-eight members of the British House of Commons, half of them Conservatives. The few people who were aware of Koestler's real rôle as an agent of the Comintern kept that knowledge to themselves. His propaganda book, *L'Espagne ensanglantée*, had been published only in German and French versions, and few people in England had read it. Thanks to Dorothy's campaign, his name was now widely known, but nothing whatsoever of his background. The Foreign Secretary, Anthony Eden, answering a Parliamentary question, announced that the Government had intervened with Franco on his behalf 'in spite of the fact that he is a Czechoslovak [*sic*] citizen'. All the public knew was that a newspaperman, the correspondent of the Liberal *News Chronicle*, had been imprisoned by the Spanish rebels and threatened with death. His case became a symbolic issue, and so the Nationalists eventually freed him in exchange for the wife of one of their leading airmen.

* *

Koestler found Dorothy waiting for him in London on his return from Spain. For a time they lived together again as man and wife, first as guests of Sir Walter (later Lord) Layton, chairman of the *News Chronicle*, and for the rest of the summer in a house which they rented at Shepperton-on-Thames. There he dictated to Dorothy an account of his prison experiences. This was first published in serial form in the *News Chronicle* and attracted wide attention. Koestler then went on to expand it on a commission from the left-wing publisher, Victor Gollancz, incorporating several chapters from *L'Espagne ensanglantée* under the title of *Spanish Testament**.

Early in September Koestler had finished his book, and he and Dorothy had once more amicably agreed to go their separate ways:

> 'All the circumstances were propitious; yet my neurotic inability to settle down with a partner for life proved distressingly stronger than affection and gratitude.'

The advance from Gollancz had been spent. He could not return to Spain as a correspondent, having signed in Seville an undertaking, as a condition of his release, that he would not 'meddle in the internal affairs of Spain'. Layton, who did not know that Koestler was a member of the Communist Party and had acted in Spain as a Comintern agent, proposed to send him to Moscow as the *News Chronicle*'s correspondent – a bright idea quashed by the editor, Gerald Barry, who knew all about Koestler's background and connections. As a compromise, it was agreed that he should write a series of articles during a tour of Greece and the Middle East.

His first stop was Paris. On the following day he was interrogated by two *apparatchiks* from the Party about his conduct in the Spanish jail. It was their task to try to satisfy themselves that he had not betrayed any of his comrades or been 'turned round' by anti-Communists. For an hour he was closely cross-examined by one of them, Paul Merker,† while the other – an apparently senior *apparatchik* who spoke German with a foreign accent – looked on. Since Koestler had not in fact given anything or anyone away while in the Nationalists' hands, he was able, it seemed, to satisfy his interrogators. But he was ill at ease during the interview. When a friendly jailer in Seville had asked him how he, an educated person, was mixed up with the Reds, he had blurted out, 'But I am no longer a Red.'

* Published in January 1938, it was widely and well reviewed. Among its reviewers was George Orwell, who a few months earlier had been wounded in Spain while fighting with the POUM militia – a mainly Catalan party of Trotskyist persuasion later suppressed by the Communist-dominated Popular Front. He was one of the very few who at the time realised the extent of, and deplored, the Russian takeover of the Loyalist Government machine and the Popular Front propaganda in support of it. Reviewing *Spanish Testament* in *Time and Tide* on 5th February, he praised Koestler's account of his experiences in prison. 'It is of the greatest psychological interest – probably one of the most honest and unusual documents that have been produced by the Spanish war.' He had reservations, however, about the earlier part – that is, the material incorporated from *L'Espagne ensanglantée* – which looked, he wrote, 'rather as though it had been "edited" for the benefit of the Left Book Club'. In this he was correct. *Spanish Testament* became a Left Book Club choice and was translated into several languages. Koestler later excised the propaganda chapters from the book now in print as *Dialogue with Death*.

† After the war Merker became a member of the East German government but was later purged.

Intending to lie, he had in fact spoken the truth. The possibility of execution had led him to examine himself during the long hours he spent by the small window of his cell, and the surges of the 'oceanic feeling' he experienced there had gradually washed away the faith in Communist dogma that had hitherto for some years sustained him.

> 'In the end Merker said that he had finished with me – but perhaps the comrade would like to ask some further questions? His voice, in addressing the other man, was slightly deferential. The other shook his head, looked at his watch and got up. The only words he had spoken during an hour were his opening phrase when Merker introduced us, "I have heard about you"; and his closing words "Good-bye" . . . Once the interrogation was over, I had a sudden intense attack of anxiety, and I noticed how unsteady my hand was as I lifted the cup of cold *café au lait*. This was the autumn of 1937; a few weeks earlier Marshal Tukhachevsky and eight top-ranking Generals of the Red Army had been shot after a secret trial; every day we heard of new arrests, accompanied by incredible and frightening accusations. The harmless interrogation of a moment ago carried a terrifying echo. It was impossible not to think how helpless one would be facing that taciturn, hard-eyed man, not at a Paris café table, but across the Prosecutor's desk in the GPU building in Baku or in the Lubyanka.'

* *

After a few days in Athens, Koestler received a cable from the *News Chronicle* instructing him to go at once to Palestine, where the Arabs, alarmed by the rapid increase of Jewish immigration and inflamed by the Royal Commission's recommendation of partition, were in rebellion against the British administration.

Eight years had passed since he had left Palestine and said good-bye to Zionism, disillusioned by the narrow chauvinism of the settlers and stifled by the hothouse atmosphere of Jerusalem and Tel Aviv. In so far as he had thought about the Jewish question at all during this period he had assumed that the answer to it, as to most other intractable problems, would be found in the global context of Socialist revolution.

But the prospect of the Socialist millennium had been receding fast. Terror reigned in the Soviet Union. In Hitler's Germany the officially sponsored persecution of the Jews was gathering momentum. For millions there and elsewhere in Central and Eastern Europe, Palestine meant their only chance of survival.

> 'Whether they were welcome or not, whether the climate and culture suited them or not, were irrelevant questions . . . In this limited, resigned, and utilitarian sense, I was still a Zionist.'

During his stay, Koestler met a number of friends and former colleagues from Berlin who had managed to escape: a former Ullstein editor, now a cloakroom attendant in the King David Hotel; a woman lawyer, now a cook in a boarding-house; the former head of the Ullstein international news service, now selling advertising space for an obscure Polish-language publication. They were all rooted in German culture, knew no Hebrew, had never been Zionists. They had survived, but in their refuge Koestler saw them as condemned to a pointless and sterile existence in a country to which they had been driven by force and not by inner choice.

Koestler was now convinced that Jabotinsky's ideal of the transformation of all Palestine into a Jewish state, with an Arab minority, was unworkable and utopian. Partition, as proposed by the Royal Commission under Lord Peel, was an imperfect solution to be sure, but it was the only one that held out any hope. The council of the League of Nations had authorised the United Kingdom as the mandatory power to draw up a detailed plan for the division of the country. The representative Jewish organisations were prepared to accept it, and Koestler believed that the moderate Arab leaders would yield to diplomatic pressure and disown the extremists. King Abdullah of Transjordan, with whom Koestler had an interview in Amman during the lull in the riots, said as much.

On his return to London he wrote a series of articles which warned of the horrors which further procrastination on the part of the United Kingdom and the League of Nations would entail:

> 'Britain must act, and act quickly,' his final article ended. 'This is an S.O.S. for Palestine.'

An S.O.S. which is still sounding, but on a different note.

# CHAPTER VII

# *1938*

ON HIS RETURN TO England, immediately after the publication of *Spanish Testament* in January 1938, Koestler set off on a four weeks' lecture tour sponsored by the Left Book Club (the Popular Front's most successful propaganda operation in Britain), directed by Victor Gollancz, Harold Laski, and John Strachey. Most of the Club's sixty-five thousand subscribers were Communists or fellow-travellers.

He was greatly touched by their eagerness and innocence. In every audience there were people who had friends or relatives fighting with the International Brigade. Ignorant of the ferocious internecine struggles going on behind the lines, as the Communists with the powerful support of the Russian GPU systematically eliminated their rivals in the struggle for power (to be exercised not in the interests of Spain but of the Soviet Union), they clung to a simplistic, heartening and unreal view of the Spanish Loyalist Army as the united rearguard of Western democracy. Koestler knew better, of course, and it was the contrast between his increasingly disturbing knowledge of the true state of affairs on the Government side and the generous innocence and ignorance of his British audiences that was eventually to lead to his apostasy.

His lectures were supposed to be on the political and military situation in Spain as seen from a strictly Marxist-Leninist-Stalinist, and therefore 'objective', point of view. It was no part of his brief to speak about his personal experiences, and any 'subjective' conclusions he might draw from them. It was his job to boost the Popular Front (ie, the Moscow) line and vilify any individuals or organisations on the anti-Nationalist side whom Moscow wished to destroy. Here, however, he was guilty of a serious transgression.

> 'At almost every meeting there was for me one critical moment. It came when somebody in the audience asked a question about the POUM, a small Leftist splinter group . . . Because of its Trotskyist leaning, the POUM was at the time treated by the Communists as enemy number one, and its members were fair prey for the GPU in Spain. It had been made a scapegoat for the anarchist

rising in Barcelona. Its leader Andres Nin, formerly Minister of Justice in the Caballero Government, had been denounced as an agent of Franco and arrested, together with a group of his associates . . . The men of the POUM had fought with great bravery and self-sacrifice at the front in Aragon (George Orwell had been wounded while serving as a volunteer in their ranks), and there was no doubt in my mind that the accusations against them were absurd and perfidious. But for a Party member to say this in public meant expulsion, with the inevitable sequel of being himself denounced as a Trotskyist agent of Franco or the Gestapo. That is why questions referring to POUM put me in a critical position.

'The first time it was asked, the question took me unawares . . . For a moment, my mind was a blank . . . Then, without conscious reflection, I took a plunge and said what I really thought. I said that I disagreed with the policy of the POUM for a number of reasons which I would be glad to explain, but that in my opinion Andres Nin and his comrades* had been acting in good faith, and to call them traitors was both stupid and a desecration of the dead . . .

'There was a short, embarrassed silence . . . Every time the question cropped up at other meetings, I gave the same answer, and every time it was received with the same embarrassed silence . . .'

No one seems to have denounced Koestler to the Party's inquisitors for his heresy, and at the end of the lecture-tour he returned to Paris to complete his novel, *The Gladiators*, in which he was working out in terms of historical fiction some of those problems of ends and means which had returned to preoccupy him with acute urgency during his imprisonment in Spain.

A good deal was happening to dispel the last of his cherished illusions. In March there was the great show trial in Moscow of the 'Anti-Soviet Bloc of Rightists and Trotskyists', during which Bukharin, Rakovsky, Yagoda and other Old Bolsheviks confessed to a variety of imaginary crimes, as a final service to the Communist cause, before their extermination. The Revolution, having butchered millions of innocents, was now devouring the revolutionaries themselves in increasing numbers.

Koestler and the other German-speaking Communist members of the writers' cell who met regularly in a private room of the Café Mephisto knew very well that nobody was safe from the Terror, however dedicated to the cause and the Socialist Fatherland he might be. One of their comrades, 'Hans', who had worked for the Communist military intelligence *apparat* in Germany under its chief, Kippenberger, had been arrested before Hitler's accession and sentenced to five years' hard labour. While Hans was serving his sentence, Kippenberger was summoned to Moscow and shot because of his reluctance to obey the GPU's directive that 'deviationists' in the party should be betrayed to the Gestapo. When 'Hans' had completed his sentence in the spring of 1938, he succeeded in crossing the frontier illegally and joining his fiancée, 'Judy', waiting for him in Paris. A few days later the German Communist Party's weekly newspaper in

* They were later shot without trial or ceremony, presumably by Comintern agents.

France published a photograph of them both on the front page with a caption denouncing them as Gestapo spies. Koestler knew the allegation to be an absurdity, but he also knew that such denunciations were often considered to be an 'objective' necessity in the case of comrades who had been exposed to the risk of contamination. In spite of this, he wrote a letter of protest to the central committee of the Party. He received no answer, and the other members of the caucus obediently turned their backs on their former friends and comrades.

Not long after this, a special meeting of the cell was summoned to discuss ways and means of implementing the latest directive from Moscow, handed down to them in the form of the Soviet Writers' Federation's new slogan: 'Write the Truth'. The proceedings were, of course, grimly farcical, since Koestler, Kisch, Seghers, Regler, Kantorowicz, Uhse and all the others were well aware of the fact that the question to which they had to find an answer was how to 'Write the Truth!' without writing the truth.

A female *apparatchik* was sent from Moscow to urge them to exercise more revolutionary vigilance. She

> 'took for her text another slogan:
>
> '"Every Bolshevist must be a Chekist."*
>
> 'We took it as quietly as if she had said: "Grow your own vegetables; the Nation needs them."'

Koestler at long last decided that he could stand no more of what Orwell was later to describe as 'newspeak' and 'double-think' when a Party official approached him shortly before he was due to give a lecture on Spain to the Association of Exiled German Writers. The *apparatchik* asked him to insert a passage denouncing the POUM as agents of Franco. Koestler refused, and also declined to let the *apparatchik* see the text of his lecture. This alone would have been enough to condemn him in the eyes of his superiors, but the concluding words of his lecture made the real nature of his apostasy glaringly obvious.

There were two or three hundred refugee intellectuals in the audience, most of them Communists or fellow-travellers. In the course of his lecture Koestler was careful not to criticise the Party. Nor did he attack Russia. But the three sentences with which he ended his speech shocked the Communists in the audience who sat on their hands while the naïve and decent non-Communist minority applauded.

The first was: 'No movement, party, or person can claim the privilege of infallibility'; the second: 'It is as foolish to appease the enemy as it is to persecute the friend who pursues the same end as you by a different road'; and the third, a quotation from Thomas Mann: 'in the long run, a harmful truth is better than a useful lie'.

* Cheka, the 'Extraordinary Commissions to Combat Counter Revolution, Sabotage, and Speculation' – in short, the secret police set up after the Bolshevist *putsch* in October 1917 to implement the Terror, and the forerunner of the OGPU, NKVD, MVD, KVD, and the present KGB.

Such heresies uttered publicly on such an occasion were certainly more than enough to guarantee his denunciation and expulsion, but he chose to forestall this by resigning.

> 'I worked on my letter of resignation all night . . . It was a farewell to the German CP, the Comintern, and the Stalin regime. But it ended with a declaration of loyalty to the Soviet Union. I stated my opposition to the system, to the cancerous growth of the bureaucracy, the terror and supression of civil liberties. But I professed my belief that the foundations of the Workers' and Peasants' State had remained solid and unshaken, that the nationalisation of the means of production was a guarantee of her eventual return to the road of Socialism; and that, in spite of everything, the Soviet Union still represented "our last and only hope on a planet in rapid decay".'

He was to cling to those last shreds of illusion until the Hitler-Stalin pact tore them away and forced him to analyse, in a series of essays,* the various fallacies to which he had been faithful for so many years.

* *The Yogi and the Commissar.*

# CHAPTER VIII

# *1938–1940*

JONATHAN CAPE, HAVING AGREED to publish *The Gladiators*, had paid Koestler £125 as an advance against royalties. Out of that sum, since the novel was being written in German, Koestler would have to find the cost of translation. That left him with just enough for six months of frugal living and enabled him to finish the book which he had been forced to abandon on several occasions, either because he had run out of money or under the pressure of his political work. The return to the first century BC filled him with peace and relief.

While he was working quietly on the last chapters of *The Gladiators*, he was contacted by his old friend Eva Weissberg who had been freed from a Soviet jail and expelled from Russia. Her husband, Alex, was still held in a Kharkov prison, accused of spying for the Germans and of fomenting an armed insurrection in the Ukraine (and also, as Koestler learnt later, of recruiting a band of National Socialist terrorists to assassinate Stalin and Marshal Voroshilov when they next went hunting in the Caucasus).*

Could anything be done to save him? Koestler, having promised to do his best but without much hope, had an idea. Since Alex was a distinguished physicist, perhaps a direct appeal to Stalin by the three French winners of the Nobel Prize for Physics – Frédéric and Irène Joliot-Curie and Jean Perrin – all of them leftists and well disposed to the Soviet Union, would have some effect. He drafted a letter and took it to Frédéric Joliot who immediately took Koestler's word for it that Weissberg was innocent of the trumped-up charges. He signed the appeal and also obtained the signatures of his wife and Perrin, although

* The GPU's object was to prepare Weissberg for the role of star witness in the trial of Bukharin. Twice he had signed a confession after several days and nights of non-stop interrogation, only to withdraw it after sleep had brought him to his senses. The GPU, having decided that he was too tough to be a good performer, left him alone thereafter. Following three years in various Russian prisons, he was handed over by the GPU to their Gestapo collaborators with many other German and Austrian Communists, Socialists and anti-Nazi refugees. He survived their attentions, played a part in the Polish underground, and escaped to the West after the War. He told his extraordinary story in *Conspiracy of Silence* (London, 1952), to which Koestler wrote a preface.

neither had even heard of Weissberg before. Einstein also wrote directly to Stalin. Although neither letter was even acknowledged, the joint protest was perhaps instrumental in saving Alex's life.

* *

As soon as *The Gladiators* had been completed, Koestler wrote a brief synopsis of a novel tentatively entitled *The Vicious Circle*. Jonathan Cape accepted the idea and Koestler set to work. All that he knew was that it concerned four or five characters under sentence of death in a totalitarian country which they had served with unquestioning loyalty, placing the interest of mankind in the future above the interests of man in the present, unhesitatingly sacrificing morality to expediency in the belief that a glorious end justifies the most inglorious means. Now, because their extinction was expedient to the cause, they were to die at the hands of men who subscribed to the same principles.

Stalin's show trials of his old comrades, whose confessions had baffled the world, was the obvious inspiration; but when he began to write, Koestler had formulated no plot and only one character was clearly established in his mind. He

> '. . . was to be a member of the Old Bolshevik guard, his manner of thinking modelled on Nikolai Bukharin's, his personality and physical appearance a synthesis of Leon Trotsky and Karl Radek . . .
>
> 'The opening sequence seemed quite obvious. When his own people come to arrest him, Rubashov is asleep and dreaming about the last time when he was arrested in the enemy's country; sleep-dazed, he is unable to decide which of the two hostile dictators is reaching out for him this time . . .
>
> 'Once the opening scene was written, I did not have to search for plot or incident; they were waiting among the stored memories of seven years, which, while the lid was down on them, had undergone a kind of fermentation. Now that the pressure was lifted, they came bubbling up, revealing their true essence and colour . . . I did not worry about what would happen next in the book; I waited for it to happen with fear and curiosity . . .'

So that most extraordinarily influential of novels, eventually to be entitled *Darkness at Noon*, began, as it were, to write itself, concentrating the author's half-conscious insights into a fearful revelation of the nightmarish realities of Communism in practice.

There were, of course, interruptions forced on him from time to time by the need to make some ready money. The first of these came in the autumn of 1938 when Willy Muenzenberg invited him to be the editor of the new German language weekly paper he had founded. This was *Die Zukunft* (*The Future*) and its aim was to work for the rapprochement of the various anti-Nazi groups in exile. By this time, Muenzenberg, having wisely declined various pressing suggestions that he should present himself in Moscow, had broken with the Comintern.

The weekly got off to a good start, with contributions from Thomas Mann, Harold Nicolson, Duff Cooper, Norman Angell, E. M. Forster, Aldous Huxley, and others. Advising Muenzenberg and Koestler on the editorial board were Manès Sperber (who by then had also left the Communist Party), 'Paul Sering' (the pen name of Richard Loewenthal), Julius Steinberg the sociologist, and Ludwig Marcuse. After a few months, however,

'. . . the paper began to go stale, as sooner or later most émigré papers do, cut off as they are from their native country, and without real contact with the country of their exile.

While I was editing it, I could only work at *Darkness at Noon* during the night – but the novel was growing on me like an advancing pregnancy, and, as I felt that the war was approaching, I wanted to concentrate on it while the going was good. About Christmas I resigned from the paper . . .'

By the end of March 1939, halfway through *Darkness at Noon*, he ran out of money again. For the third time he put on Dr Costler's alpaca jacket and spent two months writing another sex book for his cousins.

When that was out of the way he and his new girl-friend, Daphne Hardy,* drove south to the Midi in search of a place where they could live cheaply and he could work steadily without interruption. They found it in Roquebillière, a village in the valley of the Vesubie about fifty miles from Monaco and ten miles from the Italian frontier, where accommodation, food, service, and *vin à discretion* cost them only £5 a month each.

The time bought for the West by Chamberlain at Munich was running out. The Senate of Danzig had decided to join the Third Reich. All the villages of the Maritime Alps were packed with soldiers – grumbling, drinking red wine, playing cards, bored, demoralised. But Koestler and Daphne were

'. . . very happy . . . No, there would be no war. We would sacrifice another piece of our *honneur* – who cares for *honneur*, anyway? – and go on playing belotte. And writing novels and carving stones and cultivating our garden, like sensible people should do during their short stay on this earth. Besides, Hitler couldn't fight against the Soviets and the West simultaneously. And if the West made a firm stand this time, the Soviets would come in at once. There would be no war. You had only to repeat it sufficiently often, until you were sick of hearing yourself say it.

'And all the time we knew that this was our last summer for a long time, and perhaps for ever.'

On 23rd August Koestler read in the *Eclaireur du Sud-Est* that Ribbentrop and Molotov had signed a treaty of non-aggression between Germany and the Soviet Union – in effect a direct encouragement to Hitler to attack Poland. On the following day he read in *L'Humanité*, the official organ of the French Communist Party, that the treaty was the result of Stalin's supreme effort to prevent the threatening 'imperialist' war.

And so was dispelled, once and for all, the last lingering trace of the illusion which had buoyed up Koestler for years. Only a few days before he had

* A young English sculptress who had won a travelling scholarship. She now lives in Suffolk a few miles from the Koestlers' country house.

completed a long passage of dialogue in *Darkness at Noon* in which Gletkin, the OGPU interrogator, says to Rubashov, the old Bolshevik,

> 'We did not recoil from betraying our friends and compromising with our enemies, in order to preserve the Bastion. That was the task which history has given us, the representatives of the first glorious revolution.'

Now the hitherto hidden logic of events had become blindingly obvious. The summer was over. It was time to start packing.

A day or so later, still hoping that some miracle might happen at the last minute, they set off in Koestler's ancient Ford for Paris. At Le Lavandou they learned that Poland had been invaded and that the French Government had ordered general mobilisation. From Avignon onwards for miles on end they passed a stream of tanks, armoured cars, and trucks heading for the Italian border. Between Pouilly and Melun, on Sunday 3rd September, they learned that the United Kingdom had declared war on Germany, and on the last fifty miles of their journey the road was almost blocked by people escaping from the capital in their cars and in taxis.

> 'We arrived at my flat in Paris at four o'clock in the afternoon. I shook hands with our old *concierge*, she gave me a strange look . . .
>
> '"I am not allowed to tell you," she said, "but you had better leave at once. The police were here at 2 a.m. this morning; they have taken away Dr Neumann handcuffed and they wanted to arrest you too."'

Koestler was puzzled by this. Neumann, who occupied the flat next door, was a political refugee, an anti-Nazi whose loyalty to France was beyond doubt. He had hurried back to Paris from a Swiss sanatorium where he had been treated for tuberculosis, to enlist in the French army. But he was of German origin and so, technically, an enemy alien. That no doubt explained his arrest.

But why did the police wish to arrest Koestler? His nationality was Hungarian and Hungary was neutral.

Convinced that the whole matter was a mistake, he presented himself at the local police station, where the *commissaire* dismissed him irritably: 'I really don't see what you want. What do you think would happen if all foreigners came running here?' Koestler spent the night in the flat and nothing happened. Next day he and Daphne went to the *Préfecture de Police* where his identity card was renewed without comment. But Koestler was still uneasy. He telephoned a friend, Jubert, a well-known advocate and formerly a Soviet sympathiser, who gave him cold comfort. He knew of many people who had been arbitrarily arrested although their loyalty was not in doubt; many of them were personal friends of his but he had been unable to help them. The country, he said, was living under the *loi des suspects* which gave the police practically uncontrolled power over the individual.

Jubert advised him to try to get to England as soon as possible. But Koestler had already tried, without success. He and Daphne had in fact planned to go on to London, where Koestler intended to enlist in the British army. His permanent twelve-months visa to the United Kingdom had been renewed shortly before he and Daphne had gone to Roquebillière. But all existing visas to the United Kingdom had been cancelled and the British passport office required special authorisation to issue new ones. Koestler filled in an application form and asked the passport control officer how long it would be until the authorisation came through. He

> 'gave a rather discouraging shrug; he could not commit himself to a definite date, but he gave me to understand that I might have to wait for anything between three and six weeks.'

Thereafter Koestler slept with a small suitcase beside the bed, ready to go to prison at any moment. Daphne, who could, of course, have returned to England without difficulty, decided to stay with him.

* *

At half-past eight on the morning of 3rd October two policemen came to the flat and took him away.

> 'When we turned the corner of the rue de Vaugirard, Daphne still stood in the doorway with wide-open eyes, waving her hand.'

After three monotonous days at the *Préfecture* without explanation, they were taken to the Roland Garros Stadium which had been turned into a temporary internment camp for undesirable aliens. There were about five hundred of them packed into the dressing-rooms under the grandstand of the main tennis court.

Koestler spent a week there. On the day when he learned they were about to leave Paris for an unknown destination he persuaded the commandant, a decent soldier who disliked his role as jailer, to let him send one of the guards in a taxi to bring Daphne to the Stadium. He could have two minutes with her at the entrance.

> '. . . The Commandant personally escorted me to her, as the matter was against all regulations. The two minutes became five, and when they were over I knew that the Home Office had refused my application for a visa . . . and that Daphne had decided not to return to England, but to wait until I was released.'

That evening the five hundred internees were taken to the Gare d'Austerlitz where, under heavy escort, they boarded a number of third-class carriages attached to the Toulouse Express, the night train on which Koestler had frequently travelled during the Spanish Civil War to catch the 5 a.m. plane from Toulouse to Barcelona, Alicante, and Madrid.

At eleven o'clock next morning they arrived at the little station of Le Vernet in the foothills of the Pyrenees.

* *

The internment camp of Le Vernet was one of the largest in France, holding two thousand aliens. Its crude wooden hutments, roofed with waterproofed paper, and its grounds together covered some fifty acres. The camp was divided into three sections – A, B and C – each separated from the others by barbed wire entanglements and trenches. Section A housed aliens with a criminal record; Section B, those considered politically dangerous; and Section C, those against whom no definite charge could be brought but who had been judged to be suspect either on political or criminal grounds. Koestler and most of those who had travelled with him from Paris were housed in Section C. Among them were some thirty men who at some point or another during the preceding four years had been imprisoned in such German concentration camps as Dachau, Cranienburg and Wolfsbüttel, in which conditions had been, they said, much superior to those of Le Vernet.

Each hut, housing two hundred men, was thirty yards long and five yards wide. Down each side ran an upper and lower platform of planks three feet apart. Each platform was divided into ten compartments by the roof supports. In each compartment five men slept, each man having a space twenty-one inches wide. All five, therefore had to sleep on their sides facing the same way. If one turned over, all had to turn over. A thin layer of straw covered the planks. There was no other furniture in the hut. In the walls there were detachable shutters, but no glazed windows. There were no stoves and no blankets. There were no dishes, knives, spoons, forks, or soap. Those with money could purchase these and certain other items from the camp stores; others had to do without.

The normal daily ration consisted of eleven ounces of bread, a cup of unsugared coffee in the morning, at midday a pint of soup and three ounces of boiled beef, and in the evening a thin near-soup containing a few chick-peas, lentils, or vermicelli.

There were three hours of labour in the morning and three in the afternoon. The work consisted chiefly of road-building, digging and levelling the waste ground between the hutments, and various maintenance fatigues. Roll-calls were held four times a day, lasting from thirty minutes to an hour each.

Discipline was strict. The Gardes Mobiles in charge of the internees did not hesitate to strike, with fist or leather crop, anyone who fidgeted while standing at attention during roll-call or who was not in their estimation working hard enough. More serious offences were punished by confinement in the prison hut, the minimum sentence being eight days, the first day without food or drink, the next three days bread and water only. Anyone suspected of malingering was punished exceptionally severely.

On the day of their arrival they learned that their heads were to be shaved. Koestler, Leo Valiani,* a member of the Italian anti-Fascist underground who had already spent nine years in an Italian jail, and the German author Gustav Regler, drew up a petition against this indignity which was angrily dismissed.

For three years Koestler had suffered from a mild cardiac complaint. It did

* Valiani escaped from Le Vernet a year later and made his way to Britain. In 1943 he returned to Italy and joined the Resistance. In 1945 he was one of the three members of the General Insurrectional Committee which organised the rising against the Germans and ordered the execution of Mussolini and his mistress. Four years later he retired from political activity and devoted himself to writing. His books include a critical evaluation of Benedetto Croce's philosophy and *The End of Austro-Hungary* (London, Secker & Warburg, 1973).

not normally trouble him but after three days of labour with pick and spade he felt ill. There were two doctors on the camp staff – the 'bad one' who took pleasure in ignoring the most serious of symptoms and prescribing fourteen days imprisonment for malingering, and the 'good one', his young assistant. Koestler was lucky enough to be seen by the 'good one' who, after a fairly thorough examination, exempted him from work and also from marching. When he returned to the hut and found the others with whom he shared a section of planking lying grey-faced and exhausted on the straw, his happiness fell to ashes. But Valiani

> 'jumped to his feet and embraced me with as radiant a face as if the news had concerned himself . . . "You will keep the straw tidy and clean our blankets, and bribe the cooks for hot water for our tea. *En somme*, we shall exploit you and prevent you falling back into the parasitical ranks of the *bourgeoisie*."'

Thus they began to organise their lives and make the best of a bad job. The lucky few who had friends and relations outside began to receive food parcels, clothing and blankets. After a few weeks a canteen was opened in each section of the camp where those with money could buy cigarettes and some foodstuffs at an inflated price. As time went on the class distinction between the few who had money and received parcels and the majority grew increasingly marked.

In the hut next to Koestler's there were a great many German Communists, among them Gerhard Eisler, a member of the central committee of the Party. Koestler and Eisler took care to avoid each other. One day a letter from Daphne informed Koestler that American Communists had opened a propaganda campaign against the blockade of Germany and against American help for the Allies. Shortly afterwards he ran into Eisler who was cleaning out the open latrine in front of his hut. Koestler handed him the letter.

> '"And what about it?" he asked when he had finished.
>
> '"Do you agree with this?"
>
> '"Of course I do. This war is no concern of the international working class."
>
> 'We had the usual argument. Everything he said sounded utterly convincing. One could almost hear the well-oiled cogs turn in his brain and grind the words out of their meaning, turn them round and round, until it became self-evident that real Fascism meant support for the Fascists. At the end he said:
>
> '"If you were in a responsible position would you release us?"
>
> '". . . I would keep *you* behind barbed wire for the duration, under more decent conditions of course."
>
> '"Because you are a renegade skunk and afraid of us."
>
> '"Because you play into the Nazis' hands and must be prevented from it."
>
> '"Then why don't you report what I have said to your friends the gendarmes?"
>
> '"I am not an informer."
>
> '"Why not? It would be the logical inference from your convictions."
>
> '"Because I have ceased to believe that the end justifies the means – and that is why I have left the Party."

'"Petty-bourgeois liberalist," said Eisler with finality, and went on sweeping the latrine with his slow, thorough, dignified movements. I never argued with him again. He had all the advantages of his passionate error against my shaky truth.'

December came and the weather grew worse, with the temperature well below zero and icy gales blowing down from the mountains. An epidemic of dysentery broke out. The latrines were in the open air. Some of the older men could not face it and in consequence the huts grew even fouler. Morale began to collapse. One or two in Koestler's hut went mad, another committed suicide.

* *

January 1940 brought a bad time for Koestler. The 'good doctor' had gone: sickened by the conditions in the camp, he had successfully applied for a posting to a line regiment in the field. Everyone who had been exempted from work by him had been ordered to undergo a second medical examination by the 'bad doctor', who passed them all as 'fit for every kind of work'. On the following morning Koestler joined the *corvée de tintette*, the squad engaged in what was familiarly known in the British army as 'shithouse fatigue'. The tasks involved in the detail were, according to Koestler, revolting in the extreme.

He had been in the latrine squad for about a fortnight when he was told to report to Lieutenant Cosne's office. The Lieutenant had good news for him which he could scarcely believe:

'I have the pleasure to announce to you that we have just received from the Ministry of the Interior a telegraphic order for your release.'

Koestler's influential friends in London had succeeded at last.

At six that evening he was saying goodbye to Leo Valiani at the gate in the barbed-wire fence of Section C.

'"If I should ever write your life story," Koestler said, "I should put as a motto the words: 'There was a man in the Land of Uz, whose name was Job, and that man was perfect and upright.'"

'Leo smiled: "After this lived Job an hundred and forty years; and died, being old and full of days. I'll miss you. If I get transferred to the latrine squad, I might use the spare time to write an essay on Benedetto Croce's *History of the Nineteenth Century*."'

Koestler picked up his valise, went through the gate, and began his long journey in freedom back to Paris and Daphne.

# CHAPTER IX

# *1940*

Before leaving Le Vernet, Koestler had been given a document ordering him to present himself on his arrival in Paris at the police station of the XVth *Arrondissement*. There he was informed that he had to go to the *Préfecture* and have his *carte d'identité* extended. But first, he learned at the *Préfecture*, he would have to obtain a *cachet de déconcentration* – a stamped document certifying that he had been properly released from an internment camp. He was directed to Room no.34 on the fourth floor, and there he entered Kafkaland.

The young official was about to apply the rubber stamp when he paused, noticing that Koestler's nationality was Hungarian.

> '"But you are a neutral," he said in astonishment. "How on earth could they have sent you to a camp?"'

On realising that Koestler had been incarcerated in the notorious Le Vernet, his manner changed. He was empowered only to deal with enemy aliens released from ordinary camps. He would have to consult his *chef*. The *chef*, to judge by the fragments of conversation Koestler could hear through the open door, was enraged. The young man returned to say that he would have to present himself at the *Départment de l'Éloignement des Étrangers* – the office which dealt with deportation cases and which operated a new and refined form of bureaucratic torture, the *régime des sursis*. This consisted of refusing an applicant an authorisation to stay in France and then modifying the *réfus de séjour*, the equivalent to an expulsion order, with short-term reprieves, or *sursis* of different durations. Koestler's first reprieve was of twenty-four hours; his second, of five days; his third, of forty-eight hours; and so on. Each time he presented himself at the *Éloignement* he had to wait in the ante-room for seven to eight hours by way of additional torment.

Once again he slept every night with a suitcase ready beside his bed, waiting for an early-morning knock at the door.

All his efforts to struggle out of the morass came to nothing. A former Cabinet Minister took up his case and arranged for him to see the head of the intelligence department of the aliens branch of the Paris police. That official, having agreed, then found he was too busy; and five days later Koestler's flat was raided and some of his papers removed. Léon Blum arranged a meeting with the head of the aliens department at the *Sûreté Nationale*, but he too, it turned out, was too busy.

At that, Koestler gave up and concentrated his energies on completing *Darkness at Noon*.

It was a close-run thing. On 1st May, Daphne's translation of the novel from Koestler's German, was posted to Cape in London – nine days before the Germans launched their offensive against France through the Low Countries.

Sedan was evacuated. The Germans crossed the Meuse. The French fell back on the Aisne. Abbeville was taken. The Germans broke through to the Channel. Reynaud's voice was heard on the radio: 'If I were told that only a miracle can save France, I would believe in that miracle.'

But there was, of course, no miracle to believe in: the half-rotten fabric of the French polity was collapsing into panic and chaos, pushed by Hitler's Communist allies.

The police, however, were busier than ever, arresting or re-arresting suspect aliens. One morning at seven came the long-expected and dreaded knock on Koestler's door. From seven-thirty in the morning until three-thirty in the afternoon Koestler sat in the police station with the rest of the morning's haul in the *arrondissement* – thirty foreigners between fifty-five and eighty years of age. They were not allowed to move from the benches nor to get anything to eat. At three-thirty

> 'We were packed into a police van. I thought we would be taken to the Salle Lepine, but the car went down the rue de Vaugirard and then followed the *boulevards extérieurs*. "Where are we going?" somebody ventured to ask one of the hostile *flics*. "Stade Buffalo. There are some nice machine guns there; before the Boches come in, we will stand you all against the wall."
>
> 'By this time I was half drunk. For the last three months a bottle of Courvoisier had been packed in my suitcase as an iron ration for this occasion . . . The others in the car were Germans and Austrians; I was the only one in the category of Non-Enemy suspects. So far, the "enemy aliens" had been concentrated in the Buffalo . . . sports stadium in the south of Paris, and the "suspects" in the Roland Garros Stadium. On that morning, probably because of the shortage of transport, the *Préfecture* had ordered the local police stations to direct all arrested men to the Buffalo camp. But, as it turned out on our arrival, they had forgotten to inform the camp authorities at Buffalo of their changed dispositions. It was the usual French muddle. I was the first non-enemy alien to pass through the control bureau of the camp; when I put my passport on the desk and saw the official's surprised face, it all came to me in a flash.
>
> '"When and where were you arrested?" asked the official.
>
> '"In the Café Dupont, Place de la Convention, an hour ago."
>
> 'I did not for a second consciously think of my answer. The brandy did it

for me – and that sly, hairy super-ape, the subconscious. The point is that normally I am a bad actor, and if I try to bluff at poker I am always caught. It was a very odd experience.

'"Where is your *carte d'identité?*"

'"At home – 10 rue Dombasle, seventh floor. That's why I've been arrested. I just went down to have coffee after lunch and left my *carte d'identité* upstairs; there was a round-up and they took me to the police station. I asked them to let me go home and fetch the *carte d'identité* but they didn't give me a chance even to speak – they just shoved me into the car and here I am."

'. . . The man behind the desk turned my passport over and looked at my other papers: Press card, the famous letters from Influential Persons etc. Over his head, there was a clock on the wall and it marked 4.30.

'"All this is quite an amusing experience for a journalist, but the bother is that I have an appointment for five o'clock," I said – that is, the brandy said, or the hairy ape.

'"What sort of appointment?"

'"Why – the daily Press Conference at the Ministry of Information." (I had never been at the Press Conference and I had not written an article since the war started – but I had kept the Press card.)

'" . . . Look," I said. "I have got to be there at five. If you still have any doubts, send a man to accompany me home in a taxi while I fetch the *carte d'identité*. You can give me an armed escort with a machine gun if you think it necessary."

'" . . . No, I don't think that's necessary," said the man behind the desk and handed my papers back with a smile. "You are free, monsieur. Sentry, take monsieur to the entrance gate."'

* *

The time had come to go to ground. Instead of returning to his flat, Koestler sought the help of his friend Henri Membré, secretary of the French PEN Club, who agreed without question to hide him from the police. A message was sent to Daphne, who packed her bags and joined him. After a few days spent first with Membré and then with the writer, Adrienne Monnier, who contrived to obtain travel permits for them, they left Paris in an overcrowded train and got as far as Limoges.

There, for the moment, they were safe. But it could not be for long. In spite of the bombast of the official communiqués, it was all too clear that the final collapse of French resistance was imminent. They sat on the terrace of the Café de l'Orient facing the Place de la Mairie and watched the bedraggled stream of refugees pour through. Day after day they went on sitting on the café terrace in a strange lethargy of indecision. Their money would soon run out. They could not stay in Limoges indefinitely. In the north the Germans had broken through everywhere. Would they overrun all of France? Day after day Koestler and Daphne discussed the possibilities of escape. Should they try for Bordeaux in the hope of getting a passage to England? For Daphne it was the obvious solution; but Koestler, who had had his fill of internment, feared that he would be clapped into jail there; and Daphne refused to leave him. America? But they had no exit permits, no visas, no money. In a daze of indecision they watched the flood of refugees pour through the town.

But on the day they heard that Reynaud had been succeeded by Marshal Pétain and that the old man had asked the Germans for an armistice, Koestler knew that they could stay in Limoges no longer. He recalled a film he had seen a few years before, *Le Grand jeu*, in which Jean Gabin was hunted by the police. When all seemed lost, he passed by chance a recruiting office of the Foreign Legion. He went in and signed up for five years under a false name. He was asked no questions and had to show no documents. It was very simple. The recruiting sergeant, handing him his *carnet militaire*, had smiled: 'Whatever your past has been, from this moment it is dead. Here nobody will ask you indiscreet questions; in the Legion we are all *des morts vivants*.'

Was it really as simple as that? Koestler suddenly decided to put it to the test.

Leaving Daphne on the terrace, he went to the recruiting office which he had noticed earlier. A sergeant and two clerks, who looked dejected and drunk, were talking about Pétain's capitulation. The sergeant, when Koestler told him that he wished to sign up for the Legion, went red in the face.

'*Sans blague!* Just now when the war is over?'

Koestler explained that he meant the 'real' Legion, not one of the *régiments de marche* manned by foreign volunteers for the duration. 'That's different,' said the sergeant; and it was all just as simple as it had been for Jean Gabin in the film. In the name of Albert Dubert, a Swiss national and a taxi-driver by trade, Koestler signed four printed forms without reading them, underwent a cursory medical examination, and emerged from the office with a railway warrant and instructions to report to the Legion depôt at Lyon-Sathenay. But the Germans, Koestler knew, had already taken Dijon and were on the road to Lyon.

> '"Couldn't you change my *ordre de marche* for Marseille?" I asked the sergeant. "The central depôt of the Legion is at Marseille, anyhow."
>
> '"Never mind about your order," he said. "All railway traffic in France was stopped an hour ago. And tonight they'll arrive at Limoges. Good luck."'

That night Koestler and Daphne decided to leave Limoges and make for Périgueux. Koestler's plan was to report to military headquarters there. As for Daphne, once she knew what was to become of him, she would try to get back to England, or, if Koestler was to be posted to Algeria, to accompany him there and live with her sister, who was married to a Frenchman.

As the recruiting sergeant had told Koestler, no trains were running, but on the following day, having spent the night in a restaurant crowded with refugees on the southern outskirts of Limoges, they got a lift to Thiviers and completed the journey by bus. Daphne found a lodging while Koestler presented himself at the barracks.

> 'In the orderly room I showed my papers. "And what do you want?" "Instructions." The orderly sergeant stared at me, then he called: "Hi! Come here, all of you." About fifteen ragged, unshaven *poilus* were standing

around me. "Now look at him: this is Légionnaire Dubert from Berne in Switzerland, who signed up on the day of the armistice, bound for Lyon and comes to Périgueux to ask for instructions." Nobody laughed; they shrugged and went back to their benches, dragging their feet.'

After some argument, Koestler was taken on the strength and given an old uniform which made him look, Daphne observed, like Charlie Chaplin dressed as a Turk.

Two days later they were on the road again. A friendly officer had warned Koestler that the Germans were moving quickly down the Atlantic seaboard.

At noon on Sunday 23rd June, tired and bedraggled, they arrived at Bordeaux where they learned that the last ship bound for England had sailed forty-eight hours before. The Germans were said to be near the mouth of the Gironde. The harbour was cut off. The British Consul had left for Bayonne, a hundred and ten miles to the south. And then, just as they had given up all hope, they ran into an acquaintance of Koestler's, Edgar Mowrer of the *Chicago Daily News*, who was on the point of leaving for the south.

'I tried to persuade Daphne that she should go with Mowrer, who would take care of her, and leave me in Bordeaux; I knew that I could not go to Spain, whereas she might get through, and I thought that if there were still boats from Bayonne to England they would take her, but not me, and if I were there she would refuse to leave and thus spoil her last chance; so I preferred that we should separate at once. It was a long and morbid argument. Daphne cried, and I went to the lavatory and had a sort of nervous breakdown . . . Finally Daphne won and we both left in Mowrer's car.'

At midnight they arrived in Biarritz where an armed patrol stopped the car and examined their papers. Koestler was ordered out.

'I saw through a sort of mist Daphne's white face leaning out of the car . . . Then I moved along the street between the rifles: I did not turn back, but I knew that she was staring after us, as she had stared when the police had taken me from the flat in Paris . . .'

* *

After a few hours on the floor of a cell in the *gendarmerie* of Biarritz, Koestler was escorted to the Château Neuf Infantry barracks at Bayonne. There, two days later, he learned that a ship bound for England from St Jean de Luz had been torpedoed and that all on board had been drowned. Daphne, he concluded, must have been in that ship.

'. . . I hardly moved from my palliasse and was most of the time asleep or sick; I did not talk to anybody, but on the second or third evening a soldier sat down on my palliasse and began to talk to me. His face somehow reminded me of Leo Valiani's although it was clean-shaven and round. He asked whether he could do anything for me, as I was apparently ill; and when I said no, he said that this was very regrettable, as for the last few weeks he had looked in vain for somebody whom he could help, being a Father of the Order of Dominicans, mobilised as an army chaplain, but this was apparently a time in which nobody could help anybody.'

But Father Piprot did in fact help Koestler by listening to his story.

'I also told him that I thought he had turned up just at the right moment; he said, "*Le bon Dieu est un metteur-en-scène raffiné.*"'

Then and during the weeks that followed in the various *cantonnements des isolés* which housed the stragglers once they had marched out of the occupied zone, Father Piprot's conversation kept Koestler from falling into despair.

At last, while in a camp at Géronce in the Basses Pyrénées, Koestler learned that he and all the other alien volunteers were to be demobilised at Septfont in Tarn-et-Garonne. With four Spaniards, a Turk, and a Romanian, he set off early in the morning of 11th August. It took them three days and five changes of train to cover the distance of 175 miles. At the barracks Koestler was informed that the Géronce authorities were idiots: he should have been sent to the Foreign Legion depot in Marseille.

Two days later, at nine in the morning of 15th August, he walked out of the Gare St Charles.

'That first day in Marseille was full of surprises. Less than 100 yards from the steps of the railway station I heard a voice call out, "*Halt, Genosse Koestler,*" and when I had got over the shock, I saw the conspicuously tall figure of Dr Breitscheid, German Minister of the Interior in the legendary days of the Weimar Republic, barring my way . . .

'"What is this fancy dress?" he asked, looking me up and down, and I saw by his expression that my appearance must have changed. But last time we had met in Paris, his hair had not been white either, and his face had not been that sharp waxen mask. We went to his room, on the third floor of the Hotel Normandie; Mrs Breitscheid was making coffee on a spirit stove. I told them my story, and then we knocked on the wall of the next room and Comrade Dr Hilferding turned up in his dressing gown. Hilferding had been Minister of Finance in those long-vanished days; both he and Breitscheid were leaders of the German Social-Democrat Party and close friends.'

They both, Koestler learned, had visas for the United States, but the French had refused them exit permits.

'I asked Breitscheid why they did not try to get out without exit permits. Surely there must be ways of obtaining papers under false names, or crossing the Pyrenees at an unguarded mountain pass? I knew that some others had done it and succeeded. But Breitscheid would not hear of it: he still hoped that Vichy would grant exit permits; he even had promises from some French officials . . .

'When I left the Hotel Normandie an hour later, Breitscheid said: "So far there have been no demands for extradition and I do not think there will be any. It is unthinkable." '*

Having reported to the orderly room at the Fort St Jean, the Foreign Legion's depôt, Koestler went to the refectory where he had his second surprise of the day. The first words he heard after he had seated himself at the long mess-table were English: 'There's no bloody salt in the bloody soup.' His neighbours, all in civilian clothes, were, he learned, British soldiers who, captured by the Germans at St Valéry, had managed to escape to the south and were interned in the Fort. During the next few days, Koestler joined forces with four of them – three officers and a staff sergeant – who, having by some means acquired false papers, had determined to get to Casablanca. Once there, they hoped, they would find some means of returning to England.

Late one evening, towards the end of August, they succeeded in slipping out of the Fort and boarding the Oran ferry at the Quai de la Joliette. The voyage was uneventful and they had no trouble in making their way by train from Oran to Casablanca. There they approached the American Consulate, where a friendly official directed them to Mr E. E. Bullen, the English chief accountant of the Société Shell du Maroc. Bullen directed them to a certain café where they could be contacted by a Mr Ellerman who would find a way of getting them to Lisbon.

Ellerman's performance was impressive. A Portuguese fishing-boat, *El Mar Azul*, chartered by him, was lying in Casablanca harbour. Within a day or two it put to sea, packed with Koestler, his four British companions, fifty other refugees and the mysterious Mr Ellerman† himself. Four days later, it tied up in the neutral capital of Lisbon, where the British refugees were greeted by the United Kingdom's representatives and congratulated on their escape.

* Six months later, on 11th February 1940, Breitscheid, Hilferding and twenty other prominent political refugees were handed over by the Vichy authorities to the Germans.

† In fact the Baron Rudiger von Etzdorf, a member of one of pre-war Germany's leading families. His father had been a close friend of the Kaiser, and he had visited Sandringham during the reign of Edward VII. He had fought at Jutland as a German naval officer. Disgusted by Hitler and his National Socialists, he had been recruited by the British Secret Intelligence Service in 1935. In 1940 he was in Tripoli and organised an escape route for British soldiers after the collapse of France. He died in London during 1966. His younger brother, Dr Hasso von Etzdorf, was West Germany's ambassador to the Court of St James from 1961 to 1965.

# PART TWO

# *1940–1945*

# CHAPTER X

# *1940*

FOR TWO MONTHS AFTER the departure of 'Mr Ellerman', Koestler haunted the British consulate in an attempt to obtain a visa to re-enter Britain. The consular officials were sympathetic, but their recommendations to the Foreign Office went unheeded. It would seem that the Security Service had its doubts about Koestler.

In the circumstances of the time – with Germany, its eastern flank secured by the non-aggression pact with the Soviet Union, apparently on the point of invading Britain – it was inevitable that MI5 should be extremely cautious. It must be remembered that following the signing of the Ribbentrop-Molotov agreement, all Communist parties in the West had called a halt to their anti-Nazi campaign and opposed the war. Active Communists were therefore in effect enemy agents. In France they had played a considerable part in bringing about the demoralisation and defeat of the armed forces. The British Communist Party was very much smaller, of course, but it had many undercover supporters. There was no reason to suppose that they would be any less obedient than their French comrades to the dictates of Moscow. Nor could the *bona fides* of professed ex-Communists be taken for granted. In Koestler's case, the text of *Darkness at Noon* was conclusive proof of his defection from Communism, but it was still at the printers.

Also, as we now know, MI5 had been penetrated in some depth by Communists during its hurried expansion. It may be that one or other of the many traitors in the service, regarding Koestler as an enemy of the over-riding cause of international socialism, was instrumental in denying him an entry permit.

Eventually, after eight weeks of anxiety and fruitless agitation, he decided that he could wait no longer. He weighed up the alternatives before him. The first was to get out of Portugal to another neutral country where he would be safe. Through his contacts in Lisbon and thanks to the efforts of the International Rescue and Relief Committee, he had been offered refuge in the United States. But he foresaw that to run away from Europe would be to condemn himself to lifelong frustration, sterility, and self-reproach. The second alternative was to try and get to England without a visa. That, as his English contacts warned him, would almost certainly mean imprisonment or internment. He decided to take the risk.

Having no documentation other than 'Albert Dubert's' demobilisation certificate, he wrote a lengthy summary of his case and sent a copy to the Consul-General in the hope that an appropriate signal to London might with luck ease his entry into a Britain suffering, understandably, from an attack of spy-fever. With Sir Henry King's passive connivance and the help of *The Times*' correspondent, he got a seat in a Dutch aircraft bound for England.

* *

When the KLM plane arrived at Poole, the passengers were taken at once to Bristol for examination and clearance. All Koestler's fellow-travellers had valid papers and were quickly cleared. He was left alone with an immigration officer who had obviously never heard of him. If any signal had been sent to London from the consulate in Lisbon, it had not yet reached Bristol. When Koestler asked the officer whether he had received any instructions about him, he heard for the first time the excuse that had already become routine: 'No, I'm afraid not. But, you see, there's a war on . . .' Koestler then produced a copy of the statement he had typed in Lisbon. Having read through it quickly, the officer excused himself politely and after some delay returned with two of his seniors. They were wearing, Koestler recalls, 'only moderately stern' expressions. One of them said that Koestler would have to be detained. That was what he expected, Koestler replied, adding forcefully that he wished to have his case clarified and to find out why he had been refused an entry permit. 'I am here,' he said, 'to play whatever part I can in the war against Hitler.' The immigration officers received this assurance phlegmatically and had him removed to a police cell. He was relieved. The one fear that had haunted him was that sheer ignorance of his special case might lead the men on the spot to turn him back without ado and put him on the next plane to Lisbon.

After breakfast on the following morning a major of the Intelligence Corps came into his cell and told him that he was to be sent up to London under escort. That, of course, was just what Koestler had hoped for. But his nervousness got the better of him and he exclaimed: 'So long as they don't expel me! If they want to expel me they'll have to use force. You won't get me willingly on a plane back to the Continent.'

'You can put that out of your mind,' said the major in reply to this outburst, and Koestler, reassured as much by the Englishman's matter-of-fact tone of voice as by the words themselves, finally and thankfully did so.

Shortly afterwards, his escort, a tall plain-clothes policeman, turned up and they set off for the railway station. At length they arrived in London and made their way through a noisy air-raid to Cannon Row police station. Koestler spent a sleepless night in Cannon Row, and not only because of the air-raids. The mood of euphoria in which he had left Bristol soon wore very thin. His experiences so far, to be sure, were very different from those he had endured in

Spain and France. He had been treated politely, with consideration even. But here he was in jail again with no clear notion of what was likely to happen to him. Eventually his impatience swelled up into a great surge of something like panic. He hammered on the door of his cell and announced to a surprised policeman that he wished to be interrogated immediately. That was not possible, the policeman told him, adding that he need not worry since he could only be kept in Cannon Row for seventy-two hours. Koestler, unappeased, decided on a hunger-strike and ate nothing during the following day. After another sleepless night breakfast arrived – bacon and eggs – and lay untouched on the table. During his pacing Koestler looked at it from time to time. The egg, he thought, seemed to be grinning at him. He was on the point of succumbing when an officer arrived and said: 'You wished to be interrogated. Come with me, then. Your interrogator is waiting.'

Koestler was led into a room where, seated behind a table, was a person whose head was covered with a black hood. This odd and melodramatic sight gave him, he recalls, the giggles. As soon as the interrogator opened his mouth, Koestler realised that he was a German whose identity had to remain secret, no doubt for the sake of relatives still in Germany. It was obvious that he knew a great deal about Koestler, and the interrogation was a perfunctory affair.

'Your present status,' the hooded inquisitor explained at the end, 'is that of "alien refused permission to land". You will certainly be freed in due course – in a few days, perhaps, or at most a few weeks. Refugees are arriving from the Continent all the time by fishing-boats and yachts, and of course they all have to be screened, because there are spies among them, and although we know all about you, there is just no way of persuading the bureaucracy to give you a short-cut.'

Koestler was reassured by the interview. He ended his brief hunger-strike and on the following morning he was taken off to Pentonville, where he had a cell to himself.

Koestler was content enough in Pentonville. As he wrote later, if he were ever to produce a Baedeker of the prisons of Europe, he would give it three stars in spite of the regrettable state of the plumbing. What vexed him most were the sanitary arrangements, having to spend fifteen or sixteen hours in a cell with a chamber-pot full of urine and excrement, and in the morning the 'slopping-out' routine. Koestler found this so depressing that he somehow contrived to alter the rhythm of his digestive tract and arrange his need to defecate to coincide with exercise-time in the yard, where there were latrines.

He was, of course, something of a connoisseur of prisons. Physically, Pentonville left much to be desired. The jail in Seville had been much more up-to-date. There he had a wash-basin and a water-closet in his cell; and he had been able to buy wine to wash down the prison fare. Offsetting the relative physical comfort, however, there was the endless wailing of prisoners being taken out to be executed – and the fear that he might be next in line. Executions had been frequent there and unexceptional, all in the day's work for the jailers. Not so in uncomfortable Pentonville where only one prisoner – a German spy – was executed during Koestler's six weeks there.

> 'That was a ghastly morning. We all knew that somebody was going to be executed. The early morning timetable had been changed. Doors were closed quietly, not with usual banging and clashing. Warders went about on tip-toe, with long faces. The entire prison became a house of death. Years later, when I was involved in the campaign for the abolition of capital punishment, I learned that the public hangman, Pierrepoint, had observed during his testimony to the Royal Commission that the man he executed that morning was the only one of his clients who had made a fuss. "He kicked up rough," Mr Pierrepoint said. "But then he was not an Englishman. He was a foreigner."'

What struck Koestler at the time was the fact that he was in a place where putting a man to death was still regarded as a solemn and exceptional event.

> 'It made all the difference. It was, as a matter of fact, what this war was about.'

* *

Various people were active on Koestler's behalf while he was in Pentonville – Gerald Barry, editor of the *News Chronicle*, Ellen Wilkinson, the Duchess of Atholl and many other political friends.

Shortly after his arrival in the jail his English publisher, Jonathan Cape, had sent him the page-proofs of *Darkness at Noon*. Koestler corrected and returned them, enclosing an urgent plea for cigarettes. Cape sent him a box of a hundred with a note to say that the cost would be deducted from his royalties.

It was during his stay at Lisbon that Daphne Hardy learned from Cape that he was alive. Until then, each had thought the other dead. After their separation in the summer, Daphne had embarked on a ship at Biarritz which had been wrongly reported sunk. Now she had a job in the Ministry of Information and a small house in Chelsea. Their reunion took place in the visitors' room, where they had to talk through a wire-mesh screen in the presence of a warder. They found the surroundings so painfully inhibiting and anti-climactic that they decided not to meet again before Koestler's release.

Koestler had only one other visit during his stay at Pentonville. One day the Chief Warder brought him from his cell to the visitors' room where two men – one elderly, the other young – were waiting. It was immediately obvious from their conversation that they were from the Security Service, and also that Koestler's identity must by this time have been satisfactorily established by the bureaucracy. The older man began to ask him what he made of his fellow-detainees.

'You can't ask me to be a stool-pigeon,' said Koestler.

'But you want to help this country, don't you?'

'Look,' he said, 'if I am released unconditionally and offered some sort of intelligence job, I might do it – depending on the job. I came to Britain to join the army. But I certainly can't work for you while I'm in prison, for I'd feel that I was doing so under duress. Informing isn't my line, anyway.'

The elder man seemed to be pleased by this. He looked at his young colleague and smiled. 'Ah well,' he said, 'your case will be cleared up very soon.'

'Good,' said Koestler. 'In the meantime, could you give me some matches?'

* *

He was still in Pentonville on the day *Darkness at Noon* was published and reviews began to appear before his release. They were, for the most part, full of intelligent praise for its literary qualities as well as for the light it threw on the Moscow Trials and the psychology of the Old Bolsheviks who had confessed so incredibly and abjectly before being released by a bullet in the back of the neck.

Much had been written about those trials, concluded the *Times Literary Supplement*, 'but possibly this comes as near the truth as anything'.

It was, of course, an unpalatable truth to those of the Left who clung to their vision of Moscow as the secular Mecca or Jerusalem. Daniel George gave them a let-out at the end of his review in *Tribune*:

> '. . . if at the end you are not conscious of having at last received a plausible reason for those incredible confessions at the Moscow Trials, you will just have to go on saying, "Ah, but the Russians are different."'

By far the most percipient view was that of George Orwell in the *New Statesman*. From his own experience of the Communists in Spain, Orwell knew exactly what Koestler was writing about. In his earlier review of *Spanish Testament* he had dismissed the Left Book Club propaganda elements while praising the part that has survived as *Dialogue with Death*. In his review of *Darkness at Noon*, he returned to his attack on Western leftists and 'liberals' who were ready to apologise for Communist atrocities:

> 'When Rubashov gives in and confesses, it is not because of the torture – he has suffered worse at the hands of the Nazis without confessing – so much as from complete inner emptiness. "I asked myself," he says at the trial, almost in Bukharin's words, "For what am I fighting?" For what indeed? Any right to protest against torture, secret prisons, organised lying and so forth he has long since forfeited. He recognises what is now happening is the consequence of his own acts – even feels a sort of admiration for Gletkin, as the kind of subhuman being probably needed to guide the Revolution through its present stage. The Moscow trials were a horrible spectacle, but if one remembered what the history of the Old Bolsheviks had been it was difficult to be sorry for them as individuals. They took the sword, and they perished by the sword, as Stalin presumably will also, unless he should happen to die prematurely like Lenin.
>
> 'Brilliant as this book is as a novel, and a piece of prison literature, it is probably most valuable as an interpretation of the Moscow "confessions" by someone with an inner knowledge of totalitarian methods. What was frightening about these trials was not the fact that they happened – for obviously such things are necessary in a totalitarian society – but the eagerness of Western intellectuals to justify them. Correspondents of Liberal newspapers

pronounced themselves "completely satisfied" by the confessions of the men who had been dragged into the light after, in some cases, years of solitary confinement; an eminent lawyer even produced the theory that the loss of the right to appeal was a great advantage to the accused! The simultaneous cases in Spain, in which exactly the same accusations were made but no confessions were obtained, were sedulously covered up or lied about in the Left-Wing press. It was, of course, obvious that the accused in the Russian cases had been tortured or threatened with torture, but the explanation is probably more complex than that. Mr Koestler thinks, like Souvarine, that "for the good of the Party" was probably the final argument; indeed his book is rather like an expanded imaginative version of Souvarine's pamphlet, *Cauchemar en U.R.S.S.* As a piece of writing it is a notable advance on his earlier work.'

Kingsley Martin, editor of the *New Statesman*, did a great deal to promote *Darkness at Noon* which he described (correctly) as 'One of the few books written in this epoch which will survive it'.

It should be remembered that this was a period when left-wing socialists in Britain were still floating in the vacuum created by the National Socialist-Communist pact and the partition of Poland, and long before respectability was conferred upon Stalin by his ally Hitler's unleashing of the Wehrmacht and SS against him across the River Bug. Martin,* to his credit, allowed C. E. M. Joad to return to *Darkness at Noon*:

'The significance of this emphasis on means rather than upon ends is most forcibly brought out in Arthur Koestler's book, *Darkness at Noon*. To one brought up in the older tradition this is indeed a terrifying book. Its theme is the conflict in Russia between two codes of ethics, the one that respects the individual, treats him as an end in himself and seeks, so far as may be, to love him – in fact the Christian Code – and the one that treats him as an ant in the social termitary, a cog in the proletarian machine, as – it is the phrase of Koestler's new Communists – a million divided by a million, and the million citizens themselves as raw material for vivisection in the interests of the collective good. In the interests of that good, the liberal ethics of the nineteenth century, the ethics of fair play, must be replaced by the revolutionary ethics of the twentieth century. Those who have dedicated themselves to the Party must be equally deaf to the voice of love and to the call of pity; they must ignore justice and deny truth; at its behest they must rob, cheat, lie, betray, murder, and torture. What matters is not that one should be well-meaning, that one should be sincere, that one should be self-sacrificing, but that one should be objectively right. Now the path of objective rightness is laid down by the Party, and the Party is concerned not to impose virtue, but to exact obedience.'

Shortly before Christmas Koestler was summoned by the Chief Warder who shook his hand and told him he was free to go.

'How well I remember him,' Koestler recalls, 'and how warmly. He was the

* Whose mistress, Dorothy Woodman, was a Communist.

most decent of men. We all knew that he had lost his only son during the British Expeditionary Force's retreat to Dunkirk. Whether or not there were any spies among us, I don't know, but he might well in his embitterment have regarded us all as a bunch of spies, bloody foreigners, rotten Gerries. But no; he always behaved with exemplary correctness, kindness even. He made life easier for us, and, as I've said, I had no hard feelings at all about my six weeks in an English jail . . . The only unpleasant character I encountered was the prison officer who returned my civilian clothes. As you know, the little money I arrived with had been confiscated – all except a penny and a halfpenny left in one of my pockets. He fished the coins out and said: "Here's your penny ha'penny, Gerry. You won't get far with a penny ha'penny, Gerry." True enough; but I did resent, I must confess, being called a Gerry.'

So he walked out of Pentonville, a free man with a penny ha'penny, to find himself famous – not among the public at large (that was to come later) but at least in the eyes of that minority which takes an interest in ideas and those who shape them – and already, of course, to those obedient Communists and fellow-travellers still denouncing the 'imperialist' war, a traitor.

In the *New Statesman* of 28th December, Kingsley Martin wrote:

> 'I am glad to note the name of Arthur Koestler among the "internees" recently released. Why he was ever interned I dare not guess. He was one of the best of the British correspondents who fell under Franco's displeasure during the Spanish War; his *Spanish Testament* with its wonderful section on the experience of expecting death in a Fascist prison should rank among British classics. Since the outbreak of war he tried repeatedly to return to England from France in order to join the Forces but his applications were rejected. Since the end of June he had been slowly making his way from France to this country. When he arrived he was arrested and his new book *Darkness at Noon* had to be sent out while he was still in Pentonville. Now, thanks to the improving sanity of the Home Office and the British people, he is again a free man.'

## CHAPTER XI

# *1940–1943*

ON HIS RELEASE FROM Pentonville, Koestler found his way to Chelsea and Daphne. On the following day he enlisted at an Army recruiting office where he was told it would be eight or nine weeks before he would be called up. He decided to spend the time writing an account of his experiences in France. *Scum of the Earth* he would call it, and he would write it (contrary to his usual practice with any serious or lengthy work, when he preferred to work with a pen, and, like Conrad before him, seldom achieved more than 400 words a day) straight on to a typewriter – and also, for the first time, in English.

Jonathan Cape gave him an advance of £60, payable in ten weekly instalments of £5, with the final ten pounds to come on his delivery of the completed typescript. Out of the first instalment of £5 he hired a typewriter and bought some paper.

Where would he begin?

His mind went back to that marvellous and ominous summer of 1939. He had never loved France as he loved it then. He had never been so achingly conscious of its sweetness and decay.

Now, sitting in front of a typewriter in Chelsea, he recalled the curious history of the house where he and Daphne had been both sad and happy:

> 'Sometime during the last years of Victoria's reign, the Prince of Monaco had an anglicised mistress who wanted a bathroom of her own. He built her a villa . . .'

The work went well but in the middle of February his call-up papers arrived. Koestler reckoned that he needed another fortnight to finish the book. Cape wrote to the recruiting office to explain the situation and ask whether Koestler could have a deferment. He received the following reply from No.3 centre of the London recruiting division:

> '*re Arthur Koestler*
>
> 'I am in receipt of your letter of the 11th instant contents of which have been noted.

'As requested, I am therefore postponing Mr Koestler's calling-up, and would suggest that he calls at this centre when he is at liberty to join His Majesty's Forces.'

When Koestler read this civil letter he was more than ever convinced (or so he wrote many years later, not wholly seriously, perhaps) that England was bound to lose the war. At any rate, he learned that it was bad form to hurry and to appear too eager. So he took a month instead of a fortnight to finish *Scum of the Earth*.

* *

Koestler's final rejection of Communism, implicit in *Darkness at Noon*, came at a time when the Communist Party of Great Britain was instructing its members to take no part in the 'Imperialist War', not even in defence against air-raids. It was natural too, no doubt, that Koestler – an ex-Communist certainly, but still a 'progressive' and no convert to Conservatism – should be acutely sensitive both to their attacks and to the scorn of 'progressive-minded' people who had never been Communists:

'While I was a Communist, I felt surrounded by the sympathy of progressive-minded people who did not like Communism but respected my convictions. After I had broken with Communism, the same class of people treated me with contempt. The abuse that came from the Party conformed to pattern; but behind the resentment of those who had never been Communists I felt a different kind of unvoiced reproach. Ex-Communists are not only tiresome Cassandras, as the anti-Nazi refugee had been; they are also fallen angels who had the bad taste to reveal that Heaven is not the place it is supposed to be. The world respects the Catholic or Communist convert, but abhors unfrocked priests of all faiths. This attitude is rationalised as a dislike of renegades. Yet the convert, too, is a renegade from his former beliefs or disbeliefs, and quite prepared to persecute those who still persist in them. He is nevertheless forgiven, for he has "*embraced*" a faith, whereas the ex-Communist or the unfrocked priest has "*lost*" a faith – and has thereby become a menace to illusion and a reminder of the abhorrent, threatening void.'

Koestler learned this lesson sharply and sadly not long after the publication of *Darkness at Noon* and while he was still writing *Scum of the Earth*. He and Daphne lunched in Soho one day with Sir Peter Chalmers-Mitchell. Sir Peter had never been a Communist. He did not like Stalin's pact with Hitler. To Koestler he had been a warm-hearted and generous friend. But, as Koestler found, he liked people who changed their 'Clubs' even less.

After lunch the three of them were in a tube travelling towards Kensington. After the wine they had drunk at luncheon they were in high spirits. But suddenly Chalmers-Mitchell leant across Daphne and said to Koestler: 'Frankly, I did not like that novel of yours. What a pity that you sold yourself for thirty pieces of silver.' Koestler at first thought the old man was joking, but it soon became clear that he was not, and they argued across Daphne. In the end Koestler said: 'Please take that back, or we won't be able to see each other any more.' But Chalmers-Mitchell refused and Daphne and Koestler got off the train.

That was the last they saw of Sir Peter, who was run over by a bus in 1945 and killed.

* *

Towards the end of March, when he had delivered *Scum of the Earth* to Cape, Koestler returned to the recruiting office and was sent off to the aliens' depot of the Pioneer Corps in Ilfracombe. There he put on British battle-dress for the first time. Under British sergeants and officers, he and a strange assortment of fellow-foreigners learned the rudiments of foot-drill on the promenade, watched by all the retired colonels and their ladies.

Daphne, who had a job in Oxford at this time, joined Koestler as often as she could. His unit was generous with weekend passes and he already had many hospitable English friends. He and Daphne often spent a day or two with Michael Sadleir and his wife at their house in the Cotswolds, or with Cecil Day-Lewis, who was living in Cheltenham at the time. In London Cyril Connolly gave a party for him at which he met Stephen Spender, Louis MacNeice, Philip Toynbee, and many other writers grouped around *Horizon*. He also saw a good deal of Frank Owen, Michael Foot, Peter Howard, George Orwell and John Strachey.

During their first meeting in 1941, Strachey asked Koestler what he had meant by his title, *Darkness at Noon*:

> 'My mind was still so numb that the simple obvious answer meaning an eclipse of human reason, just when the enlightenment should have reached its noontide, in the coming to power of the first government to be consciously based upon rationalism, had wholly escaped me. Far more remarkable, it had escaped the author himself. Koestler told me that the title had actually been thought of by Daphne Hardy and that he didn't quite know what it meant but that it seemed to have the right ring to it.'

Once a week or so Koestler came to London to broadcast to the Continent in German, and frequently he was seconded to give talks in remote units – anti-aircraft sites in the Thames Estuary area, mobile laundry units in God-forsaken places, and the like. He always tried to keep his talk short, leaving most of the time for questions and discussion. Here he learned something about the lower strata of the English working class.

> 'For me it was an eye-opener,' he says, recalling those days, 'because in my Communist time, the proletariat had been a mere abstraction for me. My comrades were either intellectuals or Party bureaucrats, I had had no contact at all with slum-dwellers. Nor had the English middle-class until the early years of the War. Don't forget that this was a time when a pamphlet called *Our Towns* on the state of slum-children evacuated from the towns into middle-class houses throughout the countryside had shaken the nation. Most

of the children were lousy and a great many of them were not even house-trained. Their mothers, some of whom seem to have been incapable of boiling an egg, had fed them on bread and marge and fish and chips from the shop on the corner – sardines out of a tin if they were lucky. It is often forgotten now what an enormous social upheaval there was in England during the early years of the War, with the mixing of the population and the word "slum" ceasing to be an abstraction for the English middle-class. Believe me, I was no less shocked.

'And how often I was depressed by the lamentable ignorance of the audiences to whom I was supposed to talk about the nature of totalitarianism. I have a vivid memory of talking to the girls of a mobile laundry unit. Many of them could neither talk nor listen – they couldn't even look at me, just shifting their gaze about and blinking their eyes all the time, taking nothing in, showing no interest. I tried to find out whether any of them knew how the electoral system worked in England. There was a long silence but eventually one girl put up her hand. "Every town and village," she said, "has to send a Member of Parliament from each of the parties to London." I gave up. When I talked to them about concentration camps, I'm quite sure they didn't believe a word of it. It was not that they thought that I was a liar, but the very idea of a concentration camp was totally beyond their imagination.

'Only one thing made any impression on them.

'"Look," I said, 'in this country you can buy the *Daily Mirror* in the morning if you want or you can buy *The Times* or you can buy any other paper. You can buy a conservative paper or a liberal paper or a socialist paper, or a communist paper – but in the totalitarian countries you can only buy one paper and that's a Government paper."

'That somehow shocked them because the idea of a Government paper reminded them of official posters and exhortations. Well, as a result of all these experiences in the Pioneer Corps and lecturing to Army units and mobile laundry units and the like, I became a fervent supporter of the Labour Party. The once convinced Continental Communist became a fervent English-style "Social Democrat".'

* *

During 1942 Koestler was discharged (ostensibly on medical grounds) from the Pioneer Corps. He left two close friends behind – Private Szedö who is now Dr Seaton, Professor of Social Sciences at Nuffield College in Oxford University, and an Austrian, Corporal Wodak. Nearly thirty years later, at a gathering in Alpbach in the Tyrol, the Austrian Ambassador to Moscow was announced, and in came Wodak.

'How are you, Private Wodak?' said Koestler. His Excellency was indignant. '*Corporal* Wodak, if you please!'

Koestler was recruited by the Ministry of Information* where his talents could be put to much better use than in digging for victory. At this time he was also writing *Arrival and Departure*.

* Which had engineered his discharge from the army.

Early in the war, the much photographed Paget twins, Celia and Mamaine, star debutantes of the thirties, had let their house in Drayton Gardens to Cyril Connolly and Peter Quennell. When Koestler was discharged from the Pioneer Corps he moved in with Connolly and Quennell. This was his home for several months, until Daphne returned from Oxford to London. It was a vital period in the process of his anglicisation. Thanks to his friendship with Cyril Connolly, whose review *Horizon* was a literary and intellectual centre of gravity, Koestler's range of friendship and acquaintance among English writers and artists was enormously enlarged.

'Cyril,' says Koestler, 'took me under his wing. I want to emphasise very warmly my indebtedness to Cyril. Instead of spending my time in loneliness and isolation like so many exiles, or confined to an émigré clique, I was welcomed into the *Horizon* crowd. I wouldn't say that I was exactly an insider – more a strange bird on the periphery: but the important thing was that I felt at home.'

It was a busy time for Koestler, writing propaganda pamphlets, broadcasting in German, scripting radio plays and co-directing documentary films, getting on with his novel and putting his political thoughts in order. But life was not all work. There was a lively social life centred on *Horizon*, and Daphne came up from Oxford every weekend. To assuage the feelings of guilt that he was not more dangerously employed, he drove an ambulance at night and acted also as a part-time air-raid warden.

His touchiness can be seen in the following letter to X, who, resenting his relationship with Daphne, had insulted him:

> 'I don't know whether you expected an answer to your bellicose letter, but as it contains a question I might as well assure you that I certainly did not and do not intend to interfere with your friendship with Daphne; she works hard during the week and spends her weekends with me, so that she has practically no time for keeping up contacts outside Oxf.
>
> 'I am sorry you resented our meeting. By God I didn't see it that way. But now that you have succeeded so thoroughly to spoil an otherwise pleasant memory there is no more to be said about it.
>
> 'As to the White-Feather part of your letter, don't you think it is a bit unfair? I don't know how much you know about my past and I certainly don't intend to flaunt it, but I can assure you that during the last ten years I had very little opportunity for "women, drink and etceteras" as you put it. You see, for some of us "foreign gentlemen" this present war started as far back as 1933, when Hitler came to power, and if a few of us – perhaps one in a hundred among the militant Continental anti-fascists – had the luck to survive we should not be blamed so hard for it. So much for the past; as for the present it would be a very good idea if you could convince the War Office to let foreign volunteers, who are technically enemy aliens, to join the fighting Forces instead of the Pioneer Corps; I tried very hard but all I was allowed to do was Washing Dishes for Victory in the PC for a year, until I was released for my present job, equally unspectacular, which gives me very little chance of

getting myself killed, hanged or shot for the time being; for which I feel clearly apologetic towards you.'

* *

When Mamaine Paget, who had been working as a nurse in Warley Wood Casualty Hospital at Brentwood in Essex, came back to London, Connolly moved to a flat in Bedford Gardens. Koestler and Daphne, who had returned from Oxford to the Ministry of Information in London, took a house in Tryon Street, Chelsea, and there they stayed for a time until they moved into George Straus's house in Kensington Palace Gardens. Straus, the rich Socialist MP, was the chief backer of *Tribune*, for which Koestler wrote occasionally.

His versatility was given full play at this time. With Basil Wright he co-directed a documentary film on the Pioneer Corps, *Lift Your Head, Comrade*. It was one of the few Ministry of Information films to be shown in America where it had some success. In addition to his propaganda broadcasts in the BBC's German service, he wrote several scripts in English for home consumption, among them dramatised portraits of Julius Streicher and of Heydrich in a Home Service series called *Black Gallery*. They were inventive and effective, and the yellowing scripts still read quite well.

Much of his BBC work was concerned to get across to the British public the reality of the National Socialist concentration camps where the Jews were already being killed in large numbers. A play, *Protective Custody*, set in Dachau concentration camp, made a strong impact, hammering home the message that idealism and loyalty can turn ordinary civilised men into monsters of barbarism. There were still many people in Britain unconvinced by the news of atrocities being committed daily in Continental Europe.

> 'The trouble with being a contemporary in times like this,' said Koestler in a broadcast talk, 'Is that reality beats imagination at every step. Try as we may, we are unable to form a comprehensive idea of what is going on day by day and night by night in Continental Europe. For an educated Englishman it is almost easier to imagine conditions of life under King Canute on this island than conditions of life in, say, contemporary Poland.'

In the autumn of 1942 a tall aristocratic Pole named Karsky managed to make his way from Poland to London. His function in Warsaw had been that of a delegate of the Polish Government in exile in London to all the underground parties, including the Jewish Social Democratic Organisation, in Poland. He brought to London the first eye-witness account of the systematic extermination of Jews by the National Socialists. Koestler was asked to interview him and, if satisfied with the authenticity of his account, help him prepare a broadcast.

Karsky had a terrible story to tell. He was not a Jew himself and, as he told Koestler, before the war he had very little contact with Jews. In fact, he knew practically nothing about them. The sufferings of his own Polish compatriots, he admitted frankly, were nearer to his own heart. Virtually the entire Polish intelligentsia – university professors, teachers, lawyers, writers, journalists – had been arrested and imprisoned, and many had been executed. It was the aim of the Germans to deprive the Poles of their cultural standards, their traditions, their education; to reduce them to a nation of robots – a race of mediaeval serfs. But at least the majority of them were allowed to live, after a fashion.

It was very different, Karsky had discovered, with the Jews. Towards them the Germans had a policy not of mere subjugation and oppression, but rather one of cold and systematic extermination.

With the help of the Polish Underground he gained access to one of the extermination camps in the east in the guise of a Latvian special policeman. He had been, in fact, one of the executioners. When he arrived in July, the camp contained some 6,000 Jews of both sexes and of all ages, who had arrived a few days before from the Warsaw ghetto. They had been told that they were to be employed on field work and trench-digging. On their arrival they had been encouraged to write letters to their friends left behind in Warsaw, stating that they were being treated correctly and that 'deportation' was not at all as bad as they had feared. The object was to reassure the victims and keep them in doubt till the last possible moment, thus avoiding unnecessary fuss. Had they known with certainty of the horrors ahead, the Germans would have had to use much larger forces to deal with them.

The camp was bounded by an enclosure which ran parallel to the railway track at a distance of about thirty yards. A narrow corridor about two yards wide led from the gate of the camp to a point on the railway track where the trains halted. On both sides there was a wooden palisade.

At ten o'clock one morning a freight train halted alongside the camp. At the same moment the guards on the further side of the camp started shooting into the air and urging the inmates to get into the trucks, thus creating a deliberate panic in order to prevent any hesitation or resistance. The Jews were driven like cattle into the first wagon, which had halted opposite the gate. It was the standard Army wagon designed for six horses or thirty-six men. The floor was covered in quick-lime about two inches deep, but the Jews had no time to realise what this meant. When about one hundred had been driven into the truck they could only stand packed like sardines. It seemed physically impossible to press any more in, but at that moment the guards, aided by the prisoners themselves who were half-crazed by fear, began lifting those next to the truck and throwing them in. Thirty individuals, men and women, were thrown on top of the heads of the hundred already inside, some of whom had their necks broken. Then the sliding doors were closed and bolted and the train moved so that the next wagon was opposite the palisade. The same procedure was carried out again.

Altogether, Karsky told Koestler, he had counted 51 trucks which had absorbed the entire 6,000 people in the camp with the exception of some twenty or thirty who had been shot dead during the rush.

So much Karsky had heard and seen for himself. The end of the story he learned from his 'comrades' in the camp, who had been doing this sort of thing for several months, despatching one or two trains a week. The train packed with 6,000 people moved on for about twenty-five miles and halted in an open field. There it stood for six or seven days. When its doors were opened by the grave-digger squad, the Jews were dead, their bodies in an advanced state of decomposition. The quick-lime on the floor had the property of developing chlorine gas when coming into contact with water. The urine from those jammed inside had instantaneously produced the chemical reaction. While they were slowly asphyxiated by the gas, their feet were burnt to the bone.

Koestler helped Karsky to prepare a broadcast which ended:

'The latest estimate of the number of Jews executed by such methods in the systematic carrying out of Himmler's orders, is two and a quarter millions. I have nothing else to say.'

A great many people who listened to that broadcast found it impossible to digest such horrifying facts and dismissed them as propaganda. In one of the chapters of *Arrival and Departure* (the novel on which he was then working) Koestler made use of some of the information gained from Karsky and corroborated by intelligence sources. Connolly published this chapter in *Horizon*, as a result of which Koestler received many letters accusing him of atrocity-mongering and a morbid imagination. Others asked more temperately whether the episode really had any factual basis. Among them was Sir Osbert Sitwell. Koestler, who had just heard that some members of his own family had been among the victims, was stunned into replying to Sitwell by this open letter:

'In your letter you asked me the idiotic question whether the events described in the "mixed transport" were "based on fact" or "artistic fiction".

'Had I published a chapter on Proust and mentioned his homosexuality you would never have dared to ask a similar question because you consider it your duty "to know", though the evidence of this particular knowledge is less easily accessible than the massacre of three million humans. You would blush if you were found out not to have heard the name of any second-rate contemporary writer, painter or composer; you would blush if found out having ascribed a play by Sophocles to Euripides; but you don't blush and you have the brazenness to ask whether it is true that you are the contemporary of the greatest massacre in recorded history.

'If you tell me that you don't read newspapers, White Books, documentary pamphlets obtainable at W. H. Smith's bookstalls – why on earth do you read *Horizon* and call yourself a member of the intelligentsia? I can't even say that I am sorry to be so rude. There is no excuse for you – for it is your duty to know and to be haunted by your knowledge. As long as you don't feel against reason and independently of reason ashamed to be alive while others are put to death; not guilty, sick, humiliated because you were spared, you will remain what you are, an accomplice by omission.'

Karsky, driven to despair by his inability to arouse world opinion, had by this time committed suicide.*

* *

Koestler's reputation was steadily growing but in England it was still confined to that relatively small part of the population which read the weeklies and the

* Polish authorities in London say that he found a home in the US.

more serious Sunday papers. A year after its publication, *Darkness at Noon*, in spite of the enthusiasm with which the reviewers had received it, had sold barely 4,000 copies.

It was different in the United States. When the novel was published there in 1942, it was chosen by the Book of the Month Club and immediately became a best-seller. Thereafter Koestler was to have few financial worries.

In the same summer Koestler's developing political philosophy was compressed into an essay, *The Yogi and the Commissar*, which Connolly published in *Horizon.* Here Koestler, developing in concentrated form the themes that had informed *The Gladiators* and *Darkness at Noon*, criticised sharply the escapist romanticism that was beginning to run riot in Britain, and displayed the seeds that were to grow and fructify in all his later works.

At the infra-red end of the sociological spectrum stood the Commissar, the dominant figure of the pink thirties.

> 'The Commissar believes in Change from Without. He believes that all the pests of humanity, including constipation and the Oedipus complex, can and will be cured by Revolution, that is, by a radical reorganisation of the system of production and distribution of goods, that this end justifies the use of all means, including violence, ruse, treachery, and poison; that logical reasoning is an unfailing compass and the Universe a kind of very large clockwork in which a very large number of electrons once set in motion will forever revolve in their predictable orbits; and that whosoever believes in anything else is an escapist.'

At the other end of the spectrum squatted the Yogi, melting away into the ultra-violet.

> 'He has no objection to calling the universe a clockwork, but he thinks that it could be called, with about the same amount of truth, a musical-box or a fishpond. He believes that the end is unpredictable and that the Means alone count. He rejects violence under any circumstances. He believes that logical reasoning gradually loses its compass value as the mind approaches the magnetic pole of Truth or the Absolute, which alone matters. He believes that nothing can be improved by exterior organisation and everything by the individual effort from within.'

Civilised man was crowded at the centre of the spectrum. Here there was room for discussion and argument, but the argument could lead nowhere, for the real issue of the time remained between the Yogi and the Commissar, between the fundamental conceptions of change from without and change from within. No synthesis between Yogi and Commissar, between saint and revolutionary, had ever been achieved; and this, Koestler speculated, may be one of the reasons why man has made such a mess of his history. Either the means were subordinated to the end, or the end to the means.

* *

The *New York Times* asked him, as a member of the 'Left Intelligentsia', to write an article based on personal experience 'on what gives men faith to fight to the end for the democratic way'. Koestler gave the readers of the *New York Times* a dusty answer.

> 'Take one of the great episodes of this war: the tiny Greek army, of which nobody ever heard before, beating up Mussolini's crack regiments. It was almost a miracle – and yet the Greeks fought under the fascist dictatorship of the late Metaxas, a tyranny so stupid and narrow that it put *Plato's Republic* on the list of forbidden books. Again, take the latest miracle, the defence of Stalingrad. We look with humility, gratitude and admiration at the men and women of the Soviet State. Those who try to divide us from them are playing Hitler's game; but those who pretend that Uncle Joe Stalin's ways are democratic ways either are trying to be very clever or are just innocent fools.'

It was, he admitted, a very modest credo for a member of the Left Intelligentsia. His friends, he said, were going to throw stones and call him names. And many of them did so.

But Koestler continued to struggle against the wind. Not that he cut himself off from his Socialist friends who had thought of the battle for progress in the classical terms of Socialist trench warfare with neat front lines between the classes; and were now caught in a perplexing fluid war of movements with mobile units breaking loose from their social bodies: large sections of the working-class joining the Fascist ranks, radical wings of the younger Tory generation operating on the left of the Trade Unions, bureaucrats and managers establishing themselves in vital hedgehog positions.

> 'There we stand in no-man's-land, dazzled knights in rusty armour, with a well-thumbed hand-book of Marx-Engels quotations as our sole guide – the truest and profoundest social guide of the last century, but, alas! of modest use on this topsy-turvy battleground of today.'

* *

Just before he was called up and drafted into the Pioneer Corps, Koestler had met George Orwell for the first time.

> 'What appalling stupidity,' Orwell noted in his diary, 'when you have a youngish, gifted man who speaks I do not know how many languages and really knows something about Europe, especially the European political movements, to be unable to make any use of him except for shovelling bricks.'

They were to become close friends, but it took time. Orwell made a somewhat intimidating impression on Koestler at their first meeting – 'Rather cold, a real Burmah police sergeant.' While Koestler was still in the Pioneer Corps, Orwell asked him to write a booklet on the European Underground Resistance for a series which he was editing with T. R. Fyvel for Secker & Warburg. Koestler tried and couldn't finish it, because he felt it to be pure propaganda, not truth. He knew only too well how feeble the Resistance was. Orwell who had no taste for propaganda himself must have understood Koestler's reluctance.

> 'I remember saying once to Arthur Koestler,' Orwell wrote in his essay, *Looking Back On the Spanish Civil War*, '"History stopped in 1936," at which he nodded in immediate understanding. We were both thinking of totalitarianism in general, but more particularly of the Spanish Civil War. Early in life I had noticed that no event was ever correctly reported in a newspaper, but in Spain, for the first time, I saw newspaper reports that did not bear any relation to the facts, not even the relationship that is implied by an ordinary lie. I saw great battles reported where there had been no fighting, and complete silence where hundreds of men had been killed. I saw troops who had fought bravely denounced as cowards and traitors, and others who had never seen a shot fired hailed as the heroes of imaginary victories; and I saw newspapers in London retailing these lies and eager intellectuals building emotional superstructures over events that had never happened. I saw, in fact, history being written not in terms of what happened but what ought to have happened according to various "party lines".'

Orwell, like Koestler, knew what it was like to swim against the tide, and he too was learning how difficult it was to break the idea, engendered by euphoric propaganda, that Uncle Joe was, after all, a genial democrat – not a mere *de facto* and basically hostile 'ally' in the fight against National Socialism, Communism's most powerful pseudo-religious rival.

* *

Koestler knew and loved France no less than the Francophiles of the English literary establishment – 'the managerial class on Parnassus', he called it – but, having lived through its moral, military, and political collapse, he had no illusions about it. It was quite otherwise at this time with the English arbiters of literature, who tended to greet anything that came out of captive France with cries of rapture. This malady, Koestler called the 'French 'Flu' and he diagnosed it sharply in an essay in *Tribune.*

Gide's *Imaginary Interviews*, Aragon's volume of poems, *Le Crêve-Coeur*, and Vercors' *Le Silence de la Mer* had all been celebrated as literary revelations. Koestler fully shared the Mandarins' nostalgia for France and his delight in the French language. ('*L'usage du cabinet est interdit pendant l'arrêt du train en gare* means only that you should not use the toilet while the train is standing in a station, but it sounds like the pure harmonies of the spheres, especially if you have been cut off from the Continent for four years.') But that did not prevent him from pricking the three balloons.

He had read the Gide interviews greedily – with the greed, he wrote, with which one would listen for news from the planet Mars. But

> 'It was distressing reading. Gide's writings have always shown a touch of esoteric arrogance; his influence on the younger French generation was deplorable.'

In Vercors' *Le Silence de la Mer* he saw

> 'the uncannily precise repetition in 1942 of the mentality which in 1939 sent the German anti-fascists in France to concentration camps. M. Vercors has learnt as little as the squabbling French politicians in exile.'

As to Louis Aragon, the propagators of the French 'Flu felt driven to present him not only as a poet but as a hero and a martyr of the Left. Koestler exposed all this as a fantasy and a lie.

There were others he concluded who could legitimately speak in the name of France, but they were silent:

> 'All this literary ballyhoo gives about as true a picture of the common people of France as Hollywood of the underground movement in Europe. It is of no service to the French cause, and it dangerously sidetracks people's attention from the real problem which we shall have to face.'

The clearer it became that National Socialism was going to be defeated, the more Koestler grew irritated by the tone of Allied propaganda and the climate of opinion which it engendered. The West, he said, was fighting against a total lie in the name of a half-truth:

> 'We call Nazism's New Order a total lie because it denies the specific ethos of our species, because by proclaiming that might is right it reduced Civil Law to Jungle Law, and by proclaiming that race is all it reduced Sociology to Zoology. With such a philosophy there can be no compromise; it must unconditionally surrender.
>
> 'We, on the other hand, live in a climate of half-truths. We fight against Racialism and yet racial discrimination is far from abolished in the Anglo-Saxon countries; we fight for Democracy and yet our mightiest ally is a dictatorship where at least two of the four freedoms are not operating. But such is the sticky, all-pervading influence of our climate that even to mention these facts, undeniable though they are, has the effect of a provocation.'

Sentimental appeals for more good-will and co-operation between the competing partners who tomorrow would rule the world, he wrote, were naïve and pointless: governments only had a narrow margin for manoeuvring within the fatal automatism of the economic and social forces behind them. For at least fifty years it had, in his opinion, become increasingly clear that only a vigorous supranational organisation could end the global muddle by global solutions. But the truth of the matter was that 'the outstanding feature of our day is the collapse of all supranational structures'. This failure of supranationalism was more than a momentary set-back – it revealed the inadequacy of a method of approach which had dominated the Liberal and Socialist movements for the last century.

Koestler berated the shallow optimism of his fellow Leftists. What was needed was an active fraternity of 'short-term pessimists'. He felt in his bones that an era was dying. The age of religious wars had ended when secular politics began to dominate human consciousness; feudal politics ended when economic factors assumed over-riding importance; the struggles of 'economic man' would end by the emergence of the new ethical values of the new age. But he was under no illusion, unlike so many of the optimists among his Leftist friends, that the new age would dawn with the ending of the war.

# CHAPTER XII

# *1943–1944*

IN NOVEMBER 1943, *Arrival and Departure* was published. Like Koestler's two earlier novels it was concerned with the perennial problem of ends and means, the conflict between morality and expediency. But whereas in the earlier novels he demonstrated the impact on history of this conflict, in *Arrival and Departure* he attempted to transpose it into terms of individual psychology.

A young ex-Communist, Peter Slavek, escapes from an East European country (unnamed, but Hungary) and arrives as a stowaway in Neutralia (obviously Portugal). His aim is to get to Britain to join the Armed Forces. The British consul hears him out and is sympathetic. But why doesn't Peter want to have a good time like other young people? Why doesn't he try to get to neutral America instead?

> 'Well,' said Peter, 'I have been told that you are fighting a war.'
>
> 'If it depended on me,' said the consul, 'you could go tomorrow, but as things are . . .'

While Peter waits in vain for a permit to come through from London, he is befriended by a Freudian psycho-analyst of his own nationality, and has an affair with a French girl who is staying with her, waiting for her American visa to come through. When the French girl leaves, Peter has a nervous breakdown. The analyst 'cures' him by eliciting from his unconscious the fact that his earlier revolutionary Communism (for which he had suffered grievously at the hands of the security police) had been the result not of any rational belief in Marxist ideology but arose instead from a guilt complex caused by his repressed memory of an attempt he had made as a small child to blind his younger brother. Thus 'cured', Peter sees no reason why he should not go to America. America is willing to have him. But just before the ship sails he turns, runs back down the gang-plank, returns to the British consul and says that with or without a permit he will go to Britain. He gets to Britain, joins the Forces, and the book ends with Peter drifting down on a parachute into his native land.

The character of Peter was modelled, in his external aspects at least, on the young Hungarian poet Endre Havas, whom Koestler had met in London in 1941 or 1942. Although, like Koestler, he had been disillusioned by Communism, he joined the Party again during the Battle of Stalingrad, and was dropped by parachute into Hungary.*

The novel was not a popular success; it was too clever, too paradoxical, too Continental, and dared to call to account the potent totems of Marx and Freud. Most reviewers were respectful enough, but uncomprehending – their normal attitude when confronted with the work of a foreigner who gives the impression that he understands the English better than they understand themselves.

There were, of course, a few who understood what he was attempting.

'*Why Sneer At The Intellectuals?*' asked the headline over the review by Michael Foot, who, having remarked the 'horrifying detail' of the story (which, thirty years of horror later, seems mild enough), went on to say that

> 'one page of Koestler is more convincing than a thousand atrocity accounts, however substantial . . . He is the greatest foreign novelist since Joseph Conrad who has paid us the honour of writing in the English tongue.'

Elizabeth Bowen also recognised the novel's peculiar quality:

> 'Contemporary in subject, it has a background of values that do not change. The story contains – in fact, *is* – an analysis of heroism.'

Such also was the verdict of Philip Toynbee:

> 'The thesis . . . is a blind and unreasoned heroism, the heroism of Slavek under torture and inquisition. The antithesis is the revelation of childhood guilt and the explaining away of heroism as a mere mechanism of atonement. The synthesis is clear-sighted self-sacrifice.'

Koestler's schismatical restoration of the individual within the framework of the dialectic offended both Freudians and Marxists, and their weird assortment of fellow-travellers in search of certainty. Toynbee, himself an ex-Communist, regarded Koestler as probably the cleverest novelist writing in English, and in the opening of his review felt obliged to go to some lengths to indicate (such was

*In 1949, during the great purge which followed the trial of the former Minister for Foreign Affairs, Laszlo Rajk, Havas was arrested, together with virtually all Party intellectuals who had spent the years of the war in the West. He was accused of being a spy, but persisted in his refusal to sign the usual confession. Several of his fellow prisoners who were released during the revolution of 1956, and escaped to England, reported his end. Havas had gone insane under protracted physical torture. He would crawl round on all fours shouting 'Help, help. Long live Stalin.'

Paul Ignotus, former Hungarian Press Attaché in London, who had also been arrested during the Rajk purge, had seen Havas' end. In his book *Political Prisoner* he wrote:

> 'Havas, with his conspicuous appearance and the typical awkwardness of an intellectual, was a tempting target. They dragged him about and played football with his body. He was left lying in his excrement for days.'

the density of quasi-romantic fog enveloping the English literary scene) that a writer, even foreign, could be good as well as clever.

> 'In our language the word [cleverness] had become a slight – the quality suspect, if not odious. No honest instinct this, but a bubble bursting on the dough of our stupidity. In itself the word has no intellectual implication, but just as there are clever salesmen and clever politicians, so there are clever intellectuals. Koestler is one of these. His attitude is profoundly and honourably intellectual in that he sees life as a series of mental and moral problems to be solved, or at least to be clearly stated. His cleverness is shown in the subtlety of his solutions and, perhaps even more strikingly, in the clarity of his expositions. His mind is dialectical in the most reputable sense of the word . . . But suspicion of cleverness persists even among the educated, though this, I believe, is due to confusion rather than to obscurantism . . .'

The anonymous reviewer in the *Times Literary Supplement* also succeeded in seeing the essential part of *Arrival and Departure*, which, for him, had something of the atmosphere of *The Possessed* overlaid on a precarious base of Hegelian dialectic – something, at any rate, very far from 'English'. What, he asked, were the decisive counters in the revolutionary idealism of the age? On the one hand: nerves, glands, and tissues. On the other: vanity and illusion.

> 'All this Mr Koestler embodies in dramatic symbol and introspective discovery. His is a fierce and glowing heat of mind, which by this time has burned away many or most of the fancy wrappings designed to conceal the nakedness of the dream dreamt in terms of political economy. Yet he really has not gone back on his beliefs: having reduced heroism and quixotry to their neurotic elements, he restores them in the end to their moral inspiration . . . It is a difficult and imperfectly resolved fable, but with something like a hundred times as much of the peculiar meat of modernity in it as there is in the run of contemporary novels.'

Koestler's friend, George Orwell, had begun to write his masterpiece *Animal Farm*, that devastating satire on Communism (which was to have such difficulty in finding a publisher because of the officially sponsored cult of Uncle Joe and the myth of Allied-Soviet unity), when he read *Arrival and Departure*. He too knew the difficulties of swimming against the tide, but he differed from Koestler in that he still genuinely clung to the sturdy belief that an English form of Socialism could somehow reconcile social order and individual freedom and so avoid the drift towards totalitarianism (a belief he was to abandon when he came to write *Nineteen Eighty-Four*). He greatly admired Koestler but with reservations.

> 'His main theme is the decadence of revolutions owing to the corrupting effects of power, but the special nature of the Stalin dictatorship has driven him back into a position not far removed from pessimistic Conservatism.'

*Arrival and Departure*, he concluded, was not a satisfactory novel. In making Peter Slavek take his final decision ('from a mere instinct') not to shirk action and danger, Koestler had in fact made him suffer a sudden loss of intelligence. Here, for once, Orwell had missed the central point.

Orwell returned to Koestler's hedonism in the essay he wrote after reading *Arrival and Departure*. There is a passage which is worth quoting at some length (although it fails to recognise that Koestler had already rejected Utopia) for the light it throws both on Koestler in 1944 and on his most intelligent and unsparing 'Socialist' critic.

> 'To take a rational political decision one must have a picture of the future. At present Koestler seems to have none, or rather to have two which cancel out. As an ultimate objective he believes in the Earthly Paradise, the Sun State which the gladiators set out to establish and which has haunted the imagination of Socialists, Anarchists and religious heretics for hundreds of years. But his intelligence tells him that the Earthly Paradise is receding into the far distance and that what is actually ahead of us is bloodshed, tyranny and privation. Recently he described himself as a "short-term pessimist". Every kind of horror is blowing up over the horizon, but somehow it will all come right in the end. This outlook is probably gaining ground among thinking people: it results from the very great difficulty, once one has abandoned orthodox religious belief, of accepting life on earth as inherently miserable, and on the other hand, from the realisation that to make life liveable is a much bigger problem than it recently seemed. Since about 1930 the world has given no reason for optimism whatever. Nothing is in sight except a welter of lies, hatred, cruelty and ignorance, and beyond our present troubles loom vaster ones which are only now entering the European consciousness . . . The real problem is how to restore the religious attitude while accepting death as final. Men can only be happy when they do not assume the object of life is happiness. It is most unlikely, however, that Koestler would accept this. There is a well-marked hedonistic strain in his writing, and his failure to find a political position after breaking with Stalinism is a result of this. The Russian Revolution, the central event in Koestler's life, started out with high hopes. We forget these things now, but a quarter of a century ago, it was confidentially expected that the Russian Revolution would lead to Utopia. Obviously this has not happened. Koestler is too acute not to see this and too sensitive not to remember such things as purges and mass deportations for what they are; he is not, like Shaw or Laski, looking at them through the wrong end of the telescope. Therefore he draws the conclusion: This is what revolutions lead to. There is nothing for it except to be a "short-term pessimist", i.e. to keep out of politics, make a sort of oasis within which you and your friends can remain sane, and hope that somehow things will be better in a hundred years. At the basis of this lies his hedonism, which leads him to think of the Earthly Paradise as desirable . . . All revolutions are failures, but they are not all the same failure. It is his unwillingness to admit this that has led Koestler's mind temporarily into a blind alley and that makes *Arrival and Departure* seem shallow compared with the earlier books.'

*　　*

Now that no excuse remains for ignorance about the horrors of Communism in action, there would be little point in detailing at tedious length the extreme hostility of English Marxists to Koestler's work. Two examples, both products of the mid-fifties, will suffice.

> 'Koestler,' wrote Jack Lindsay, 'is an interesting example of the way in which the "renegade rebel" ends by projecting on to socialism the constrictions, distortions and regimentations which he has reacted against in capitalism. Indeed, he may be said to parody the whole process so obviously that one can scarcely believe it. His admirers have written that he has had the advantage of suffering under Communism and so can write of its cruelties with special knowledge. But in fact he has suffered only under fascism – at the hands of Franco and the anti-Communist French police in 1939. What he experienced in Franco's jails he then used as documentary material to blacken the Soviet Union!
>
> 'No wonder he decides in *Yogi and Commissar* that the imperialist Blimp is after all not such a bad fellow and that there is room for Koestlers in his world.'*

Arnold Kettle offered a rather less crude assessment:

> 'The two qualities which strike one most, perhaps, as one surveys the period, are narrowness and pessimism . . . But are they not, perhaps, mere words, expressive of what one reader happens to find unsympathetic? It seems to me that one cannot avoid the issue by such arguments. That the work of, say, Aldous Huxley, George Orwell, Arthur Koestler, Graham Greene and Evelyn Waugh is in its total effect pessimistic, that the picture of the human situation that emerges from the novels of these writers is in the last degree unhopeful and, as a result, unhelpful, is not a matter of mere opinion but is as clearly demonstrable as any statement of literary criticism can well be. The point is not merely that the material with which these writers are concerned is unsympathetic that they write about a society which manifests all the classic aspects of decadence; what is significant is that the writers themselves partake overwhelmingly in the values of the society they depict. They are not simply writers describing decadence, they are decadent writers.
>
> 'And why not?, the question will be asked, what's wrong with pessimism and decadence? The simple answer, I think, is that such attitudes are unhelpful and in consequence life-denying.'

Unhopeful? In the short term, and justifiably as it turned out, yes. But unhelpful? From the standpoint of 1980 it would be difficult to think of a more inept description of Koestler's earlier writings.†

* *

In the process of his anglicisation, Koestler concluded that the arms of England should be supported by the ostrich as well as the lion and unicorn. He recalls the time when Stalin, having given the word for the Poles of Warsaw to rise against

* *After the 'Thirties*, London, 1956.
† *An Introduction to the English Novel*, Vol. II, London, 1953.

the Germans, ensured their destruction by having the Red Army under the Polish Quisling, Marshal Rokossovsky, rest on their arms reversed on the other side of the river during the slaughter. (It has recently been revealed that this was one of the fruits of the secret wartime collaboration of the Gestapo and the NKVD.)

Koestler considered this a crime worse than the Germans' destruction of Lidice and wished to denounce it in *Tribune*. But *Tribune*'s chief backer, George Straus, would not permit it – just as Victor Gollancz and T. S. Eliot would not publish Orwell's *Animal Farm*. Nothing to irritate the jovial pipe-smoking Uncle Joe, or embarrass the American authorities (and to a lesser extent the English) who considered it expedient to appease him at all costs.

'*Déjà vu!*' Koestler says sadly today, contemplating the West's vulnerability in the age of one-sided 'détente'.

* *

On 10th January 1944, Cyril Connolly gave a party in his Bedford Square apartment. It was here that Koestler had first met the identical Paget twins, Mamaine and Celia, in whose house in Drayton Gardens Koestler had stayed for some months in 1942 after his discharge from the Pioneer Corps.

They were beautiful and cultivated young women, eleven years younger than Koestler. Their childhood had been saddened first by the death of their mother a week after their birth and by that of their father, Eric Morton Paget, when they were twelve. A village schoolmaster had seen to the earlier years of their education, two English boarding-schools and a *pensionnat de jeunes filles* in Lausanne to the later. After their presentation at court, readers of glossy magazines and the gossip columns of the daily press came to expect the regular appearance of the Twins who always dressed alike and had identical hairstyles. Mamaine modelled once for a Harrods advertisement, but no one could tell that it wasn't Celia.

Such exposure gave the impression that the Twins were the late thirties' equivalent of the Bright Young Things of the twenties; but this was far from the truth. Their formal education had included no Latin, Greek, mathematics, or science; but they had enjoyed ample time to read voraciously in French and English and both played the piano well, practising for hours every day. They loved the country, but walking, bird-watching, and photography were more to their taste than hunting and shooting. In conversation with writers, artists, and intellectuals they could hold their own unaggressively but vivaciously, being modest in their own ambitions. They fitted easily and most decoratively into the circle that had formed itself around Cyril Connolly and those who contributed to his *Horizon*.

When Koestler met them, his long affair with Daphne was breaking up. Mamaine was unattached. Celia, who was married, recognised the immediate mutual attraction between Koestler and her sister. A few days later Connolly brought them together again at a dinner-party in the White Tower restaurant. That night they became lovers. So began the most profound, stormy, disturbing, and in the end, saddening of Koestler's many love affairs. Between them there was, of course, the attraction of opposites – the 'rootless cosmopolitan', as Koestler liked to describe himself, and the indubitably upper-class English girl. Each had much to give the other. Koestler, although none could have guessed it from his accent, was already being anglicised; Mamaine was to hasten, and guide, the process. For her part, Mamaine was to have her intellectual horizons widened by her association with a man fanatically dedicated to a wide variety of intellectual vocations and missions. What they had in common, deriving from different causes, were chronic insecurity and anxiety; but whereas Koestler was hardly ever ill, and disposed of an energy that sometimes seemed superhuman, Mamaine (who suffered from bronchial asthma) was hardly ever well, and tired easily.

It was this that was to part them in the end, not Koestler's sexual infidelities which she overlooked tolerantly as affairs of no consequence. She would have liked to have children, but Koestler had made it clear from the beginning that there would be none. He would, he said, make a bad father. His books would be his only children and Mamaine was to help him bring them forth. Nor, for some years, was there to be any thought of marriage. Koestler had long been parted from his wife Dorothy, but there seems to have been no contemplation of divorce. It was a hard enough bargain he struck with Mamaine, but she accepted it cheerfully for many years – and even after their parting, years later, they were to remain close friends.

# CHAPTER XIII

# *1944–1945*

'IF I FORGET THEE, O Jerusalem, may my right hand forget her cunning.'
Koestler had not forgotten the menace to European Jewry, but his interest in Zionism and Palestine had been largely superseded since the late twenties by his Communist activities (the Soviet Union was then intensely hostile to the Zionist cause); his tribulations in Spain and France; his early experiences in England. The old obsession was sharply revived in 1942 after his release from the Pioneer Corps. When he had last heard of his mother, she was staying with her sister in a small village in Czechoslovakia where her nephew was the local doctor. Where were they now?

In the course of his work for the Ministry of Information he came across many of the early first-hand and well-authenticated accounts of the accelerating progress of the National Socialists' policy of extermination. He became an active member of the Anglo-Palestine Committee, a pressure group which worked in close conjunction with the Jewish Agency, whose own intelligence service provided an abundance of information about the horrors already inflicted on the Polish Jews, the threat to those who still survived in the countries of Eastern Europe not yet overrun by the Germans, and the rapidly deteriorating situation in Palestine. For a long time he refrained from attacking Britain's Palestine policy in public, but behind the scene he worked – under the nominal supervision of Chaim Weizmann, the elderly and unmilitant head of the world Zionist organisation – with such people as Israel Sieff, Michael Foot, Kingsley Martin, Tom Driberg, David Astor, Victor Gollancz, and Moishe Shertok of the Jewish Agency (later as Moshe Sharrett to be the first Foreign Minister of the State of Israel).

Another member of the committee was Guy de Rothschild, whose ship had been torpedoed in mid-Atlantic while he was on his way back from the United States to join the Free French. At the moment the torpedo struck, Rothschild had been reading *Scum of the Earth*, and when he was pulled out of the water five hours later, covered with oil, he vowed that if ever he reached London safely, Koestler would be one of the first people he would contact. His sister Miriam, who knew Koestler, brought them together and they soon became close friends.

The influx of Jews and Jewish capital into Palestine during the twenties and thirties benefited the Arabs economically and in some other respects; but such benefits failed to offset the resentment inevitably aroused by the cultural clash between the bustling, efficient, and (in Arab eyes) vulgar incomers, with their Western Socialist values, and the native Palestinian peasants, many of them Christians, who were still for the most part living in a feudal age. By 1936, when the Jewish community had grown to half a million, the native Palestinians were in a state of virtual rebellion.

Furthermore, ships full of refugees from Germany were arriving off the coast of Palestine, only to be turned away by the Royal Navy. In the House of Commons the Colonial Secretary was asked what would happen to them.

'They would,' said Mr Malcolm MacDonald, 'be sent back to where they came from.'

Did that mean the concentration camps of Germany?

'The responsibility,' Mr MacDonald replied, 'rests with those responsible for organising illegal immigration.'

In other words, the answer was yes.

The refugee ships were still being turned away. In December 1941, a small Danube cattle-boat, the *Struma*, had staggered across the Black Sea to Istanbul with 769 men, women and children. For two months she lay there while the Jewish Agency tried in vain to persuade the mandatory authority to issue permits for the deck-cargo of desperate humanity to enter Palestine. In the end the Turks ordered the ship to leave, and a mile from the coast she foundered. There was one survivor.

This and similar incidents ensured a revival of anti-British terrorism in Palestine.

* *

The situation for the Jews still alive in Europe was uglier still, and Koestler, like the other members of the Anglo-Palestine Committee, was well-informed about it. In Britain and America, Zionists and their non-Jewish sympathisers (whatever the views of the latter as to the future of Palestine) had done their utmost – with little official support – to arouse the public to some sense of the reality of what was happening, but somehow public opinion was either unwilling or unable to accept and digest the appalling reality of death-trains criss-crossing Europe, of extermination-factories, of genocide – carried out not by hate-crazed maniacs but by pedantic bureaucrats implementing a carefully calculated and co-ordinated plan.

A small group of the Anglo-Palestine Committee, including John Strachey and Koestler, prepared a memorandum for the British Government urging the bombing of the death-factories in Upper Silesia and Poland by the American Air Force. This, they argued, would be a spectacular act of political warfare. So far, official reaction to the massacre of racial and national minorities had been confined to humanitarian protests. But such an operation would translate those protests into terms of military action. The mere mention of the slaughterhouses in an Allied Air Force communiqué would dispel the widespread incredulity about the matter, and demonstrate that the Allied Powers meant business in fighting such atrocities. This would arouse a strong echo in world-wide public opinion. Just as the outcry of protest about the torture of British prisoners-of-war by the Japanese, and about the shooting of RAF officers in Stalag 3, had had a restraining effect on Japanese and German methods, so it would be reasonable to assume that the repercussions on world public opinion of such an attack from the air would have a restraining effect on Hitler's extermination policy. It would also strengthen the hand of the more conservative circles in Germany which had always been in opposition to the policy but had not been able to take a stand against it.

Such an attack (Strachey and Koestler argued optimistically), by emphasising the importance which the Allies attached to the matter, might even lead to an abandonment of the extermination policy in the hope that it might facilitate more favourable capitulation terms. Moishe Shertok, among others, favoured the scheme.

But nothing came of it.

* *

For some years Koestler had been gradually developing the notion of two planes of existence, the tragic and the trivial, and the line of intersection along which the genius walks when most inspired. Feeling his way towards a general theory of creativity, he had been collecting and reading a formidable library of works in English, French and German by established authorities on, among other subjects, psychology, physiological psychology, neurology, psychopharmacology, telepathy, evolution, aesthetics, anthropology, heredity, and extra-sensory perception.

He would soon, he felt, be able to work up his notes into a work which would establish him as a scientific thinker. But this was a task which could not be tackled among the distractions of London. This was no doubt in his mind when he told the readers of *Horizon* that the state should provide a writer with 'a retreat in the country – an isolated cottage with quiet and reasonable minimum comfort'.

With the help of friends he found such a place – an old farmhouse called Bwlch Ocyn on the hillside near Blaenau Ffestiniog in North Wales – and took a lease for a few years. But he was not ready to move there.

He was obsessed by an itch to return to Palestine, to see for himself what was happening there, to gather material for a book – and also to contact the Irgun Zvai Leumi (his sympathies with which he had never hidden, because it was the successor of Jabotinsky's movement). On the other hand, like Weizmann, with whom he was on friendly terms, he was in favour of partition; and he thought that he might be able to change Menachem Begin's mind on that score.*

Weizmann agreed: 'Talk to those mad friends of yours', he told Koestler, 'and try to make them see that partition is the only chance of a peaceful settlement.'

* Begin was then in hiding with £5,000 on his head.

But under whose auspices was Koestler to get to Palestine? Lovat Dickson, of Macmillan publishers, approached the British Council, only to hear from John Hampden:

> 'Your letter about Arthur Koestler I passed on at once to the people directly concerned, and although there is unanimous agreement about his capability, there is, I am sorry to say, no possibility of our sending him out to Palestine on behalf of the Council because of his Hungarian nationality. If he were to make his own way to Palestine there would be no objection to our representative there securing his services locally.'

It was then suggested to Koestler that he should approach *The Times*. There he met Donald Tyerman. Koestler told him that he was in favour of partition of Palestine and that he wanted to go there and see what he could do. Tyerman gave him a letter of accreditation as *The Times*' special correspondent. Weizmann obtained a permit from the Colonial Office for him, on the understanding that he was going to try to talk sense to the Irgun Zvai Leumi.

There was a possibility (which came to nothing) that Mamaine would find some way of joining him in Palestine later.

Just before he left England Koestler heard from the International Red Cross that his aunt and cousins had been sent to Auschwitz and killed. He had no definite news of his mother, who had been staying with her sister, but he assumed that she too had been deported to Auschwitz.*

On the 20th December, Koestler embarked at Liverpool on the S.S. *Exeter*. The voyage was uneventful until the convoy arrived in the Mediterranean, where it was attacked by U-boats, the ship behind the *Exeter* being torpedoed.

The *Exeter* arrived at Alexandria towards the end of the first week in February and Koestler went on to Jerusalem by train. On the evening of his arrival he attended a party given by the Mayor, a former American foreign correspondent, Gershon Agronsky. There, as he wrote, he met 'all Jerusalem' – acquaintances whom he had not seen for years, officials of the British political warfare service, Ministry of Information officials, innumerable politicians. As soon as he had settled in at the Hotel Eden he cabled Mamaine: 'Come soon'.

The first few days were hectic. In spite of the tension (or perhaps because of it), Jerusalem at that time was a lively place. There were many parties, many receptions, much social diversion. At the Hotel Eden he was contacted by many people, including representatives in disguise of the Irgun and the Stern Gang.

After two or three weeks of social (and discreet political) activity in Jerusalem, Koestler got away to tour the *kibbutzim* in Galilee and collect material for the novel that was eventually to be published under the title *Thieves in the Night*. He chose as the setting for that book the *kibbutzim* Ain Hashofeth and Ain Geb, the latter the home of Teddy Kollek (now the Mayor of Jerusalem).

From time to time Koestler interrupted his work on the novel to make contacts with the extremists. This was a delicate business, for at that time the Jewish Agency and Haganah were cooperating with the British Authorities.

* Mrs Koestler survived the war and came to live in England.

He knew from Teddy Kollek, who was second-in-command of the Jewish intelligence organisation, that the organisation had handed over to the British authorities all that was known about Irgun and its leadership.

To complicate matters, the head of the CID in Jerusalem, who had rather a bad reputation about third-degree methods of interrogating terrorists, was taking a lively interest in Koestler. (He knew, of course, that Koestler was on the Zionist side and had a certain sympathy for Irgun.) On the very evening when Koestler had arranged to be picked up by the Irgun and taken off for a secret meeting with Menachem Begin, this officer was sitting in Koestler's flat, drinking scotch with him and complaining, 'What a bloody country!' Fortunately, he left only a matter of minutes before the Irgun agent arrived.

Koestler was taken by the agent in a car to another street in Jerusalem. There they got into another car, and then, after a short drive, into a third car which took them to the outskirts of Tel Aviv. There again they changed cars. In all, five cars were used before Koestler was led into the dark room where Menachem Begin was waiting for him. They had a long and more or less amicable conversation, but Begin refused to be persuaded that it would be sensible to settle for partition.

Later, in very similar circumstances, Koestler met David Yellin, the head of the Stern Gang. He had no more success with him.

Koestler shut himself up with his impressions and pads of lined paper, feverishly working on *Thieves in the Night*; making notes for the book he intended to write one day about the history of the British Mandate and the tragic complexities and consequences of Israel's return to the Promised Land; longing for Mamaine; finding some solace in an affair with an attractive girl on the High Commission staff; being irritated by a former boy-friend of Mamaine's, a rich young man criss-crossing the Middle East in his own light aircraft and dashing off pro-Arab despatches for a popular London paper; growing sick of the Palestine hothouse, the internecine feuds, the opposing fanaticisms, the pusillanimity of the Administration, the awfulness of British wives – the hopelessness of it all.

A note of anguish (unusual in Koestler's intimate correspondence, where the tone is generally one of self-protective reserve) began to creep into his letters to Mamaine, whom he called 'darling Mermaid'.

'God bless you. I wish, I wish, I wish you were here . . .'

* *

On 8th May, Germany capitulated. In Britain Churchill went to the country and was defeated. Labour – the friends of Zionism and bitter critics of the White Paper – came to power with a large majority. Hopes were high that there would be a dramatic change in British policy. In 1939 there had been some seven million Jews in Europe (excluding the Soviet Union). A million had survived, 700,000 of whom were in 'Displaced Persons' camps. The Jewish Agency applied for 100,000 immigration permits to Palestine. The Colonial Office offered 1,500 – 'the last available under the White Paper'.

When the new Parliament was opened in London, there was not a word about Palestine in the speech from the Throne. Labour in office, it soon became clear, was not going to sing the Zionist songs it had sung so fervently in Opposition. The new Foreign Secretary, Ernest Bevin, was openly and bluntly hostile to the Jewish Agency and its claims. Haganah ended its truce with the British forces and began to collaborate once more with the Irgun.

Koestler was still in Jerusalem, immersed in his book. After a long and exhausting day of writing he scribbled to Mamaine:

> 'Darling Mermaid, This is just a line to tell you that I am still alive and that I still love you. I got a heap of letters from you including the one which you wrote on a sleepless night after VE-day and which broke my heart. But it is a good idea to write when one is feeling miserable and I don't mind – on the contrary . . . I am only living for my book. If it is as good as I sometimes think it is, then it is damned good – what a bright and modest sentence. But my head is reeling with tiredness – I wrote seven hours non-stop, without noticing it, and now I get a sudden and savage craving for you . . . I have asked for a passage in September, and I hope I shall get it.
>
> 'God bless. It's getting hot here. I am more and more convinced that it's a blessing you didn't come here; the climate would have killed you. How is Celia? And Plesch? And John Strachey? Do go on writing nice gossipy letters; you have no idea how I enjoy them.
>
> 'Bye, angel, I am getting sentimental and falling asleep.'

Koestler's attitude to both official Zionism and the British administration was one of *odi et amo*. Official Zionism, as embodied at the top in Chaim Weizmann, believed (ostensibly) in a policy of minimum pressure behind minimum demands (i.e. the partition or cantonisation of Palestine). The Irgun (with which the Jewish Agency and Haganah now maintained contact) believed in a policy of maximum pressure behind maximum demands. Koestler, his political acumen telling him that the correct policy for the Jews to adopt was one of maximum pressure behind minimum demands – i.e., for a negotiated partition of the Holy Land – was a voice crying in the wilderness between the hard men of the Irgun and the respectable front-men of the Jewish Agency. He was increasingly alarmed by what he considered the almost unanimous and irrational anti-Jewish sentiment pervading the British Administration – and also by the infiltration of Communists into the Ministry of Information services.

From time to time he came across old friends whom he had not met since the fall of the Weimar Republic; among them was Dr Magnus, who had sat on the board of Ullstein Verlag when Koestler was employed by the chain. He now earned a meagre living in the streets by selling cigarettes from a tray.

As the draft of his novel neared its end, his depression deepened. On 1st July he wrote to Mamaine:

> 'I get rather depressed here lately, and longing to be back . . .'

Five weeks later Koestler managed to get a seat on an aircraft leaving for England. A girl-friend drove him to the airfield. Before they parted he bought a copy of the *Jerusalem Post* and learned that the city of Hiroshima had been destroyed by an atomic bomb.

'That's the end of the world war,' were his parting words to the girl, 'and it's also the beginning of the end of the world.'

# PART THREE

# *1945–1950*

# CHAPTER XIV

# *1945*

MAMAINE WAS WAITING FOR Koestler, and their reunion in London dispelled any uncertainties about their relationship.

Bwlch Ocyn was ready for them but Koestler had work to do in London before they could leave for Wales. In addition to the draft of the novel, *Thieves in the Night*, Koestler had brought back from Palestine a mass of information about the rapidly deteriorating situation. He urged Chaim Weizmann and the Anglo-Palestine Committee to adopt a clear-cut policy of maximum pressure for a partition of Palestine that would give the Jews the Negev. He argued that if this could be done rapidly, and the British ban on immigration lifted, the Arabs would probably, after a brief period of unrest, accept the *fait accompli* and learn to live with it. The longer London hesitated, in its fear of offending the Arabs, the remoter would be the possibility of reaching a relatively peaceful solution.

He condensed his information and arguments into two long articles which *The Times* published anonymously. Although they were obviously written from a Zionist point of view, they were fairly temperate in tone and did not underestimate the strength of the Arabs' understandable resentment of the increasingly powerful and aggressive foreign body planted in their midst. Nevertheless, he pointed out, the Arabs had shared the benefits of the rapid economic development of the country by the Jewish incomers, especially the last pre-war wave of relatively wealthy Jews from Germany and Eastern Europe. After centuries of stagnation, the Arab population, between 1922 and 1942 had doubled. Most of the diseases endemic throughout the rest of the Middle East had been eradicated. The influx of Jewish capital had given the country a well-balanced economic structure.

On the other hand, Koestler admitted, it would be foolish to underestimate the power of new-found Palestinian nationalism. The Zionists argued that it was not their aim to 'take the house away' from the Arabs but rather to add new floors to it. But that image in itself contained the essence of the Arab objection:

> 'There is hardly a nation in the world which would willingly acquiesce in new dwellers establishing themselves "on top" of it. In private conversation Arab

leaders admit the economic advantages derived from Jewish immigration; but they argue that no nation will sell its aspirations to independence and sovereignty for the sake of hospitals, schools, and metal roads . . . No economic advantages can counter these Arab fears or appease their violent xenophobia. "We want neither their honey nor their sting" is an Arab saying quoted to your Correspondent by a moderate Arab leader.

'Thus eight years after publication of the Palestine Royal Commission's report, the incompatibility of claims, the antithesis of Zionist achievement and Arab traditionalism, the pressure of homeless Jewry's distress against the closed doors of their promised homeland continue. The political deadlock is complete.'

If the Palestine problem were considered in isolation, then right was opposed to right in the clash between Arabs and Jews. But if the picture were widened to include the Arab world as a whole, then Palestine shrank to a bare two per cent of the total area inhabited by Arabs – while for the Jews it represented all their hopes of ever recovering a national home.

There were signs, Koestler optimistically conjectured, that if partition were enforced, the leaders of the Arab League would confine themselves to vocal protests. Perhaps he was right, but it seems unlikely.

* *

By the beginning of October Koestler and Mamaine were installed in Bwlch Ocyn. A lot of work was needed to make the old farmhouse comfortable and the draft of *Thieves in the Night* had to be revised, cut, revised again and retyped before Koestler could get down to the intricate work on the psychology of creativity that had been gestating for years. They had scarcely unpacked their cases before visitors began to descend on them. There was a large and growing correspondence to be dealt with. And Koestler was still feverishly preoccupied with the Palestine situation.

Before leaving London, his relations with Weizmann had become strained, partly because the old man still resented his friendship with Jabotinsky, but more immediately because during their last meeting Koestler had reproached him bluntly with political quietism, deploring what he considered to be the Zionist Movement's shortcomings in the field of propaganda and public relations.

Koestler understood, of course, that Ernest Bevin's impatience with the Zionist movement reflected the conviction of Whitehall that Britain's interests in the Middle East and beyond demanded a conciliatory policy towards the Arabs. But such a policy, in his view, would in the end prove self-defeating. The most urgent necessity, he considered, was to reawaken and mobilise the traditional pro-Zionism of the Labour Party and bring this to bear on the Executive. Weizmann was shortly to address the Labour back-benchers, and Koestler noted his fear that 'the old man in present state of nerves might not fully exploit the opportunity'.

On 3rd October he wrote a long letter to Victor Gollancz in the form of an aide-memoire of points 'which I think should be taken into consideration in his speech . . . I felt that if it comes from you . . . it will cut more ice and meet with less resistance than coming from me.'

Weizmann, he suggested, should admit frankly that any solution imposed by Britain would involve a degree of injustice and then go on to assert that the undeniable injustice that would be inflicted on the Arabs by the partition of Palestine would be small compared with the injustice that would flow from any alternative. He should analyse the legal, moral and (above all, as seen from the point of view of British interests) political aspects of the Zionist case:

> 'The Balfour Declaration was motivated half by romantic sentimentality and half by "*Realpolitik*" (c.f. Lloyd George's evidence before the Royal Commission, Royal Comm. Rept. p.23). Zionist propaganda always uses the sentimental arguments and neglects the "real-political" ones, – that is, the emphasis on the strategical importance to the British Empire of having a beach-head of a compact European highly industrialised population at their focal centre of communications. The basic point is that there is a community of interest between the British and us, and that we are reliable partners – if for no other reason than because there is nobody with whom we could double-cross them. A weak Jewish Palestine is an irritant to the Arabs and therefore a liability to the Empire. A strong Jewish Palestine will be an asset.'

*Realpolitik* indeed. But that was not the style of the Grand Old Man of Zionism. If he had taken that line what effect would it have had on the Parliamentary Labour Party? It would probably have shocked most of the back-benchers, whose sympathy with Zionism was essentially sentimental and who would surely have been much too squeamish to stomach the implications of Koestler's harsh line. As for Attlee's administration, it was not to be budged by such arguments any more than by the American President's electoral calculations.

The Ironic Spirit of history saw to it that Koestler's arguments would in time be accepted not by pro-Zionist Labour but by Anthony Eden's Conservative administration, when the final bankruptcy of Whitehall's policy of 'appeasement' was confirmed by Nasser's hostility, and the British and French joined forces with Israel in the ill-judged, ill-timed, and (on the Anglo-French side) lamentably executed Suez operation.

# CHAPTER XV

# *1945–1946*

KOESTLER'S RELATIONSHIP WITH GEORGE ORWELL gradually ripened into something close to intimate friendship. 'Close to', because Orwell's distrust of that hedonistic strain he rightly discerned in Koestler combined with his own unrelenting masochism to create a protective palisade of reserve even more forbidding than Koestler's insecurity and touchiness. But the anglicised and puritanical Scot and the half-anglicised and neurotic Hungarian Jew understood each other very well, Orwell's critical insight into the strengths and weaknesses of Koestler's work being matched by the latter's insight into the psychology of his critical ally.

For Orwell 1945 had been a year of both tragedy and success. In March his wife, Eileen, had died, leaving him with their ten-month-old adopted son. In August, *Animal Farm* had been published by Secker & Warburg (having been turned down on political grounds by Gollancz, Cape and Faber).

During the autumn Koestler invited him to Bwlch Ocyn, and on 17th October Orwell replied:

> 'Do look me up if you're in town. It's ages since I saw you. I am nearly always at the above, as I don't go to an office now. I can't remember when it was I last saw you. You knew I lost my wife early this year, didn't you? My little boy is 17 months old and very well, and walking quite strongly. I have just started writing for the *Tribune* again, but I am not doing any editing. You must write for *Polemic*, the first number of which you saw, I dare say. I am doing an article on *The Yogi and the Commissar*, at least on one aspect of it, for *Commonwealth*, also going to lecture on it to some youth league or something. There's also a longish essay on you in the book of reprints I am publishing about the beginning of next year. This was written for *Focus* but hasn't appeared there yet. The essay was written before *The Yogi and the Commissar* appeared.
>
> 'Don't fail to ring up if you are here. I'd love to come to Wales some time but I can very rarely get out of London.'

In his essay on *The Yogi and the Commissar*, Orwell pointed out that many reviewers had assumed that Koestler had come down heavily on the side of the Yogi; he corrected this misapprehension in a shrewd passage:

> 'Actually, if one assumes the Yogi and the Commissar to be at opposite points of the scale, Koestler is somewhat nearer to the Commissar's end. He believes in action, in violence where necessary, in government, and consequently in the shifts and compromises that are necessary from government . . . No one is less likely than Koestler to claim that we can put everything right by watching our navels in California. Nor is he claiming, as religious thinkers do, that a "change of heart" must come *before* any genuine political improvement.'

*   *

After Christmas, when their usual horde of visitors, Orwell among them on this occasion, departed, Koestler got down to work on the revision of *Thieves in the Night*, trying to accomplish as much as possible before Mamaine left for Switzerland, where she had been advised to spend a month or two for the sake of her health. She and Koestler were happy, but sometimes she found their occasional evenings of conversation with highbrow friends a little wearing:

> 'Life has been very pleasant lately, except for an awful spell of highbrow social life with Polanyi, the Crawshay-Williams, and Bertrand Russell. The latter came to lunch with us and we invited him just when we had nothing. Misi Polanyi dined with us and we with him, and he and K. had endless conversations about the weight of various articles, the mismic field, the impossibility or not of formulating any extrapolation which would predict the movements of electrons or God knows what. What with this, a dash of semantics, more physics, and emergent vitalism with Russell etc, a discussion with the latter on politics came as a great relief to my weary brain. But my inferiority complex about my ignorance and general dumb-ness is worse than ever.'

Over the Christmas holiday Koestler and Orwell had discussed the possibility of forming a new League for the Rights of Man that would be proof against Communist infiltration. On his return to London, Orwell drafted a memorandum and sent it off to Bwlch Ocyn for Koestler's comments, adding that he was shortly going to discuss the project with Barbara Ward and Tom Hopkinson.

The draft noted that even in Western countries there had grown up a certain contempt for democratic traditions, and a habit of sanctioning tyrannous practices which only a few years before would have raised an outcry:

> 'In this country the majority of people are largely uninterested in and even unaware of their own democratic rights, while a considerable section of the intelligentsia has set itself almost consciously to break down the desire for liberty and to hold totalitarian methods up to admiration. Over considerable portions of the earth not merely democracy but the last traces of legality in our sense of the word have simply vanished. But instead of this fact awakening the traditional indignation of the western peoples, the normal reaction is either

> apathy or a certain admiration for what it has become usual to call political realism. As a result, we see liberal newspapers making themselves the advocates of totalitarian diplomacy and bodies such as the League for the Rights of Man and the National Council for Civil Liberties, which were started to defend the individual against the arbitrary action of the state, ending up by pursuing objects which are almost the exact opposite of those for which they were originally founded. Since Nazism collapsed, the one great power with a totalitarian structure is the U.S.S.R., and it is chiefly in the form of uncritical admiration for the U.S.S.R. that totalitarian ideas establish themselves in the western countries. Meanwhile, the gradual decay of democratic sentiment, of human decency and the desire for liberty goes on . . .'

Koestler, who approved the draft, showed it to Bertrand Russell and tried to enlist his support; but Russell, while agreeing with the aim of the proposed movement, considered the approach futile.

> 'He thinks that it is too late,' Koestler wrote to Orwell, 'to start any sort of ethical movement, that war will be on us soon, and that more directly political action is necessary to prevent it.'

Russell suggested that a conference should be called to be addressed by a dozen experts, himself among them but he was unwilling, being tired and overworked, to take on any burden of organisation.

> 'I believe,' Koestler wrote to Orwell, 'his idea for a conference can be fitted into our plan and that people at such a conference would be in favour of initiating an organisation on our lines . . . I hear that Silone is coming to London and I hope you will be able to have a talk with him and see his reactions. What was the outcome of your lunch with Tom and Barbara Ward?'

Koestler's letter crossed one from Orwell:

> 'I saw Barbara Ward and Tom Hopkinson today and told them about our project. They were both a little timid, chiefly I think because they realise that an organisation of this type would in practice be anti-Russian, or would be compelled to become anti-Russian, and they are going through an acute phase of anti-Americanism. However they are anxious to hear more and certainly are not hostile to the idea.'

Bertrand Russell then sent Koestler 'a very depressing text for discussion' (as his secretary described it), arguing that the only way in which great wars could be prevented would be the establishment of

> 'an international government with a monopoly of serious armed force . . . one that really governs, not an amiable facade like the League of Nations, or a pretentious sham like the United Nations.'

It was a politically unreal and in parts almost hysterical document – but it was something, after all, to have the support of a world-famous philosopher and Grand Old Man who had reached the age which in England transforms eccentricities and inconsistencies into sanctity; and the paper contained at least one sentence that Koestler was able to extract for propaganda purposes:

'The difficulty is to persuade the human race to acquiesce in its own survival.'

He and Orwell went ahead with their plan to convene a small conference of like-minded intellectuals to be held over Easter in Merioneth.

* *

In the Anglo-Saxon world Koestler had made himself even more unpopular among Stalin-cultists with an article, 'A Way To Fight Suspicion', published simultaneously in London and New York. Since this has never been collected, and because it is no less valid in the age of pseudo-détente following the Helsinki Conference (which it anticipated) than it was at the beginning of the Cold War, I make no apology for reproducing it:

'In 1938 we were appeasing the German mania of grandeur; to-day we are appeasing the Russian mania of persecution. Yet as long as this pathological condition lasts, all hope for genuine world co-operation is illusory.

'During the war, pressure was brought upon our Press and Radio not to utter any criticism which might upset our Soviet ally's delicate temper. Books critical of the Stalin regime were withdrawn from publishers' lists; and mention of the fact that it was a dictatorship, any reference to Russia being communistic, or having ceased to be communistic, wanting international revolution, or abandoning international revolution, had to be carefully avoided. The Press, led by Lord Beaverbrook, built up the myth of jovial "Uncle Joe" whose pipe outrivalled in popularity even Churchill's cigar and Roosevelt's cigarette holder.

'But as it passed through the filter of the Soviet censorship and through the controlled channels of the Tass Agency, the gentle cooing of the Western voices became transformed into the barking of mad imperialist dogs. The Battle of Britain and of the Seas, the campaigns in North Africa and Italy, were played down by the filter until they were hardly audible, while the clamour for the "second" front gave the Russian people the impression that there was only one, and that they were fighting alone.

'The majority of Soviet citizens have never heard of Dunkirk, of Bataan, of Alamein; what they heard were reports from Cairo that the British were negotiating a separate peace, that the Americans were dropping arms to the Fascist Warsaw maquis, and that we were sitting back in our armchairs watching the Russian people bleed to death. Nothing that the Western powers did or did not do, nothing that they said or did not say, could influence Russian suspicions – for they are an artificial growth, a hothouse plant unaffected by the real temperature outside the glass walls.

'There were two reasons why the common man in the USSR had to be vaccinated with the serum of distrust against foreign influences. The first was external, the second internal.

'The external reason was, in the early days, real enough to warrant caution in dealings with the capitalistic world. The Western powers had supported the armies of the counter-revolution during the Civil War of 1917 – 21; they persecuted Communists; they waited hopefully for the collapse of the Soviet regime and tried in various ways to speed it up. . . . All this gave the infant revolution a kind of traumatic shock. To live it down would in any case have taken considerable time. For internal reasons, which I shall discuss presently, the Soviet leaders were interested not in living down, but in perpetuating the trauma. They kept the memory of the "Capitalist intervention", the slogans of an "Anti-Soviet Crusade", and of the "Cordon Sanitaire" ever-present in the people's mind; they systematically developed it into an obsession.

'Now let us compare this development with the evolution of public opinion in the West. The Western countries had, of course, as sound reasons to be suspicious of Russia as the other way round. Up to the middle 'Thirties the avowed aim of the Communist International was the violent overthrow of their regimes. The wave of strikes and abortive revolutions which swept over the world in the wake of the Russian revolution provided the equivalent traumatic shock for the countries of the West.

'However, by the middle 'Thirties the average common man with average common sense had lived down that trauma. He was able to do that because a free press, free discussion, uncensored books, had gradually enabled him to see things in their proper perspective. . . .

'Thus the original shock was gradually lived down in the West, while it was artificially fanned and preserved by the centralised propaganda apparatus of the Soviets. Why? We now come to the internal causes for his attitude . . .

'The Five-Year Plans, instead of lifting, had to lower the living standard of the people. To the leaders this was a logical and unavoidable consequence of their long-term policy. But it would have been too much to expect the illiterate masses to understand the paradox that the workers and peasants in a socialist country were worse off in food, clothing and housing than the workers and peasants under the capitalist yoke. The opportunity of making comparisons would have meant a constant provocation and would have overtaxed the ordinary man's powers of thinking in abstractions. Russia had embarked on an unprecedented adventure, leaving the fleshpots of Egypt behind, and it was only logical that the fleshpots should be kept out of the people's sight while they were led through the desert towards the distant goal.

'Thus the iron curtain was lowered round Russia. No Soviet citizen, except on special mission, was allowed to leave the frontiers of his country, or to make friends with foreign journalists and engineers in Russia. Non-fraternisation was the motto of Russian contacts with the outside world during the lifetime of a whole generation. The State monopoly in information, the campaigns and stunt-trials against "foreign saboteurs", gave the Russian people a grotesquely distorted picture of conditions in the West; in this hothouse climate of propaganda, the seeds of suspicion sprouted into a tropical plant.

'So much for the genesis of suspicion. What can we do to break it down?

'Mere gestures of goodwill are futile. If tomorrow the complete blueprints of our atom plants were handed unconditionally on a silver plate to M. Vishinsky, *Pravda* would inform the Russian people that "the irresistible pressure of the Communist Party and of the toiling masses had forced the imperialist American Government to capitulate to their demands"; and things would go on exactly as before.

'In short, palliatives would not help. The Soviet Government has achieved, for the first time in history, a complete State monopoly not only over the production and distribution of goods, but also over the production and distribution of ideas, opinion and emotions. World peace can only become a reality if suspicion is abolished. Suspicion can only be abolished if the Soviet Government can be induced to turn the masterswitch of their propaganda factory.

'How can the Soviet leaders be induced to do this? The first necessity is that our own statesmen should realise that no political treaties and trade agreements can guarantee peace as long as this world remains psychologically divided into two worlds, with persecution-mania on one side, growing alarm on the other. The conclusion and aim of this article is a plea to politicians for the inclusion of the psychological factor in their power-calculations, as a factor equal in importance to Air Forces and Navies. *More precisely: that psychological armaments should be made an object of international negotiations and of political bargaining just as armaments in the air and on the sea; and made subject to as clearly defined clauses as, for instance, naval armaments are.*

'By "psychological armaments" I do not mean criticism directed by one country against another. This democratic right is as vital on the international as on the national scale, and such criticism cannot do much harm if the country criticised has full facilities of stating its case before the public of the country from which the criticism comes. But it becomes poisonous if the country attacked is deprived of this right of defence – as the Western countries are at the present in the Soviet Press, which prints M. Vishinsky's speeches but suppresses Bevin's replies, prints statements by E.L.A.S. [the Communist-led "People's Liberation Party" active in Greece in the 1940's] but suppresses those by the Greek Government, and so on.

'The measure of "psychological armament" is the extent to which a government obstructs the free exchange of information and ideas with the outside world. A country which builds a Maginot line of censorship from behind which it fires its propaganda salvoes is committing psychological aggression. Since the end of the war, the USSR has raised certain claims in South-Eastern Europe, the Middle and Far East and North Africa. The Western Powers, who have no territorial counterclaims to make, should table instead a demand for psychological disarmaments, including:

(a) free access for foreign newspapers, periodicals, books and films to the USSR;

(b) such modifications of the Russian censorship (if censorship there must be) as to permit the free circulation of information about the outside world throughout Soviet territory;

(c) free access for accredited journalists, parliamentary committees, etc., to Russian-occupied territory;
(d) the abolishing of restrictions on travel for foreigners in Soviet territory, and for Soviet citizens abroad;
(e) active cooperation with the Western Powers in the organisation of "vacations abroad" schemes, on a mutual exchange basis, for students, teachers, writers, workers and professional men.

'I do not know whether this is a counter-revolutionary, Trotskyite, or Fascist suggestion; but I do know that if it were carried out, if the doors of the hothouse were opened to the sun and fresh air of the world's natural climate, the next war (which will mean the end of us all, including the people of Russia) could be avoided. Psychological disarmament would almost automatically lead to material disarmament, and the enormous Soviet potential thus diverted into productive channels would lead to a rapid rise of the standard of living of the Russian people, and make isolation the more superfluous. The present vicious circle would be reversed.

'Nobody in his senses will expect the Soviet leaders to agree to this easily. Hence the suggestion that psychological disarmament should be made a bargaining object in all future negotiations, and given high priority on the political agenda. The demand for the free circulation of ideas across frontiers, for restoring the arrested bloodstream of the world, should be raised at every meeting of the Big Three, the Security Council, the Committees and Assembly of the United Nations; it should be made the pre-condition of concessions in the geographical, economical and scientific field. To get it accepted, the use of all levers of pressure, political and economical, would for once be morally justified.'

* *

Among their many other preoccupations, Koestler and Orwell continued to spend much time and energy in refining – with the help of Michael Foot, Jennie Lee, Bertrand Russell and others – their ideas for the new League for the Rights of Man. It was to be called either the League for the Defence and Development of Democracy or (Koestler's preference) the League for the Freedom and Dignity of Man. It was to be an international organisation to which existing bodies with compatible aims in various countries could be affiliated; and somehow or other it was to be rendered proof against such Communist infiltration as had worm-eaten the old League and was now rotting organisations like the National Council for Civil Liberties. This involved them in much correspondence and many meetings. Papers had to be prepared for the Easter conference in Merioneth which Bertrand Russell had suggested.

The indefatigable Duchess of Atholl, chairman of the British League for European Freedom, was sympathetic, and appropriated for her own organisations some of Koestler's and Orwell's ideas. Contacts were made with other anti-totalitarian movements, among them the American Union for Democratic Action and the International Rescue and Relief Committee (both of which saw in the British Labour Government a countervailing force against the Stalinist agents already threatening Western Europe).

A great deal of effort went into enlisting the support of liberal and left-wing intellectuals (such as Victor Gollancz) who had grown out of their pre-war gullibility about the nature of the Soviet Union – not always an easy task, for many of them, especially in the scientific and academic communities, were already resentful and fearful of American power and inching towards the defeatist 'better red than dead' position.

Among the many people Koestler had conferred with during the week or so he spent in London with Mamaine, after her return from Switzerland, were Rodney Phillips, proprietor of the magazine *Polemic* (for which Mamaine's twin sister, Celia, worked), and its editor, Humphrey Slater, painter, author, and ex-Communist. Phillips, Koestler understood, was ready to meet the cost of the Easter conference, and Slater was to make room temporarily in *Polemic*'s office for the League's secretary. For all the muddle and frustration that inevitably attend the formation of a new movement, things were beginning to move; and Koestler and Orwell had hopes that, after the conference, the finance needed to launch the League would be forthcoming from Edward Hulton and Victor Gollancz.

On 13th March Koestler and Mamaine returned from London to Wales.

> 'My God,' Mamaine recorded, 'it was cold when we arrived back here; I put on twice as many clothes as I ever wore in Switzerland, and yet I shivered for two days. Now thank God it is warmer. But I must say coming back here from Switzerland makes one realise what an austere life K. and I lead.
>
> 'I work hard on secretarial work for K. etc., now I am going to start helping him with his book.'

They began to prepare their spare rooms for the six to ten people whom they were to put up during the conference (eight hotel rooms were booked for the others). Koestler reported progress to Rodney Phillips, reminding him to find, if he could, the constitution of the old League for the Rights of Man, and to bring a draft constitution for the new League.

> 'Special emphasis,' he wrote, 'should be laid on a formula which would permit whole bodies like the Pen Club or the Freedom Defence League to affiliate without giving up their independence.'

Orwell, who had been ill ('something vaguely called gastritis, which means something wrong with your belly – I suppose if it was your head they would call it cephalitis and so on'), sent Koestler further details about the International Rescue and Relief Committee and the Union for Democratic Action:

> 'While I was still in bed an American called Henson came to see me and tell me about an American organisation along partly the same lines as our own, with which we obviously should be affiliated . . . The purpose of the International Rescue and Relief Committee, as I understand it, is to assist victims of totalitarianism, particularly in such matters as giving relief to destitute people, helping political refugees to get out of totalitarian territory,

etc. He impressed upon me that this is very definitely a non-Stalinist organisation, that they know all about the Stalinists' ways and are keeping them out of it, and that the organisation is anti-Stalinist to the extent that the people they assist are largely Trotskyites etc. They appear to have considerable funds at their disposal and are therefore able to help people in a solid way. The organisation to which the other enclosed draft refers, the UDA, is, I gather, in some sort of loose tie-up with the IRRC, but I understood him to say that Stalinists or fellow-travellers have not been completely excluded from that one.

'He asked me about our organisation, and I told him how far it had got and who was associated with it . . .

'I won't write more now because I still feel a bit sick.'

In his reply, Koestler, having assured Orwell that he would be welcome at any time if he wanted to convalesce, added that he had booked rooms for the Easter conference and was corresponding with Phillips about the technical arrangements. But Phillips and Slater (stimulated by A. J. Ayer) had been having second thoughts. Slater wrote to Koestler saying he continued to approve of the project, but that he felt it would be damaging to his magazine *Polemic*'s independence if it were to be too closely associated with the League. The withdrawal of Slater and Phillips was the beginning of the collapse of the conference. Others dropped out, and eventually Koestler was forced to cancel the hotel bookings.

* *

However, he had at last begun his first draft of *Insight and Outlook* – 'an inquiry into the common foundations of science, art, and social ethics' – that seminal work of synthesis from which Koestler's later scientific writings were to flow. The research involved was prodigious, the writing slow and difficult. Mamaine typed and re-typed draft after draft from Koestler's indifferent handwriting. Sometimes she was stuck at the typewriter for hours on end while he dictated, very slowly, the thoughts and insights he was painfully reducing to clarity. The house had to be run (with little help), meals cooked, numerous guests looked after. In addition to the work on *Insight and Outlook*, there was a large and rapidly growing correspondence to be dealt with. All letters had to be answered.

*Darkness at Noon* had become a phenomenal success in France, and this helped enhance Koestler's reputation at home. To those whose eyes were being opened to the true nature of Eastern totalitarianism he had become a kind of guru. His play *Twilight Bar* had to be revised and translated for production in Paris later in the year by Jean Vilar, director of the Compagnie de Théâtre – 'problablement la plus sortable', Koestler's friend André Malraux assured him, 'qu'il y ait en France à l'heure actuelle; à peu près l'équivalent de ce qu'était le Vieux-Colombier, au temps de Jacques Copeau.'

The area around Bwlch Ocyn had become a kind of intellectual kibbutz, and the Koestlers' evenings of relaxation (sometimes ending unfortunately when Koestler had a few drinks too many) were full of political, philosophical, scientific and psychological disputation.

In addition to all this, Koestler was more than ever obsessed with the task of arousing the West to the dangers threatening it. Somehow or other the new League had to be brought to birth, and a petition drafted ('to be signed by at least a hundred leading personalities') urging the government to take the lead in trying to persuade the Soviet Union to dismantle the rigid wall of censorship which kept its subjects in total ignorance of what was happening outside. On this there were many discussions with Bertrand Russell, many drafts to be typed and re-typed. As secretary, mistress, cook, hostess, and keeper of the peace, Mamaine was more than earning Koestler's dedication of *Insight and Outlook* to her 'for her remarkable patience with this book and its author'.

Russell now had some second thoughts, and, after a mildly acrimonious exchange of letters, proposed that Koestler draft the position in his own way and seek general support from other intellectuals. Koestler accepted Russell's decision graciously enough but made it clear that he had no intention of abandoning the struggle to get group action under way.

Towards the end of the month Koestler turned again to another of his preoccupations – Palestine. Drawing on his voluminous notes, he prepared a detailed brief urging the immediate partition of Palestine. He spent a few days with Michael Foot and Richard Crossman at the latter's country house polishing it into a memorandum, *Labour's Pledged Word*, for circulation to all members of the Parliamentary Labour Party. It was later published by Victor Gollancz as a pamphlet, *A Palestine Munich*, under the names of Foot and Crossman alone. (Koestler having already expressed himself so forcefully and controversially on the subject, it was thought prudent not to have his name attached to the pamphlet, although he was in fact the principal author of it.)

Back at Bwlch Ocyn in June, Koestler was up to his eyes in work again. The domestic situation was somewhat complicated by a visit from Daphne and her husband. Mamaine's patience for once was strained:

> 'Daphne is very nice indeed and I get along fine with her. But K. has been in an absolutely fiendish temper, so life has hardly been worth living. I told him before they came that if I felt like doing some housework while they were here he was not to interfere, as I refused to have Daphne spend her entire holiday cooking and washing up; so I begged K. just for once to desist from his nagging on this subject. But has he done so? Not for one minute. I would go on strike if it were not that poor Daphne and Henri must eat. For once I really do feel that K is being rather selfish; it doesn't really interfere with his life in the least if I occasionally work in the kitchen, which is miles from his room, but he talks as if he couldn't have a quiet moment for clattering pots and pans. I am quite determined not to have K dictate how I shall spend every minute of the day, nor at what time of day I do which work, and I told him that if he wanted *me* to make an effort not to (for instance) make a fuss when he drives the car when he is drunk (which the other evening led to his ditching it), then *he* must make an effort not to nag me about every single meal we ever have.

'However, this is only because he is doing hellish work, correcting endless French versions of his books and play, and therefore can't get on with his book; by Thursday he should have finished and then his temper will improve – I hope; otherwise I shall soon retire to a mental home.'

Koestler's temper was improved by a letter from Victor Gollancz announcing that he was 'tremendously in favour' of the new League and that 'this should be pressed on with immediately'.

In his reply, Koestler dropped a broad hint that Gollancz should take over the organisation, to which Gollancz's reaction was chilly.

Koestler's campaign petered out; but his energies were to find an outlet four years later when Stalin's intensifying of the Cold War led to the creation of the Congress for Cultural Freedom.

# CHAPTER XVI

# *1946–1947*

FRANCE WAS BECKONING KOESTLER and he was anxious to answer the summons. The hedonist in him, bored and irritated by the austerities of the 'land of virtue and gloom', anticipated with relish the fleshpots of the 'land of bread and wine'. The country which had treated him so harshly in 1939 and 1940 was now ready, he thought, to welcome him back as a celebrity. While zealous members of the powerful Communist Party regarded him, correctly, as an implacable enemy, many of the less fanatical fellow-travellers in the intellectual community were anxious to meet him.

In Britain his name was known to thousands; in France, to hundreds of thousands. Britain, for all its enormous economic and industrial difficulties, was disciplined and stable: therefore boring. France, undisciplined and corrupt, was still in turmoil: therefore stimulating. The sales of *Le Zéro et l'infini* (the French title of *Darkness at Noon*) were still soaring. *Arrival and Departure* was also a best-seller, although not on the same spectacular scale. The translation of the collection of essays and articles, *The Yogi and the Commissar*, had been corrected by Koestler and would soon be published.

His own inclinations apart, there was a pressing reason for his presence in Paris. The production of his play *Twilight Bar* had been fixed for October. This was the revised version of the fantasy – or 'escapade in four acts' – *Bar du Soleil*, which he had dashed off in Moscow in 1933 and which his friend Andor Németh had translated into Hungarian. Németh, having sold the play to Budapest's leading modern repertory theatre, the Belvárosi Szinház, was then to appear on the bill as co-author. That production, it will be recalled, had fallen through, because the director, having read Németh's text, decided that it was both too weak and too leftist.

During his flight from France in 1940 Koestler lost the typescript and in London three years later he re-wrote it from memory.

> 'The idea was that a pair of scouts from an alien planet land on earth in search of colonising space for their overcrowded world. They explain that only happy planets have a cosmic right to exist, and give mankind a last chance to

organise its happiness within three days – or else it will gently be put out of its miseries, and the earth turned to better use. Faced with this ultimatum, the government resigns, the opposition washes its hands of the issue, and the dilettantes take over at last, appointing a crazy poet called Glowworm to be Dictator of Happiness. And lo, it works, to everybody's surprise: money is abolished, all taboos are smashed, all curtains raised. Alas, at the end of the three days it transpires that the scouts are impostors; and as there is no longer any need to be happy, the old order is restored and everybody goes back to his former miseries.'

Koestler himself, or so he said years later, had no inflated ideas of the play's merits. He had rewritten it mainly for his own amusement, describing it as a diversion, and one completely without literary pretensions. Slight though it was, it was now about to be staged by one of France's most brilliant young directors because its author's name happened to be very much *en vogue*, and Koestler took it seriously enough to wish to have a hand it its direction during the final stages of rehearsal.

As for Németh, Koestler had heard nothing of him since 1939.

Early in September Koestler went up to London to see about his French visa. When Mamaine had seen him off on the train and returned to the farmhouse, she pondered a letter from Celia urging her to take a firmer and less submissive line in her relationship with him, to give more weight to her own interests. Mamaine gave this a good deal of thought, not for the first time, but on reflection rejected the advice. There would be no point in always thinking about one's own interests, she wrote to Celia, if one really wanted to live with someone as difficult as Koestler. The centre of his life was his work. His work meant everything to him. When his work was going well he was happy, whatever else was going wrong. He wanted her not merely to be a collaborator in his work but to make it the centre of her life as it was of his. If she bothered about anything other than this, she explained, getting lunch for example, he naturally became impatient since this meant she was not concentrating enough on his work. The physical side of married life could not last forever. There had to be something else to share, without which there would no longer be much reason why they should stay together, and that something was his work. Mamaine accepted this because, she told her sister, she considered Koestler a thoroughly worthwhile person.

And that, for the moment, was that.

Koestler returned from London without his visa and in a furious temper. The French consular authorities in London had been distinctly unhelpful. In spite of his fame, or notoriety, as a vehement anti-Communist, he was still listed by the bureaucracy as an 'undesirable' because his police dossier in Paris showed that he had been interned at Le Vernet. From Wales he continued the negotiations by letter and telegram in a mood of mounting anxiety and frustration. He was plagued, as Mamaine noted, by 'an archetypal neurosis, having been through so much *Scum of the Earth* stuff'. To relieve the tension he had frequent recourse to the bottle. Mamaine took it in her stride.

One evening they dined with Richard Hughes and his wife at their house on the estuary opposite Portmeirion. Koestler got drunk and on their way back along the sand he kept falling down. He walked off a wall on to non-existent steps; then he disappeared briefly into a hole on the beach; and shortly afterwards he found himself up to his waist in the sea. 'It was all great fun!' Mamaine noted. But desperation returned with the hangover in the morning. *Twilight Bar* was already in rehearsal at the Théâtre de Clichy. The director, Jean Vilar, was having trouble with the actors. The author's presence was urgently required.

At the end of the month, when he had almost given up hope of setting foot in France again, the bureaucracy suddenly decided that he was not, after all, a dangerous agent of the Kremlin. The visa came through and he and Mamaine went up to London. On Tuesday 1st October Koestler left for Paris on the Golden Arrow. Mamaine stayed behind in London, intending to join him in a week's time.

* *

There was much bitterness in the intellectual atmosphere of Paris. The intoxicating camaraderie among people of widely divergent views that followed the expulsion of the Germans had long since evaporated, thanks largely to the determined excesses of the Communist Party. All over France its members, relatively few of whom had played any real part in the resistance movement, had emerged to settle old scores against 'collaborators', many of whom were guilty of nothing more heinous than being 'bourgeois'. The far more serious crimes of Communist collaboration with the occupying forces during the period of the German-Soviet pact had been conveniently forgotten, of course, although the French Communist Party's treasonable support of the Stalin-Hitler alliance had been a major factor in the demoralisation of the French nation and its armed forces.

But the social round in Paris was undeniably stimulating. Koestler the celebrity plunged into it with gusto. The hedonist in him had free reign and the entries in his diary for the first few days are no more than a stuttering and scarcely coherent catalogue of names, meals, drinks, parties, quarrels, hangovers. Three days after his arrival in Paris he sent Mamaine a telegram saying:

'Am very happy amidst terrific bally hoo
much love tenderness from big lion Koestler.'

The play was not going well. The opening was postponed at Koestler's insistence while two new actors were found and the production re-shaped. Then, to Koestler's amazement, his old collaborator, Németh, suddenly appeared in Paris, having read of the forthcoming première. Németh was destitute and Koestler paid him a substantial sum to give him time to write a book and find his feet again. The next day Németh and his wife left for Budapest and certain persecution by the Communist authorities. The whole incident depressed Koestler further.*

* In July 1953, Koestler noted in *The Invisible Writing*, Németh was a destitute old man, huddled in a café, unknown and forgotten. In November of the same year he died, aged sixty-two.

To assuage the feelings of guilt conjured up by the nightmarish encounters with his old friend, and to keep the dark devils of depression at bay, he crammed his days and nights with frenetic activity. He had a sudden, short and intense affair with the blonde Russian wife of a journalist, and a number of more or less desolating encounters (sometimes in the company of Camus) with whores. There were horrendous drinking bouts, ferocious quarrels, fearful hangovers. All the time, at the back of his mind, was the fear that *Twilight Bar* was going to be a disastrous failure. He knew also (enough of the English temper of pragmatism having rubbed off on him) that he would never again feel entirely at home in the intellectual life of Paris, among people like Sartre and Simone de Beauvoir, so wilfully abstract and, at bottom, frivolous, nihilistic and irresponsible.

Also, he had come greatly to rely upon Mamaine. In Paris he attempted to shake off this reliance, but without success. The more frenziedly he fled from himself, disgusting himself in the process, the more sharply he realised just how much he had changed in recent years – and how much England in general and Mamaine in particular were involved in that change. Through the frantic shorthand of his diary entries run the twin threads of exasperation and desperation:

> 'At 12 Németh. Lunch at Voltaire Bistro; get tight . . . driven . . . to Vilar where don't open mouth during dinner . . . Ghastly lunch with S . . . Drinks at Barley's [Barley Alison's] with Camus, radio chap, etc. . . . terrible discussion and home. . . . Long explosive intensive dinner with Malraux, crowned by Madeleine playing "La Revolution"; "Alors on va devenir fasciste?" "ça s'appellera par un autre nom." Langage du destin. . . . Bistro Calvados – ghastly postscript . . . depression rock-bottom. . . . Lunch Mediterranée Malraux, Madeleine, Alixe [de Rothschild]. . . . was happier before war at 5 francs 50. . . . Dinner Sylvain [Mangeot], Tanja – ghastly Russian restaurant – abruptly home; nuit blanche de St Petersburg. . . . Camus. Lunch alone. . . . *Time* – idiotic interviewer. . . . Not a minute's rest from 12 a.m. till 3 a.m. . . . Dinner at Sperber's. . . . despair. . . . champagne in loge. . . . showdown with copain. . . . Row with Camus. . . . Lunch with Hans [Hans Schultz, who had been Muenzenberg's secretary in the Western department of the Comintern] until 9 p.m. . . . Great scene . . . with Simone and Sartre; sleep there . . . Dinner Munjo [Manès Sperber]; make nasty scene; somehow patched up. . . . Success gold turning to merde, or rather to dust . . . Incident with Roumanian social democrat who shouts "Merde, plus facile d'être homme de lettres que d'être homme!" . . . Dinner with Camus . . . home with depression . . . Two nightmare hours with Simone . . . later go off alone to Carrefour Boulevard Edgar Quinet, entertain two tarts one fat the other thin to chicken and assiette anglaise, two pimps quarrel beat each other blood washed up with monkey speed, try to bc vicious don't succeed, home depressed . . .'

These and other such hastily scribbled notes express all too clearly the misery of frustration and inadequacy that was the melancholy reality behind the aggressively touchy, not to say arrogant, façade he presented to the world.

In the middle of October Mamaine announced that she was about to leave for Paris. Koestler, thankfully, sent a telegram:

'Mood brightening wire exact hour and place arrival love.'

She arrived in Paris at three o'clock in the afternoon of Thursday 17th August, and was drawn into the whirlpool without delay. Koestler was in a bad state by this time – physically exhausted by the various excesses of the past fortnight, tired of the personal publicity in which he had at first revelled, depressed by the poisonous political atmosphere and the near certainty that *Twilight Bar* was going to be a flop.* However, Mamaine's arrival was celebrated with a pub-crawl in Montmartre, ending up at Chez Victor where they diverted themselves by watching, through an alcoholic haze, an aging *grue* guzzling snails.

While Mamaine remained in Paris for a holiday, Koestler returned to London for a week to deal with the great pile of correspondence that had accumulated at his agent's office, before returning to Bwlch Ocyn and the resumption of work on *Insight and Outlook*. His Zionist novel *Thieves in the Night*, which had already sold 50,000 copies in the United States, came out in London during the week. Not altogether surprisingly – since it portrayed with marked sympathy the violent militancy of the Irgun Zvai Leumi against the mandatory authority of the United Kingdom as well as the Palestinian Arabs – the English reviewers received it with much less enthusiasm than their American counterparts.

The reviews from the United States were 'enthusiastic to good', he reported to Mamaine, but in England 'tepid to lousy'. Fortunately in the same ratio as being a *vedette* in Paris had depressed him, 'this mud-slinging rather exhilarates me, so the two cancel out'.

Besides, some 20,000 copies had been sold a day or two after publication, thus dispelling any doubts he may have had about the book's commercial prospects. That apart, London seemed unexciting after Paris. He saw 'all the usual people' but found the social round rather dull. The only engagement which merited the description 'pleasant' in a letter to Mamaine was a dinner-party given by Hamish Hamilton at which Bruno Walter was a fellow-guest.

He advised Mamaine not to stop in London on her way home – 'it's too depressing'.

His spirits lifted almost as soon as he got out of the train at Llangollen. And driving from there to Bwlch Ocyn by way of Penmachno in clear sunshine, he noted with pleasure how the heather, gorse, bracken were all now in their full autumn colours. Looking at the countryside with fresh eyes, he was surprised to see, as if for the first time, how beautiful it all was.

And then, as he neared Bwlch Ocyn, he felt such a happy pang of homecoming that his month-old depression lifted at once. At the farmhouse he found to his relief that all was well. Thanks to the domestic help, he found everything dry and tidy. The dogs were in good shape, the car was still in working order, the hens were doing well (he found about forty eggs) – '. . . so everything looks bright'.

* It was.

Among the letters waiting for him at Bwlch Ocyn was one from Malraux which gave him a good deal of pleasure. Koestler in his depressed mood had given his friends the impression that it would be a long time before France saw him again. But Malraux, pointing out that the imminent appearance there of *The Yogi and the Commissar* would stir up a great deal of controversy, predicted that it would not be long before he returned. Not so, Koestler replied: he would be far too busy with *Insight and Outlook*. But Malraux maintained (correctly, as it turned out)

'. . . with the authority of a fortune-teller, that you will be back in Paris within six months. As for me, alas, I do not count on going to England before the end of the year: exactly for the same reasons as you. I am very anxious to finish my book on Art, but I believe that God wills otherwise.'

Like Koestler, Malraux – more intimately involved in political action which estranged him from those who once regarded him as a comrade – was coming under increasingly savage attack from the Communists and their fellow-travellers.

'Is it necessary to tell you that . . . I have been called, with a certain regularity, a snake-in-the-grass . . . ?'

* *

Koestler had succeeded George Orwell as the London correspondent of the progressive New York magazine, *Partisan Review*. On his return from Paris he found a reminder that copy for the first of his 'London Letters' was urgently required. Conveniently enough, *Partisan Review* at the time was preparing a symposium on 'the future of Socialism'. Koestler therefore chose to enlighten its progressive readers about the condition of England under the Socialists whose electoral victory in 1945 had inspired one of the successful candidates (not a proletarian extremist but a middle-class lawyer) to cry exultantly: 'We are the masters at the moment!'

Although Koestler was ostensibly a supporter of non-totalitarian Socialism and in his opinion the English people in 1945 had recorded the sanest vote in their history, he was no more enthusiastic than the average Conservative about the way in which the new masters had set about the transformation of society.

If the excitement of Paris had combined with the political and moral corruption of France in general to drive him almost to the brink of a nervous breakdown, the dullness of London (about which he had complained to Mamaine) and the grey and decent dreariness of the country as a whole seemed to strike him as even more oppressive. Compared with France, where the black (or free) market had virtually supplanted the controlled one, and where anything could be purchased by those who had the money to pay, Britain was a model of virtue and probity; the morale of the 'masses', who grumbled certainly but nevertheless accepted the austerities of rationing and the irritations of controls, was firm and sound. Koestler found this profoundly depressing because in his opinion it was based on 'resignation, puritanism, and lack of *joie de vivre*' rather than foresight and voluntary sacrifice. And according to his cursory analysis, the reason for this dull acceptance of the 'bad life' was the depressing fact that 'the people in the suburbs and working class districts' had never known the 'good life'.

It was all (of course) basically the fault of 'decades of capitalist management', but the new leaders of the Socialist Era were also at fault in failing to inspire the 'masses'. Why hadn't the Government retained the services of Mr Billy Butlin, the inventor of holiday camps for the lower classes, or studied the admirable aspects of the Nazis' 'Strength through Joy' organisation? Why did Socialist Britain make motion pictures about Henry VIII and Lady Hamilton instead of such equally thrilling subjects as Robert Owen, Karl Marx, Keir Hardie, and the Tolpuddle Martyrs? Why was the *Daily Herald* (the Labour movement's mouthpiece) the dullest and drabbest newspaper in the country? At the beginning of the year, after decades of socialist agitation, the coal industry had been nationalised. But instead of the kind of pageantry a Hitler or a Mussolini would have staged to impress such an historic event on the national memory, there was only Major Attlee mumbling that the National Coal Board was 'going to bat on a sticky wicket, but I think it will score a great many sixes'.

The varicose veins of the endlessly queuing British housewife, he considered, would be more appropriate than the lion and the unicorn as emblems of contemporary Britain.

And so it went on, a drizzle of glum complaints as dull as the alleged dullness of the country. Koestler blamed the 'typical Labour politician' for making the 'typical mistake of equating gradualism with dullness', but failed himself to offer any suggestions (other than hiring Billy Butlin, making movies about the Tolpuddle Martyrs, and studying 'Strength through Joy') as to how the gloomily virtuous and puritanical scene could be brightened, and reformist Socialism made rather more inspiring. It seems most likely that the muddled and patronising content of the article and its bilious tone were merely reflections of his own frustrated hedonism and unacknowledged disillusionment with Socialism of whatever variety. Towards the conclusion he asked:

> '*Who is going to protect the workers in the Workers' State?* The question is less paradoxical than it sounds, and I have found no answer to it in Labour's blueprints of the future . . .'

* *

Apart from two brief excursions to Paris and an occasional flying visit to London, the rest of 1947 was spent at Bwlch Ocyn, wrestling with the draft of *Insight and Outlook*. The spartan existence imposed great strain on them both, sometimes alleviated, occasionally exacerbated by their visitors and by other demands on Koestler's attention which – although he had determined to concentrate all his energy on the book – he felt unable to refuse.

The worsening situation in Palestine was a constant source of concern. After the ship *Exodus* with its four thousand Jewish refugees had been turned away and sent back to Germany, Koestler wrote a long article for the *New Statesman*, entitled 'Letter to a Parent of a British Soldier in Palestine'.

> 'Every morning when you open your paper,' it began, 'you feel sick with fear that your boy might have been kidnapped or blown to pieces by Jewish terrorists. I am a person who sympathises with the terrorists, and though I disapprove of their recent methods, I might have become one of them – by force of circumstances . . .
>
> 'I am not speaking lightly of terror; during several years I have lived in the same anxiety, for persons near to me, which you feel for your son. The persons were my mother and her family; the danger which threatened them, as Jews in German-controlled territory, was death by poison gas or quicklime. My mother was the only one who escaped.
>
> 'Obviously you will answer that these regrettable deeds were committed by the Nazis and not by the British; that one of the reasons your boy fought this war was precisely to save those unfortunates. . . .'

But the Jews of Palestine, Koestler asserted, had no reasons for gratitude to Britain. Between the wars they had to provide their own protection because permanent military garrisoning of the dispersed settlements would have required a standing army out of all proportion with Britain's peace-time establishment. That was how the Haganah had come into existence.

> 'Up to 1939 it was tolerated and even encouraged by the authorities as a kind of semi-legal Jewish Home Guard. It rendered useful services to the British during the Arab riots and during the war; in fact, the Zionists turned out to be your only reliable allies in the Middle East, as Lloyd George and Balfour had foreseen.'

Having described the turning away in the spring of 1939 of three ships packed with Jewish refugees from Europe, he went on:

> 'Try to put yourself into the place of a Jew of your own age on the jetty of Haifa, shouting and waving to a relative – your son for instance – on the deck of one of those ships . . . a few years later you hear that he has been gassed in Oswiecim. If, instead of Smith, your name were Schmulewitz, it might have happened to you. Something on the same lines happened, among others, to a man whom I met in Palestine two years ago; he told me that his mother and three brothers had been killed "by German sadism and the British White Paper". His name is Friedman-Yellin, and he is head of the so-called Stern Gang.'

But now, he wrote, the patience of the Jews was exhausted, and as a result they had shown themselves capable of fighting as ruthlessly and savagely as any other people driven to despair.

> 'Political terrorism has not been invented by them, as the penny press tries to make people in this country believe; it is as old as injustice and oppression which are its cause . . .'

With bitter invective he listed the pledges made and broken by successive British Governments, culminating in Foreign Secretary Ernest Bevin's rejection of the Anglo-American Commission's recommendations in 1946. He had pledged himself to carry out their suggestions if they were unanimous; they *were* unanimous and they were not carried out. Now the matter had been passed to the United Nations, but Bevin reserved the right to accept or reject the verdict. The methods employed by Bevin to sabotage any constructive solution – to get out of the Labour Party's, the Labour Government's and indeed his own personal commitments – resembled more than anything, Koestler wrote, 'the subterfuges of a Jewish pettifogger'; and it was not surprising that the Palestine Jews suspected Bevin's latest move as merely another subterfuge to gain time and continue a policy based on principles which his colleagues in the Cabinet had branded, before they came to power, as morally and politically indefensible.

What could be done to stop the vicious circle of terror and retaliation? The first was to present the United Nations with constructive proposals for a just partition of Palestine, to be enforced if need be with international help; and the second was to raise the monthly immigration quota from 1,500 to 5,000 during the period of transition. It was, he declared, as simple as that.

> 'If you refuse, you will have to take the consequences, which may be more serious than you think.'

Koestler's polemic – astutely mixing, as one of his critics observed, 'the old political Zionist arguments with sentiment and emotion' – had the desired effect, and a great many readers of the *New Statesman* reached for pen and paper, some to order large quantities of offprints, others to support or refute the arguments. Kingsley Martin, the editor, published two mildly critical letters by Philip Mumford and Oliver Coburn which drew some heavy sarcasm from Koestler:

> 'I don't want to be harsh, nor court a libel action, by suggesting that Mr Mumford and Mr Coburn possess all the requisite qualifications for joining the Foreign Office Middle East Department.'

But there were many more correspondents who wrote directly to Koestler to say that their eyes had been opened by his version of Britain's policy in Palestine.

* *

Domestic life at Bwlch Ocyn had its ups and downs – rather more of the latter, perhaps; but Mamaine continued to weather the storms and make the most of sunny spells:

'March 18th, 1947: Tuesday

> 'Teddy Kollek turned up on Saturday for the night, and he and K got frightfully drunk, in fact I have never in my life seen K so drunk – I had gone to bed, and they just went on drinking Armagnac which Teddy had brought, and not noticing it because they were discussing Palestine, and when K came up to bed he was green in the face . . . Consequently he had a bad attack of anxiety neurosis next day; and of course it was a perfectly dreadful day, for

there was a 90-mile an hour gale and as we were frying our dinner on the sitting-room fire there was a loud crash, and half the big 17th century west window fell in on us, followed by lashings of rain.'

'Friday 20.3.47

'K has been in a bad temper for about a week, but is improving now. Anyway I take his outbursts much more philosophically than I used to. He got furious the other evening because he wanted to go to Oakeley and I didn't seem enthusiastic . . . it seems to me a waste of time to sit at a bar drinking and talking to boring people; but I quite see that K, who sits all day in his tiny room, occasionally feels like an outing, especially as he likes drinking, so off we went in the end, and had quite a pleasant evening.'

* *

They had a week's break in Paris. This was shortly after General de Gaulle's formation of the *Rassemblement du Peuple Français* – the inauguration, that is, of Gaullism. She enjoyed their holiday a good deal more than Koestler, who was depressed by the undercurrents of violence, the instability of the 'third force' coalition government, the growing threat of the Communists who had recently been expelled from it, and the sinister *sancta simplicitas* of Sartre and Simone de Beauvoir.

* *

Back at Bwlch Ocyn, Mamaine tackled her chores cheerfully:

'22.5.47

'. . . poor K is in despair, his brain is simply not functioning at all, and he still can't get back into his work; it is now over 2 months since he was working properly, so you can imagine the state he's in, and how impossible he is. But it will come all right soon no doubt . . .'

'May 26th 1947
Monday

'Arthur is still depressed and morose. I always have doubts about his ultimate sanity when he is like this. It seems to have lasted a long time this time; nearly three months I should think. However we now work all morning and from about 4 till 7.30 on the book, which is making slow but steady progress . . .'

'May 27th 1947

'Misi [Prof. Michael] Polanyi has just been to dinner with us. Today he was more interesting and slightly less woolly than usual, mainly because K made him talk about two subjects in which he is interested, namely, extra-sensory perception (or allied topics) and religion. For believe it or not, K has now only one interest: mysticism. He also believes in miracles. He had lunch in London with 2 psychologists, one a specialist in miracles, and the latter said "there is no logical reason *not* to believe in them"; this is also K's view. There is a man called Dr Rhein [sic] in Duke University, U.S., who has demonstrated that if one is throwing dice and *wants* say a six to turn up, it will do so by a significant proportion above the laws of probability; thus proving the influence of mind over matter. K is feverishly reading books about Yoga. Of course he is greatly disappointed in them all . . .

'Apart from this, K has not yet recovered his normal interest in life, and yesterday complained that he hadn't been able to experience real rapture about anything for over a year. E.g. to really enjoy listening to music. He complained that he has no intake to feed his output, so to speak. He certainly seems to get little or no stimulation from people. He bewailed the collapse of all his heroes, and said how awful it was to have nobody to look up to.'

* *

They returned to Paris where they saw a good deal of Camus and his wife Francine, now their closest friends there. Koestler, although he had once told an American journalist that if he were a Frenchman he would rather live in exile in Patagonia than in France under de Gaulle, was now, under Malraux' influence, coming round to the view that sooner or later the General would be called on to save France from civil disorder and a Communist takeover.

Camus, although he disliked the *Rassemblement du Peuple Français*, was moving, against his will, in the same direction. His relations with Sartre and Beauvoir and the *Temps Modernes* group were growing more strained than ever, although a certain friendship still subsisted. What he and Koestler had in common politically was a clearheaded and unequivocal hostility to Communism. He was impatient with the sophistries of Sartre and Beauvoir and was apt to lose his temper with them when they suggested that the extreme left offered less of a totalitarian threat than de Gaulle and his supporters.

* *

Koestler's anxiety to open the eyes of confused or complacent idealists to the reality of the threat from the East was sharpened by the reestablishment in October of the Comintern (dissolved by Stalin during the war as a sop to Western public opinion) under the title of the Communist Information Bureau, or Cominform.

Throughout the year, of course, Moscow had been working through the national Communist parties and their agents in the trades unions to subvert the legitimate governments of Western Europe, all of which were wrestling with economic crisis: but the resurrection of the Comintern in its new guise was a clear sign that the Kremlin was going to intensify its efforts – the 'Truman Doctrine' notwithstanding – to extend the Soviet Union's *imperium* still farther westward before the Marshall Plan could be implemented effectively and the democracies helped to their feet. In Greece the Moscow-backed Communist bid had been checked by the United States, which had taken the task over from the United Kingdom earlier in the year. Now it was France and Italy that were most at risk from their fifth-columns. (Britain might also seem on the brink of economic collapse, but it was fortunate in having a stable and staunchly anti-totalitarian administration, and powerful trades union leaders ready to counter the tactics of the minuscule but menacing Communist Party's industrial *apparat.*)

In Paris, Koestler had discussed with Malraux and others the possibility of forming an organisation of intellectuals to counter the propaganda of the Communists and fellow-travellers and demonstrate to self-indulgent 'liberals' the folly of their fashionable anti-Americanism. From Wales he wrote to Malraux asking for news of developments. Malraux, who shared de Gaulle's distaste for the United States but welcomed Koestler's reasoned support for Gaullism as the least of the evils facing France, wrote:

> 'I haven't replied to you earlier because I had to have another word with the friends we met together; I saw them again yesterday evening and found them somewhat surprised by the events that had taken place between our two cocktail parties.
>
> 'For the rest, what you say is perfectly correct and we entirely agree that the General must make a speech next month at Le Creusot, after he has addressed, together with your humble servant, the intellectuals at the Palais de Chaillot on the 27th. On the other hand, you'll see the text of Wednesday's press conference (the General's, that is).
>
> 'Our friend Sartre continues to play the fool; but if Gaullism should win millions of votes they'll be laughing on the other side of their face in St Germain des Prés where we're regarded as pretty feeble in point of morale. By God, I hope it does! Monsieur Nadeau in *Combat* has been explaining that I'm on the way out, that I no longer write, in short that I'm become a complete imbecile. And he drops this brick, naturally, on the very day that my *Psychology of Art* is published.'

* *

The final struggle with the text of *Insight and Outlook* combined with the generally depressing news of the world to make Koestler more than usually touchy and irritable.

> 'I am afraid,' Mamaine recorded, 'he is starting a period of very bad temper, but perhaps it will blow over. I just try to shut my eyes and ears and withdraw into my shell. I feel pretty dismal . . .'

Koestler and Mamaine had more or less made their plans for 1948 by this time. First they would spend a month or two travelling in France and Italy; then Koestler would undertake a six-weeks' lecture tour in the United States, to enlighten the 'liberals' there; on his return they would be able, they hoped, to visit Palestine; and thereafter, possibly, they would take a house in France.

## CHAPTER XVII

# *1947–1948*

IN THE LAST DAYS of 1947 Koestler completed *Insight and Outlook* and handed a copy to Cyril Connolly to read. He also delivered it to his publishers. He and Mamaine then set out on their travels. First, there was a round of parties in London. And then there were more parties in Paris to be enjoyed before they began their journey south to Italy. Mamaine had been rather apprehensive, not without reason, about Koestler's behaviour in Paris; but on this occasion all went well. There were no outrageous scenes, no furious rows, no embarrassing approaches to other women. Harmony was restored.

Koestler had agreed to write a series of articles for the *Observer* about the social and political scene in France and Italy. It is very clear from the almost invariably disgruntled and dejected jottings in his notebook (even when allowance is made for the fact that he very seldom, in such hastily scribbled notes, recorded whatever had reassured or pleased him) that he considered both countries far advanced in decay. He noted his political and sociological impressions, if not exactly on the Tragic, certainly on the profoundly Pessimistic Plane.

But at the same time he was also, like Mamaine, though reluctantly and at times, it would seem, almost against his will, in holiday mood (now that the *magnum opus* with which he hoped to widen and deepen his reputation was with the publishers). Although France and Italy struck him as so close to chaos and revolution that he entitled the draft of his first article 'Journey through Fear', it is evident from Mamaine's diary that their travels were traced for the most part across the Trivial Plane.

On their way south to the Riviera and Italy they stopped at Pouilly-sur-Loire. It was here, on Sunday 3rd September 1939, that Koestler and Daphne Hardy, on their way back from the Midi to Paris, had stopped for lunch

> '. . . in a sunny garden overlooking the river and surrounded by vineyards. It was our last halt before Paris; in a few hours we would reach our journey's end. We had smoked ham and a bottle of Pouilly *fumé*, the wine that makes you happy and wise like no other wine in the world. We looked at the river,

and emptied the bottle to the last drop; and then, shortly before Melun we met two cars with people shouting excitedly to us; and when we stopped a mile further to fill up, the woman at the petrol pump told us that Britain had declared war on Germany.'

Mamaine found it beautiful and Koestler observed that the Pouilly *fumé* was still delicious, and still cheap.

Another stop was Villefranche because of a puncture. While the repair was being made they had drinks in a café with three talkative *cocos* (Communists) who were already tipsy. After a few more glasses of harsh Rhône wine, one of the *cocos* pulled out his Communist Party membership card, brandished it, declared to the world at the top of his voice:

'Thorez disgusts me! Moscow disgusts me! But the others disgust me even more. So what am I to do? Long live Thorez!'

This, in Koestler's view, was the voice not of revolutionary enthusiasm but of lassitude and despair, of a dying civilisation's nostalgia for the apocalypse.

Finally, after a week, they arrived in Florence.

At this point Koestler's own diary became even gloomier than usual. The puritan strain in his nature was obviously at odds with the hedonist.

If anything could re-convert one to Communism, he wrote, it was Florence. Immortal in stone but putrid in flesh, he detected an unholy alliance of Fra Angelico and traveller's cheques.

And so he brooded on the agony of civilisation . . .

The impossibility of having a holiday . . . Decline of the West . . . Survival of the dullest?

The depth of his pessimism is evident in the rough draft of an article based on those glum and jaundiced jottings:

'. . . as the kaleidoscopic jumble of impressions begins to settle down, one basic pattern emerges and dominates all others: the conviction that what is happening now and here is not a post-war symptom and passing crisis, but the irrevocable end of a form of civilisation which, for better or worse, was our own.

'Of all the towns Florence was perhaps the most perfect symbol of this civilisation. Once the torchbearers of the European Renaissance, its people have gradually come to base their living on the unholy union of Fra Angelicos and traveller's cheques. Both the parasitic nature of liberal capitalism, and the civilised form of existence which it nevertheless produced, were embodied in the social structure of the town. Today, the monumental state apartments of the Signoria are occupied by the Communist mayor.

'If he represented a truly revolutionary movement which had a new form of life to offer, the Communist successor of Lorenzo the Magnificent would make one feel jubilant. But not even red-scarfed coco friend of Villefranche has any such illusions. The peasants of Tuscany and the dockers of Le Havre and the white-collar workers in their nameless misery in the nameless little town vote Communist, as opposite social numbers vote for de Gaulle or the

Vatican: propelled not by attraction but by revulsion. And so, slowly, fatally, with momentary standstills and shortlived interludes of optimism, the process of polarisation continues.

'A century ago Marx predicted this polarisation into two opposing camps, but he did not foresee the infernal twist which history would give to his prophecy. How hopelessly naïve the Marxian schema of exploiters versus exploited appears today, when the strike-tactics of the revolutionary bank-clerks in Milan are determined by secret cabinet-decisions of an imperialist power three thousand miles away, and the political orientation "left" has become synonymous with the geographical direction "east". In the Marxian schema a dying order is replaced by an utopian new world; today an old form of civilisation is dying, but the only revolutionary alternative is Balkanisation of the West and the Police state.

'And the Third Force, which in the opinion of well-meaning Labourites is destined to fill in the vacuum? The fact is that this vacuum does not exist as a social reality: exasperated masses never yearn for a middle way; it only exists in the wishdreams of a minority of the progressive intelligentsia, including my own. If one means by "third force" the unstable parliamentary coalition on which the present French government rests, then one may as well trust one's fortune to a tight-rope walker over the Niagara falls; if one means by it the quarrelling splinter-groups of the dissident French Trades Unions or of Saragat's independent Socialists, then your hopes are only a little less quixotic than if you expected world salvation from the ILP. Through the optimistic telescope of the British Labour man-in-the-moon all this may not look serious, or at least provide an excuse for evading decisions which go against Western Europe three years after V-Day; if his progress from words to action moves at the same speed, there will be no field for action left east of Calais.'

* *

On his way home (Mamaine had left him to stay with friends in Trieste) Koestler spent a week in Paris. It did nothing to raise his spirits. In Italy he had been alarmed by the strength of the Communist Party. This in turn aggravated his already considerable exasperation with the fellow-travellers in France, and even more with the 'Third Force' Socialists. His conversations with friends circled almost exclusively around the burning questions: Would Western Europe fall without a fight to the Soviet Union's proxies? Or would there be general war? And would there be civil war? And would the United States use the atomic bomb? Was the apocalypse at hand? He found his friend 'Chip' Bohlen, the American Ambassador, in a panic. Even he was saying privately: 'Let's drop the bloody things on Baku and have finished with it.'

Nor did London do anything to dispel his gloom:

'Thursday 4th: Dinner and night club . . . couldn't stick it, home . . . Friday 5th: Escaped from Gargoyle [the outré drinking-club] . . . Saturday 6th: Lunch Cyril [Connolly], then with Frank P. [Lord Pakenham] to Dick [Richard Crossman]. Frank thinks 25% chance war this year . . .'

On Saturday he wrote to Mamaine to tell her that his US visa had not yet arrived and that the projected American journey was still uncertain. But he didn't

> 'care a hoot, for if the American lecture tour falls through, I shall still get the visa sooner or later and *Life* will always be willing to pay the expenses of the trip . . .
>
> 'Hope you are having a lovely time. Am as usual when back from the Continent at rock-bottom of depression. Both Macmillans [the publishers] and Strauss [Eric Strauss, psychiatrist] absolutely enthusiastic about the book [the typescript of *Insight and Outlook*]. That's the only bright spot in this world of utter gloom. Things here have gone so much worse since we left that pity made me recover some of my lost affection for this country.
>
> 'Am feeling lonely without you – sign of age.'

He tackled an official at the American embassy about the missing visa. No luck. 'Almost given up hope,' he noted again in his diary. It seemed almost certain that the *Queen Mary* would sail on Friday without him.

But the American Ambassador in Paris had been pulling some extra strings. On Thursday evening – on his return from a 'frightful French film about a blind sculptor played by frightful Jean-Louis Barrault' – there was a telephone call to say that his visa had come through.

On Friday morning there was a 'frightful rush and embarkation *Queen Mary*'.

He was sadly disappointed in the great ship:

> 'Instead of luxury, Lyons corner house; instead of glamour stars, ship apparently packed with Board of Trade officials cum families.'

So he spent most of the following day in his cabin, oppressed by the 'lost-dog feeling' he usually suffered from when he was on his own.

However, he emerged at last from his cabin and found himself (according to his diary) the centre of attraction of a distinguished, if oddly mixed, group of passengers: Alfred and Blanche Knopf, the New York publishers; George Lane; Adolph Zukor, the Hollywood movie producer; John Foster Dulles of the US State Department; General Sir Frederick E. Morgan, formerly General Eisenhower's chief-of-staff; Eric A. Johnston, administrator of the US Stabilization Agency; and other Very Important People.

The conversation, he noted, ranged far and wide – from the possibility of enforcing the postponement of the Italian elections to Sir Stafford Cripps' willingness to ban the import of American films to the United Kingdom even if this should mean the bankrupting of distributors and exhibitors.

Both Knopf and Zukor urged him (he noted) to go to Hollywood and write really good screenplays for the movie industry. He was needed there. All Hollywood movies, they said, stank. Zukor said that his own movies stank. The whole industry stank. And the primary cause was the lack of such talent as Koestler's. To refuse, Knopf and Zukor asserted forcefully, was selfish. It was his duty to join Huxley, Isherwood and the like in Hollywood.

When he informed them that, having other matters on his mind, he had no difficulty in resisting the temptation, he was aware of 'a great feeling of virtue'. But it was not quite enough to offset the malaise that still affected him:

> 'Headache and depression,' he jotted down on Monday the 15th. 'Off the waggon tomorrow – it's time, too. On the other hand don't want to become enslaved again to alcoholic schizophrenia. . . . Saint, artist, chronicler, hedonist? Forty-three, and still in search of one's leitmotif.'

Not only that, but also

> 'Still no feminine solace.'

* *

Mamaine in the meantime was enjoying herself enormously in Trieste:

> 'For instance, on Wednesday we all went to Venice – the Joyces, the Sulzbergers [Cyrus Sulzberger of the *New York Times* and his wife, Marina], Gastone, and I – in two cars, stopping on the way in a field for a picnic . . . Gastone . . . is an Italian diplomat, aged about 43, and he is quite wonderfully sweet and nice and amusing and intelligent and everything else: I simply adore him, and so does everybody . . .'

* *

During the morning of Thursday 10th March Koestler disembarked from that seaborne 'Lyons Corner House' the *Queen Mary*, and entered for the first time what he was to describe again and again in his diaries and correspondence as the 'delectable nightmare' of the United States of America.

# CHAPTER XVIII

# *1948*

WHEN KOESTLER ESCAPED FROM Marseille to Lisbon in 1940 he could have found refuge in the United States under the auspices of the International Rescue and Relief Committee, which had already come to the aid of many of his old friends, also former Communists. But, like the hero of his novel *Arrival and Departure*, he had chosen instead to throw in his lot with the embattled British.

Although his former faith in Communism had been replaced by uncompromising detestation, he was still a 'Socialist' of sorts and already had many friends and supporters, some of them extremely influential, in the Labour Party. He would feel more at home among them, he believed, than in the great transatlantic (and then still neutral) citadel of capitalism.

But now, eight years later, he was sadly disillusioned by the post-war Labour Government's failure (as he saw it) to capture 'the goodwill of the electorate, the benevolent neutrality of the Little Man, and the sympathy and hopes of the European Left'. He was deeply depressed by the greyness and austerity of life in Britain; by the lack of emotional appeal in the Government's gradualist and bureaucratic approach to the 'Socialist transformation of society' (something he still hankered after, with one part of his mind at least); and by its inability or reluctance to assume the leadership of Western Europe and bring about its unity. He was increasingly alarmed by the apparent vulnerability of the European democracies to the threats, internal as well as external, from the totalitarian East, and he was also profoundly angered by the anti-Zionist attitude of the Foreign Secretary, Ernest Bevin.

By the spring of 1948 he was desperately impatient. Truman's America, unlike Warren Harding's three decades before, was at last resisting the temptation to retreat into isolationism. The brief euphoria of victory and goodwill towards Uncle Joe had at last been dispelled by the manifest and implacable hostility of the Soviet Union. America, now openly assuming the leadership of the non-Communist world (and the chief hope of the Zionists) and demonstrating its readiness to defend the integrity of Western Europe, had become more attractive to him.

In 1940 he had declined the offer of an American visa because, among other reasons, he knew that

'. . . to run away from Europe now would mean to condemn myself to lifelong self-reproach, frustration and sterility.'

But now a growing sense of despair about Europe in general and England in particular was drawing him towards the power and confident dynamism of the United States.

Not that he wanted, as he had often told Mamaine, 'to run away from Europe' altogether. Perhaps the ideal solution to his personal problems would be to spend half the year in America and half in France? In both countries his books had been enormously successful, and in both he was far more of a 'public figure' than in England.

Mamaine was doubtful. Would he find the hectic atmosphere of the United States congenial? Anti-Communism there seemed to be verging on the hysterical, and Socialism itself had become a dirty word. Would the unrestrained commercialism of the New World be any more agreeable than the infuriating muddle of the 'land of virtue and gloom'?

The opportunity to find out for himself had come with a second invitation from the International Rescue and Relief Committee – this time, now that *Darkness at Noon* had made him a celebrity – to undertake an extensive fund-raising lecture-tour on behalf of the Committee (and in the process to warn America's 'confused liberals' about the deadly realities of Communism, the nature of which many of them still tended to confuse with their own benignly naïve idealism).

He had readily agreed to do so, declining to accept any fees. *Life* magazine had offered him exceptionally generous payment for an article. This would cover his expenses.

* *

Met at the Cunard Pier on the Hudson by Sheba Strunsky of the IRRC and James Putnam, his editor at Macmillans, his American publishers, Koestler was whisked off to the Ambassador Hotel where he endured his first American luncheon – 'rich and tasteless' was his verdict on it. This was followed immediately by his first American press conference. He took the trouble to record in his diary the reaction of one typically 'confused-liberal' reporter to his remark that the frightened people of Western Europe looked upon the Americans as their only hope of salvation.

'"Do you really believe that we can help Europe with our dirty hands?"'

When Koestler asked him to explain what he meant by 'dirty hands', the reporter explained,

'"Well, I mean our policy in Greece, and in Palestine, and backing up Franco, and the way we treat Negroes and Jews. We are dirty all over, and when we pose as defenders of democracy it is sheer hypocrisy."'

Having disposed briskly of this 'soul-searching fallacy' – high on the list of the many 'liberal' misconceptions he had come to dispel – and brought the press conference to a close, Koestler spent the next hour or two dictating to the secretary who had been engaged for him. She turned out to be virginal, long-nosed, innocent, addicted to psychoanalysis, and a lodger in a women's hostel.

She would not do, he decided.

His good humour, to judge from the jottings in his diary, was slightly restored by dinner with the editors of *Partisan Review*, William Phillips and Philip Rahv, and their wives, and then by a party attended among others by James Burnham (whose *Managerial Revolution* Koestler had much admired, and who was to become a close associate in the fight against Communist influence among Western intellectuals), Delmore Schwartz, Elizabeth Hardwick, Daniel Bell, and the philosopher Sidney Hook – 'who attacked Burnham and me and to whom I was rather rude'.

In the recollection of one distinguished academic who was present, the party was far from successful. Not for the first time, and certainly not for the last, Koestler's efforts to overcome the shyness and diffidence that had plagued him ever since adolescence conveyed an unfortunate impression of arrogance.

So ended, in the early hours of Friday morning, his first day in America.

The days that followed were no less hectic. His arrival in New York City had been well publicised by the IRRC and Macmillan, and he was besieged not only by reporters but by many old friends from Europe who had also succeeded in escaping both from the Nazis and their former Communist associates. In his hotel room the telephone rang incessantly. What he described as 'nightmare mail' kept pouring in.

He replaced the unsatisfactory long-nosed virginal addict of psychoanalysis with a 'charming, nice, calculating Kentucky girl' who was, he learned, in the middle of divorcing the musician she had married after a long affair (as he noted carefully) with a married man.

She would not do either, he decided on reflection.

Apart from the calculating Kentucky girl's long-nosed and virginal predecessor, virtually everyone he met or heard from seemed to be painfully entangled in marital or extra-marital problems of one sort or another.

There were a few exceptions, of course, to what seemed to be the general rule of emotional untidiness and disruption. A letter from Iowa, reminding him of his carefree Communist days in Berlin, came from one of the few who had settled down happily into capitalistic domesticity:

> 'Many times in the years since I first discovered *Darkness at Noon* – in fact with the reading, enjoyment and digestion of it and each subsequent book – I have had the impulse to write. – But I didn't know where to reach you – and then war intervened. However, I have always thought you would come to this country eventually.
>
> 'Koestler, do you remember our brief friendship in Berlin when we were young and not always gay? – I've often thought of those days . . .

'It is trite to say "how things have changed – the world, and you and I." But so they have – far more than either of us could possibly have foreseen seventeen years ago!

'If, on your lecture tour, you should come close to Des Moines I would like very much to see you and to have you become acquainted with the rest of my family – my husband [a colonel in the US Army] and my young daughters...'

This correspondent, unlike so many of his old associates from pre-war days, had obviously found a niche in the New World into which she could fit herself happily. Koestler was never to 'come close to Des Moines', but her letter moved this least sentimental of men and he kept it carefully among his papers – as a token, perhaps, of that ordinary and more or less contented domesticity to which he was, and always had been, a stranger.

There was a remorseless succession of receptions and meetings and luncheon, cocktail, dinner, evening, and all-night parties, during which he kept himself going with pep-pills. And he had, of course, not always in the best of moods, to make himself available to the reporters dispatched to extract copy from 'the most notable visitor to enliven the local publishing scene in many months' (as one of them described him). Most of them wanted to know his views on Palestine. They included a reporter from the *Herald Tribune*.

'"I have supported the case of partition," he [Koestler] replied, "and emotionally I feel strongly in favour of a Jewish State. Yet the Russian danger is so urgent that I wouldn't hesitate to sacrifice the Palestine issue to this larger issue if I were convinced that a Jewish Palestine would strengthen the Russian position.

'"In fact, however, I am convinced of just the opposite. I am convinced that a Jewish Palestine would be a bridgehead for the Western powers and that appeasing the Arabs will have the same results as all appeasement policies have had in the past."

'Mr Koestler, who used to be a journalist and still writes occasional newspaper articles, eyed the reporter's notes and said: "You know, I think it would help if my secretary took this down in shorthand and gave you a transcript. This is Miss Marcia Dorwin, she is the third secretary I have had in four days. The others were worn out."

'With Miss Dorwin transcribing, Mr Koestler said;

'"Now, you should ask me this question. I will ask it for you: If you think that the Jews of Palestine would strengthen the anti-Communist front, then how do you explain that Soviet Russia and the American Communists are backing the Zionist case? Is that question too long? How long should questions be from the standpoint of a city editor?"

'The reporter said the question was all right, and Mr Koestler continued:

'"The answer is that there is no contradiction. The classic pattern of Soviet politics is always to take a position which causes maximum embarrassment to the Western powers, quite regardless of the merits of the case they are backing. The Soviets are backing the Jewish case in Palestine simply because the Western powers have put themselves into the wrong on that issue."

'With the help of Mr Koestler, the reporter phrased the next question: "What do you think will be the effect of the present American policy in Europe as regards Russia?"

'"To put it into one word: a great sigh of relief," said Mr Koestler. "The developments of the last few weeks culminating in your President's speech and the declaration on Trieste will fill the frightened peoples of the West with a new hope. You saw the first reactions in Italy; you will soon see similar developments in France. People are learning to hope again."

'Asked about his working methods, Mr Koestler said: "When I write a book, first I write it in longhand, then I type it, then I give it to the professional typist.

'"And when I write a newspaper article, I make three drafts of it," he concluded, looking hard at the reporter.'

In spite of his general disapproval of reporters, especially those who were unable to record his words in shorthand, Koestler (no more inclined than his publishers, in fact, to underestimate the importance and value of publicity) gave them as much time as his other activities allowed. And the newspapers certainly gave him a 'good press', filling columns not only with his insistent warnings to their liberal readers that Communism, far from being merely a manifestation of the 'extreme left', was no less dangerous than National Socialism, and with his unstinted praise for American democracy as Europe's 'whole hope of survival and salvation', but also with his comments on many less weighty matters.

The *New Yorker*'s reporter (who saw him as 'a small, tense, restless man in his middle forties, with brown hair, blue eyes, and a pleasant German-Hungarian accent; a chain-smoker; and a frequent taker of aspirin') asked him the customary question – what did he think of New York?

'"It is certainly a cozy town," he said. "Nothing functions. The hot water is often cold. The elevator bells do not ring. Messages are not delivered. Everything is, in short, entirely un-American. I welcome this un-Americanism. I was prepared to develop an inferiority complex because of the great efficiency that I had heard existed in the United States."'

When the man from the *New York Times* put the same mandatory opening question to him, Koestler confided that

'New York doesn't seem strange to him. . . . The fact that . . . he has many friends here – friends he hadn't known, but whose books he had read or with whom he had been in correspondence, so that meeting them was like picking up in the middle of an interrupted conversation – makes him feel familiar and at home.'

He declined only to discuss specific European political problems other than the Communist menace. 'I am a philosopher and literary man, not a politician,' he told the correspondent of the *San Francisco Chronicle* (who obviously thought this an odd remark from the author of *Darkness at Noon* and *Thieves in the Night*).

France, he told the *Chicago Tribune*, was the scene of the most significant literary movement in Europe – a renaissance far more vital than anything to be found in Italy or England (or America for that matter, although he urged that Hemingway – 'still the greatest living writer' – should not be underestimated). Far and away the most important literary figures to emerge were Malraux, Sartre and Camus; and

> '"Of these the greatest is Camus. His new work, 'La Peste', is almost a masterpiece, a classic."'

He was questioned about existentialism.

> '"Existentialism? As a vital literary movement it never existed. It is a 'kaffee-haus' affair. But as a writer Sartre is volcanic."'

Harvey Breit of the *New York Times Book Review* asked him what he thought of the opinion held by many intellectuals that his *Darkness at Noon* along with Malraux's *Man's Fate* and Silone's *Bread and Wine* constituted the most powerful triad of the time.

> 'I don't think I'm up to them artistically and there is no false modesty in what I am saying. Politically it is something else again. I may be more penetrating on that level.'

In England, he added (modestly, or sardonically), critics considered it blasphemous to link him with Malraux and Silone.

Why was he so unpopular with the British? Mr Breit enquired:

> '"The British don't care for the political novel. The writing that goes on in England is very beautiful, with something of the fragrance of old vines [sic], but it is still the sensitive lady living out her life in a most sensitive way and all political realities are evaded . . . The American and French reactions to 'Darkness at Noon' were quite opposite to the British response." With reprints, it is estimated, Mr Koestler's novel has reached a sales total of half a million copies in the United States alone. In France 400,000 copies of the novel have already been sold.'

Most of the reporters gave generous advance publicity to *Insight and Outlook*, scheduled for publication in the autumn. According to the *New Yorker*, this was

> '"My life's work," he said, popping an aspirin into his mouth. "It is a treatise analysing the psychological roots of ethics, social behaviour, artistic creation, and scientific discovery. It is an original theory of mine that has been maturing for fifteen years. I call it bisociative psychology."'

He had finally, the *New York Times* reported, got down

> 'to work on it five years ago. He sat down, then, and resumed his studies in biology, neurology and psychology, in an effort to determine the scientific basis of ethical behaviour.'

But the book was not in fact, he told the *Herald Tribune*,

> '"as erudite as it sounds; it's written so that the average educated person can understand it with a little attention . . . it runs to 500 pages, took five years to write – and, I suspect, will sell about 500 copies."'

* *

There were so many demands on his time that he was finding it difficult to prepare the lecture – billed as *The Radicals' Dilemma* – which he was to deliver shortly at the Carnegie Hall to an audience (it was expected) of three thousand. Two days after his arrival he had

> 'started dictating lecture under shower of telephone calls, visitors . . .'

but his third secretary was able to get no more than a few tentative sentences down in shorthand before he had to break off for cocktails with James Burnham and his wife, followed by 'lunch with Bill Donovan in his wonderful Riverside apartment'.

This was an important engagement. General William J. Donovan had directed the Office of Strategic Services under Roosevelt during the war, and then, under Truman, had created the Central Intelligence Agency in 1947. In Paris, it will be recalled, Koestler and Malraux had discussed with certain others the need for an organisation that would effectively counter the influence that the Cominform's 'peace' propaganda was successfully exerting on parts of the intellectual community of the West – particularly on the more naïve or timid artists and academics (and especially, among the latter, the scientists and technologists) whose prestige in their own fields was well deserved but whose simplistically idealistic or utopian notions of the political process, untempered apparently by any understanding of the advantages conferred on the functionaries of totalitarianism by the fact that the 'public opinion' behind them was entirely State-manufactured and State-controlled, were undeniably dangerous. Koestler had recently met Ambassador Bonner in Italy and Ambassador Bohlen in Paris. He had talked with John Foster Dulles during the voyage to New York. It would have been strange if Bill Donovan had not been anxious to hear Koestler himself on the question of how the Cominform's propaganda onslaught should be countered.

Much was to flow from their conversation over and after luncheon that day, but all Koestler recorded in his diary was:

> 'Discussed need for psychological warfare. First-rate brain.'

His jottings about less momentous but increasingly numerous encounters were equally laconic.

* *

And so Friday 26th March arrived and his lecture was still unwritten. Perhaps it was as well he had not succeeded in dictating it, as he had attempted, a few days earlier, because he would probably have been obliged to recast it daily in the light of his arguments, frequently heated, with a succession of *Angst*-ridden 'liberals', both native Americans and newcomers.

For almost all of them the Communist God of materialistic and deterministic rationalism had failed. Many of them were lapsed (or lapsing) Trotskyists. But they still had a certain attachment to the vanished certainties and to those who still clung to them. They were much more alarmed, Koestler found, by the harshly inquisitorial methods of the Congressional Committee on un-American Activities and by the Hollywood purge of Communists and fellow-travellers in the motion-picture industry (which in those days was almost as influential as the television is now in shaping as well as reflecting the general attitudes of a public which knew very little about the realities of the world beyond their own small patch of the vast continent), than by the threat to Western Europe.

Koestler himself was opposed to those fanatical and ignorant anti-Communists who were attempting to whip up a mood of war hysteria throughout the United States. But knowing from bitter personal experience the inhuman realities of Socialist totalitarianism in action (about which there was an astonishing ignorance in America), he was even more concerned about the confusion into which so many members of the 'progressive' intelligentsia had fallen, and about the various fallacies with which they either tortured or comforted themselves (and which he had identified during the innumerable discussions he had had since arriving in the city).

He was no less aware than they of the imperfections and contradictions of American society as shaped by dynamic 'capitalism', and of the injustices committed in the name of anti-Communism, but for him they were wholly insignificant when compared with the atrocious repression that was commonplace in the Soviet Union and its satrapies. And so it was to the 'Babbits of the Left' – the new phrase he coined for the 'confused liberals' and 'muddled radicals' – that he decided to address his lecture.

After luncheon with James Burnham (perhaps the staunchest of his allies) and a siesta, he made his way alonc and on foot to the Carnegie Hall, pulling his thoughts together and listing the points he wished put across as forcefully as possible.

The hall was packed. To speak extemporaneously, and at length, on a difficult subject to an audience of three thousand, and not in one's native language, proved to be a difficult business, and it was not made any easier by a defective microphone. Koestler, who dislikes public speaking in any language and has always been acutely self-conscious about his heavy middle-European accent in English, was extremely nervous. Behind him on the platform were prominent exiles from Bulgaria, Estonia, Jugoslavia, Poland, Spain, Czechoslovakia, Lithuania, Latvia, Romania and Hungary, and, among the many distinguished Americans, General William J. Donovan.

On the spur of the moment Koestler decided that an informal approach would effectively disguise his nervousness, so, instead of standing behind the table and orating, he walked round to the front and seated himself on it, his legs swinging free. From that position he chatted colloquially, without bothering much about the length of his sentences or their syntactical coherence, as if he were addressing three rather than three thousand. There were some who thought this altogether too casual (Koestler had not yet realised that on such occasions Americans are sticklers for formality), but on the whole it succeeded. He got his points across, and the newspapers efficiently smoothed away the roughnesses and ragged edges of his speech.

His basic message was simple. The power-vacuum in Central and Western Europe created by the two world wars had inescapably linked the fate of the United States with that of the European continent. There would either be a *Pax Americana* or there would be no peace at all. No single nation in history had ever borne such a burden.

> 'It is the more unfair to you as yours is an adolescent civilisation, with adolescent enthusiasms and adolescent pimples. The task of the progressive intelligentsia of your country is to help the rest of the nation to face its enormous responsibilities. The time for sectarian quarrels in the cosy no-man's-land of abstract radicalism is past. It is time for the American radical to grow up.'

And so the 'Babbits of the Left' had to get 'seven deadly fallacies' out of their thinking.

The first was the confusion of 'Left' and 'East'. Whatever democratic radicals meant by 'Socialism', it did not exist in the Soviet Union, and the Cominform's policy was in no respect 'Socialist', whatever their understanding of the term.

Next came the 'soul-searching' fallacy, as exemplified by the reporter who had asked him how the Americans, with their dirty hands, could help Europe. A few years back, Koestler said, this would have run:

> 'We have no right to fight Hitler's plans of sending the Jews to the gas chambers so long as there are "Restricted" hotels in America [i.e., which do not accept Jews] and so long as Negroes do not have absolute equality here.'

Closely related was the fallacy of the false equation – the notion that there was nothing to choose between Soviet totalitarianism and American 'imperialism'.

> 'The American fellow-traveller has never lived under a totalitarian regime, so when he draws comparisons he mostly doesn't know what he is talking about . . . In American elections political machines may distort the people's will. In Russian elections 99½ per cent vote for the one official list – the remaining half of one per cent presumably being in bed with influenza.'

Next came the 'anti-anti fallacy':

> '"I am not a Communist. In fact, I dislike Communist politics, but I don't want to be identified with anti-Communist witch-hunting. Hence I am neither a Communist nor an anti-Communist, but an anti-anti Communist. If W. R. Hearst says that twice two is four, I shall automatically hold that twice two is five, or at least four and a half."'

The laughter which greeted this sally prompted him to remind his listeners that the roots of this particular fallacy were deep in all 'progressives', himself included, and he told them of the chagrin he had felt some years before when a 'doddering elder' came up to him in a London club, tapped his shoulder, and condescendingly remarked: 'Well, young man, I am glad that at last you have come round to see reason. I myself knew twenty-five years ago what Bolshevism means, and it's never too late to repent.'

> 'You can't help this sort of thing; you can't help people being right for the wrong reasons . . . Being against our will in one camp with the Hearst press or Senator McCarthy does not mean that we identify ourselves with their ideas and methods . . . If you are sure of yourself – politically and ideologically – you will no longer be frightened to say that twice two makes four, even if Colonel McCormick says the same.'

And then there was the sentimental fallacy. The Communists, after all, had been allies in the 'anti-Fascist struggle', and it was hard to tear up the roots of old loyalties. But

> '. . . our bedfellows of yesterday do not, of course, share this emotional squeamishness. Over the slightest disagreement they will denounce us as Fascists, spies, and traitors. These emotional ties are one-way ties and it is essential to bear in mind that they are entirely irrational . . .'

Related to the 'soul-searching' fallacy and that of 'the false equation', was the 'fallacy of the perfect cause'.

> 'History knows no perfect causes, no situation of white against black. Eastern totalitarianism is black; its victory would mean the end of our civilisation. American civilisation is not white but grey . . . The choice before us is merely that between a grey twilight and total darkness. But ask the refugees who manage to escape, at the risk of their lives, from behind the Iron Curtain into our grey democracy, whether this choice is worth fighting for. They know. You don't.'

The last, and according to Koestler the most dangerous, fallacy was the confusion between short-term and long-term aims:

> 'Your leftist Babbit may refuse to fight against the short-term emergency until he has finished the job of creating a perfect government in his country – in a hundred years or so. The opposite danger is to become so obsessed with the immediate emergency that all principles of the long-term struggle are thrown overboard. Ex-Communists and disappointed radicals are in a particular danger of toppling over to the other extreme . . . to defend our system against a deadly threat does not imply acceptance of everything in the system . . . and, vice versa, that our criticism of the shortcomings of this system does not free us of the shortcomings of defending it, despite its ambiguous greyness, against the total corruption of the humanitarian ideal.'

Towards the end of his speech Koestler was at pains to emphasise that he had been addressing himself to the Left as a man of the Left:

'I may have been harsh to the left Babbit; it was a brotherly harshness. To the Babbit of the Right I have nothing to say; we have no language in common.'

It may have been this which prompted the two bewildered policemen present as his bodyguard to ask him as he left the stage whether his lecture had been pro-Communist or anti-Communist.

* *

Offstage the past was waiting for him in the shape of a score or so of his former comrades – female, most of them. Five of these ladies accompanied him to the celebrity dinner which James Putnam had arranged at the 21 Club. He found the cacophony of talk about the old days exceedingly tiresome. The dinner-party, in consequence, dragged. But the evening might yet be enlivened by a visit to a certain night-club which featured an especially spectacular striptease. On the way, they called at a bar for a sustaining drink. Here a woman, half-seas over and swaying on her stool, recognised the celebrity and addressed him loudly thus:

'You are Koestler. The trouble is, my analyst doesn't like you.'

An accolade of sorts.

* *

Koestler left New York to repeat his message in Washington. He met plenty of opposition, particularly from old comrades.

He touched briefly on the question of the Hollywood purges of known or suspected Communists which had deprived many of their livelihood in the dream-factories which were undoubtedly most influential in shaping, directly or subliminally, the attitudes of the majority. His next lecture was to be given in Hollywood, where the actor Robert Montgomery was to be in the chair. He read a letter Montgomery had forwarded to him:

'"I am in receipt of your circular letter asking me to purchase tickets for a lecture by Arthur Koestler. You must have got hold of the wrong mailing list. Your speaker, Koestler, cannot claim my support in as much as he is to my mind one of the most dangerous reactionaries loose in the world today and a man who has not hesitated to slander the Jews as well as the International Brigade of the Spanish Republican Army in which I had the honour to serve in 1938."'

The author, Koestler told his audience, was well known to him. He was a courageous man and he had fought well in Spain. He obviously believed in the things he said. He believed that Koestler, a Jew, slandered the Jews; that he was a dangerous reactionary; that the International Rescue and Relief Committee (which had in earlier years rescued so many from Fascism and National Socialism) was a Fascist organisation. Why?

'He is not in the pay of Moscow. That is nonsense. He has been deprived of his job. He was a scenario writer in Hollywood. He was purged because of his convictions which were a continuation of the convictions for which he fought in 1938 in Spain, risking life and limb. He was slow in realising that the Soviet Union was not what he thought it was – that it was not for Socialism, for freedom, for a new conception of the human idea but for a new form of a Panslavic police state. He was slow in realising it, but that is all.'

Koestler had much more sympathy for the purged script writer than for the New York 'liberal' whose typically muddled objections to his mission he had quoted earlier:

'"I don't think the Kremlin is a perfect ruler for Europe but I am inclined to think that the people of Europe would be even worse off under the domination of Wall Street. Monsieur Thorez is not a perfect leader for France, but he is preferable to Monsieur de Gaulle. Maybe Signor Togliatti hasn't a 100 per cent clean record but Signor de Gasperi has a 100 per cent dirty record."'

The author of this, Koestler commented, was the type of man who equated the Hollywood purges with the Moscow purges. For him there was no choice between the Kremlin and Wall Street, no choice between the farcical proceedings in Hollywood (where, after all, no corpses had been left behind) and the Moscow purges which had resulted in the condemnation and execution of most of the Old Bolshevik leaders of the revolution. For this type of person, Koestler went on, the Kremlin's deportation of hundreds of thousands and the incarceration of 10 per cent of the Russian people – twenty million or so – in forced labour camps could be equated with conditions in the United States.

'That is the perfect fool – the Left Babbit . . . a very dangerous man, the more dangerous as he is usually well-meaning.'

* *

The four days Koestler spent in Washington were no less hectic than his stay in New York. In addition to the daily round of 'working breakfasts', tedious press conferences, luncheons, cocktail and dinner parties, there were many meetings during which he was closely questioned by politicians, State Department officials, presidential aides, intelligence officers, and trades union officials (who were, although it seems that he did not know it at the time, also agents of the Central Intelligence Agency).

For picking his brains as they did, a friend observed, they should have paid him a hefty fee. But Koestler, alarmed by their ignorance of the real complexities of the situation either in Europe or the Middle East, was content to enlighten them gratis, although he was often enough exasperated to the point of anger by the extraordinary naïvety he encountered. After lunch with a senior State Department (or possibly a CIA) official (concerned with 'security and counter-espionage and God knows what') he noted:

'Knows nothing about anything; burns with zeal to start witch hunt in administration. Told him can't X-ray what goes on in a little child's head, but that very few of the vague fellow-travellers would actually turn traitor against their country.'

* *

He spent a fortnight in California, lecturing, party-going, seeing the sights from San Luis Obispo in the south to San Francisco in the north.

On the whole he found the atmosphere provincial and disagreeable:

'Local politics the one and only obsession into which all jealousies and venom projected.'

His spirits were restored briefly by the beauty of San Francisco, but after two days of press conferences, receptions, parties and arguments, he concluded that he had had enough.

'For first time hardly able to sleep . . . nearest to nervous breakdown.'

On Tuesday 13th April he telephoned Sheba Strunsky and told her to cancel the rest of the trip. After a lengthy discussion he relented to the extent of agreeing to keep his engagements in Chicago and Boston. However, 'sick to death of it all,' he scribbled in his diary: 'decide on the spur of the moment to go [between two lectures] to Salt Lake City.'

He found the Mormon capital a 'most unremarkable town' where the 'historic' monuments were no more than sixty or seventy years old. There were other disadvantages, he discovered. The city was dry except for beer. Liquor could only be bought with a special licence between 1 and 8 p.m. He hired an obliging young cab-driver who tried to find him a bottle of whiskey, but without success. They then drove out to a country club, which turned out to have no hard liquor. Returning to an 'uncanny' café in the city, the cab-driver warned him:

'"These two blocks to be avoided – you know, tough women, tough men; before you have time to roll your sleeves up you are knocked out cold." In café everybody carries bottle in brown paper . . . horrible mixture of puritanism and vice . . .'

On that dour and censorious note he went to bed and had his first good sleep for days. He was greatly relieved to be on his own, free of bear-leaders, lion-hunters, contentious drunks, inefficient organisers, and the incessant grinding of the publicity-machine. The prospect of a whole day without press conferences, interviews, receptions, cocktail parties, and tedious conversation filled him with pleasure. But not even here could he get away from reporters.

He took a cab out to the Great Salt Lake and decided to have a dip. As it happened, he was the first bather of the season; someone spotted him and a reporter and photographer were summoned, and on the following day the inhabitants of Salt Lake City learned that the first person to immerse himself that year in the chill waters of the Great Salt Lake was one Mr Brown, a London dentist. 'That's fame!' Koestler jotted in his diary, pleased with his little trick.

In Chicago, of course, he was once more on the merry-go-round, but the jottings in his diary show he had recovered from the exasperation that had threatened to overwhelm him during the exhausting weeks in New York, Washington, and California. Back in New York on Monday 19th April he worked quietly on the article commissioned by *Life* – an extended version of his lectures.

That completed, he flew to Boston where his talk was well received. There and in Cambridge he enjoyed himself in the company of writers and scholars. 'Once more reviving in academic atmosphere,' he noted thankfully.

The last fortnight of his visit he spent in New York, leaving it once only with the Burnhams for a visit to the Institute for Advanced Studies in Princeton where, as in Cambridge, he had some stimulating conversations on the theories of human creativity he had sketched at length in *Insight and Outlook*.

A round of leavetaking parties occupied much of his last few days: 'end-of-holiday feeling,' he jotted. He had, in spite of all his reservations about the way of life, succeeded more or less in coming to terms with America.

> 'I can't tell you,' he wrote to Mamaine shortly before he left, 'about all the tentative projects which have developed during my stay. My ideas at present are that we should both come here late in the autumn for approximately six months and then see how it goes . . . I have made friends with a lot of people and am mostly enjoying myself . . .'

On the evening of Sunday 9th May, James Putnam accompanied him to the airport, both of them cheerfully drinking Bourbon from the bottle.

* *

In his last letter to Mamaine from New York Koestler had described himself as 'your loving and homesick spouse'; and on the day before his return Mamaine, staying with Sonia Brownell (later to become Mrs Orwell) in London after her holiday in Trieste and Paris, had noted:

> 'Arthur is coming back tomorrow morning, thank God. I am longing to get out of London and be settled back in Wales.'

But his homecoming was not quite the happy event both had anticipated. Mamaine was less than enthusiastic about Koestler's plans for their future:

> 'We are migrating to the States, I mean emigrating, early next year, if I still feel I can stick the prospect by then; the idea is to live in New England for 9 months of the year, and travel in Europe, for the other three.'

By 15th May they were at Bwlch Ocyn again. Looking back on the past few days, Mamaine recorded:

> 'It was pretty grim when K arrived back in the worst possible mood . . . So I tried to sit back and wait till he recovered, which he has now done – but it took a week during which I despaired once again of ever being able to stick it out. For during the whole of this week the nice K hardly put in an appearance for one single second; but on the contrary everything was wrong and I was nagged from morn to night, and finally when we got back here K said he despaired of ever being able to lead a tidy and organised life with me . . .'

What Mamaine did not realise when she wrote this was the extent to which Koestler, during his absence in America, had become increasingly preoccupied again with the chaotic state of affairs in Palestine during the final and ineffectual phase of the British mandatory authority. The announcement from London that the UK's mandatory authority would end on 15th May 1948 intensified the hostilities between Jew and Arab, and casualties mounted rapidly as the Zionists brought in 'illegal immigrants' at a growing rate and the Arab states increased their support of the Palestinian Arabs with a volunteer force after the Jewish declaration of the State of Israel. The worsening news drove all other pre-occupations out of Koestler's head.

Although it soon became apparent that the Jews (with the exception of those in the Old City of Jerusalem who had been forced to surrender to the Arab Legion) were holding their own, his conscience was tortured. What was he, who had so passionately advocated the Zionist cause, doing in Wales when the new-born state was in danger? Should he not be there, reporting its struggle for survival? When he discussed his dilemma with Mamaine, she urged him to go and insisted that she would accompany him.

By the end of the month arrangements had been made: the Israeli authorities agreed to admit them, and Koestler made arrangements to act as correspondent for the *Manchester Guardian*, *Le Figaro*, and the *New York Herald Tribune*, additional articles to be syndicated widely by the Paris agency, Opera Mundi.

# CHAPTER XIX

# *1948*

On Tuesday 1st June 1948, Koestler and Mamaine received their visas at the Paris office of the Jewish Agency in the Avenue Wagram. Mamaine's was the fifth to be issued since the declaration of the new State of Israel, Koestler's the sixth.

Two days later – under a cloud of deadly hangovers acquired at farewell parties given by James de Rothschild and others – they boarded a chartered Dakota at Le Bourget; and on Friday at four in the afternoon, after a long and uncomfortable flight by way of Marseille, Rome, Athens, and Cyprus, they arrived at Haifa.

In addition to his heavy journalistic commitments, Koestler had decided to write a book* on the conception, gestation, and birthpangs of Israel. The first part, 'Background', was to bc a survey of the developments which had led to the foundation of the state. Over the years he had done a great deal of research on the historical aspects, and had the material at his fingertips. The second part, 'Close-Up', was to offer 'a close and coloured, but not I hope technicolored, view of the Jewish-Arab war and of everyday life in the new state'. The third and final part, 'Perspective', would be 'an attempt to present to the reader a comprehensive survey of the social and political structure, the cultural trends and future prospects of the Jewish State' – and the likely repercussions of its existence on the Jews who elected to remain in the *Galuth* (exile), while supporting Eretz Israel from the lands of their adoption.

The copious journal which he had begun in Paris before boarding the aircraft, together with the long series of articles he had contracted to write, were to form the raw material out of which the second and third parts of the book were to be shaped. It was his intention to complete the book by the end of the year at the latest – a formidable task.

Koestler began his researches with long conversations with wounded Haganah soldiers recuperating in Haifa, filling his journal with accounts of their experiences in the early fighting against the Lebanese and Syrians.

* *Promise and Fulfilment – Palestine 1917–1949*, London and New York 1949.

> 'This evening,' Koestler noted on the evening of their arrival, 'a Haganah soldier with a bullet-wound in his lung told me, as we were sitting on the starlit terrace . . . where I am writing this . . . of his experience during the first night of the Syrian invasion into Israel: "I was lying with my platoon on a hill in the Jordan Valley near the communal settlement of Shar al Hagolan. I am myself a member of the commune . . . I am the cowman . . . The Arabs had cut off the spring which supplies the water of the commune, and our imported Dutch cows there were dying of thirst. They had cost a lot of money those Dutch cows, and our commune has very little money. Now while we were waiting for the Syrian tanks, each time the guns were silent we heard the cows complaining in a chorus. Whenever I heard them I was unable to take the guns and the war very seriously, and was unable to make up my mind which was the real reality, so to speak: the tanks or the wailing of the thirsty cows." '

From him and other convalescents Koestler gathered that the morale of the Syrian and Lebanese invaders was as low as that of the Jewish defenders was high. One of them had been among the fifty-two Haganah men who had successfully defended the settlement of Ramat Naphtali against the assault of fifteen hundred Lebanese infantry backed by thirty to forty medium tanks. According to his account, the Jews

> 'found to their amazement that whenever a single man of the attackers was hit he threw his arms into the air in a theatrical fashion, yelled "Allah!", whereupon the whole line came to a standstill or started running back. Then armoured cars advanced, put themselves between the stockade and the wounded man, pulled the wounded man inside and drove back. After that came the next attack: advance, one or two "Allahs!", reflux, armoured cars acting as ambulance. Soon accustomed to this game, the defenders now let the enemy advance to a 200 yard enclosure and took a heavy toll of them. After three hours the Lebanese became fed up with the game and vanished.'

Many of Koestler's friends and acquaintances in Tel Aviv from whom he immediately began to collect material about the early stages of the war, and the emerging political forces in the new state, supported the Revisionist Party and its military wing, Irgun Zvai Leumi, under the leadership of Menachem Begin who had inherited the 'maximalist' policies of Jabotinsky. Although Koestler had long since been converted to the idea that Palestine should be partitioned between the Jews and Arabs, and although he deplored the Irgun's massacre of the inhabitants of Deir Yassin, he still had considerable sympathy for Begin and his movement. In Haifa he had talked with a wounded member of the Palmach (the élite shock-troops of the Haganah recruited from the extreme left-wing Socialist parties, Hashomer Hazair, Poale Zion, and Achtut Avada Bey), who had assured him that 'the Irgunists are Fascists,' and who

> 'spoke with glee about mutual fights and kidnappings and seemed quite cheerful about the prospect that once the Arab war is over the accounts with Irgun and Lekhi [the terrorist Stern Group] will have to be settled.'

Koestler was the most distinguished foreign correspondent in Israel. His arrival had been widely publicised. He was, or had been in the past, on friendly terms with the men who were now members of the provisional Government. Every taxi-driver in Tel Aviv knew the author of *Thieves in the Night*. But his reputation cut no ice with the bureaucrats of the Public Information Office who were no more helpful to him than they were to the rest of the journalists kicking their heels in Tel Aviv.

Although he could get no information worth filing out of official sources (perhaps because, as he noted in his diary, he was 'already suspected of being an anti-Soviet agent of Bevin'), he kept his growing irritation in check. A few more days of frustration, however, exhausted his patience with the virginal innocence of the Public Information Office and he wrote a long letter for publication in the *Palestine Post* criticising the provisional Government's catastrophic ineptitude in the field of public relations. Muddle was wearing out the patience of journalists sympathetic to Israel and confirming others in their hostility. This resulted in a long and engagingly frank reply by the Director of the Public Relations Office.

> 'Mr Koestler,' he began, 'deserves our thanks for having raised a very urgent problem. Moreover, his accusations are substantially correct. Our Public Information Service is decidedly underdeveloped and inadequate. This is well-known to the Government and it is the task of the undersigned to do his utmost to improve it.'

But the State of Israel, he went on, was only five weeks old. The former administration of the country having been 'deliberately dissolved and destroyed by the mandatory power before and until May 15', the Government was faced with the task of building from scratch a complete state with all its institutions. Besides, the State of Israel numbered only about 600,000 Jewish inhabitants (with another 100,000 isolated in besieged Jerusalem).

> 'The question is not to decide whether a Ministry of Information has to be established, but to find dozens or hundreds of suitable officials, liaison officers, translators, typists, messenger-boys, etc; of renting offices, of putting the telephone lines into working condition, in short, of overcoming all the overwhelming difficulties of shortage of manpower and material.'

As to the atmosphere of secrecy shrouding the Army:

> 'There is no doubt that the criticism of "the habit of conspiracy" is to some degree justified. The Haganah was able to leave the underground only five weeks ago, and it has not yet found time to change all its traditions of anonymous and unrewarded service. This, too, will no doubt be achieved in the course of time.'

Koestler's first clash with authority elicited the soft answer that turned away wrath. For the moment. The inordinately complex intricacies of Israeli politics – the main topic of lengthy conversations with Jewish friends and other correspondents on the terrace of the Kaete Dan hotel and elsewhere – were beginning to exasperate him. He and Mamaine were relieved to find a friend on the staff of Count Bernadotte, the UN mediator. This was the young Greek, Alexis Ladas, the brother of Mrs Cy [Marina] Sulzberger. They had a pleasant dinner with him at the Kaete Dan:

> 'Already after three days in this country it is a relief to have dinner with a non-Jew – like glass of water after salty dish . . .'

* *

There followed a ceasefire, and after much involved negotiation Koestler succeeded in obtaining permission to leave Tel Aviv for a brief tour of the Lebanese and Syrian frontiers; and on 19th June he and Mamaine set off with a Haganah escort called Shlomo.

> 'His surname we never found out, nor that of any of the officers and local commanders with whom we talked and travelled along the fronts. It was all part of the atmosphere of dark secrecy in which Haganah shrouded itself . . . a source of endless muddle and confusion. As we proceeded on our journey to Galilee, our escort Shlomo would get out in various towns and villages, hail a soldier, go into a conspiratorial huddle with him about the probable whereabouts of headquarters – where he was to get his security briefing and some more permits, if not an additional field security escort. After driving about for a while in quest of HQ, when Shlomo felt that the trail was getting hot, he would leave the car and continue his search on foot, so as not to betray its location. We were drifting along on our journey in a kind of elusive and fluid universe in which there were no fixed points of support . . .'

Koestler was able nevertheless to fill his journal with many eye witness accounts of the headlong flight (or expulsion) of most of the Palestinian Arabs and the Israelis' subsequent defeat of the Lebanese, Iraqi, and Syrian invaders. In Haifa he pieced together the extraordinary story of how the Haganah had succeeded in putting its seventy thousand Arab inhabitants to flight by cunning propaganda – using the local radio station and loudspeaker vans – rather than by force of arms. In this the Jews were greatly helped by the prior departure of Arab notables in motor yachts laden with their families, furniture, and valuables. It was more or less the same story, he discovered, in the other mixed towns during the civil war period. Palestinian Arab morale had collapsed everywhere under the simultaneous impact of the desertion of the *effendis*, of panicky rumours, and of Jewish improvisation and propaganda.

One of the first *kibbutzim* Koestler revisited during this tour was Ain Hashofet – the original of Gan Tamar in *Thieves in the Night*. The *kibbutzniks* here were members of Hashomer Hazair, a doctrinaire revolutionary Socialist group which had formerly been opposed to the idea of a Jewish state, favouring instead united action by both the Jewish and the Arab 'toiling masses' against both the capitalists and the *effendis* – a Marxist programme utterly remote from reality.

He and Mamaine were given an icy reception:

> 'In the secretariat one man refused to shake hands, the other said "Pity you didn't announce your visit" – implying that I would have been told that the

visit was undesirable. At last Jonah turned up, who admitted that the book [*Thieves in the Night*] may have acted as an "eye-opener" to "a few million gentile readers", but that's no excuse for my crime. The crime is that [in the novel] (a) the girls in the kibbutz are not pretty enough; (b) that all kibbutzniks are abnormal; (c) that only the Etzel [Irgun] people are heroes . . . The fantastic thing is that Hashomer Hazair has really been proved wrong on every single point of their programme: bi-national state, peaceful co-habitation with the Arabs, impending Arab Marxist revolution, etc. etc. But would never admit that even to themselves, and hence according to the classic psychological pattern of the bad loser, only get more venomous (cf. Mr Bevin). Jonah's first remark was "well, what are you doing?" "Writing the second volume." "Well, I hope you will do better this time."'

The next few days were spent in an extensive tour of settlements and towns in the north which had seen heavy fighting, Koestler filling his journal with material for his book.

* *

In the afternoon of Tuesday 22nd June, Koestler and Mamaine made their way back from Upper Galilee to Haifa. During the journey they heard disquieting rumours of armed clashes between the Haganah and Irgun Zvai Leumi. In Haifa these were confirmed. Koestler feared that the outbreak of civil war was imminent.

'Very alarmed,' he noted that evening. 'One of the most dreadful things is when one's own prophecies, in which others wouldn't believe, come true; for then one feels it as a personal failure not to have succeeded in making others aware of the danger. If anybody was justified in committing suicide, it was Cassandra.'

Serious fighting had broken out between government troops and a shipload of Irgun supporters bringing in arms. Faced by overwhelming forces, the Irgun leader Menachem Begin ordered his forces not to resist Government orders. The ship, the *Altalena*, was shelled by Haganah artillery. Next day a unit of Palmach broke up the Irgun's headquarters, smashing the furniture and tearing up the files while Begin's men stood by, white-faced and silent, watching the destruction.

During the following day, by which time Koestler had interviewed dozens of people about the incident and amassed forty foolscap pages of detailed notes which pointed to the conclusion that, far from planning a *putsch*, the Irgun had been guilty of nothing worse than walking naïvely into a trap set by the Government, he was taken by a courier to a flat in Tel Aviv where

'I saw Menachem Begin for the first time in my life. I had actually talked to him before, but without seeing him – in a dark room in Tel Aviv in 1945, when he was the man most wanted by the British Police, with £5000 on his head. On that occasion we had argued for about an hour in the pitch darkness which Irgun's conspiratorial precautions prescribed. I had tried to convince him that England was one thing, the Palestine Administration another; that with the end of the war the White Paper would be abolished, and that Israel's future was that of a Dominion in the British Commonwealth. Begin had said in substance that he didn't believe British policy would change, even if Labour came into power; but that even if I were right, his job was to fight the Palestine Government and that he couldn't get his boys to risk the gallows by telling them that it was all a temporary misunderstanding and the English ultimately very nice people.

'Judging by his voice coming across the table in the dark, I had imagined the owner of the voice as a tall, ascetic-looking man with a fanatic expression. Actually he is rather short, thin, frail, very short-sighted, with a gentle, earnest young schoolmaster's face. Obviously voices, like cigarettes and food, change their flavour in the dark. His manner is that kind of self-assured awkwardness which comes to people who, by achievement, have learned to find a *modus vivendi* with their own shyness. He talks as thoughtfully and unfanatically as his propaganda is bombastic and violent; he wears the loose, ill-fitting clothes of a scholar, and has the scholar's dry charm. We got on much better than at the time when he had been the Invisible Man, and I took down his version of the *Altalena* and counter-checked it again.'

Koestler filed a long dispatch in which he criticised the Government for over-reacting:

'. . . There is an uneasy lull in Tel Aviv today. The atmosphere ominously recalls Barcelona in 1937, when clashes between the anarchists and the Government fatally undermined the resistance of the Spanish Republic. Though there is no immediate danger of civil war, the internal situation is so serious that a disclosure of the full truth about the events culminating in [the] savage street and beach fighting is essential in the very interest of the future of the young State of Israel. So far this has not been done by the Government, whose statements, it must regretfully be said, are self-contradictory and misleading in several essential points.'

He then went on to confirm from his own independent investigations the truth of Begin's statement about Irgun's negotiations with the Government and

'. . . the fact that the Government's sudden order to open fire took even the local military and civilian authorities by surprise, as, until receiving the order to fire, these had collaborated with Irgun in unloading the . . . *Altalena*.'

The ship, with its nine hundred young immigrants of all parties, with millions of pounds' worth of desperately needed arms purchased before the truce, represented six months' effort of French Jews and Gentiles. As to the smouldering rivalry and resentment between Irgun and the Government,

'Perhaps a generous gesture of the Government towards Irgun recognising its past merits might have healed the wounds. Unfortunately the Government party seemed more concerned with settling old accounts than with national unity.'

Koestler's article, widely syndicated throughout Western Europe and America, did not endear him to the provisional Government and its supporters, but it was undoubtedly effective in persuading Ben Gurion and his colleagues to moderate their attitude towards Menachem Begin and so consequently in making it possible for him to speed up the dissolution of the Irgun and the full incorporation of all its armed forces in the national army.

Koestler, undeterred by private warnings and public criticisms, continued to dig for the facts and to speak and write the truth as he saw it. In a letter to the *Jerusalem Post*, replying to an article by its London correspondent, he wrote:

> '. . . there are two ways of loving one's country, the soft and the hard way. The soft way is that of the foolish mother who believes that her child is an infant prodigy. For thirty years Zionist propaganda has been based on this type of sloppy adulation of the Palestine *Wunderkind*. Every cow . . . every reclaimed marsh, every stone in Tel Aviv, has been boosted ad nauseam, as if nowhere else in the world have marshes been reclaimed and towns built on sand. And woe betide the friend of Israel who dared to suggest that the hideous architecture of Tel Aviv could be improved, or the grotesque methods of [proportional] election to the country's representative bodies be revised.
>
> 'The second type of patriotism is nourished by a hard and bitter love, which experiences the shortcomings of one's country as a personal humiliation. All propaganda derived from this attitude puts the harmful truth before the useful lie. In the long run, as history shows, it is the only type of propaganda which produces lasting results.'

The *Post* in the same issue countered with a long editorial chiding Koestler for his support of the Irgun and ending:

> 'The wide circulation in this country of his in part critical novel, *Thieves in the Night*, and the free discussion of his controversial opinions are enough to show that his opposition has plunged him into intolerance.'

Koestler let it rest at that. The atmosphere of crisis soon lifted. Within a week or two the Irgun battalions were fully incorporated in the national army. Begin was in the process of forming his organisation into a legal political movement which eventually emerged as the Freedom Party, the one specific feature of whose otherwise 'vaguely progressive, eclectic, and colourless programme' (as Koestler described it) was the uncompromising demand for a Jewish State on both sides of the Jordan.

The Arabs refused to agree to an extension of the truce. Fighting was resumed. Tel Aviv was bombed and a score or so were killed. But the expected Arab *Blitzkrieg* did not materialise and the Israeli forces had little difficulty in improving their position. Within nine days the Arabs had agreed to another truce. Life in Tel Aviv returned to normal and Koestler settled down to the production of a series of long articles on the political, economic and cultural aspects of the embattled state, some of which were to involve him in heated controversy.

As the work continued, Koestler became increasingly irritable and difficult to live with, until Mamaine could take it no longer. She set off for Cyprus and a holiday. She came back in good form:

> '. . . I feel that I shan't be here very much longer, and this gives me the strength to bear the remaining weeks or months. Whether to go to England, or to accompany K to America, is the problem about which I'm now puzzling, and rather think I shall do the latter, for the time being. . . . I may return to Europe in the middle of October to pack up Bwlch Ocyn and make arrangements for K and me to stay somewhere in France till we go to America in January – K would stay here till the middle of November. He says that if he gets a job at a university – which he hasn't yet got – the term only starts in February, and there would be no point going much before as it's so expensive and so cold: better stay a month or so near Paris if we can borrow or rent a house, which I think we can: Winkler said something about our sharing his, which is somewhere in the Fontainebleau direction as far as I can remember.
>
> 'We went to Haifa for two nights this week, and K got FRIGHTFULLY drunk at the house of a psychoanalyst, whom he didn't know at all; then I abandoned him on Mount Carmel, and he returned next morning in company with a priest, who had discovered him sleeping under a tree and taken him for a tramp. K had explained that he was a famous writer, to which the priest replied "Oh yeah?" or words to that effect. The priest then took him to a monastery where he met another (English) priest of 81 (the first was French). K said to him that several young English writers had become converts to Catholicism, and the old priest said "Oh, yes, a fellow called Chesterton's one isn't he?". I suppose he thought G.K.C. was still alive and only about 30.
>
> 'Alexis has been in Rhodes since my return – I crossed him in Haifa on my way back (by air, in a very small plane, from Nicosia) . . . I met Menachem Begin at a party, who was charming . . . My Hebrew is very elementary but I understand a bit now.'

On 3rd October she left for England to pack up their belongings at Bwlch Ocyn and then to await Koestler in Paris. A fortnight later he followed her amidst a storm of protests against a series of articles in which he had criticised the inadequacies of cultural life in Israel. The draft of *Promise and Fulfilment* was not quite complete, but he knew how it was to end.

In his evidence to the Anglo-American Committee of Enquiry, Chaim Weizmann had said despondently, 'I believe the only fundamental cause of anti-semitism – it may seem tautological – is that the Jew exists. We seem to carry anti-semitism in our knapsacks wherever we go . . .'

Now that the state of Israel was in existence, Koestler concluded, and likely to become an entirely 'unJewish' country within a generation or two, the time had come for the Jews of the Diaspora to break the vicious circle of being persecuted for being 'different', and being 'different' by force of persecution. They must arrive at a clear decision:

> 'They must either follow the imperative of their religion, the return to the Promised Land, or recognise that that faith is no longer theirs. To renounce

the Jewish faith does not mean to jettison the perennial values of Judaic tradition. Its essential teachings have passed long ago into the main-stream of the Judeo-Christian heritage. If a Judaic religion is to survive outside Israel, without inflicting the stigma of separateness on its followers and laying them open to the charge of divided loyalty, it would have to be a system of faith and cosmopolitan ethics freed from all racial presumption and national exclusivity. But a Jewish religion thus reformed would be stripped of all its specifically Jewish content.

'These conclusions, reached by one who has been a supporter of the Zionist Movement for a quarter-century, while his cultural allegiance belonged to Western Europe, are mainly addressed to the many others in a similar situation. They have done what they could to help to secure a haven for the homeless in the teeth of prejudice, violence and political treachery. Now that the State of Israel is firmly established, they are at last free to do what they could not do before: to wish it good luck and go their own way, with an occasional friendly glance back and a helpful gesture. But, nevertheless, to go their own way, with the nation whose life and culture they share, without reservations or split loyalties.

'Now that the mission of the Wandering Jew is completed, he must discard the knapsack and cease to be an accomplice in his own destruction . . .'

# CHAPTER XX

# *1949*

STALIN WAS TIGHTENING THE screws at home and throughout the lands which were now in effect being incorporated into the new Soviet Empire. Elsewhere in Europe (with the exception of Jugoslavia) the national Communist Parties took their lead obediently from Moscow. So did such trade unions as were either openly Communist-controlled or covertly manipulated. In their task of disrupting the economy and weakening public morale they were assisted not only by 'crypto-Communists' in positions of power or influence, and other fellow-travellers, but also by an impressive stage-army of innocent and well-meaning progressives of one sort and another whose idealism (or dislike of the United States and what they imagined it to stand for) induced them to ignore or minimise the threat from the East. Many such people were usually to be found among the leading supporters of the various Communist 'front' organisations.

With the benefit of hindsight we can see that during this period it was the initiative, resolution, and generosity of the United States which preserved the integrity of Western Europe, restored the morale of its democratic majorities, and encouraged its constituent states to take the first tentative steps towards unity. For a generation at least, Western Europe had been saved from incorporation in the Soviet Union's sphere of influence by the process of 'Finlandisation', and perhaps even from civil wars and 'liberation' by the Red Army and the KGB's specialist airborne divisions.

In France the European crisis was at its most acute. It had not yet recovered from the moral and military collapse of 1940 and the humiliation of occupation. It was smarting still from the self-inflicted wounds of the post-liberation period during which the Communists (who had played so large a part in 1939 and 1940 in bringing about the *débâcle*) had settled many old scores behind the smokescreen of the Resistance myth. The inherent chauvinism of most of its intellectuals permitted them neither to feel any obligation to the British and Americans for clearing the Germans out of their country nor to express gratitude to the Americans for their economic help. General de Gaulle, biding his time in the wings with the *Rassemblement du Peuple Français*, was generally regarded by the intellectual community with feelings which ranged from sour suspicion to fanatical hatred. The Fourth Republic – with its endlessly reshuffled coalition cabinets of Socialists, Radicals, and the *Mouvement Républicain Populaire* – was proving to be no less unstable than the Third.

It was to counter the West's new-found determination to resist Soviet pressure that Russia launched through the Cominform, with the support of its proxies in the national Communist parties and 'fronts', its powerful 'peace offensives' ('peace', of course, having the now familiar connotations of non-resistance to Communism). Although the French Socialist Party (like the leadership of the British Labour Party and the overwhelming majority of its supporters) was strongly anti-totalitarian, most left-wing intellectuals in France – addicted to various admixtures of Marxist abstraction and full of nostalgia for the cosy atmosphere of the pre-war Popular Front – were willing enough to play along with the Communists.

Koestler, who had chosen to settle in France for a time before moving to the United States (if he could succeed in getting permission to take up residence there: not easy for an ex-Communist and former Comintern agent) was often to find it no less exasperating than the dull, decent complacencies and essential conservatism of England.

Earlier in this year, before his trip to America, he had analysed the situation in France:

> 'Just as the storming of the Bastille was not a local French event,' he wrote, 'but the symbol of the collapse of the feudal system in Europe, so the present situation in France is like a dramatisation on the stage of all the relevant contradictions and conflicts of the post-liberal era . . . it is the glory and tragedy of French genius to serve as a burning lens of Western civilisation.'

The crisis, Koestler argued, had no more been 'caused' by war-inflicted losses in capital substance (for France had emerged from the war with a structurally intact and essentially sound economy) than the crisis of 1789 had been 'caused' by the salt-tax or the Court's extravaganzas. It marked the end, rather, of an era in the economy of Europe:

> '. . . the crisis can be eased by foreign aid and other palliatives, but it cannot be solved within the framework of French economy alone . . . blueprints for a French recovery can only make sense within the framework of Western Europe, including Western Germany, as an economically integrated unit.'

This argument, as may be imagined, did not endear Koestler to his left-wing acquaintances any more than to the supporters of de Gaulle.

As for the Communists, they presented the same dilemma to France as the National Socialists did to Germany in 1930 – with this difference, that while the National Socialists frankly professed their intention to destroy democracy, the Communists posed as its defenders.

Sartre and Simone de Beauvoir were among those who disapproved of

Koestler's analysis. They disapproved even more of his tolerant assessment of de Gaulle and the movement he led.

In the summer of 1947 the Gallup Poll had asked two questions. To the first: 'Do you wish to see de Gaulle return to power?' the answers were: *Yes*, 30 per cent; *No*, 50 per cent. The second question was: 'If there existed only two political groups in France, one Gaullist and the other anti-Gaullist, which would you choose?' Here 40 per cent opted for the Gaullist alternative and 30 per cent for the anti-Gaullist – ie, for the Communists and fellow-travellers.

Those curious results, in Koestler's view, indicated that Gaullism – a 'movement without a profile' – was essentially a movement towards the lesser evil.

* *

Koestler and Mamaine had decided not to stay in Paris itself (where little work would have been done), but somewhere in the country not too far from the capital, and preferably on the banks of the Seine. While they were looking for a house to buy, they stayed in a cottage in the grounds of Chartrettes, a *château* owned by Paul Winkler* looking across the river to the Forest of Fontainebleau.

They shared a sitting-room and dining-room with Ripka, a Czech politician in exile, and his wife. Their social life was lively. From Koestler's diary:

'*July 19th*. Dick and Zita Crossman, Michael and Jill Foot for weekend. Bertaux and Colonel George for lunch; then dinner Place de Tertre (Montmartre) – same plus a few others. Later Lapin Agile [Cabaret] soupe à l'oignon. All highly enjoyable, except Dick and Zita piqued and jealous about presence of French friends.

'According to Ménard, Ripka has been appointed Prime Minister of Czechoslovak government in exile (the third). Ménard's comment: "You know these people as emigrés – they are dim, pathetic, *pas sérieux*. Then they go home and become Ministers and make History. Then they return to exile – dim, pathetic, *pas sérieux* as before."

'*July 30th*. Bertaux's story of Clemenceau having to fly, which he hated, admonishing the pilot: "Fly very cautiously, very slow and very low!"

'Ripka's stories of Munich: Daladier constantly drunk (made drunk by Goering); Bidault photographed so drunk that two men had to hold him up; Bidault leaving one of the notorious Kremlin banquets asking a French-speaking, gaping officer, "*Dîtes donc, mon brave, où est ce qu'on trouve un bordel dans votre sacrée ville?*" Getting on slowly with novel . . . Reading *Bengal Lancers* first time. Wrote article for *Figaro*. Wrote "memoirs of a tight-rope walker" for Jamie [Hamish Hamilton] anthology [*The God that Failed*].

'Bernard Shaw on his 93rd birthday called Stalin "mainstay of peace". Clowning through three-quarters of a century, never tiring of it. Still the naughty, naughty little boy. The most over-estimated writer of his time – Thomas Mann publishes pompous interview refusing to apply for permission to visit Buchenwald concentration camp because "do not want to embarrass authorities", but accepts Soviet zone literary prize. Says something about Stalin inspired by higher ideals than Hitler.'

* Head of the Opera Mundi agency, and now co-proprietor of *France-Soir*.

Although her health was indifferent, the damp atmosphere exacerbating the asthma from which she suffered, Mamaine was happy enough at Chartrettes to begin with:

> 'We have a cook who does all the cooking and shopping for all, and a *femme de ménage* (Polish) who does the rooms. We are ¼ mile from the Seine, over which our rooms look. They are very nice and comfortable and our bedroom, which is also my working-room when I am not working with K, has a wood fire which one can keep going all day, as there is plenty of wood. The park is simply lovely, mostly woods and alleys of different kinds of trees – limes, chestnuts, etc. One can easily walk about in it for half an hour or more without going out of it . . .'

Eventually Koestler and Mamaine found a house, Verte Rive, at Fontaine-le-Port on the Seine, and arranged to move in at the end of January. That, combined with the hectic rush to complete the typescript of *Promise and Fulfilment* and a stream of visitors kept them on edge, as Mamaine recorded:

> 'As we seem unable to finish this blasted book, I doubt whether we shall be in England before the end of the month or beginning of Feb. . . .
>
> 'In spite of all our hard work, the book still isn't quite finished, so I don't suppose we shall be in London before about the middle of the week after this one – e.g. round Feb. 3rd or 4th . . .
>
> 'We haven't poked our noses outside the house for ages, and are both rather tired, especially K. However we really have nearly finished now . . .
>
> 'Is not Mr Bevin an unspeakable swine? to come out now with the statement that if fighting should break out again in Palestine Britain wouldn't be able to stand aside . . . What have we come to when that maniac can make England go to war against the Jews without anybody being able to stop him? When we heard his iniquitous statement, and the bunch of lies which preceded it, K nearly hit the ceiling with rage . . .'

By the end of the month the last page of *Promise and Fulfilment* had been typed and they had taken over Verte Rive.

'Furniture hasn't arrived yet, bare floors and walls echo every sound. Very irritable and unbalanced,' Koestler jotted in his diary.

On 3rd February he and Mamaine left by car for London. After ten days of crowded social life he returned to the Hotel Montalembert in Paris, leaving Mamaine to follow in a week or so. People in London had depressed him (with a few exceptions, such as T. S. Eliot, who earned the relatively high praise in his diary of "nice, unpompous"). John Strachey, for example, he found complacent. He had no idea that in France no independent Left survived. And if Strachey, he noted, the most cosmopolitan member of the Cabinet was as ignorant as that – 'God help us!'

*Insight and Outlook* had just been published in the United States and was received with something less than enthusiasm.

> 'The reviews in *Time*, *Newsweek*, and *Herald-Tribune* are as stinking as could be expected,' Koestler wrote to Mamaine, 'but I don't seem to mind. I got

over the depression as soon as I got back to Paris and spent a series of pleasant evenings with Sperber and other old friends popping up, with wise talk and moderate drinking.'

A few days later Mamaine returned from London and joined Koestler at the Hotel Montalembert:

> 'K has gone to dine with Sperbers and other old-time German pals, so I didn't go as their German jabbering about old friends bores me, when I understand it . . . K is in fine form, though he says everything is going very badly . . . He is unbelievably sweet and easy to get on with . . .'

* *

Koestler had told Mamaine that he didn't mind what the reviewers were saying about *Insight and Outlook.* Simone de Beauvoir had a different impression. He was worried, she thought. He was always going to the desk of the Pont-Royal, she wrote, to see if his publisher had sent him any clippings. Her friendship with Koestler, and Sartre's, had been cooling for some time because of his anti-Communism and his friendship with Malraux. But Koestler, she thought, was unwilling to see that friendship die. His efforts involved, according to Madame de Beauvoir's account, rather more than 'moderate drinking' on occasion:

> 'He wanted to repeat our night at the Schéhérezade. We went with him, Mamaine, Camus, Sartre and myself – Francine wasn't there – to another Russian nightclub. . . . In a tone more hostile than the year before, he returned to the theme of "No friendship without political agreement." As a joke, Sartre was making love to Mamaine, though so outrageously one could scarcely have said he was being indiscreet, and we were all far too drunk for it to be offensive. Suddenly, Koestler threw a glass at Sartre's head and it smashed against the wall. We brought the evening to a close: Koestler didn't want to go home, and then he found he'd lost his wallet and had to stay behind in the club; Sartre was staggering about on the sidewalk and laughing helplessly when Koestler finally decided to climb back up the stairway on all fours. He wanted to continue his quarrel with Sartre. "Come on, let's go home!" said Camus, laying a friendly hand on his shoulder: Koestler shrugged the hand off and hit Camus, who then tried to hurl himself on his aggressor; we kept them apart. Leaving Koestler in his wife's hands, we all got into Camus' car; he too was suitably soused in vodka and champagne, and his eyes began to fill with tears: "He was my friend! And he hit me!" He kept collapsing onto the steering wheel and sending the car into the most terrifying swerves and we would try to haul him up, completely sobered by our fear. During the next few days we often went back to that night together; Camus would ask us perplexedly: "Do you think it's possible to go on drinking like that and still work?" No. And in fact such excesses had become very rare for all three of us; they had some meaning when we were still refusing to believe that our victory had been stolen from us; now, we knew where we stood.'

The political differences between Sartre and Koestler deepened rapidly:

> 'Koestler', in Madame de Beauvoir's version, 'was now declaring that the best solution for France at that time, all things considered, was Gaullism. He had several arguments with Sartre. One day, when I happened to be in the bar of the Pont-Royal with Violette Leduc, he came up to me with a member of the RPF in tow. The latter immediately attacked me point-blank: publicly, Sartre was opposing de Gaulle; but the *Rassemblement* had contacted him, made him offers that would be very worth his while, and, in sum, he had promised to support the movement. I shrugged my shoulders. The Gaullist refused to let the matter rest and I grew heated; Koestler listened to us with a smile on his lips. "All right! Make a bet on it," he said. "I'll be a witness to it. Whoever is in the wrong will buy a bottle of champagne." At that I left. When Sartre challenged him about his attitude, Koestler replied laughingly that one should always be prepared for anything from anyone, and that I had taken the matter too seriously. "It's just a woman's squabble!" he ended up . . .'

* *

Koestler and Mamaine went off in their new Citroën (the first new car Koestler had ever bought) to their new house at Fontaine-le-Port. Conditions were spartan. Their furniture had not yet arrived. Koestler found it difficult to get down to work again ('carpets, bookshelves, furniture looming like nightmares').

Koestler's crisis of confidence was soon to be displaced by anxiety about Mamaine. A sudden and violent attack of asthma began a long period of illness from which she was never to recover completely:

> 'Arthur,' in Mamaine's words, 'was wonderful as usual and rushed about getting things from various chemists in Fontainebleau etc. and ringing up doctors – a frightful sweat as we have no phone. I shall be up by Sunday . . .'

But on Monday she was

> 'Still in bed and beginning to feel that I shall never be out of it – having apparently got into one of those states when one never seems to make any progress. I still don't really feel well enough to get up, though I am not suffering in the least. It is too annoying, because poor Arthur has been left to do all the unpacking and arranging of the furniture by himself, including all the books of which we have over 2,000; it is nearly killing him. Simultaneously the proofs of the Palestine book have started to arrive, so he is in a real flap. Thirdly, Jim Putnam also retired to bed with gastric flu or something; and the cook is quite off her head and is driving us all off ours . . .
>
> 'It is evening now and I am feeling much better; shall definitely start getting up tomorrow . . .
>
> 'We've just been having a conference with Jim who wants Arthur to cut and change his Palestine book radically; I think I have found a good compromise solution. *Insight and Outlook* won't be out in England till the end of May now – they are incredibly slow, it's most annoying.'

Within a day or two Mamaine had a relapse and became so dangerously ill that she was moved to the English Hospital in Paris. After a month of treatment there, she had recovered sufficiently to return to Fontaine-le-Port.

Mamaine's proposed visit to the mountains had to be abandoned because of her continuing illness. At the end of May Koestler took her to London and left her in the care of an asthma specialist, Dr Croxon Deller, in a West Hampstead nursing home.

As for himself, on his return to Verte Rive, he

> '. . . settled down to work surprisingly quickly this time, and feel quite happy . . . I spent two lovely days at Whitsun sailing up and down the river past Samois, for nine hours on Sunday and seven hours yesterday, and got frightfully sunburnt. Now Daphne* has come and put an end to the vacation, and I am back at work again . . . Thank God the days of gloom seem to be over . . .'

Undeterred by the indifferent reviews of *Insight and Outlook* and his irritation with his London publishers, who had written to say that they would not be able to publish *Promise and Fulfilment* until September, Koestler was hard at work on various projects in addition to conducting a voluminous correspondence. His novel *The Age of Longing*, in which he dramatised – with Paris as the setting – his thoughts and feelings about the deepening crisis in the West, was taking shape.

His long-delayed divorce from Dorothy was at last going through and would be completed (he wrote to Mamaine) by the beginning of October.

Mamaine made good progress in London and Koestler continued to work hard in spite of a fierce heat-wave and the visitors who descended on him at weekends. He had at last brought himself to revise the French version of *Promise and Fulfilment*:

> 'I am redictating practically the whole book,' he wrote to Mamaine, '. . . translations are just never any good unless one does them oneself and as we are now living in France, I want this to be a really good book, which I hope it will be. But it is a very awful sweat . . .
>
> 'The Gaullists are rather in a mess; they may or may not recover. As for Rousset, he is certainly more enlightened than Sartre but still far from seeing light . . .
>
> '. . . I am rather harassed – I gave [Mme] Grandin [the cook] next Saturday and Sunday off and now a whole invasion is announced: Plesch, Jamie Hamilton and Robin Ironside, Dominique etc . . . Much love, darling, from getreuen Gatten.'

* *

By the middle of August, Mamaine was back at Verte Rive and in good spirits, although her recovery from her own illness was impeded by various domestic

* Daphne Woodward, who acted for a time as Koestler's secretary.

strains: 'servants, dogs on heat or having puppies, painters in the house, mad furnishing drive' – and a constant stream of visitors . . .

> 'K is rather irritable these days. I don't think he has opened his mouth once today except to shout at me or nag about something – most wearing. If I don't rest he nags me, and if I do he grumbles because I haven't done this or that. – However, I am cheerful though rather énervée . . .'

* *

Now it was the turn of the English reviewers to savage *Promise and Fulfilment*.

> 'Poor K is most depressed about having had such bitchy reviews in English papers, it seems to him they are full of venom, which indeed they mostly are, because the English have such a bad conscience about Palestine and simply won't admit it. As a result K is more violently anti-English than ever. I fully sympathise with him, but at the same time am terribly irritated by his going on about it . . . I suppose if one was French, and one's husband kept on day and night telling one how dishonest and cowardly the French were, and how shamelessly they had capitulated to the Germans whenever they got a chance, etc., one would feel the more irritated because one couldn't very easily defend them . . .'

There was, however, a cheerful item of news for her:

> 'The divorce will be through in a week or so. I don't know yet how long after that it will take to get married, or what we shall do in the way of a wedding feast.'

* *

During the greater part of November, Mamaine was in London, undergoing diagnostic examinations in a nursing-home and having troublesome wisdom-teeth extracted.

Early in the following month she was back in France, feeling better, her resilience restored, and recording the vicissitudes of *La vie de Bohême*.

## CHAPTER XXI

# *1949–1950*

On Friday 23rd December Koestler went by himself to Paris to see friends with whom he was thinking of staying when Mamaine went off to the Alps on her doctor's advice. He told her that he might spend the night at their place and come back in time for lunch on Christmas Eve.

Lunchtime on Saturday came and went. Koestler had not turned up; nor had he telephoned. Mamaine, with his recent succession of 'blinds' fresh in her mind, was worried:

> '. . . by lunch time I was getting rather apprehensive, since I felt sure he would have rung up if he had intended to stay in Paris for lunch, or even be late for it. The afternoon wore on, as they say, and still no sign of K, and by 5 o'clock I was pretty well resigned to widow-hood, and impatient to know the worst.
>
> 'The telephone rang; I rushed to it, and a gruff and unfriendly voice said, "*Votre mari m'a demandé de vous prévenir de ne pas vous inquiéter à son sujet.*" "*Mais d'où téléphonez-vous?*" I said, "*et où est-il?*" "*Je ne peux pas vous dire,*" replied the voice. I tried a few more questions, but the chap would only say, "*C'est tout ce que je peux vous dire, Madame.*"
>
> 'At this moment the Vallons turned up, and I talked to them for an hour while waiting to see if K would return . . . but by 6 still no K, so I rang Bertaux to see if he had any news, and Vallon rang a friend of his at the *Préfecture* in Paris: the latter knew already that K was lying in jail.
>
> 'It turned out that he was driving back from the evening with the Weisweilers, which had become rather a blind, at 4 a.m., and finding himself at Charenton, which isn't at all on the way here, he realised that he was in no fit state to drive, so stopped the car and went to sleep. He was found there by some policemen, who took him to the local Commissariat; there he awoke at 11. Taken before the Commissaire – still fairly *alcoolisé* – K asked for permission to ring me; and when they refused it, he socked the Commissaire.
>
> 'The end was, that (after, I think, the intervention of the chap at the *Préfecture* and Bertaux) he was released, and came back in time for a late dinner. But this rather terrible story – terrible because now K has to appear

before the *correctionnelle* and may get a prison sentence, though probably *avec sursis* – was really a blessing in disguise, because the tyre of one of the front wheels of the car was about to puncture, and would certainly have done so on the way back, which if he'd been going fast, and as it has a front-wheel drive, would most likely have killed him.

'K was most shaken and has resolved in dead earnest to give up drink and ration himself to 3 brandies an evening at most. I really do think this has done the trick, so I am glad it happened, because he has been drinking much too much again lately and I doubt if anything less than a major shock of this kind could have provided the necessary incentive for him to take a firm line with himself. It was really *wonderful* when he did turn up, none the worse except for a few bruises inflicted on him by the police, because knowing how reliable he is about ringing up I had been imagining all sorts of ghastly things; I thought he must have got into a drunken *bagarre* with some toughs, who had probably turned out to be Communists as well and had beaten him up or something – otherwise I couldn't explain why he should have been unable to ring me up himself . . .'

Two or three days passed before the newspapers got hold of the story. When they did, there was a rich crop of mainly good humoured news items under such headlines as *Le Yogi et le commissaire (suite)*. Apparently under the impression that no further action was to be taken against Koestler, the Communist press spluttered with indignation. Under the heading of *Un spiritualisme à base de spiritueux, L'Humanité* asked how a foreigner, a Hungarian with a British passport, felt free to ignore the law and behave like a lunatic. And who were the contacts in high places who got him out of jail so quickly?

'All is clear when you realise that we are talking about the Trotskyite Arthur Koestler, the specialist in anti-Sovietism, the licensed insulter of the French people. Ah, the anti-Soviet forces choose their heroes well. Since he was at Charenton, Koestler could have been put up at a famous establishment there [a mental hospital]. But no doubt England the prude has need of him and his vices.'

* *

On 2nd January Mamaine left for her holiday with Prince and Princess Louis of Hesse in the Bavarian Alps and Koestler, having retained a lawyer, Maître Torrès, to represent him in the Charenton affair, settled down to work on *The Age of Longing*, helped by his new secretary, the 22-year-old Cynthia Jefferies, a pretty and efficient girl who had spent her childhood in South Africa (where her Irish father was a surgeon) except for two years at Lady Walsingham's School in England. He reported to Mamaine:

'7th January 1950

'Here is weekly digest no. 1. The Crossman anthology [*The God that Failed*] is just out in the USA and *Time* had a good review of it. In the same issue they also had a bitchy paragraph about Charenton.

'No news from the Crossmans; an announcement about the elections is expected any day now. I rang up Torrès who had no definite news yet about whether I will have to go to Court; he will probably know next week.

'Munio is here until tomorrow in a mellow mood . . .

'The weather has changed to clean Spring sunshine and my mood has much improved . . .'

Most reviewers of *The God that Failed* singled out Koestler's contribution as exceptionally important.

'One of the most handsome presents,' Rebecca West wrote in the *New York Times*, 'that has ever been given to future historians of our time.'

The success of the anthology, and in particular the special attention paid to the contribution by the author of *Darkness at Noon*, naturally enraged Communists and fellow-travellers – and also disconcerted their 'liberal' appeasers in the United States and Western Europe.

Koestler was also at this time under attack in Israel because of the concluding chapter of *Promise and Fulfilment* in which he stated his conviction that, with the establishment of the state of Israel, Jews in the Diaspora must:

'. . . either follow the imperative of their religion, the return to the Promised Land, or recognise that that faith is no longer theirs.'

This renunciation of Judaic 'racialism', coming from one who had been so active in the Zionist cause, gave great offence (and was to give even greater offence a few years later when he developed the theme in his essay, *Judah at the Crossroads*).

A Tel Aviv newspaper presented the drunken episode at Charenton as a consequence of his apostasy:

'The "painful incident" shows with what eagerness he pursues his new course of assimilation.'

On 21st January, only a few days before Mamaine was to go into a sanatorium in the Alps, George Orwell died suddenly in London. He was one of the very few Englishmen for whom Koestler – the hard-edged Continental intellectual – felt affection and admiration in equal measure; and the news of his death, at the age of forty-six, came as a shock:

'Orwell's death,' he told Mamaine, 'was a very bad shock, but I got it out of my system by writing an obituary article for the *Observer* – David [Astor] asked for it.'

His article was a moving tribute to that awkward and stubborn genius, devoid of self-love and self-pity, and so severe towards his friends as at times to seem almost inhuman. But this, Koestler wrote, was only towards his friends. He was

'. . . full of understanding sympathy for those on the remote periphery, the "crowds in the big towns with their knobbly faces, their bad breath and gentle manners; the queues outside the Labour Exchanges, the old maids biking to Holy Communion through the mists of the autumn mornings . . ." Thus, the greater the distance from intimacy and the wider the radius of the circle, the more warming became the radiations of this lonely man's great power of love.'

* *

On 1st February Koestler appeared in court in Paris, charged with striking a policeman. The case was adjourned for a month.

Mamaine returned in good time, and on 1st March accompanied Koestler to court:

'He was in an awful flap because he was so terrified he would be forced into an undignified, schoolboyish position by the magistrate making dirty cracks at him and being unable to explain the real reasons for having socked the cop, which are his old prison experiences, since to explain these would sound dramatic.'

There was also the possibility of a prison sentence of up to a year – the punishment which the Communist press had been clamouring for. Reporters and photographers were present in force. But it was all over in a few minutes, the proceedings enlivened only by a schoolboy howler on Koestler's part.

When the president of the court asked him if he had had too much to drink, Koestler (whose normal daily language had long been English) replied '*C'est correct*' – which in French means 'that's good behaviour.' 'On the contrary,' said the president smiling; 'hitting a police officer is not at all good behaviour!'

At this Maître Torrès leapt to his feet. 'My client meant to say "*c'est exact*". He was using an English expression.' He went on to remind the court that 'Arthur Koestler has known the horrors of prisons too well not to become a little disturbed by waking up in the jug.'

Koestler apologised and the court, after a brief deliberation, fined him 10,000 francs (£10).

The French press did what they could with the story – *Après 'Le Zéro et L'Infini' – le zéro de conduite; Le Yoghi rosse le Commissaire;* so the headlines ran.

The Communist press was not, of course, so good-humoured. 'Can you imagine a demonstrator who had struck a policeman getting away with a 10,000 fr. fine?' asked *L'Humanité*. 'Just imagine,' exclaimed *Droit et Liberté*, having berated Koestler as a '*juif antisémite*', 'what would have happened to an ordinary peace-fighter!'

* *

To celebrate the happy ending of the *histoire mi-cauchemar, mi-comédie* (as Koestler described the incident in a letter of thanks to Maître Torrès), he and Mamaine went off with Paul Willert and the Winklers on a sightseeing trip to Bourges and the Loire.

Spring had come early. The sun was shining. Koestler was in the best of moods. Mamaine, in good health again, was happy and vivacious, looking forward to the long-delayed wedding. When they returned to Verte Rive they found a packet of clippings among the mail – *The Gladiators* had recently been reissued and was, Mamaine noted, 'having *glänzende* reviews'. Everything was going well for them both.

'Oh life is wonderful these days,' Mamaine wrote on 28th March; and indeed all her writing at this time reflects vividly that combination of intellectual curiosity and country-girl simplicity which endeared her to all who knew her and which seldom failed to lift Koestler's spirits, even when the threatening clouds hanging low over the political scene tempted him to brood on that question which Malraux had put to him at their first meeting in 1937:

'. . . mais que pensez-vous de l'Apocalypse?'

Koestler's divorce from Dorothy came through at long last. Mamaine could scarcely believe it.

> 'I have fixed for us to be married at the British Consulate in Paris today fortnight, April 15, in the morning. So I think we really have made it . . . I am really getting almost superstitious after all the setbacks and delays we have had. We have given up the idea of having a party, and personally I feel no urge to do so, *au contraire* . . .'

At eleven o'clock in the morning of 18th April, Koestler and Mamaine were married at the British Consulate, their friends the Winklers acting as witnesses. The protracted celebrations that followed culminated in another incident that may also be fittingly described as *mi-cauchemar, mi-comique*.

After the ceremony, Mamaine recorded:

> 'We went and drank some champagne and then went for lunch to a wonderful restaurant near the abattoirs called Le Cochon d'Or. Here we had a really terrific lunch which we all enjoyed no end. We stayed in Paris for the afternoon and had a rather peculiar evening with Stephen Spender and a married couple called Berlier, the woman of which is American and an ex-girl-friend of Stephen's – she was very nice; we all had dinner together at the Oanette. K was fairly plastered (we had been drinking at the Flore with these people, A. Calder-Marshall, an American woman, and a frightfully *louche* German Communist, ex-comrade of K's, whom for some reason K got very sentimental about, much to everybody else's embarrassment and boredom).
>
> 'I enjoyed the evening because I do like Spender (he had been down to lunch with us the day before, and even K thought him very nice), but a typical incident occurred at the end of dinner, which was, that M. Berlier . . . took offence at one of K's drunken remarks and walked out in a huff, dragging his wife with him, leaving K staring wide-eyed as he had simply no idea what the whole thing was about. The fact was, that he had been teasing the nice Mrs Berlier about something and wanted to say to her husband "*vous n'y êtes pour rien*", but instead of this he said "*quant à vous, vous ne comptez pas*", which of course infuriated Monsieur B.
>
> 'We then went on to the Saint Yves, which is now a *boîte chantante*, as Cynthia, who was with us, said it was fun; but K didn't like it and wanted to go

to the Lapin Agile. Here the 2nd typical incident occurred, for I knew full well that if we did this K would insist on driving there and back, and felt that drunk as he was I simply couldn't face such a long drive with him at the wheel, so I started to procrastinate, at which K walked off himself. Stephen, Cynthia and I followed soon after, saw K sitting in his car, he said "I'm going home, are you coming?" I said yes if you let me drive, and at this, as foreseen, he drove off, so Cynthia and I spent the night with Stephen in a flat which had been lent to him.

'It was lucky Cynthia was there as otherwise I should have had to go to a hotel which is a bore after midnight if one hasn't got a room. Sunday morning Cynthia went off early and I had breakfast in a café on the *quais* with Stephen and went with him to see an exhibition of German primitives at the Orangerie. (He said: "I've always wanted to spend the night with you, it's too bad it was your wedding night"). For some reason this was quite extraordinarily nice; Stephen is so easy to talk to and one can talk to him about anything . . .

'The fact is, that unfortunately K is at present having one of his "mad fits", and has been for some time; it is the first one since we were in Palestine. This makes him very unpleasant, and is the reason why whenever we go to Paris he gets stinking and behaves abominably.'

On her return to Verte Rive, Mamaine found Koestler 'very remorseful and full of self-loathing'. Why was it, he asked her, that whenever they went out in the evening he got drunk, in spite of the resolution he had made after the 'painful incident' at Charenton? But Mamaine understood very well the strains and stresses that stretched his temper so often at this time to breaking point. His novel *The Age of Longing* was still unfinished; his old scientific obsessions were beginning to reassert themselves; his genuine desire for a life of tranquil domesticity with Mamaine was at odds with his nostalgia for the free and easy days of promiscuity before the war; and he was a public figure at the centre of fierce controversy. It is not surprising that he should have been 'in an awful state of nerves' during those days.

Koestler, as always, judged himself ruthlessly. Mamaine did not judge him at all: she was content to accept him as he was, knowing what lay behind those 'mad fits'. Not that she was meek and submissive when he saw fit to pick a quarrel. She was capable of giving as good as she got, and then letting off steam at her typewriter. But her true feeling for Koestler she expressed movingly in a note which immediately followed the description of a particularly ferocious row.

'In fact I am awfully happy with K simply because I do love him so much, not a day goes by without my thinking what happiness it is for me to be with him. As a matter of fact whatever happens to me from now on – and I have no reason to suppose that anything awful will – I shall consider my life has been well spent since I have spent six years of it with K. For apart from anything else I greatly believe in K as a writer, and I would do anything, even leave him, if it were necessary to help him fulfil what I believe to be his destiny. I should count myself and my life of little importance in such a case.'

Koestler quickly recovered from his 'mad fit'. They had decided that when he had got the novel into more or less final shape he should go off by himself to the Pyrenees, there to regain in solitude his equilibrium. As it turned out, there was no need for such an eremitical remedy. Instead, he and Mamaine went off to explore Alsace – a trip which they both greatly enjoyed.

If Mamaine had any worries about her relationship with Koestler, or her health, she did not record them at this time. Now that she was married, a slightly more housewifely note makes itself heard:

> 'Imagine the expense of life here: in the last few weeks – having had quite a lot of guests – we have been spending an average of 30,000 frs. (£30) a week on housekeeping alone, excluding heating, telephone, light and all extras; yet we don't live luxuriously by French standards, eat only rice or macaroni or eggs etc for lunch, don't buy much fruit, and hardly ever any *charcuterie*, and I haven't been drinking at all during this period. It really is too awful . . .'

# PART FOUR

# *1950–1954*

# CHAPTER XXII

# *1950*

BEHIND THE SHAKY FAÇADE of Western unity, with all its easily penetrated gaps and cracks, an epidemic of moral flabbiness was spreading thoughout the intellectual community. A marked symptom of this malaise was the increasing readiness (anxiety in some cases) to avert the gaze from the huge chancrous ulcers on the menacing face of the Soviet Union and peer through a magnifying glass at the comparatively insignificant blemishes on the bodies politic of Western societies. This was especially true of vaguely 'progressive' academics and scientists (and even of many Protestant clerics, of the type later to be described as 'trendy'), many of whom seemed inclined to the view that 'capitalism' – and, above all, American 'capitalism' – was even more to blame for the dangerous state of the post-war world than Communism. (A fairly good case for this argument could be made out, of course, on the basis of the ailing Roosevelt's infamous sell-out to Stalin at Yalta and its disastrous political and strategic consequences; but this was not what the 'progressives' of 1950 had in mind.)

Throughout the various opinion-forming communities of the West there existed an undeniable tendency to avoid the main issue of survival and concentrate inquiry and discussion on whatever seemed necessary to put liberal democracy's admittedly imperfect house in order, while ignoring or minimising Communism's messianic determination to see the structure razed to the ground and rebuilt in its own jailhouse image. Through its 'peace' campaigns, skilfully mounted and orchestrated by Cominform 'fronts' (which had little difficulty in recruiting eminent dupes, who failed to realise the Newspeak significance of the word 'peace' in this connexion), the Soviet Union was exploiting this situation with a good deal of success. In some respects its success in this field posed a greater threat in the long term than its tireless subversive activities among Western trades unions and Socialist parties.

How could this be countered? This, as we have seen, was the question that had long exercised Koestler. For many years it had been the dominant theme of his political writing. How could those who created the climate of opinion in the

West be brought together, induced to sink for the moment their relatively petty differences, persuaded to look the evil of Communism in the face, and, whatever their reservations about the existing order in their own societies, to demonstrate loudly and clearly their determination to stand firm for 'relative freedom against absolute tyranny'?

During his lecture tour of the United States he had laboured hard to disabuse the 'Babbits of the Left' of their deadly naïve illusions and to instil into the less blinkered 'liberals' the courage of their liberal convictions. His strenuous arguments had naturally attracted the attention of American officials whose chief concern was the countering of Soviet influence, direct or disguised, among influential individuals and institutions in Western Europe. In New York City, it will be recalled, he had had a long and apparently satisfactory talk with General William J. Donovan, who had directed the Office of Strategic Services under Roosevelt, and later, under Truman, presided over its transformation into the Central Intelligence Agency. His advocacy of more intelligent, vigorous, and effective psychological warfare in defence of western values and interests, as opposed to the panicky whipping up of war hysteria, had greatly impressed Donovan (as it later impressed the officials whom Koestler met in Washington – rather more, it would appear, than the knowledge and intellectual quality of some of those officials had impressed Koestler). It had also impressed James Burnham, an influential convert to anti-totalitarianism whose works Koestler admired and who became a close friend and associate. Burnham, Professor of Philosophy at New York University, was a knowledgeable and valued consultant to the Office of Policy Coordination, the division of the Central Intelligence Agency responsible for organising, financing, and administering (in close liaison with certain European intelligence services, and especially the British) the counter-offensive against Communist penetration in Western Europe.

Koestler's ideas were shared by a few intellectuals untainted by the prevailing moral timidity and pusillanimity, and by none more keenly than those ex-Communists like himself who had looked into the heart of darkness and understood the supreme importance of mobilising informed public opinion without creating a war-hysteria – and who rejected the desperate idea of a pre-emptive nuclear strike against the Soviet Union that had been advocated by some (and supported for a time by Bertrand Russell).

Among the most vehement of them was Ruth Eisler (alias Fischer, under which name she had published her authoritative account of the Comintern's cynical manipulation and betrayal of the German Communist Party, *Stalin and German Communism*), whom Koestler describes as 'probably the most brilliant woman in Communist history'. She and her two brothers, Gerhard and Hanns, the three children of an eminent Viennese sociologist, were indeed a remarkable and repellent trio. Koestler had known them all during his Communist days in Berlin, and Gerhard later at Le Vernet.*

Ruth ('a short, stout woman,' in Koestler's description, 'with an explosive temperament'), a ferocious revolutionary in the Luxemburg mould, had

* see p. 54 above.

been one of the leading founders of the Austrian Communist party. Later, in the Weimar Republic, she became chairman of the Berlin Communist Party, a Reichstag deputy – and, honour of honours, a member of the Comintern praesidium until Stalin had her removed because of her 'left deviationism' (ie, 'revolutionary internationalism' as advocated by Trotsky, Zinoviev, Kamenev and the like) as opposed to Stalin's theory of 'Socialism in one country'.

One of Ruth's brothers, Gerhard, was also a member of what Koestler describes as the 'high Comintern aristocracy'. He too incurred Stalin's displeasure – his heresy, however, as opposed to his sister's, being 'right deviationism' (ie, a belief in 'moderation' vis-à-vis the peasants and industrialisation, as advocated by Bukharin, Rykov, Tomsky, and other such opponents of 'leftists' in the Leninist-Trotskyist tradition). Unlike Ruth, however, he succeeded in crawling back into Stalin's good books – and to such an extent that he had the honour of being sent by the Comintern in 1929 (after Stalin had defeated all his opponents and established himself as the absolute and undisputed tyrant of all the Russias) to China. There he assisted Chiang Kai-shek and his Nationalist Party to liquidate (ie, to massacre) the Chinese 'leftist' Communists in Shanghai who were in rebellion against the Stalin-Chiang Pact of 1927 (a forerunner, as Koestler points out in *The Invisible Writing*, of the Stalin-Hitler Pact twelve years later and the subsequent collaboration of the NKVD and the Gestapo). During 1940, in the French concentration camp of Le Vernet, Koestler met him for the last time. Gerhard had been playing a key Comintern role in France, persuading the French Communists to stick to the Stalin line and sabotage the war effort. It is remarkable that the French authorities did not summarily dispose of this venomous Stalinist spy and *agent provocateur*.

Gerhard's ruthlessness in the Stalinist service, and in particular his brilliant success in liquidating the 'deviationist' Communists in Shanghai, inspired his brother Hanns – a revolutionary composer whom some considered superior to Kurt Weill – to collaborate with Bertolt Brecht in the production of *Die Massnahme*, a *Lehrstück*, or 'didactic piece' entitled in its English translation *The Punitive Measure*. As to which of the two – Eisler and Weill – was the more gifted of Brecht's musical collaborators in his works of Communist propaganda, I am not competent to judge. But I am in no doubt that there is little to choose between them, and Brecht for that matter, as moral gangsters – in certain respects more dangerous than, say, the apolitical gangsters of Sicilian and Neapolitan extraction then active in the United States (which, in its innocence, offered refuge to all three Eislers as well as to the odious Brecht). *Die Massnahme* is a peculiarly revolting hymn of unswerving obedience to the Communist Party Line, however monstrous the means employed to secure the end required by the Leader. Koestler did not exaggerate when he remarked that it reads like 'a glorification of the anti-Christ'.

Unlike her brothers, however, Ruth Eisler, following her excommunication by Stalin, progressed by way of a vehement Trotskyist anti-Stalinism to an even more vehement outright anti-Communism. Whether prompted or not by cooler heads, she was one of those who helped to prepare the ground for the kind of action Koestler had been advocating, although she had to be kept well in the background in order to avoid frightening off the more timid among the 'confused liberals'. Among those whom she consulted were Melvin J. Lasky, a young American ex-leftist writer employed by the US Military Government in Berlin to edit the anti-Communist German-language monthly, *Der Monat*; Franz Borkenau, another historian of the Comintern; and Koestler himself. Following a meeting with Lasky and certain others in Frankfurt-am-Main during August 1949, she wrote a memorandum for circulation in the appropriate quarters, urging the organisation of a demonstration in Berlin which would open a full-scale counter-offensive against the Soviet Union's propaganda onslaught. Whether or not this memorandum is the seed that grew into the Congress for Cultural Freedom is a question that must for the moment remain unanswered. Certainly the copy of it in Koestler's archives is the earliest reference in writing which I have seen.

Ruth Eisler's 'explosive temperament' can be felt in her proposals that:

> 'The congress should: 1) proclaim the liberation of Europe and Russia from the Stalinist party-dictatorship; 2) fight openly against the Russian system because of its imperialistic and totalitarian character; 3) emphasise the friendship with all Russian liberation movements inside and outside the country.'

Such a 'declaration of war' would be quite enough, she added, for there was no point in wordy speculations about the nature of a post-Stalinist future. What was absolutely essential was to hold the Congress in Berlin ('at the very doorstep of Russia') and ensure its maximum impact 'by the presence of ex-Communist personalities from all quarters who would use their experiences in addressing themselves to the Stalinists'.

* *

The translation of the idea into action was put in the deft hands of the late Michael Josselson, at that time a senior cultural official serving with the US Military Government in Berlin.* His superiors agreed that, given the consent of the courageous *Burgermeister* of Berlin, Ernst Reuter, the United States would finance the operation. After some months of delicate negotiations, during which a number of prominent writers and academics and anti-totalitarian trades union leaders had agreed to lend their support, Reuter, in the spring of 1950, proposed publicly a great demonstration in the Western sector of Berlin – an island of freedom behind the Iron Curtain – at which a representative gathering of democratic intellectuals would show their solidarity with the beleaguered Berliners. Melvin J. Lasky was appointed executive secretary. An international

*Josselson unhappily did not live to see the publication of his biography of Barclay de Tolly, the Russian general of Scottish-Lithuanian extraction, whose part in the expulsion of Napoleon's *Grande Armée* from Russia has been overshadowed by Tolstoy's adulatory depiction of Prince Koutouzov in *War and Peace*.

committee was formed and honorary chairmen appointed.* Invitations were sent out. The rally was set for the week 24th to the 26th June.

* *

In fact, as his diaries show very clearly, much of the strategic planning was formulated by Koestler in Verte Rive, as witness the following jottings:

> 'Raymond Aron and James Burnham came for talks to prepare Berlin Congress which already riddled with usual jealousies and muddle. Proposed some time ago creation of "Free Europe Anthem" by Benjamin Britten and Louis MacNeice. Of course, nothing came of it . . .
>
> 'Wrote under great difficulty . . . two speeches for Berlin Congress . . .
>
> 'The Berlin Congress (starting next Monday) is driving me crazy. The organiser's fantastically inefficient; D. a French literary hack whom we engaged as Press agent has vanished after extracting 20,000 francs advance; and so on . . .
>
> 'As Burnham cabled: "Can amateurs inherit the world?"'

* *

Arrived in Berlin, Koestler soon sailed fiercely into battle. He had heard that Gerhard Eisler, now the chief East German propagandist, had been describing the delegates to the Congress as 'American police spies and literary apes'. So, when an interviewer from Berlin radio arrived to record Koestler's first impressions, he went for his former friend in 'vulgar *Berlinisch*'.

> 'We are happy to welcome you back to Berlin,' said the radio interviewer to Koestler, 'where you no doubt have many old memories. What, do you feel, is the importance of this Congress for Cultural Freedom?'
>
> 'I feel,' Koestler replied, 'that our Congress works not only for cultural freedom but also for peace. Nowadays, the word peace is used in a sense that is as different from the original one as faked currencies are from the real ones. It is a sort of black market way with words. And words are dangerous.'

Did Koestler think that the Congress was going to have a special importance for the people beyond the Iron Curtain?

> 'I hope that it will be of importance. It does seem to me that the way my ex-friend Gerhard Eisler reacted to the news about our Congress proves that his people are afraid. I have just seen a press cutting in which Eisler calls us literary apes and spies for the American secret police. When these people start using that sort of language, it always means they are afraid. Are you by any chance listening, Gerhard? Do you remember when we were together in

* The committee consisted of Julian Amery, Irving Brown, Margareta Buber-Neumann, James Burnham, Josef Czapski, Sidney Hook, Arthur Koestler, Eugen Kogon, Karel Kupka, Haakon Lie, Nicolas Nabokov, Boris I. Nicolaevsky, André Philip, Theodor Plivier, Herbert Read, Denis de Rougemont, David Rousset, Carlo Schmidt, and Ignazio Silone. The eminent philosophers who lent their weighty moral support in the capacity of honorary chairmen were Benedetto Croce, Salvador de Madariaga, Karl Jaspers, John Dewey, Jacques Maritain, and Bertrand Russell.

the concentration camp of Le Vernet, in France, in 1940? We were carrying shitbags to and from the latrines, and you asked me what I would do once freed, and I said: "I'll join the Army to fight against National Socialism". You laughed in my face and said "You are a hopeless, petit bourgeois romantic". I suppose you have changed your opinion again, and will change it once more. But what you said about us, about our Congress, shows that you are still trembling, you poor dogs, as soon as the word "freedom" is pronounced.'*

At the Congress, all shades of opinion were represented, from the extreme conservatism of certain American participants to the utopianism of the left-wing (but non-totalitarian) social democrats of western Europe. There were also those who tended to be extremely cagey about anything that might be regarded as excessive provocation to Stalinist Russia. So far as all the invited members were anti-totalitarian, they were on the side of the angels; but they were, most of them, each in his own sphere, men of eminence, of strong personality and equally strong convictions. The task of organising a programme that would both allow them all to express their opinions and yet in the end arrive at an impressive degree of unanimity must indeed have been a daunting one. From almost the first moment of his arrival Koestler became the dominant figure both in public (when the full force of his rhetoric was unleashed) and, even more so, behind the scenes.

By lunchtime on Sunday, the atmosphere, already tense, had been heightened by the news coming through of the Communists' invasion of South Korea. Stalin, stalemated for the moment in the West, obviously intended to test the Americans' resolution by proxy in the East. Could this lead to the third World War?

On Sunday evening Koestler got down to business with fellow committee members Sidney Hook, James Burnham, Irving Brown,† and Melvin Lasky. They agreed to form themselves into an unofficial steering committee, to meet every night and plan the tactics for the sessions of the following day. He insisted that the Congress press officer should redraft his plans, to ensure that the Congress's various sessions would be properly reported in the press and on radio. He also produced the draft manifesto, which he had some time before roughed out on his own initiative, for distribution among all the members of the Congress.

Koestler's conspiratorial experience gained during his membership of the Communist Party was proving very useful. He knew how he wanted the Congress to end, and he was determined to have his way. He knew that without a very tight organisation behind the scenes, manipulating each day's events, the Congress would probably fizzle out in a welter of confused generalisations. Also, he had no intention of allowing the work of the Congress to end with the speeches that would be made at the last public meeting.

It seems to have been a fairly stormy meeting that Sunday night, with Sidney Hook and Irving Brown backing Koestler strongly, and Burnham tending to move off the main point. When Mamaine got back to the hotel after midnight,

* See pages 54–55 above.

† Roving ambassador of the powerful American Federation of Labour.

she found 'K. still making politics with Irving Brown at the bar, also Arthur J. Schlesinger Jr., and [Saul] Levitas; bed 2.30'.

Koestler had already prepared the speech that he was to deliver at the first public meeting on the Monday afternoon in the Titania Palast, but on Monday morning, in the light of the news coming through from Korea, he rewrote it and had it typed in German and English for circulation. In the meantime the other members of the Congress who could read German, and especially the 'confused liberals' among them, were pondering the way in which the newspapers in the Eastern Zone of Berlin were dealing with the news from Korea. According to the Communist press, the North Koreans had embarked on a glorious war of liberation of their fellow countrymen against the malignant puppets of American imperialism.

Not far from the Titania Palast, in the Soviet sector, a huge 'peace meeting' had been held and attended by many thousands. There John Peet, an Englishman who had formerly been the Reuter correspondent in Berlin and who had gone across to the Communists, made a ferocious speech against the Congress. From the platform he denounced his former press colleagues who were present to report the meeting, while the frenzied audience of Nazis-turned-Communist screamed 'hang them!' 'to the gas chamber with them!' and similar pleasantries.

The Koestlers finished their work on the speech just in time for a quick lunch before the opening meeting at three o'clock in the Titania Palast.

Mamaine noted:

'Took along Herbert Read who'd just arrived from England and had lost his ticket for the meeting. Speakers: Reuter, Silone, Rousset, K., Hook, Czapski, Kanellopoulos, Alfred Weber, and Haakon Lie. Orchestra behind speakers played *Egmont* at the beginning and *Leonora* at the end. In spite of great heat, audience listened attentively even to long rather academic speech largely about German guilt, by old Weber, and to all the other speeches, of which some (especially Rousset and Silone's) were very poor. Great enthusiasm for K.'s speech; he and Silone seemed to be the popular heroes so far. K., got down by the heat, took off his jacket and spoke in shirt sleeves.'

* *

'Since the earliest days,' Koestler said, 'the teachers of mankind have recommended two diametrically opposed methods of action. The first demands that we should refuse to see the world divided into black and white, heroes and villains, friends and foes; that we should distinguish nuances, and strive for synthesis or at least compromise; it tells us that in nearly all seemingly inescapable dilemmas there exists a third alternative which patient search may discover. In short, we should refuse the choice between Scylla and Charybdis and rather navigate like Odysseus of the nimble wits. We may call this the "neither-nor" attitude.

'The second, opposite advice was summed up two thousand years ago in one single phrase: "Let your communication be, Yea, yea, Nay, nay; for whatsoever is more than these, comes from evil." This we may call the "either-or" attitude.

'Obviously humanity could not have survived without taking both methods into account. By neglecting the first advice, men would long ago have torn each other to pieces. By neglecting the second, man would have forsaken his dignity and moral backbone, and lost his capacity to distinguish between good and evil.

'It is equally obvious that each of the two tenets has a different field of application. To enumerate these would be a tedious and pedantic undertaking, and frequently there is conflict between both methods within the same field. Our concern here is with action in the political field. And there it seems that the first method is valid for long-term planning with a certain elbow-room in space and time, and that the second is valid in immediate and vital emergencies when, in Beethoven's words, "Fate knocks at the gate of existence".

'In such an emergency, the threatened individual or group or civilisation can only survive if it acts with the unhesitating assurance of an organic reflex. The nerves of all living organisms function according to the so-called all-or-nothing law; they either react to a stimulus for all they are worth or do not react at all. And it is not by chance that the calculating machines called electronic brains are constructed according to the same "either-or" principle. They perform immensely complex functions, but each time a decision is required of them, they act according to the Gospel of Matthew.

'In vital emergencies like the present, when man stands at a crossroads which only leaves the choice of this way or that, the difference between the very clever and the simple in mind narrows almost to vanishing point or even turns to the latter's advantage. It is amazing to observe how in a crisis the most sophisticated often act like imbeciles. Imbued with the mental habits of the "neither-nor" attitude, of looking for synthesis or compromise – a profoundly human attitude of essential value in its proper field – they are incapable of admitting, even to themselves, that there are situations in which an unambiguous decision is vital for spiritual and physical survival. Faced with destiny's challenge, they act like clever imbeciles and preach neutrality towards the bubonic plague. Mostly they are victims of a professional disease: the intellectual's estrangement from reality. And having lost touch with reality they have acquired that devilish art: they can prove everything that they believe, and believe everything that they can prove. Their logic reminds one of the German student's old nonsense song:

*The elephant has his tail in front and his trunk*
*is at his rear; But when he turns round his trunk*
*is in front and his tail is at his rear.*

'Don't misunderstand me: I know that many of those who are not here with us today cherish freedom too, and are rather frightened of the fate which might befall them if everybody imitated their attitude of contemplative detachment. It is only that they haven't yet learnt that there is a time to speak in relative clauses and a time to speak in terms of Yea and Nay. For destiny's challenge to man is always couched in simple and direct language, without relative clauses – and requires an answer in equally simple terms.'

Mamaine noted:

'Great applause when he said: "Let their communication be Yea, yea, Nay, nay."'

* *

On Tuesday morning Koestler attended the social-science panel of the Congress. During the session there was a curious incident. Professor Thirring, the Viennese atomic scientist, a naïve member of the Cominform-inspired 'Peace' movement had prepared and circulated a paper in which, while appealing to the Soviet Union to end the cold war, he accused Western intellectuals of adding fuel to the flames. He had not believed that the Soviet Union could possibly take part in military aggression. Shaken however by the news from Korea, and having been subjected to the attentions of Sidney Hook and Koestler the night before, he withdrew his paper.

The low-key interventions by A. J. Ayer and Trevor-Roper were not well received. They were concerned to debate the niceties of choice open to man within relatively free societies rather than the possibly demoralising effects of such debate in the light of the Communist threat. But Koestler's view – that the overwhelming issue was simply the defence of relative freedom, whatever form it took, against absolute tyranny – was clearly gaining ground.

After lunch, Koestler visited the headquarters of the *Kampfgruppe gegen Unmenschlichkeit*, where he was much impressed. He found that they had files covering the individual activities of some 44,000 Communists and informers in the Eastern Sector of Berlin, and also card indices detailing the fate of 27,000 people who had been arrested in the East Zone. According to the *Kampfgruppe*'s statistics, there was a mortality rate of 80 per cent in the Soviet controlled concentration-camps.

* *

The unofficial steering committee's meeting that night was held at Lasky's house in Zehlendorf. The main topic of the discussion was the manifesto which Koestler had already drafted, and by four o'clock in the morning he had persuaded them to approve it. Three hours later he was out of bed rewriting the manifesto yet again, and translating it into German and French. By one o'clock in the afternoon he had finished the job, and Sidney Hook had persuaded Silone to agree to the wording. In the afternoon there was a meeting of the political panel, chaired by *Burgermeister* Reuter at which the main speakers were André Philip, Haakon Lie, James Burnham, and Koestler.

In the light of the international situation three decades later, it is unnecessary to apologise for reproducing Koestler's speech *in extenso*:

'The thesis which I wish to put before you,' said Koestler, 'is that the antinomies "Socialism and Capitalism", "Left and Right", are rapidly becoming meaningless, and that so long as Europe remains bogged down in these false alternatives which obstruct clear thinking, it cannot hope to find a constructive solution for its problems.

'The term "Political Left" originated, as you know, with the distribution of factions in the French National Assembly after the Revolution in 1789. At the beginning of the nineteenth century it spread over the Continent and was applied to that section of a country's legislature which sat to the left of the President's chair and was traditionally associated with liberal and democratic opinions. Gradually, the word came to mean the radical or purist or extremist wing of any ideological school or movement, whether liberal and democratic or not. Later on it was used in an even more vague and metaphorical way; and the more it was drained of meaning, the stronger became its emotional appeal. At the beginning of the last war there existed about half a dozen political parties in France, all of them conservative to reactionary in their programme, all of them seated in the right wing of the Chamber, and all of them carrying the word "Left" in their names.

'I mention this development as a semantic curiosity and because of its relevance to the present situation. For to this day European Liberals and Social-Democrats refer to themselves as "the moderate Left" which, if words are to be taken seriously, must mean that they differ only in degree but not in kind from their neighbours of "the extreme Left". And "the extreme Left" is still regarded as synonymous with the Communist Party, in spite of the fact that virtually every tenet in the Communist credo is diametrically opposed to the principles originally associated with the Left. In short, the term "Left" has become a verbal fetish whose cult sidetracks attention from the real issues. It is at the same time a dangerous anachronism, for it implies the existence of a continuous spectrum between liberal progressives and the worshippers of tyranny and terror, and such is the magic power of words over the mind that European Socialists who think of themselves as "men of the Left" were unconsciously led from a fallacious verbal identification to a real feeling of solidarity with the Communists. They may feel critical or even hostile towards their "extreme" neighbours of the Communist Party; they retain nevertheless an ambivalent neighbourly feeling for them, a conviction of "having the same historical roots", of being, after all, "on the same side of the barricades".

'A good many American liberals fell into the same emotional trap during the thirties and even later. The victim of the witch-hunt supplied the whip which scourged him and became an accomplice in his own perdition. However, the relative safety and prosperity of that continent made the confused American liberal gradually accessible to reality and enabled him to get out of the trap, while a major portion of the French and Italian Left, and a smaller portion of the British, exposed to the neurosis-forming climate of Europe, have remained in it.

'In the past it was always "the Left" who protested loudest against tyranny, injustice, and infringements of human rights. The failure of European "Leftists" and American liberals to lead the fight against the worst regime of terror and despotism in human history created a strategic vacuum on the ideological battlefield. This vacuum was filled by the Christian Democrats in Italy, the Gaullists in France, by Senator McCarthy and his associates in the U.S.A. McCarthyism represents the wages of the American liberal's sins. If today everywhere in the world the parties who claim to represent the "moderate Left" are beaten or in retreat, it is because they were found wanting in the most crucial issue of our time.

'Europe has developed a political climate in which words are no longer taken seriously. The ideological chaos created a semantic inflation and a semantic black market where words are traded at a meaning-value entirely different from their official quotation: where war is prepared by peace petitions, police states are labelled popular democracies, and "Leftism" means benevolent neutrality towards despotism.

'At first sight the alternative "Capitalism or Socialism" appears much more concrete and meaningful than "Right or Left". But on closer inspection it will be found that the term "Socialism" has suffered a semantic decay similar to that of the "Left". German National Socialism, Russian Soviet Socialism, French Socialism which is Marxist with a pinch of salt, British Socialism which is Christian, non-Marxist, Fabianist, and heaven knows what, all derive their emotional dynamism from the fetish-power of the same word, attached to quite different meanings.

'However, let us leave semantics aside, though it is an essential branch of political hygiene. If we are not too pedantic, we may hope to agree at least on some rough-and-ready definition of what Socialism really means and on some common denominator for the aspirations of the various existing Socialist parties.

'Let us turn first to the field of *international* politics. One of the basic elements of Socialist thought, from Spartacus' slave revolt to Thomas More's Utopia, from the primitive Christian communities to Marx, is the brotherhood of man. In the past, Socialists have always fought against parochialism, chauvinism, aggressive nationalism and have preached internationalism, cosmopolitanism, the abolition of ideological and political barriers among nations. But do they still?

'In the Union of Soviet Socialist Republics the word "cosmopolitan" has become a term of abuse, and chauvinism has reached a hitherto unprecedented peak. At the same time at the recent Paris Congress of the French Communist Party a banner was stretched across the hall which read: "The true internationalist is he who is prepared unreservedly, unhesitatingly, and unconditionally to defend the U.S.S.R." So much for the Russian version of Socialist internationalism.

'In the Western world the only great power with a Socialist Government is Great Britain. The Labour Party won the elections a few weeks after the end of the war in the still strongest country of Europe, and just at the decisive moment when it no longer needed a Socialist training to understand that Europe must unite or perish. Never before in history was Socialism offered such a chance. Yet from the moment it came to power, the Labour

Government has deliberately obstructed every effort towards European unity. The non-Socialist Governments of France, Germany and Italy have proved themselves more internationally minded than the Socialist Government in England.

'Of course Britain has a particularly difficult position between the Continent and the Commonwealth; and there are always plausible arguments for avoiding decisions which would require a certain amount of historical imagination. But the essential point is that the victory of British Socialism has not abolished British insularity; it has, on the contrary, strengthened and deepened it. It was Churchill the Conservative, not Attlee the Socialist, who started the United Europe movement which led to the Council of Strasbourg; and when the movement got under way, the Labour Party's attitude to it remained consistently hostile. The reason for this was explained in a statement by the National Executive Committee of the Labour Party issued in June, 1950. "No Socialist government in Europe", the decisive phrase in the statement runs, "could submit to the authority of a [supranational] body whose policies were decided by an anti-Socialist majority."

'What this amounts to is simply a mild British version of the Russian "Socialism in One Country" policy. The Russian veto in the United Nations finds its equivalent in the British veto against the political and economic unity of Europe.

'It need not be emphasised that there is a world of difference between the British and the Soviet regimes. My comparison refers merely to one specific aspect: the collapse of the cosmopolitan élan in the Socialist movement. This process started almost a generation ago, in 1914, and has now reached a stage where we can see the paradoxical phenomenon of capitalist America being prepared to make sacrifices in national sovereignty which Socialist Russia refuses, and of British, French, and German Conservatives pursuing a more internationally-minded policy than their Socialist opposite numbers. In other words, *Socialism has lost its claim to represent the international trend of humanity*. As far as the integration of our world is concerned, the Socialist-Capitalist alternative has become void of meaning.

'Is it meaningful when applied to *domestic* policy?

'As regards political and intellectual freedom, there is no relevant difference between Socialist Britain and the capitalist United States. And in the domain of unfreedom there is little to choose between Socialist Russia and Fascist Spain. Again the real division cuts across the abstract frontiers between Socialism and Capitalism. Only one field remains where the alternative is apparently still relevant: the economic field.

'Theoretically there is an unbridgeable gulf between nationalism of the means of production on the one hand, and private ownership, profits, and exploitation on the other. But in fact recent developments have abolished the static trench-warfare between the classes and have transformed it into a fluid war of movement. As the question is too complex to be treated here in any systematic manner, I must confine myself to a few remarks in shorthand, as it were.

'First, even Marx and Engels knew that nationalisation itself is not a panacea. It is useful to recall Frederick Engels' remark that if nationalisation were identical with Socialism, then the first Socialist institution must have been the regimental tailor. In fact, the Soviet workers do not own their nationalised factories any more than a sailor of the Royal Navy owns the battleship in which he serves. The people's control over the battleships, railways, factories, coal mines, which they theoretically own, depends entirely on the political structure of the state. In Russia, where the Trades Unions have ceased to be an instrument of the working class and have become an instrument for the coercion of the working class, the theoretical owners of the factories and of the land have less influence over management, and work under worse conditions, than their comrades in any Western country. On the other hand, trust managers, factory directors, and "proletarian millionaires" (an official Russian term) form a privileged class, just as much as and more so, than in Capitalist countries. To be sure, their income is called salary and not profit, but again this distinction is merely abstract. Nor is, on the other hand, the factory owner in Capitalist countries any longer able to draw unlimited profits from his enterprise or do with his workers what he likes. I refer you to James Burnham's analysis in *The Managerial Revolution* of the relevant changes in the meaning of the term "ownership" in recent times.

'Generally speaking, nationalisation without an appropriate change in political structure leads not to State Socialism but to State Capitalism. The difference between the two cannot be defined in economic terms; it is a matter of democratic controls, of political freedom, and cultural climate. A nationalised economy in itself may serve as a basis for a totalitarian autocracy of the Russian type or even for a Fascist regime.

'Equally problematic is the question just how much nationalisation makes a country socialist or capitalist? British Socialism nationalised the railways, but France and Germany had state-owned railways long before. The total nationalisation of all means of production and distribution has been recognised as unworkable even in Russia. The alternative is no longer nationalisation or private economy in the abstract; the real problem is to find the proper balance of state ownership, control, planning, and free enterprise. And the search for this delicate balance is again not an abstract but an empirical pursuit. Apparently each nation has to work out its own formula, for there are many imponderabilia which enter into the equation.

'As an example of the complex reality masked by the "Capitalism versus Socialism" slogan, one may quote food-rationing. Food-rationing – which means state control of distribution – worked very satisfactorily in puritan England under Conservative and Socialist governments alike. But it broke down completely in Italy and France, both countries with a highly individualistic and resourceful Latin population. Obviously, far-reaching inferences must be drawn from this fact concerning the balance of state control and free enterprise appropriate to each of these countries. In short, even in the purely economic sphere we are not dealing with a clear-cut alternative between Capitalism and Socialism, but with a kind of continuous rainbow spectrum whose shape and colour are largely determined by psychological and other factors not contained in Socialist theory.

'What I have said should not be misinterpreted as an apology for Capitalism or as an attack on Socialism. My point is that this alternative is rapidly becoming as antiquated and meaningless as the dispute between Jansenists and Jesuits or the Wars of the Roses. Nor did I mean to say that it always was meaningless. I said it is becoming meaningless, because it operates with rigid nineteenth-century conceptions, and does not take into account new realities which have emerged since and new conflicts which cut across conventional boundaries.

'It is not a novelty in history that a real dilemma which once seemed all-important is gradually drained of its meaning and becomes a pseudo-dilemma as new historical realities emerge. People lost interest in waging wars of religion when national consciousness began to dawn on them. The conflict between Republicans and Monarchists went out of fashion when economic problems became all-important. The examples could be multiplied. Every period seems to have its specific conflict which polarises the world and serves as an ideological compass in the chaos – until history passes over it with a shrug and afterwards people wonder what they were so excited about.

'It is a further fact that some of these great ideological conflicts are never decided; they end in a stalemate. In successive centuries it looked as if the whole world would either become Islamic or Christian, either Catholic or Protestant, either Republican or Monarchist, either Capitalist or Socialist. But instead of a decision there came a deadlock and a process which one might call *the withering away of the dilemma*. The withering, or draining of meaning, always seems to be the result of some mutation in human consciousness accompanied by a shift of emphasis to an entirely different set of values – from religious consciousness to national consciousness to economic consciousness and so on.

'This "and so on" poses a problem which we are unable to answer with certainty. We cannot foretell the nature of the next mutation in the consciousness of the masses, nor the values which will emerge on the next higher level. But we may assume on the strength of past analogies that the battle-cries of economic man will appear to his successor just as sterile and pointless as the Wars of the Roses appear to us.

'Two short remarks in conclusion. First, it is necessary to qualify the statement that the apparently decisive conflicts of a given period tend to end in a stalemate and wither away. This did indeed happen in the past, but only in cases where the forces in the conflict were fairly balanced. Europe remained Christian because the Arabs never got to Paris and the Turks were beaten back at the ramparts of Vienna. There are other less-edifying examples of history solving its dilemmas. The conclusion is obvious.

'In the second place, though we cannot foresee the values and spiritual climate of post-economic man, certain conjectures are permissible. While the majority of Europeans are still hypnotised by the anachronistic battle-cries of Left and Right, Capitalism and Socialism, history has moved on to a new alternative, a new conflict which cuts across the old lines of division. The real content of this conflict can be summed up in one phrase: total tyranny against relative freedom. Sometimes I have a feeling in my bones that the terrible pressure which this conflict exerts on all humanity might perhaps represent a challenge, a biological stimulus as it were, which will release the new mutation of human consciousness; and that its content might be a new spiritual awareness, born of anguish and suffering, of the full meaning of freedom. And I don't mean by that, freedom from want, freedom from fear and the rest. Since the dawn of civilisation people have fought under the slogan of freedom; but it was always freedom from some particularly irksome oppression, freedom in a restricted, negative sense. I mean freedom in a much deeper and fuller sense than any we can conceive today, or see realised anywhere in organic nature. If that is the case, then we are indeed living in an interesting time, and the answer which we shall give to destiny's challenge is not without import for the future of our species.'

* *

After the speeches several people intervened, most of them attacking Koestler, some defending him. Borkenau created something of a sensation by saying he was glad that the Americans had sent troops into South Korea and thus avoided another Munich. At this Rousset protested loudly, at which there were many cries of "Hear! hear!" and much table-thumping from A. J. Ayer and Hugh Trevor-Roper. After some commotion, the meeting went on with speeches in defence of America's action by Schlesinger, Kogon, Lasky and Julian Amery.

In Mamaine's view (borne out by later events), Koestler's speech on the meaninglessness of Left and Right, and the withering away of such dilemmas in the face of the threat from the East, was the most effective. It was certainly the focal point of the Congress.

Mamaine had been sitting near Silone, who passed her a note saying: '*Arthur serait un bon député socialist Italien*.' Mamaine scribbled: '*Pourquoi?*' Silone replied with: '*Nous disons toujours: (a) Le vieux socialisme est moribunde* [sic]*; (b) Le Labour a trahi le socialisme.*'

* *

That evening Mamaine and Koestler went to hear *Fidelio*, and at the interval they ran into Rousset who laughed off his anti-American speech:

'After all,' he said, '*we* can't be the ones to declare war in Korea.'

After the opera, Koestler went off as usual to the steering committee, and contrived to get general agreement on the constitution of the organisation that he wished to see set up following the Berlin Congress, with an office in Berlin and one in Paris, and money to be raised to found intellectual reviews in various countries in order to counter the defeatism and neutralism gaining ground among the intelligentsia of the West. Koestler's determination was continuing to carry the day, but the ramblings of some of the other members of the steering committee were beginning to irritate him. On his return to the hotel, he told

Mamaine that the reason was that the only people with *real* political experience were himself and Irving Brown.

On Thursday morning Koestler went off early to a meeting to organise the great public demonstration gathering to be held that afternoon in the Funkturm Gardens, which was to culminate in the presentation of the Congress Manifesto. After a great deal of confusion, an editorial committee was appointed with Koestler as chairman. The only serious opposition to the manifesto came from A. J. Ayer and Hugh Trevor-Roper, but by one o'clock unanimous agreement had been achieved on all points, except one, of Koestler's draft. The exception read:

> 'Totalitarian ideologies which deny spiritual freedom do not enjoy the right to citizenship in the free Republic of the Spirit.'

Koestler's intention in drafting this sentence was somehow to distinguish between the rich and desirable diversity of opinions held and expressed in any free community and those intellectually dishonest and spiritually corrupt contributions made by totalitarian propagandists; but some members of the Committee, in particular Ayer and Trevor-Roper, held that this could be taken as advocating a witch-hunt against Communists, perhaps even a banning of Communist parties and a proscription of Communist and fellow-travelling literature. After a heated discussion it was agreed to submit the point to the editorial committee of the Congress in the afternoon.

Before this, however, there was a big luncheon party given by General Bourne, Commandant of the British Sector, for Koestler and Mamaine and the English members of the Congress, including three Members of Parliament – Julian Amery, Christopher Hollis, and Harold Davies. The officer who had arranged the luncheon had unfortunately forgotten to assign A. J. Ayer a place at the table, whereupon Ayer told him twice: 'I consider this extremely rude.' The same officer had put Koestler on General Bourne's right, which Koestler found embarrassing and liable to create further hostility to himself. The general's extreme Englishness amused cosmopolitan Koestler.

> 'He is a one-armed sweet old boy,' he jotted in his diary, 'who, as Peter Tennant (now political adviser in Berlin) later told us, had disconcerted his Russian opposite number by firing questions at him like, "where did you go to school? Which party do you belong to? What are your recreations? Are you a cultural bloke or do you like sport?"'

At the session of the editorial committee in the afternoon the controversial sentence about totalitarian ideologies was briefly discussed and dropped (much to James Burnham's surprise) by Koestler; so complete unanimity prevailed (or so it seemed).

* *

At the demonstration in the Funkturm Gardens there was an audience of 15,000 people. Koestler read out the Manifesto which was greeted with thunderous applause:

'We hold it to be self-evident that intellectual freedom is one of the inalienable rights of man.

'Such freedom is defined first and foremost by his right to hold and express his own opinions, and particularly opinions which differ from those of his rulers. Deprived of the right to say "no", man becomes a slave.

'Freedom and peace are inseparable. In any country, under any regime, the overwhelming majority of ordinary people fear and oppose war. The danger of war becomes acute when governments, by suppressing democratic representative institutions, deny to the majority the means of imposing its will to peace. Peace can be maintained only if each government submits to the control and inspection of its acts by the people whom it governs, and agrees to submit all questions immediately involving the risk of war to a representative international authority, by whose decision it will abide.

'We hold that the main reason for the present insecurity of the world is the policy of governments which, while paying lip-service to peace, refuse to accept this double control. Historical experience proves that wars can be prepared and waged under any slogan, including that of peace. Campaigns for peace which are not backed by acts that will guarantee its maintenance are like counterfeit currency circulated for dishonest purposes. Intellectual sanity and physical security can only return to the world if such practices are abandoned.

'Freedom is based on the toleration of divergent opinions. The principle of toleration does not logically permit the practice of intolerance.

'No political philosophy or economic theory can claim the sole right to represent freedom in the abstract. We hold that the value of such theories is to be judged by the range of concrete freedom which they accord the individual in practice.

'We likewise hold that no race, nation, class or religion can claim the sole right to represent the idea of freedom, nor the right to deny freedom to other groups or creeds in the name of any ultimate ideal or lofty aim whatsoever. We hold that the historical contribution of any society is to be judged by the extent and quality of the freedom which its members actually enjoy.

'In times of emergency, restrictions on the freedom of the individual are imposed in the real or assumed interest of the community. We hold it to be essential that such restrictions be confined to a minimum of clearly specified actions; that they be understood to be temporary and limited expedients in the nature of a sacrifice; and that the measures restricting freedom be themselves subject to free criticism and democratic control. Only thus can we have a reasonable assurance that emergency measures restricting individual freedom will not degenerate into a permanent tyranny.

'In totalitarian states restrictions on freedom are no longer publicly understood as sacrifice imposed on the people, but are on the contrary represented as triumphs of progress and achievements of a superior civilisation. We hold that both the theory and practice of these regimes run counter to the basic rights of the individual and the fundamental aspirations of mankind as a whole.

'We hold the danger represented by these regimes to be all the greater since their means of enforcement far surpasses that of all previous tyrannies in the history of mankind. The citizen of the totalitarian state is expected and forced not only to abstain from crime but to conform in all his thoughts and actions to a prescribed pattern. Citizens are persecuted and condemned on such unspecified and all-embracing charges as "enemies of the people" or "socially unreliable elements".

'We hold that there can be no stable world so long as mankind, with regard to freedom, remains divided into "haves" and "have-nots". The defence of existing freedoms, the reconquest of lost freedom [and the creation of new freedoms] are parts of the same struggle.

'We hold that the theory and practice of the totalitarian state are the greatest challenge which man has been called on to meet in the course of civilised history.

'We hold that indifference or neutrality in the face of such a challenge amounts to betrayal of mankind and to the abdication of the free mind. Our answer to this challenge may decide the fate of man for generations.

['The defence of intellectual liberty today imposes a positive obligation: to offer new and constructive answers to the problems of our time.]

'We address this manifesto to all men who are determined to regain those liberties which they have lost and to preserve [and extend] those which they enjoy.'

Koestler ended by crying '*Die Freiheit hat die Offensive ergriffen* – Freedom has taken the offensive.' He had indeed had his way, although at the cost of much resentment, mainly on the part of some English and Scandinavian members of the Congress.

'This manifesto,' Mamaine noted, 'was really almost entirely written by K. and pushed through by him, Burnham, Brown, Hook, and Lasky by forceful offensive tactics so that virtually no opposition was encountered though Silone had obviously come prepared to make some.'

* *

For Mamaine on the Thursday evening after the mass meeting there was a party at an hotel on the Wannsee:

'The whole of this Congress is in a way rather like one long party, at which one is always having drinks and meals with various groups of people, mostly old friends, with real parties thrown in at intervals.'

Her husband, however, had rather more serious business on hand. Two days before, several members of the Congress had been invited to meet the chemist Professor Havemann and the philosopher Professor Holitscher, both ardent supporters of the Stalinist regime in Eastern Germany, at the Hotel am Zoo.

Koestler described the encounter in his diary:

'We arrived at the Hotel am Zoo about a quarter to 8 and found a host of journalists, photographers, and radio people. After some fuss we sat down at a round table surrounded by this press crowd – on the one side Havemann and Holitscher, on the other Lasky, Hook, Nicolas Nabokov, Irving Brown, and I. Havemann objected that we were "four against two", so Irving and I got up grinning and sat in a corner. Next Havemann read a statement to the press to the effect that they had never issued an invitation and first thing he had learned about this alleged invitation was through the press, and that we were meeting by pure chance as he happened to be having tea with friends in the Hotel am Zoo. Lasky and Sidney tried to pin them down as to whether they considered Stalin to be the greatest living geneticist, philologist, etc. Havemann tried to evade [the question and] to bring in the hydrogen bomb. But as Hook and Lasky, with their dynamic temperaments, prevailed at the microphone, Havemann declared he must have dinner first and proposed continuing at 11 p.m. Hook offered sandwiches, but to no avail. Holitscher declared "You are not a Professor of Philosophy because a) you have bad manners, as you hit the table, and b) you have lied about the invitation," – and left the table. Havemann said that he would turn up at 11 but did not, so Lasky had the empty chairs photographed. As they didn't turn up Lasky rang up Havemann, and found that he was at Eisler's.'

* *

By this time, the main work of the Congress had been completed. The various factions had composed their differences sufficiently, for the moment, to support the manifesto and to join in sending the following message to writers, artists, and scientists in the Soviet Union and its subjugated satellites:

'This is a declaration of international solidarity. It is a proof that the present great world conflict is not between East and West or between peoples or cultural traditions. We deny the charge that we who are gathered here from many lands are enemies of the Russian people or of the other Slavic peoples. On the contrary: there are among us representatives of the Slavic nations of the East. And in unison with them we are sending this call to our friends, our colleagues in all lands where cultural freedom does not exist.

'We pledge our moral and material support to all those who assert their right to freedom against oppression. We earnestly hope that they may all soon live in freedom and may again join with us in the enjoyment of our common spiritual heritage.'

This reflected, in a diluted form, the conviction of Koestler (ahead of his time, as usual) that the menace of Communism could only be dispelled in the end by an ideological challenge generated *within* the Soviet Union and its satellites.

It had also been confirmed that the Congress for Cultural Freedom should continue as a permanent organisation, with offices in Berlin and Paris, arranging conferences and sponsoring magazines which would be open to all intellectuals of the West opposed to totalitarianism.

* *

On Friday, Koestler visited the Free University* to talk with the students. Their attitude reinforced his impression of the Berliners' physical and moral courage, and confirmed his idea that the cast of German thought had undergone a radical change in the past five years.

> 'I have probably never,' he jotted in his diary that evening, 'had an audience more mentally alert and conscious of its moral responsibility than the students of the Free University and the various student resistance groups who are working in the East Zone, nor met such a good cross-section of people from taxi-drivers to radio reporters, news editors and University professors. Of course there is also a kind of natural selection at work – a third of the population, the soft and flabby element, has left for the West and only the determined remain – like an outpost, or a garrison of a besieged city which in fact is an island 100 miles behind the Iron Curtain. If one remembers how frightened distant France is of a Russian occupation one can appreciate the determination it needs to live here.
>
> 'The further fact which makes the Berliner of today such a remarkable phenomenon is the constant contact with the Eastern Zone – with Soviet reality. There are at least a score of different groups who all in one way or another are carrying out underground work in the Eastern sector – student groups, who remain decentralised and work independently of each other, the *Kampfgruppe gegen Unmenschlichkeit*, and the various party organisations. For these groups and their periphery which in one way or another involved almost the whole population, freedom is not a word but a reality, and so are democracy and the rest.
>
> 'But the decisive fact in the mentality of the Berliner is something entirely new in the German mentality: unity between abstraction and reality. As far as political concepts go, the previous paragraph explains the process. But it is particularly striking when speaking *sub specie aeternitatis* with students and University professors. Empiricism – no longer Hegel and Kant – but Hume and Locke and intensity of experience, form the pattern for a new type of Europe.'

* *

The publisher Suhrkamp suggested to Koestler that he ought to meet Bertolt Brecht, but Koestler declined for two reasons: first, he felt he had nothing in common with a man who could still stick to Stalinism although his girl-friend had 'disappeared' in Russia and was probably dead; secondly, either the meeting would have to be secret (and Koestler did not want to burden himself with the responsibility of acting as Brecht's confessor) or it would have to be semi-official – and therefore pointless. Koestler was free to say what he liked, but Brecht was not, and therefore there was no possibility of a genuine discussion on the level of sincerity.

On the following morning there was an odd incident. A youth from the Young Communist organisation in the Soviet sector arrived with a bunch of flowers for

* Later subverted for a time by DDR's agents and the *Schili* (or Radical Chic) of Berlin.

Mamaine. Having presented them politely, he turned from Mamaine and said to Koestler:

> 'I've read *Spanish Testament* and I feel sure you can't be a police spy as they say you are, but you must be still on our side really.'

Koestler took up the point and tried to engage the boy in friendly conversation, but found only

> 'a nice little robot-brain . . . complete conditioning in the Brave New World sense.'

To every argument of Koestler's in favour of freedom the boy had a stock response:

> 'Yes, but we don't need it: we are in a period of transition.'

Later in the day the Koestlers went to a reception given by Peter Tennant, Deputy Commandant and political adviser to General Bourne. The main topic of conversation, dominated by Koestler, was not the Congress but the increasingly alarming news about the Russian-backed North Korean Communists' invasion of South Korea, and its international repercussions.

> 'Just as K was talking about the situation,' Mamaine noted, 'a typical upper-class woman with a white face, string of pearls, small hat, etc. came in saying: "I'm sorry I'm late but Alan has been playing cricket." We laughed but she did not see the joke.'

That evening the Koestlers joined the Silones, Burnhams and others at Lasky's house for a dinner party which was intended to be something of a celebration. But Koestler – in reaction to the intense effort he had exerted during the past few days – was depressed and upset, and the result was unfortunate. Mamaine's diary has a brief but ironically evocative entry:

> 'Not a very gay party though K did his best to make it so by drinking a considerable amount of wine. He spent a good part of the evening repeating over and over again to Silone that though he had a great fraternal feeling for him, Silone had made things rather difficult for him – for example, by reading a newspaper all through the first meal we had had with him in Rome, and also by always behaving as if he were a broad-bottomed Abruzzi peasant and K was some kind of cosmopolitan gigolo. Silone was obviously very bored by this but made some kind of friendly answer, which however did not satisfy K as he was too drunk to understand it, so he went on repeating his accusation, with some effect apparently for we were told that after we left, Silone said: "He seems to think that I think he's a gigolo." K very unhappy because he thought real fraternal feeling missing . . .'

Mamaine's jotting ended on a slightly terse note:

> 'Kept me awake till 3.30 talking about this.'

Next morning Koestler was suffering from a bad hangover, in spite of which he made a rousing, and enthusiastically received speech to a gathering of Hildebrandt's *Kampfgruppe*. Following this, he noted in his diary:

> 'If Berlin survives, of which there is little chance, a new European spirit might be born there.'

Reminded of this a quarter of a century later, Koestler smiled wryly. West Berlin has survived, its native stubbornness reinforced by the American guarantee. A successor to *Burgermeister* Reuter, Willy Brandt, later became Chancellor of West Germany and did more than most European politicians to try to create a new European spirit at the same time as he attempted to establish an easier relationship with East Germany and other Russian satrapies. But he was to be politically wounded and his *Ostpolitik* damaged by the vulnerability of non-totalitarian Socialism to Communist penetration, and by the violence of such Trotskyist groups as the *Rote Armee Fraktion*.

New versions of old heresies were injected into the Free University by successors of the students who had impressed Koestler so profoundly in 1950, buoying him out of depression and giving him hope for the future. And what has become of the 'new European spirit' today, as narrow nationalisms reassert themselves, and, lulled by reluctance to realise that the word '*détente*' has connotations in the totalitarian world very different from those attached to it in the languages of relatively free societies, Western Europe – the cradle of modernity – shows signs of falling apart?

# CHAPTER XXIII

# *1950*

AT SIX O'CLOCK ON Sunday evening the Koestlers left Berlin by plane for Frankfurt, and thence home to Fontaine-le-Port on the Seine.

The weeks that followed were for Koestler a frenzy of organisational and administrative activity. The Congress for Cultural Freedom had come into being as a permanent international organisation, but flesh had to be put on the bare bones of the idea. The international committee had to be enlarged, national committees formed, offices set up in Berlin and Paris, money found, publications planned, French intellectuals rallied in support of the Congress under the banner of *Amis de la Liberté*.

Out of the intensive planning – most of it directed and much of it actually conducted by Koestler himself in Verte Rive – came *Preuves* (in France), *Encounter* (in England), the taking over in Berlin of *Der Monat* (which had been founded and was still edited by Melvin Lasky), *Cuadernos* (a Spanish language magazine published in Paris), the Italian *Tempo Presente* which was edited by Silone and Nicol Chiaromonte and *Quest* (in India).

Koestler's files, full of plans, questionnaires, lists of equipment required for the offices – down through every detail to petty-cash books and boxes (and 'bottle of whisky for Executive Committee members and favoured guests') – bear witness to the single-mindedness with which at this time he canalised his analytical and creative energies away from his many other literary, scientific and philosophical pre-occupations into the business of getting the Congress solidly established.

Hugh Trevor-Roper, like A. J. Ayer, had been uneasy in Berlin about the dominant influence of Koestler. Although he had subscribed to the manifesto, he wrote an account of the Congress in the *Manchester Guardian* which was critical to the point of hostility of its 'political' character and of the reaction of German audiences to speeches at the public meetings:

> 'Hysterical German applause. . . . echoes from Hitler's Nuremburg. . . . anti-Russian, perhaps ex-Nazi, and hysterical with a frontier hysteria.'

He seemed particularly resentful about the prominent part played by the ex-Communists, Koestler especially. He was obviously (and understandably) dubious about the zeal with which a convert will attack the faith which formerly had his allegiance. But he certainly minimised the fact that many of the ex-Communists present had a much more intimate knowledge of Soviet reality, including the concentration camps in the Siberian Arctic,* than he.

Melvin Lasky was quick to counter-attack, suggesting in a letter to the editor of the *Manchester Guardian* that

> 'if the audience during the Congress week in Berlin reminded Mr Trevor-Roper of Hitler's Nuremburg, then at least one reader of his book has been forced to doubt whether he really knew what *The Last Days of Hitler* were like, or the first days, or any day.'

The tone of Mr Trevor-Roper's account, said Lasky . . .

> 'indicates that he is substituting for the witch-hunt against Communists another witch-hunt of his own, namely a witch-hunt against ex-Communists.'

The attitude imputed here to Trevor-Roper was already fashionable among liberal intellectuals in the United States, and was soon to be rendered even more intensely respectable by the crude antics of Senator McCarthy.

Trevor-Roper was not content merely to denounce the ex-Communists in the columns of the *Manchester Guardian*. A reasonably favourable report of the Congress in *The Economist* inspired a stern letter of correction from him. This in turn drew a letter from Melvin Lasky.

> 'Koestler,' Trevor-Roper had written, 'particularly attacked the Socialist alternative as no better than neutrality.'

> This, Lasky replied, was a misrepresentation:

> 'What Koestler had said was that the apparent policy of the present British Government in maintaining (or giving the impression thereof) a certain aloofness from Continental affairs was contributing to a situation of West-European weakness and even despair in which the neutrality idea could flourish.'

Lasky had other sharp observations to make on the terms of discourse offered by Trevor-Roper, which allowed him to credit (or discredit) a fictitious faction with far-fetched and indefensible positions, and so

> 'to demonstrate the flexibility and open-mindedness of one's own liberalism.'

Given the evidence that has come to light, from Russians as varied in kind and quality as Khrushchev and Solzhenitsyn, as well as from such Western scholars as Robert Conquest (not to mention the abundance of scarifying information that

* Of course, one must remember that three decades ago many Western 'liberals' of both conservative and social-democratic tendencies were reluctant to believe in the existence of such institutions, suspecting that they were the inventions – like most of the atrocities allegedly committed by the NKVD (now KGB) – of embittered ex-Communists in the pay of the American Central Intelligence Agency.

has more recently been circulated in the Soviet Union in the *samizdat* writings of dissidents smuggled out to the West), the quibbles of such safe and secure intellectuals as Trevor-Roper in 1950 seem almost indecently complacent.

Hindsight suggests that if it had not been for the efforts of Koestler and others who shared his knowledge, and who had the courage to speak the unwelcome and uncomfortable truth in a manner that would allow them to be misrepresented as fanatical extremists, the well-meaning – though 'woolly' or 'confused' – liberals of the West might very well have accelerated the erosion of our will to survive.

*  *

Apart from the *New Statesman*, *Manchester Guardian* and the *Economist*, the British press had shown relatively little interest in the Berlin Congress and the permanent organisations which Koestler was planning. It was a different story on the mainland of Western Europe, where the doings of intellectuals were (and are) in general taken rather more seriously. The Communist press, of course, was violently hostile, but there was also a good deal of disapproving comment by Socialists and 'confused liberals' ('mushheads' as James Burnham described them in private conversation).

The French press in particular concentrated its attention on Koestler, in no doubt that he had masterminded the Berlin demonstration and was at the centre of the movement that had grown out of it.

*L'Observateur* headlined Michèle Barat's article:

*K.K.K. 'KOESTLER'S CONGRESS' IN BERLIN*
*or*
*THE MEETING OF THE ENEMY BROTHERS*

'So, Mr. Koestler,' it ran, 'this was the K.K.K. Congress – KULTUR? KAMPF? KOESTLER? And KOREA, added Koestler, thus stating quite clearly his "cultural" position. A political manifestation, an enormous demonstration of America's will to fight the Soviet power on every level: that was what this Congress was all about, notwithstanding the presence of many a man of good will who had come in all good faith to talk about spiritual matters and the defence of cultural freedom. With Korea looming in the background, the atmosphere was already extremely tense when, on the third day, the masks were dropped and Koestler – in the name of democracy and liberty – launched an impassioned attack against the fundamental principles of intellectual freedom, ie. tolerance and respect for the thought of others.

'Two parties emerged during the Congress: the extremists or "totalitarians" with Koestler and the Americans, and the moderates, federalists, Socialists and others like Silone. Koestler's Congress was in reality a battle between those who, in order to fight against the totalitarianisms, will use the same weapons as the totalitarians, and the "good democrats", the Europeans, caught between the blocks of East and West. Neither on principles nor on methods could the adversaries reach agreement on a common action for an effective and positive fight against *the* totalitarianism.

> 'A marvellous speaker, a great comedian, full of dodges and tricks, Koestler drew tremendous applause. Wily demagogue that he is, Koestler is a devil, and devilish are his methods, his attacks against his friends whom he almost regards as traitors.'

There spoke the authentic voice of that neutralism which Koestler was convinced could only in the end deliver the liberal democracies into the hands of their implacable enemies.

André Stil's article in the Communist *L'Humanité*, headlined *Koestler with the Whip*, reflected, naturally enough, the general line of the Cominform's counter-attack:

> 'In the Western sector of Berlin a curious Congress for "Cultural Freedom" has just closed its assizes. The cream of "Marshallising" and "Atlantic-pactisising" "intellectuals" attended – in particular the traitor Koestler, Burnham, A. Philip, C. Schmidt, J. Romain, D. Rousset – 150 in all, philosophers of the absurd, novelists of decadence and of ugliness, theoreticians of the "inevitable" atomic warfare they long for.
>
> 'The most striking aspect of the Congress was Koestler's violence. For hours on end he cracked the whip of American directives over the heads of the western "intelligentsia". This was not to the liking of the "neutralists", dreaming of a neutral Europe between the USA and USSR; and the congress ended in an uproar.'

At the foot of M. Stil's diatribe, *L'Humanité* commended to the faithful the 'excellent booklet' by Jean Kanapa, *The Traitor and the Proletarian*, or *Enterprise Koestler & Co. Ltd.*, (one of the many ferocious pamphlets denouncing the defector who had dared, in *Darkness at Noon*, to expose the inner nature of Stalinism), and an equally violent attack on James Burnham by Pierre Courtade which had been published in *La Nouvelle Critique*.

At press conferences and interviews in Paris (some of them quite fairly reported), Koestler ignored the vehement personal attacks on himself and fought back hard against the interpretation of the Congress placed upon it by the Communists, their fellow-travellers (witting and otherwise), and the 'confused liberals' who hankered after a neutral Europe and did not wish to hear about the innumerable concentration camps in the Soviet Union where millions had already perished and millions of slave-labourers were still slowly dying.

The Berlin Congress, Koestler pointed out to *Combat*'s reporter, far from ending in 'appalling uproar', had unanimously adopted a manifesto in which Western intellectuals had said goodbye to neutrality in the matter of cultural freedom and abandoned their defensive posture. It was *Liberty*, he said, hammering home the point for the hundredth time, that had taken the offensive. Of course there had been many differences of opinion and emphasis. But on the overriding issue – 'relative freedom versus absolute tyranny' – there had been complete agreement. Of course he and Silone were not in agreement about everything, but it was nonsense to exaggerate their disagreements into a fundamental ideological conflict. They had both, he told *Combat*, served on the committee of the continuing Congress, preparing plans of action to be financed by each member's contributing one per cent of his annual earnings.

* *

The French Communist press intensified its campaign of vilification. *L'Action* denounced Koestler violently. *L'Humanité* published a large-scale map of the region around Fontaine-le-Port with an arrow pointing to Verte Rive, Koestler's house:

> 'This is the headquarters of the Cold War,' ran the legend. 'This is where Chip Bohlen, the American Ambassador, trains his para-military Fascist militia.'

Koestler's gardener and cook packed up and left, having been warned that the house might be blown up at any moment. Anonymous threats were regularly received by telephone.

Cynthia, who was still acting as his part-time secretary, had a Rumanian friend in Paris who tried to dissuade her from working for Koestler, because of the danger. Was the fence around the grounds electrified? he asked her. Did Koestler carry a revolver? Did he have a bodyguard?

In fact, Koestler had declined the offer of a bodyguard and rejected the advice that he should carry a revolver. He ignored the campaign of silent intimidation conducted by ugly customers sent by the Communist Party to keep the house under surveillance, and sailed his canoe on the Seine during his brief spells of relaxation. Often in the evening, with the garden lights blazing, he and Mamaine and Cynthia would sit on the terrace, looking across the water into the darkness of Fontainebleau Forest – an easy target for any assassin.

There was no point, Koestler told himself, in thinking about personal security. It could only lead to persecution mania. If the Communists wanted to get him, they would get him, whatever precautions he took.

So he went on planning and publicising the work of the Congress to counteract the eroding effect of the Stockholm and other Cominform-directed 'peace' campaigns, ignoring the quibbling of those liberals and socialists who had had second thoughts on their return from Berlin.

* *

At this stage Koestler suffered from what he called 'a kind of nervous crack up'. He resigned from the Executive Committee of the Congress and made plans to return to England. First he and Mamaine went off for a holiday in the Pyrenees, returning by way of the Dordogne, and arriving back at Verte Rive towards the end of the first week in September. Mamaine then left for England while Koestler, at Verte Rive, with Cynthia's help, got down to research on what was intended to be a development and refinement of the psychological and philosophical themes sketched in *Insight and Outlook*.

But within a day or two, he was drawn back into the Congress affairs by a letter from James Burnham:

> 'Your resigning from the Executive Committee must absolutely not stand. That, after all, would be close to the symbolic liquidation of the Congress.

You were the most prominent participant in the Berlin proceedings, and the destiny of the Congress is closely bound to you. As for "not being active" – you know very well that, even if you must be quiet for a period, you will still be on the average much more active than the other Committee members . . .

'Since I've been back in this country, I have worked on the problem of getting a solid (however small) nucleus of support here. This has seemed to me essential. It is now, I think, assured, provided that the European side doesn't collapse wholly.

'Without inserting all transitional steps in the argument, let me then, Arthur, urge you: don't, please, pull out; withdraw your resignation . . . even if for a while you can't do anything (after all, it could not be valid until presented to the full Committee).

'You will recall that you and I spoke of the possibility of your making a short business trip to this country this autumn, to confer on Congress matters and on the more general subject of which the Congress is a part. I continue to think that that would be a really excellent idea. I think that the whole setup can be made much clearer on both sides (there were insuperable handicaps to clarity at Berlin and this summer); and it would be very valuable if you could discuss some of the problems seriously with seriously interested people.'

Koestler had already decided that he could not, after all, cut himself off completely from the movement which had come into being largely as the result of his own efforts. But his reply to Burnham was non-committal. He had just been on the point, he told Burnham, of writing to say that he would be arriving in New York on 26th September on a private visit (he had to see his American publishers and agent).

'So there's no question of a "business trip",' he wrote; 'but thank you all the same for your invitation. I hope we shall have the opportunity of discussing the points raised in your letter at leisure and in a more relaxed atmosphere than over here . . . I am glad for purely psychological reasons that I got your letter before you knew of my trip.'

At this time Koestler was also much concerned about the plight of dissident intellectuals who had contrived by one means or another to escape from the Stalinist desert only to find that the rich oases of the West offered them only a few drops of water. Koestler was himself prepared to do more than make speeches, write pamphlets, organise conferences, and plan new publications. He was ready to put his hand into his own pocket, both to support the Congress and to help refugees from Communism, and he expected other successful writers to do likewise – especially best-selling American authors, a number of whom he approached. He wrote to that effect to Ernest Hemingway, ending up

'I hope you don't resent my approaching you. You will appreciate that I refrain from any sob-talk and attempt at persuasion. I can think of fifty valid reasons why you should not be interested in this whole business. Whatever your answer I will regard it as a strictly private letter.'

There is no record of any reply from Hemingway, who presumably had his own reasons, valid or otherwise, for failing to interest himself in 'this whole business'.

* *

Before leaving for America, which involved a Kafka-esque encounter with American consular authorities, Koestler had arranged a brief visit to London where Mamaine was busy making appointments with Geoffrey Crowther, Barbara Ward, Bertrand Russell and others.

> 'Drinks H. Macmillan and J. Amery on Wednesday, drinks David Astor on Tuesday.'

The meeting with Bertrand Russell was especially important. Largely as a result of A. J. Ayer's and Hugh Trevor-Roper's versions of the Berlin meeting, Russell had announced the removal of his name from the list of six distinguished philosophers who were the honorary Chairmen of the Congress's International Committee.

Koestler having been persuaded to withdraw his own resignation from the Executive Committee, it was now his task to persuade Russell likewise to return to the fold.

> 'If you will agree to meet,' he wrote to Russell on 13th September, 'I shall not attempt to persuade you but to put facts before you which have been considerably misrepresented in England.'

Russell agreed to a meeting at which Koestler, accompanied by Arthur J. Schlesinger, Jr, succeeded in convincing him that he should withdraw his resignation. On the following day, Koestler wrote to him gratefully:

> 'Both Arthur Schlesinger and I were very happy about the result of our pilgrimage to you. Your withdrawal from the Congress would have caused other members of the Committee to wonder why, and would probably have brought the roof down over our heads. The whole thing is still a very tender plant; we have little money, only a scant paid personnel and no Cominform behind us. But if we can produce results during the next six months, support will grow rapidly, for there is a vacuum in Europe and a reasonable chance that we can fill it.'

In Paris, Cynthia had been pressing the American Consul about the missing visa and wrote to Arthur with the unwelcome news that he would have to go to the US Embassy in London and renew his application. Koestler did so, and permission came through from Washington, but too late for him to sail on the *Ile de France*, so Koestler arranged instead to fly to New York on Saturday, 28th September.

His last few days in London were soured by a violent quarrel with an old friend. He and Mamaine were staying with Richard and Zita Crossman. One evening they dined with the Crossmans at the House of Commons, the other guests being John Strachey, Arthur J. Schlesinger, Jr, and Raymond Aron. A political discussion between Strachey and Crossman on the one hand and

Koestler on the other (all three at their most argumentative and aggressive) rapidly developed into an acrimonious argument, which in turn, fuelled by a great deal of drink, flared up into a furious slanging-match. According to Koestler's diary, Crossman and Strachey stubbornly defended British isolationism, their arguments becoming more absurd as the evening progressed. At length Koestler reproached the Labour Party for having done nothing to counteract Communist influence in the European trades unions, leaving the job to the unions of the capitalist USA, and also for backing the pro-Soviet Nenni in Italy against Saragat. At this, Crossman, who was fairly drunk, accused Koestler of 'anti-British lies'.

> 'I asked him to withdraw this, which he refused, so Mamaine and I walked out of the dinner and in the middle of the night moved our luggage from the Crossmans' house to the Grosvenor Hotel; and the next day we moved to David Astor's house . . .'

As usual after such incidents, Koestler wrote a contrite letter to his hostess. Zita replied at once:

> 'Dearest Arthur – Your affectionate and wise letter was a great comfort when I was feeling so utterly devastated. I cannot bear to lose a friend and particularly the idea of losing you left an aching void. I didn't sleep all that night.
>
> 'You are right about you and Dick being better apart during the present political weather but it is only with bitter disappointment that I admit this. It is so lovely having you around and I was so looking forward to days of special warmth and gaiety in the house.
>
> 'We shall always love you dearly.'

* *

On Sunday, Koestler sent Mamaine a cable from New York:

> 'Most enjoyable journey via Iceland and Greenland ring Ma [Koestler's mother]* love.'

Mamaine replied briefly on Monday:

> 'Do have a lovely time and don't kill yourself with work' –

adding without comment that she had given the Crossmans Koestler's address in New York, to which she had forwarded a letter written by Crossman on Friday in the House of Commons:

> 'Dear Arthur – let me first apologise for my ill-manners, even less pardonable since I was your host. It was my fault that the dinner broke up as it did and it probably wouldn't have if both of us had been on the cider-waggon. My feeling for you is based not on compatibility of views but on incompatibility! You provide that opposition, and I still hope that this is a basis for genuine friendship. After all, it *was* a good discussion last Monday, and I believe you too learnt something from it. I did!

* Then living in Hampstead.

'Anyway, have a good time, and be ready to try once again when you come back. Though I agree that for Europeans, the English are even worse when they are articulate . . .'

But that ferocious altercation in the Palace of Westminster, as Koestler recorded later, had brought to an end

'. . . the friendship with Dick, in spite of the letters from Zita and Dick himself. After my return to London I made several overtures to Dick for resuming relations, but nothing came of them . . .'

# CHAPTER XXIV

# *1950*

AMERICAN PUBLIC OPINION, CONDITIONED by wartime propaganda, had been slow to recognise, after the defeat of the Axis powers in 1945, that Stalin had bamboozled President Roosevelt at Yalta and that the Soviet Union had been, and remained, implacably hostile to the Western democracies, and especially to the United States. But the subjugation of Eastern Europe, the attempt to draw Greece and Turkey into the orbit of the Soviet Empire, the subversive activities of the Western Communist Parties, the rabid rhetoric of the Soviet Union's representatives at the United Nations, the Berlin Blockade, the explosion of the Soviet Union's first atomic bomb, the Russian-sponsored invasion of South Korea – all these and many other manifestations of the Soviet Union's ambitions during the first five post-war years dispelled America's euphoria and hardened its determination to support President Truman's policy of 'containment'.

By 1950 American public opinion was fiercely anti-Soviet. The destruction of former illusions about the real nature of the Soviet Union's attitudes was quickly followed by a growing fear that the United States itself might soon be endangered from within by a Communist fifth column. Had the Executive Branch been lax in guarding against the penetration of government departments and agencies by Soviet spies and sympathisers? A rapidly increasing number of people suspected that this was indeed the case, and their suspicions were duly reflected in the Congress. The Legislative Branch had taken to asserting itself more vigorously on questions of loyalty, security and subversion. Fear fed on fear. On 23rd September 1950, over President Truman's veto, the Congress passed into law the Subversive Activities Control Bill (popularly known as the McCarran Act) aimed at the repression of Communism within the United States. This gave still more power to Senator Joseph R. McCarthy's elbow.

And five days later Koestler arrived in the United States.

* *

Koestler's first visit to the United States, in 1948, had been sanctioned on condition that he maintained, during the two months granted him, 'the specific status of lecturer for the International Rescue and Relief Committee'. As we have seen, however, no objection was raised during this period to his strenuous efforts to arouse democratic Socialists and liberals to the reality of Stalinist tyranny and its threat to the West.

His second visit however

> 'was predicated upon an order of the Assistant Commissioner of Immigration . . . to the effect that the stay was for the sole purpose of arranging for the publication of a novel and for the theatrical production of a prior work.'

The novel in question was *The Age of Longing*, and the 'theatrical production' was Sidney Kingsley's dramatisation of *Darkness at Noon*. Both projects indeed required Koestler's presence in the United States, and both indeed involved him in much time-consuming and nerve-racking activity. But they were far from being the 'sole purpose' of his visit.

For one thing, he was determined to obtain the right of permanent residence in the United States, a right that could be granted only if the Congress were to pass, with or without the signature of the President, a private Bill. For another, he intended to publicise his Fund for Intellectual Freedom, by which commercially successful authors in the West would help exiles from the Soviet Union and its satrapies to get their works into print. (Koestler had already made over to it all the royalties that would be forthcoming from the dramatisation of *Darkness at Noon*.)

And then, of course, there was the need, as his friend James Burnham had put it, 'to confer on Congress [for Cultural Freedom] matters and on the more general subject of which the Congress is a part' with 'seriously interested people'.

Here, of course, he had to walk carefully. He was already liable to be smeared as McCarthyite by those 'confused liberals' of the north-eastern seaboard whose distaste for the uncouth and unpleasant Whittaker Chambers and his accusations of treason against Alger Hiss helped them greatly to sustain their disbelief in the well-authenticated guilt of that socially superior lawyer and former Presidential aide.

Koestler was not unaware of this particular hazard. During his first visit to the United States, at a cocktail party in New York City, a woman journalist had attacked him 'with some vehemence'. She said that

> 'people who had once been Communists should shut up and retire to a monastery or a desert island, instead of going around "teaching other people lessons".'

The publication of *The God that Failed* in the United States had coincided with the second trial of Alger Hiss. Both events were linked in many publications, including the Latin American edition of *Time* dated 9th January 1950. This confusion inspired a woman of German origin, a former Communist Party member now living in South America, to write to Koestler, urging him to condemn the disgusting Whittaker Chambers ('the real villain because he didn't keep his mouth shut about things past and done with') and to defend the well-meaning Hiss 'on ground of his motives'. Like herself, she elaborated,

> 'probably, sometime between now and then, when Alger Hiss changed his mind as so many did who had been Communists in good faith, he was in no position to announce that change . . .'

Koestler, having pondered this woman's plea and concluded that it did indeed represent, although no doubt in a somewhat overstrung manner, the vague feeling of unease which the Hiss trial had induced in many people on both sides of the Atlantic, wrote an article which was published during February 1950 in the *New York Times*.

It did not endear him either to those Americans for whom the god had not yet wholly failed or to those (like Koestler's correspondent) who for a variety of reasons – chief among them, no doubt, the preservation of their self-esteem – had good reason to fear the confessions of converts such as Whittaker Chambers:

> 'The outstanding aspect of the trial was that it was not a case of the State calling a citizen to account for an alleged crime. It was a public and deathly duel between two individuals, one persecutor, one persecuted . . . the whole picture became distorted by the public's emotional reactions to these two so utterly different human types . . . the persecuted Hiss appeared as the prototype of the decent, modest, hard-working, well-spoken, happily married, idealistic American liberal who, even if assumed to be guilty, could not be suspected of having acted for any base reasons or for personal gain. His persecutor, on the other hand, appeared as a man who unblushingly admitted having committed perjury, travelled with forged passports, lived with mistresses under false names, and was described by some academic gentlemen as a psychopath. To put the whole matter in a nutshell: from the spectator point of view the casting of the parts was wrong – Chambers should have got the part of Hiss and Hiss the part of Chambers . . .
>
> 'Hiss stubbornly persisted in his error; Chambers confessed and recanted his past. One would think that this decisive fact should have tilted the balance of sympathy towards Chambers. Yet . . . If you feel contempt for the renegade Chamberses and Kravchenkos, then you should feel sympathy for the loyal Ribbentrops and Lavals; and *vice versa*, if you condemn people for having "collaborated" with a totalitarian regime, then you must acquit those who have deserted such a regime . . .
>
> 'Chambers and Kravchenko and the rest of us who have once borne allegiance to the "God that Failed", will always be looked upon as unfrocked priests. This would be without much interest if it merely concerned the few individuals in question. In this case the simplest solution for these would be to follow the last journalist's advice and satisfy the demands of good taste by retiring to a desert island.
>
> 'But if Chambers had followed this advice, his repentance would have become meaningless, for the public would never have learned certain facts which it was essential for it to learn. And the same is true of Kravchenko, and

Barmine, and Silone, and Gide and the others. My correspondent asks why they can't "keep their mouths shut about things past and done with" . . . The answer is, simply, that these things are neither "past" nor "done with" . . . only those who have worked inside the totalitarian machine know its true character and are in a position to convey a comprehensive picture of it . . .

'The decisive fact about Chambers is that he has performed a service of great social utility . . . The public is entitled to feel attracted or repelled by him, but it is not entitled to let its bias interfere with its judgement: to talk of betrayal where loyalty would mean persistence in crime, and to defend the agents of an evil regime on the grounds that those who denounce it are not saints.'

Such logic was certainly not to the taste of the kind of soft-centred 'liberals' who found it comfortable to conclude – because Senator Joseph McCarthy struck them as repellent in his person, vulgar in his speech, and irresponsible both in his allegations and in the conduct of his investigations – that the danger he ranted about could therefore safely be discounted or dismissed.

But since there was nothing remotely 'McCarthyite' about Koestler or his incisive arguments, no 'liberal', however 'confused', could invent a smear that would stick. And if, in his anxiety to see the democracies of the West sink their petty differences and re-arm themselves both physically and psychologically against the Soviet threat, he was a 'scaremonger' (the view, as we have seen, of some of the English academic liberals who attended the Berlin Congress of Cultural Freedom), then he was not alone.

Four days after his arrival in the United States, the *New York Times* published an article by Paul-Henri Spaak, the President of the European Assembly, which began:

> 'The Russians have 175 divisions, of which more than twenty are armored; they possess 20,000 fighter aircraft. Opposite them the peoples of Western Europe who spend millions and millions of francs on their armies, could only put into the field absolutely inadequate, ridiculously weak and disparate forces, incapable, in a word, of opposing an invasion with the slightest chance of success.'

The Brussels Pact, he went on, had been signed more than thirty months before; the North Atlantic Pact had been signed eighteen months before; and what had been achieved?

> '. . . a tremendous expenditure of energy in meetings, in words, and in the setting up of committees and sub-committees.'

Re-reading this article thirty years after its publication, and with so many of its questions still unanswered, is an uncanny experience:

> 'It would be a dreadful thing for our countries if our people should believe that a foreign army deployed over Europe could bring them either a higher ideology or greater material advantages. That is why the defense of Europe is intimately bound up with propaganda in favor of the moral and political values which are those of the West . . .'

Why, Spaak asked, should the responsible statesmen who had signed or approved the Brussels Pact and the North Atlantic Treaty be incapable of drawing the logical conclusions from their tests?

Not that the problem of the defence of Europe could be solved by the mere creation of a good army.

'. . . It also means, and perhaps above all, the consciousness that Europe exists and that it deserves to exist.'

Koestler, in his efforts to arouse the intellectuals of the West to the reality of the danger which their own complacency made the more menacing, was in good company.

* *

Mamaine's acknowledgement of Koestler's cable announcing his safe arrival had included the admonition that he should not kill himself with work; but Koestler, far from taking it easy, threw himself into a frenzy of activity as soon as he had slept off the travel fatigue.

Mamaine sent a mild complaint:

'Darling – Absolutely no news, so this will be like the letters you usually write me – just saying Darling, no news, love, etc . . .'

She hoped, however, that he was having fun: and so he was, after his fashion. He spent his first week at the One Fifth Avenue Hotel. He had stayed there in 1948 and enjoyed it. But in 1950, with all his new commitments, it was inconvenient, and with great relief he moved in with James Putnam, an old friend and his former editor at Macmillan, at 31 West 12th Street. Once installed, he cabled Mamaine apologetically:

'First week frightful rush wrote two articles started correcting novel continue saving the world shall write long letter tomorrow much love.'

But another three days were to pass before he found time enough to report in detail:

'Sweety, This is my first quiet morning to sit down and write letters. I got caught up in a whirl of Congress, Macmillan, world-saving etc. From the moment I arrived, complicated by flat-hunting and writing two articles in that first week here, the *Observer* review* (I trust it appeared), and a very long and well thought-out article for next Sunday's *New York Times*, launching the "Legion of Liberty" project,† for the writing of which I had to consult several experts, including a general. The people I talked to say it is the most sensible project of its kind – there are others by Ely Culbertson, Sen. Lodge, etc., but much more difficult to realise. Several people are going to put it up to several people in Washington – and that's probably as far as it will go, given the chaotic conditions there, but since Berlin I am inclined to think that if one has a sensible idea it is worth trying to put it in an effective way, even if the chances are only 1%.

'I'll try to get some order into this letter, by headings.

* of Bertrand Russell's book *Unpopular Essays*. . . .

† For a multinational European Army of volunteers.

'*The flat situation.* I found an ideal temporary solution. Jim Putnam is now definitely divorcing, and I am sharing his very lovely flat, which is ideal for work – I have a bedroom and a detached workroom of the small size I like, the walls all surrounded by books. I pay half of the rent, 75 dollars a month (I mean my share is 75) which is dirt cheap for New York. Furnished flats are all round 300 a month – which is over hundred guineas! Jim has got a much better job than at Macmillans and is on the wagon again (I stick to beer) and we are getting on well.

'*But* the flat is too small for three; so when you come over I shall have to get a furnished flat; and it may take two or three weeks to find one. Generally some people always leave New York just before Christmas and are willing to let their flats, but now in October flats are extremely scarce. So I shall have to know well in advance about your plans. If you are enjoying yourself in London, don't hurry. How long I myself shall stay I don't know yet. It depends mainly on the visa business. The preliminary steps have been taken, but it may turn out a long business. I shall know more in about a fortnight.'

* *

Among the first to welcome him to the United States were his two principal collaborators in the tricky task of setting up a permanent international organisation on the basis of the Berlin Congress – Arthur J. Schlesinger, Jr, and James Burnham.

The latter, who was then living in Washington and had the ear of many 'serious persons', greeted him with a programme of travel, writing and speaking.

Koestler made no complaint. He was active not only in the long-term strategy of the Congress for Cultural Freedom but also in the planning and supervision of its tactics and day-to-day administration. He worked closely with Irving Brown of the American Federation of Labour and Jay Lovestone of the International Lady Garment Workers' Union (through which the Central Intelligence Agency's financial support was channelled to the Congress for Cultural Freedom) as well as with Burnham and Schlesinger.

* *

Koestler soon learned to avoid being drawn into protracted discussions with the many individuals and institutions bombarding him with invitations, suggestions and arguments, and to decline the more or less peremptory requests for opinions, prefaces and personal appearances that rain upon the writer who has become a public figure. But it was not always easy to avoid giving offence, especially to those regrettably self-important academics or businessmen who obviously thought that he should be flattered by invitations to travel a thousand miles and give (for a very nominal fee) an after-luncheon talk, or to set aside his own work for weeks and prepare a course of free lectures. He also ran into trouble with friends who felt themselves neglected.

'Almost a week has passed since your arrival. You promised to call me. Where are you?' – 'Would you be so good as to get in touch with me between twelve and two . . .' 'Would appreciate your wired or phoned response.'

So it went.

Meanwhile, things were going well with the Fund for Intellectual Freedom.

> 'Aldous Huxley has donated ten per cent of his American income,' Koestler reported to Mamaine. 'Dos Passos agreed, and is now figuring out what percentage he can spare; Jim Farrell ten per cent Continental royalties . . . Attorneys are busy drawing up the donation forms and by the end of this month I hope the whole thing will get going, provided Graham Greene gets Forster and Rebecca West. Could you ring him to move him into action. Tell him that since my last letter Dos Passos has given his formal agreement.'

By now, lawyers had completed the complicated job of arranging the legal incorporation of the Fund for Intellectual Freedom, Koestler had recruited voluntary workers to run it, and was organising the press conference at which it would be announced.

> 'In Germany,' he wrote, 'we have actually started paying out the first 1000 dollars to buy a Russian printing press which will publish the works of Russian émigré writers and thus give them a living and an incentive to work. There are various first-rate people among them who were condemned to sterility, and regard this little enterprise as the beginning of a new life.'

In Louis Fischer he had found, he thought, an 'ideal' general secretary for the Congress for Cultural Freedom, and Arthur Schlesinger had agreed to take on the responsibility for the American branch. 'To persuade these two took some time,' he noted, laconically.

There was no need for the Congress for Cultural Freedom to sponsor a periodical in the United States, where the support of the *New Leader*, *Partisan Review* and *Commentary* was assured.

His publisher's enthusiasm for *The Age of Longing* was growing greater day by day; he had decided to make it even better by extensive revisions in galley proof (a luxury still possible a quarter of a century ago); and both *Harper's Magazine* and *Commentary* were going to run excerpts from it in advance of publication.

It seemed increasingly likely that his friends would be able to drum up support in Congress to pass a private act giving him the right of permanent residence in the United States.

His next book – the autobiography which Cynthia wanted so badly to type – was beginning to take shape in his mind.

> 'Give Cynthia my love,' he asked Mamaine, 'and send me her address, so I can send her a postcard with a skyscraper view.'

* *

Koestler had been spending the last weekend of October in the country with friends. Hearing that an unusual and attractive property in the Delaware river – Island Farm, a leaf-shaped raft of park and woodland, a mile in length and half a mile at its widest – was up for auction on the Saturday, they took Koestler along. For themselves it was simply an agreeable excursion and they thought it might also amuse their guest. Three months before, the owners of the island had refused an offer of 72,000 dollars for it. But things had gone badly with them since and now they were obliged to sell at any price.

When Koestler and his host and hostess (the Loewengards) arrived at Island Farm on the Saturday afternoon the sale was beginning and there was no time to look round the house or over the grounds and the various outbuildings. But Koestler's first impression had been that it was the island of his dreams, and it was reinforced by the details attractively set out in the auctioneer's brochure.

When the bidding opened at 25,000 dollars, Koestler on a sudden impulse offered 26,000 dollars. The Loewengards, seeing that he was determined to get the property, assured him that he could safely go to 50,000 dollars. Koestler made a mental note to stop at 42,000 dollars, the sum that his New York publishers were holding to his credit. Twenty minutes after the sale began the last of his rivals dropped out at 40,000 dollars; and for 41,000 dollars Koestler found himself the owner of a restored and modernised farmhouse, a large barn, five poultry houses, a four-car-garage, a workshop, corncrib and potting shed, 65 acres of arable, 40 acres of tall timber, 7 acres of gardens and lawns round the building, an avenue lined with fruit trees running almost the entire length of the island, and a ten-ton capacity Roebling steel suspension bridge connecting the island with the Pennsylvania shore.

Had he been rash? he wondered. No: the Loewengards knew what they were talking about. And any doubts that arose as he wrote out the cheque for the deposit were dispelled by an inspection of the house and grounds –

> 'the kind of place,' as the auctioneer's brochure put it, 'people dream about, but never believe they will ever really find . . . In the peaceful seclusion of the island, the rest of the world might well be thousands of miles away . . .'

But Philadelphia was only 34 miles to the south, New York City 60 miles to the north, and Princeton within easy reach.

Back in New York on Monday, he dictated a letter to Mamaine explaining – lest she should think that he had gone off his head – that the acquiring of Island Farm was the most reasonable and inspired transaction of his life:

> 'I am only free to dispose of my dollars while I am still a resident abroad. If and when we return to England I should have to surrender my dollars to the Treasury. The only property which does not have to be surrendered is immoveable property (bridges, islands, etc.), so, after boring consultations with experts I decided that I must buy a house or a farm . . .'

After the auction, he wrote, a prospective buyer who had turned up too late offered him 46,000 dollars on the spot.

> 'So from an investment point of view the island – which is going to be called Treasure Island – is all right . . . As for living, everybody told me that it is quite exceptional in this country where there are no hedges, no privacy, and the countryside a maze of autobahnen and drive-ins and pump stations. The really nice thing about it is that it is neither flashy nor dingy Bwlch Ocyn.

The main house is just the right size and very charming indeed, equipped with oil central-heating, electrical cooking ranges, etc. etc.

'I don't want to do anything about Treasure Island until you come over, but my idea is to cut down the corn, plough it all up and convert it into pasture and lawns, put a couple of hundred sheep on it – not to mention bees ducks dogs and tortoises, and have one couple looking after the whole thing whether we are present or absent. It doesn't tie us down in the least as no maintenance is required. And if one wants to leave it alone for a month or a year one just locks the bridge.

'I can't go on with this letter now. I am sending it through David Astor because though I was told that I am allowed to do this while I am a resident abroad it is advisable to keep it as quiet as possible – keep that in mind when you write.'

Mamaine's immediate reaction was to send off a telegram:

'HOW WONDERFUL YOU ARE A CLEVER FELLOW LOVE REPEAT LOVE.'

But this was followed by a letter which, beginning with another declaration of her approval and delight, went on to reveal an unmistakable bewilderment:

'What I most want to know is, where oh where are we going to live in the future? And will the place we live in have some sort of outhouse where I can put a piano? Will it have a wonderful working room for you? Are we likely to live in a place which will not cause me to be ill all the time? But no of course not – only the Seine is that sort of place I think. I can't tell you how well I am here, although only a few yards from the river [the Thames]. I have got much fatter too. This is not without importance from the point of view of one's happiness and general Weltanschauung . . . I have also got a few years younger, which is nice, as one usually grows older all the time . . . Please Darling do write a long letter soon and tell me what you are doing and your plans for the future, it is hell having simply no idea what you are doing or where you are or anything.'

How painfully her mind was divided is clear from the letter she dashed off on the evening of the following day:

'. . . This is only a scribbled line to say that I really am *so* pleased about what you have done. I have read the document [the auctioneer's brochure] you sent me via David about 25 times and each time seems more wonderful and dreamlike.

'Also, David wrote saying you were in good form and behaving with admirable restraint. I am seeing him next week to find out more.

'One of these days we must discuss when I am to join you . . . I am so happy here, and have established for myself such an agreeable way of life, that I am reluctant to move into the uncertainty of New York. The chief reason is of course the piano – I feel I *must* go on working here with Joe [Joseph Cooper] for another couple of months at least . . . The day I started all my fears and worries of the last year vanished completely . . . It seems to me now that I really have been rather unhappy for some time – but of course it's only relative. No blame attaches to you of course, you have been a very great prop, besides you are my chief happiness . . .'

Six days went by and still no more news from Koestler. On 15th November she wrote:

'Darling, I haven't had a letter from you for ages, except the one I got through David [Astor], which was dated Oct. 30th, and I am getting most impatient for news. As far as I am concerned you are floating about in a void, I have no idea where you are or what you're doing. So please do write if you have not done so when you get this, and add a few words in your own writing if it is not too much trouble, many thanks chum.'

This crossed with a letter from Koestler, who had recently returned to New York from a stay in Washington:

'I have two long letters of yours (October 30 and November 5) to answer . . .

'I had a letter from Graham Greene who whittled down his promises to the Continental rights, minus France, for his next book. I guess Catholics feel so sure about their distant future that they don't feel the need to buy protection. Anyway he says there should be more than £1000 coming on that book which is not too bad. The newspapers here are publishing facts about the F.I.F. next week; David Astor promised to get something into the *Observer* and I am seeing [Alan] Pryce-Jones tomorrow for the *Times Lit. Sup.* I don't think you should approach Forster, etc., until something has appeared in the papers. Agnes Knickerbocker has taken over the whole job from me as Voluntary Honorary Executive Secretary and is functioning very efficiently . . .'

Early in December Mamaine went to Paris and cabled Koestler to say that she would be arriving in New York by air on 27th December. He wrote

'Darling: I just got your cable, announcing your arrival on the 27th, and am very happy at the prospect. I suggest that we stay in New York until January first and then move to the Island. You will have the opportunity of driving to town whenever you like . . .'

Mamaine left London Airport on 26th December beset by many doubts and apprehensions, but determined to make the best of whatever Koestler and America had in store for her.

She seems to have taken New York City, which usually administers a sharp cultural shock to the European visiting it for the first time, in her stride.

# CHAPTER XXV

# *1951*

THE MOVE TO ISLAND FARM marked for Koestler the beginning of the end of a period of extraordinarily varied and intense activity in the world of politics. The contemplative and speculative writer was trying to gain ascendancy again over the man of action, but it was a hard struggle.

During the hectic weeks in New York his mind had often returned restlessly to the many unwritten works that obsessed him – the autobiography which was to be a candid self-portrait of a typical Central European intellectual in the tormented landscape of *l'entre deux guerres*; the study of the astronomers who had revolutionised cosmology and laid the foundations for the mechanistic and determinist philosophies of the eighteenth and nineteenth centuries; the more recent discoveries in physics and the life-sciences which had created a counter-revolution against established orthodoxies; the mysteries of man's unique creativity – his predicament and his glory.

His novel about the collapse of Western Europe, *The Age of Longing*, he had written amidst innumerable distractions out of a profound sense of disgust, despair almost, with the apparent frivolity and helplessness of intellectuals in the face of the totalitarian adversary. Once he had finished correcting the proofs he felt that he had done more than his fair share of attempting to disperse the clouds of unknowing into which so many had retreated.

He had earned the right to withdraw from politics and polemics and allow his deeper interests to claim his attention. His longing to have his books and papers about him in a quiet place where his energy would not be fragmented by the demands of so many was intensified by his correspondence with scholars who shared his conviction that the old frameworks of knowledge had to be broken down and the new scientific discoveries given coherence in new syntheses, which would in turn provide the basis for a philosophy to counter the nihilism implicit in positivist empiricism.

The inevitable exasperations of political activism had suddenly seemed unbearable when, in October, he read a letter from his friend Professor Michael Polanyi, thanking him for the loan of Verte Rive.

'The 40 days which I stayed altogether in your home have produced three chapters à 7,000 words of "The Justification of Belief" – which seems to have come to stay as the title of my Gifford Lectures.* I may add that at the end of these 20,000 words I feel more rested than when I started. I do not think that I ever had – nor expect ever to have again – such favourable conditions of work.'

Polanyi went on to praise the collection of scientific and philosophical works in the library at Verte Rive. This whetted anew Koestler's frustrated appetite for the research that he had been able to pursue only in a desultory fashion since his completion of *Insight and Outlook*.

Koestler had discussed with Polanyi his ambition to deepen and expand his theories of creativity through further studies of the evolution of the brain, an enterprise in which he hoped to enlist a neuro-physiologist as collaborator. Polanyi – whose intellect encompassed many disciplines and whose lively Hungarian imagination was (like Koestler's) the opposite of that of the super-specialist content to know more and more about less and less – thought that there was a likely man at the University of Chicago and asked Professor Edward Shils to confirm this.

'I regret to say,' Polanyi wrote to Koestler, 'that I had no reply so far from Ed. Shils to my enquiry about a neurologist for collaboration with you. He is a most devoted friend but a capricious correspondent. I have meanwhile mentioned the subject to another Chicago man, David Grene, who is in Paris just now. He thought the chap I was thinking of was called Novick and was attached to Szilard in the Biophysical Institute in Chicago. Please send me a postcard to Manchester if you wish me to pursue the matter further, which I shall be very glad to do. However, the simplest approach might be to ask Shils to give *you* the answer to my enquiry. By this time he will have such a bad conscience about it that he will do something really useful. It would be a pity to waste this accumulation of potential energy.'

The accumulation was not to be wasted, although more than ten years were to pass before its potential began to be realised (most notably in *The Act of Creation* and *The Ghost in the Machine*). The scholar Polanyi had been thinking of was not in fact Aaron Novick but Paul Weiss, another intimate in Chicago of that eccentric Hungarian genius Leo Szilard (who, like Koestler, had begun by studying physics and engineering in Budapest). Twenty years later Koestler was to convene a conference of fifteen eminent scientists at Alpbach in the Austrian Tyrol at which vigorous expression was given to the growing discontent with the residual mechanistic concepts of nineteenth-century physics and the resultant crudely reductionist philosophy with its determinist bias. It was Paul Weiss, the professional, who was to open that conference, honing the cutting edge of the blade that Koestler, the amateur, had forged against outdated orthodoxies which were still dangerously entrenched, particularly among behaviourists.

But all this lay far in the future. And 1951 was not to be the peaceful year he hoped for.

* *

* Published in book form under the title *Personal Knowledge*.

Mamaine was (apparently) delighted with her new home in the middle of the Delaware River and intrigued to learn that, although its postal address was New Jersey, the island was in Bucks County, Pennsylvania (the original of her friend Edmund Wilson's *Hecate County*) – 'full of intellectuals and smarties and show people and everything else.'

Koestler's major need now was the speedy passage of the private bill designed to get round the McCarran Act and give him, although a former Communist, the right of permanent residence in the United States. Although he had many good friends both in the Administration and the Congress, and no lack of other influential friends who would support the legislation with sworn affidavits, due process had to be observed, bureaucratic hurdles cleared, and time and energy expended on diplomatic lobbying.

The capable New York lawyers who were handling the matter for him, Robert Morris and Martin Richmond, had arranged for a Republican, Owen Brewster, to introduce the bill in the Senate, and for a Democrat, Laurie C. Battle, to introduce it in the House of Representatives. They were confident enough about the probable outcome of this unusual piece of bipartisan legislation, although it was expected that the Department of Justice would object to it on strictly legalistic grounds – but they could not, of course, guarantee its success. Mamaine noted on 4th January:

'I'm afraid K's bill may take ages and ages to come through, and it is by no means easy – his is literally only the fourth case of this kind to have existed so far . . . I was interrogated by the immigration officer the other day, and so was K . . . However, it may not have reached a stage where we can go away by the end of March, when we intend to return to Europe . . . If K gets stuck here, which I hope for his sake he won't, I will come anyway in the spring to take steps about selling Verte Rive. We don't think there is much point keeping it if we don't intend to live there, and for my part I don't really want to spend more time than I can help there because of the climate, while K is rather browned off with France altogether.'

The preparation of the document necessary to support the bill was an inevitable distraction. On 3rd January, Robert Morris wrote to Koestler:

'I spoke to Mr Metz [of the Immigration Department] this morning and they still have not found the biographical memorandum which our office records show was sent to them last Thursday. However, I have had another copy made up and sent it to him . . .

'When the record is completed, Mr Metz will require your presence in New York again to sign the final record, to be fingerprinted and several other routine procedures. At that time, I think it would be best that we obtain for you, and I suppose for Mamaine, Alien Registration cards.'

And the following day:

'I received a call from Mr Metz this morning, who said that he would like you to come in next Tuesday, the 9th. At that time we will have to get a Certificate of Good Conduct from the Police Department; you will have to be finger-printed; you will have to submit a notarized certification of assets and you will have to sign the completed examination.

'I suggest you meet me at my office at 10 o'clock on Tuesday morning. We will then proceed to the Police Station and then go from there to Immigration. Please confirm this schedule . . .'

So it went on.

Sidney Kingsley's dramatisation of *Darkness at Noon* opened on Broadway in the middle of January. By this time he and Koestler, who disliked the script intensely because of what he considered the political naïveté of various scenes invented by Kingsley, were no longer on speaking terms.

On 18th January Mamaine noted:

'The play of Darkness at Noon came on last week in New York with Claud Rains as Rubashov, and appears to be a success, though I suspect that it is too intellectual even in the Kingsley version to have a very long run. All our earnings from it go to the Fund for Intellectual Freedom, anyway. We have not seen the play yet but intend to go next week.'

Her comment, once they had seen the play, was brief and to the point:

'The play was rather awful, but it is rather a success I think.'*

Robert Morris thought so too. He had asked Koestler to arrange tickets for a few influential Congressmen, including Richard Milhous Nixon, who would be testifying on his behalf. One of them, detained in Washington, gave his tickets to Morris who wrote enthusiastically:

'I saw your play Saturday night and I thought it was sensational . . . I think the play dramatises your contribution to the Anti-Communist cause very well.'

Such praise, although it echoed the general view of all except Communists and 'confused liberals' still to some extent under the wartime spell of Uncle Joe, tended to exacerbate rather than soothe Koestler's irritation with Kingsley.

* *

However, Koestler could not escape completely from the demands of the Congress. Denis de Rougemont from the Paris executive had written to tell him that the executive committee would shortly be meeting to organise a conference to be held in Paris during 1951, and that it was proposed to invite Jean-Paul Sartre, Simone de Beauvoir and Thomas Mann to attend. Koestler replied tersely:

'Regarding the list of people you intend to invite to the Paris Congress:

'The American list does not seem to me very representative. I am sure that the New York Committee of the Congress will be able to make more complete suggestions.

* She was right. It ran for eighteen months on Broadway and earned 40,000 dollars for the Fund for Intellectual Freedom.

'As to the French list, I am definitely opposed to inviting Sartre and Simone de Beauvoir. The same goes for Thomas Mann.

'Our manifesto repudiates *expressis verbis* neutrality on the issue between relative freedom and total unfreedom. People like Sartre, Simone de Beauvoir and Thomas Mann have done everything in their power to confuse this issue and can only bring confusion to the Congress and to the minds of everybody who reads about it. If you insist on taking this course will you please accept my resignation from the Executive Committee.'

He sent copies of Rougemont's letter and his reply to Pearl Kluger, the executive secretary of the American Committee for Cultural Freedom, who said in reply that

> 'We* are all in agreement with you on the matter of Sartre, de Beauvoir and Mann, and thank you for calling it to our attention as we were not informed that it was even being considered. I am enclosing copy of a letter I today sent to de Rougemont.'

A further letter from Koestler to Jay Lovestone of the International Lady Garment Workers' Union shows some unease about the US Government's method of funding the Congress for Cultural Freedom:

> 'It should also be mentioned that the latest report of the Secretariat of the Congress contains a disarming phrase: "the budget of the Congress for the next six months has been submitted to Mr Irving Brown and approved by him". I wish to make it clear that this is neither an attack on Irving nor does it imply that to accept help from American, French, Italian or other trades union movements is in any way disreputable or politically objectionable. But to hand arguments to one's enemies on a silver platter in this way betrays a political naïveté which must make the prospect of any effective political fight appear hopeless.'

Koestler was well aware that the funds were being provided not by the American trades union movement but by the American tax-payer.

* *

Many years later, in 1972, when it was conventional wisdom among liberals as well as leftists to regard the Central Intelligence Agency as a demoniacal conspiracy, a young Benedictine historian wrote to Koestler from Minnesota, seeking (in the way of American post-graduate students) copious information to fill out his doctoral dissertation. What in particular he was looking for were the connections, if any, between the theme of 'the end of ideology' (much debated in the fifties) and the Congress for Cultural Freedom.

> 'I hesitate to ask about CIA involvement,' he wrote (having already done so at length and in detail), 'because it is still such a touchy subject, but there is no way to avoid it.

* Sidney Hook, Charles S. Johnson, H. J. Muller, Reinhold Niebuhr, Arthur Schlesinger, Jr, and the many distinguished politicians, writers, artists, academics, actors, businessmen and trades unionists serving on the committee.

> 'In what I have read, I have generally found the men involved hesitant to speak of the CIA and a little defensive (understandable because usually they were being attacked). What I would like to get at, and may never get at, is the rationale behind the acceptance of CIA support for those who knew of that support. There must have been a cogent, very persuasive rationale at that time, and I think that is historically important. I find it hard to believe it was an unthinking decision to accept CIA support. And what did CIA support mean in practice? I do not know if you knew of the CIA involvement or not. I would be eager to hear anything you had to say on the subject if you knew. Or if you found out only later, I would be interested in your reactions. In any event, I would be grateful for any comments you care to make on the CIA issue.'

Koestler in his reply, having observed that a written reply to all the reverend student's questions would run to book length, went on to say:

> 'However, I do not want to give you the impression of wanting to evade the CIA question. I knew from the beginning that there was American government money behind the Congress for Cultural Freedom and had no objection to this as long as there were no strings attached. I did not know until the scandal broke that the government agency in question was the CIA. My reaction to the disclosure was that it had been a clumsy and bungling way of channelling funds – why can't you have a British Council or Alliance Française?
>
> 'The Berlin Congress in 1950 appointed a five-man executive committee consisting of Irving Brown, representing the Dubinsky-Lovestone Lady Garment Workers' Union; Sidney Hook, Melvin J. Lasky, James Burnham and myself. I was told that the money came from Dubinsky and I suspected that the State Department might channel some funds through Dubinsky. But as I said, I did not care for the reasons just mentioned. Had I known that the money came from the CIA, I would have told the American members of the committee to make a more proper and logical agreement.
>
> 'Financially I was not a beneficiary but a contributor to the CCF. Had I been a beneficiary, I would probably have taken a less broad and more puritanical view. How much others knew I do not know . . .'

Another, but much more welcome, distraction was the progress of the Fund for Intellectual Freedom which was now being run in Munich by Louis Fischer's wife, Markoosha, from the offices of the International Rescue and Relief Committee. Koestler, as well as being the founder of the FIF, was also its most generous benefactor. Among the others who had so far agreed to contribute a fixed percentage of annual income were Aldous Huxley, James Farrell, Graham Greene*, John Dos Passos, Stephen Spender and Budd Schulberg. Only three months after the foundation of the FIF, Mrs Fischer had already launched a 260-page Russian-language literary monthly, *Literaturny Sovremennik*, edited by Boris Yakovlev, as an outlet not only for refugee authors but also what we now

* In fact, Graham Greene never made any contribution whatsoever to the Fund.

call *samizdat* material – 'some works', as Mamaine put it, 'by Russians still in the USSR who write tripe for official publications but good stuff for themselves'. As the Fund grew, help was extended to refugees from the Soviet satellites, providing them with typewriters, advances on work in progress, research grants, and sickness benefits. It was already a success story, and all the more so in view of the fact that no attempt was made to raise money from the public at large, from official agencies, or from foundations.

* *

As the publication of his fifth novel, *The Age of Longing*, approached, Koestler prepared a few pages of notes for the press interviews to which he knew he would be obliged to submit. They open with an explanation of why he wished to divide his time between the United States and Europe.

A political writer of our time, he wrote, could hope to get a balanced picture of the world only if he knew America not as a visitor but as a resident involved in everyday life. And he must know Europe in the same way. The hopelessly distorted and one-sided view which the European held of America and the American of Europe was one of the main sources 'of political and cultural confusion of our times'.

The remainder of his notes, anticipating the question: 'How far has your present extended stay altered your views of this country and in particular of the literary scene?', consist of a reasoned criticism of American competitiveness, so effective in industry and commerce, on imaginative writers.

* *

Distractions of one kind or another made it difficult to get ahead with his autobiography (which he had already started and abandoned three times) or with his research for the sequel to *Insight and Outlook*. His temper grew short. Mamaine noted:

> 'I should think I have written about thirty letters today for K. I never get through my work, and K is in a rotten mood as a result of living in such a disturbed environment for so long. The other day when Agnes [Knickerbocker] and he and I were having dinner in the kitchen he suddenly worked himself up into a rage and stampeded about knocking things over (having knocked over the kitchen table and bespattered us all with wine). Agnes and I spent the rest of the evening mopping up wine, whiskey, brandy, blood, glass and china; K also broke a couple of chairs and a lamp, and almost broke his foot kicking at things, so is now limping about. He has hardly spoken to me since, i.e. for two days; I am hoping this state of affairs will not last too long. There was no apparent reason for his outburst nor for his behaviour since . . .
>
> 'I saw Edmund [Wilson] in New York last week and met his wife, who is charming. He wants me to go up and spend a day with them, but god knows when I'll be able to get away owing to the impossibility of leaving K with nobody to look after him . . .'

A fortnight later, however,

> 'K has solved a problem in connection with his work which was worrying him, and seems to have become human again and even rather nice – I don't know if it's a permanent improvement or only very temporary.'

* *

In the middle of March, the author Budd Schulberg and his wife Vicki, who lived not far away, came to dinner. Schulberg wished to discuss the progress of the Fund for Intellectual Freedom.

This was to precipitate the worst row that Mamaine and Koestler had ever had:

> 'We had a really AWFUL and catastrophic evening. . . . everything went as wrong as it possibly could. It started by K being very aggressive and trying to bully Budd; Budd refused to be bullied and became rather evasive, this made K worse; everybody got rather drunk (except me) . . . and I was almost driven mad, on the one hand by fury with K for being so rude and as I thought spoiling his case by bullying and shouting, on the other by Budd's evasiveness . . . When they had left K and I had a really major row in the course of which we decided to separate, and then decided not to – at least K thought we had decided not to, but I didn't realise this till the next day . . . However, K said the usual things, and I said that I wouldn't mind leaving him if I had somebody else to live with, but frankly could hardly face the prospect of living alone, which I hate, and which is for a woman in our civilization such a terribly difficult thing to do for so many reasons. K said he understood this and appreciated my honesty about it; he then suddenly seemed to feel the air had been cleared and all would be well, so after shouting at me a bit more he pushed off, but by that time I had started to feel that perhaps I really should have the courage to leave K now, and not postpone the inevitable. It was a dark night, pouring with rain, and a strong gale blowing, however I put on a lot of clothes and wandered off down the island and back, but was too worn out to think clearly. Ever since, things seem to have gone all right and K has been affectionate and cheerful. But God, how many more of these scenes will I have to go through, and how will this whole thing end? One thing K agreed about was that he couldn't live with any woman, however perfect . . . I also said that I sometimes wondered if we had the right to bugger somebody else's life up as he was buggering mine, and K rather agreed about this too. Well, we will see what happens. There is no doubt, as we both said, that we *are* awfully fond of each other and would miss each other desperately. But aren't I fighting a losing battle against dehumanisation, I sometimes wonder?'

Both Koestler and Mamaine were still suffering from what is now often described as 'cultural shock'. It is clear that Mamaine's enthusiastic descriptions of Island Farm and its surroundings were in large part expressions of her determination to make the best of a bad job. Although she had found much to admire in America, its values and manners were very different from those of

Europe, and the effort of attempting to adjust to them imposed a great strain, both physical and psychological. Koestler also was struggling against a certain disillusionment, and this exacerbated the irritability caused by the constant interruptions of his writing.

> '. . . I see,' Mamaine wrote, 'that K is getting very impatient to get back to Europe himself, and if he really wants to a way will be found, no doubt. The pressure of this god-forsaken country is getting him down . . . in general the externalising influence of everything, the difficulty of leading anything approaching a simple life, and the impossibility of solitude, contemplation etc. even when one lives damn it all on an island. K and I feel exactly alike on these things and we also both feel that it is a good thing to live here some of the time because one can't really know what the world is like if one doesn't face up to the worst aspects of it; but we would like to spend at least six months every year in Europe, *faute de quoi* we would feel trapped and imprisoned by cars and gadgets and washing machines and television.'

They went up to New York to dine with Senator Brewster and the lawyer, Robert Morris. They tried to find out when Koestler's bill was likely to come up, but neither could tell them. Koestler, who was growing perturbed by the hysterical excesses of the anti-Communist movement in the United States and by the rigidly bureaucratic implementation of the McCarran Act, spent the greater part of the evening trying to persuade Brewster and Morris that a change of emphasis on the part of the Republican Party vis-à-vis Communists and ex-Communists would do it no harm. But most of his arguments went disregarded.

* *

A series of lectures in Manhattan had been arranged by the Committee. The themes were 'Freedom and Social Progress', 'Freedom and Social Responsibility', and 'Freedom and Myth'. The lecturers were Max Ascoli, Daniel Bell, Peter Viereck, Lionel Trilling, Elliot Cohen, Jacques Maritain, Allen Tate, William Phillips, Arthur J. Schlesinger, Jr, Diana Trilling, Sidney Hook and Koestler – an exemplary assemblage of liberal and progressive opinion. The lectures were well received.

But Koestler was all too well aware that the excesses of Senator McCarthy and his supporters, and of the American bureaucracy, were no less effective in blurring and distorting the CCF message than the counter-propaganda of the Cominform. The innocent as well as the guilty were being punished by the more naïve and enthusiastic (or simply opportunistic) anti-Communist crusaders; and American consulates abroad, interpreting the McCarran Act much as fundamentalists interpret Holy Writ, were denying visas not only to those who might reasonably enough be suspected of subversive intentions but also to those whose goodwill could only be called in question by political morons.

* *

Koestler wrote to Robert Morris, explaining the reasons, both political and private, why he and Mamaine would have to leave for Europe before the end of

May at the latest, and urging him to do whatever he could to ensure that he would not be denied a return visa in the autumn.

A few days later he and Mamaine drove to Washington to see a few friends and, with their help, engage in a little discreet lobbying. The capital was still reverberating from the shock of President Truman's dismissal of General Douglas MacArthur from the command of the UN forces in Korea.

At cocktail and dinner parties in Washington Koestler came across many who shared his dismay at the President's decision (if not always for the same reasons) and agreed with his pessimistic appreciation of its likely consequences in Europe. Senator Joseph McCarthy assured him, as he noted without comment, that

> 'the same people who have betrayed Asia (meaning Acheson) would also betray Europe.'

Koestler tried to interest Senator Henry Cabot Lodge, Jr, in his idea of a multinational Western European defence force; but Lodge ('a smooth, smug, worldly type of Senator which we haven't met before') was too preoccupied with his own notion, embodied in the Lodge-Philbin Act, of recruiting large numbers of foreign volunteers for service with the American army, to pay much attention.

Much more amusing was the following weekend which they spent in Cambridge, Massachusetts, as guests of the Schlesingers. Mamaine wrote:

> 'The Cambridge weekend was unmitigatedly enjoyable. We landed in a dinner party consisting of Thornton Wilder (who is sweet); Archibald MacLeish . . . with whom I got on rather well on the subject of Rilke and St. John Perse; Mary McCarthy and Boden Broadwater; . . . a nice young man, former member of the Komsomol, George Fischer, son of Louis; and a very nice and intelligent neurophysiologist called Mollie Brazier . . . We took Cynthia, who stayed in a hotel. Mary McC. and Boden took her and me for a sight-seeing tour of Cambridge and Boston, which are lovely towns, the latter very Henry-Jamesian looking with street after street of tall narrow eighteenth-century houses. A vast cocktail party was also given in our honour by the Schlesingers, I couldn't say who came to it, *lauter* academic characters I suppose. We flew back to New York as we had a lunch date with Sidney Hook on Monday.'

* *

The weeks went past without firm news of the bill's progress. They postponed their departure for Europe and Koestler got on with the draft of the first volume of his autobiography. But as the end of May drew near it was decided that something would have to be done about the house in France.

Then a plan to mount an arts festival in Paris under the auspices of the Congress for Cultural Freedom was put to Koestler. He was doubtful of its value and in the end chose this moment to withdraw from the executive committee, pleading (fairly enough) pressure of work. Koestler agreed to remain a member of the international committee but his resignation from the executive marked in effect the beginning of his withdrawal from the political arena.

* *

On 11th June Pat McCarran submitted to the Senate the Judiciary Committee's favourable report on Koestler, recommending the passage of the bill to give him the right of permanent residence in the United States. Among those whose supporting affidavits were printed in the report were L. Hollingsworth Wood, chairman of the International Rescue and Relief Committee; Saul Levitas, executive editor of the *New Leader*; Norris B. Chipman, counsellor of the US Embassy in Rome; Robert P. Joyce, a member of the policy planning staff of the State Department; Bertram D. Wolfe, chief of the Ideological Advisory Unit of the State Department's international broadcasting division; Melvin J. Lasky, the editor of *Der Monat*; Raymond E. Murphy (who did not specify his occupation in Washington, but whose connection with the intelligence apparatus was scarcely a secret); George P. Brett, president of the Macmillan Company, Koestler's American publishers; and Jay Lovestone, executive secretary of the Free Trade Union Committee, an affiliate of the American Federation of Labour.

They all expounded at some length their firm conviction that the passage of the bill would be in the best interests of the United States. In spite of this formidable support, and also in spite of his attorney's statement that 'Since Mr Koestler's arrival in the United States . . . he has clearly shown a willingness to serve our Government in its effort to combat Communism' – a service which 'has also been rendered to those private groups who have undertaken this important task' – the Department of Justice, faithful to the letter of restrictive legislation, opposed the measure.

In his letter to Senator Pat McCarran, the Deputy Attorney General, Peyton Ford, pointed out without comment that Koestler's admission to the United States on 23rd September 1950 had been 'for a temporary period not to exceed 4 months' and that his stay 'was for the sole purpose of arranging for the publication of a novel and for the theatrical production of a prior work'.

So the issue was, technically at least, in doubt. But not for long. On 21st June the Senate, acting over the objections of the Justice Department, passed the bill unanimously. The measure then went to the House of Representatives, but since there seemed to be no obstacle there to its passage, it seemed safe at last for the Koestlers to leave for Europe. Cynthia went first, on the 27th, followed by Koestler and Mamaine on the 31st.

They would all three, Koestler hoped, be back at Island Farm by the beginning of October.

# CHAPTER XXVI

# *1951*

MAMAINE STAYED IN LONDON with her twin, Celia, before joining Koestler at Verte Rive. As she had feared, the humid climate of the Seine made her unwell and after a week or so she returned to London. During her stay, she and Koestler laid their plans for the coming months. Verte Rive was definitely to be sold and they would sail for New York, with all their belongings, in the *Ile de France* on 7th September. Cynthia, who had agreed to accept full time employment as Koestler's secretary, would accompany them. They would be followed as soon as possible by the cook and gardener, Anna and Maxime Mouttė who had also agreed to throw in their lot with the Koestlers in America. In the meantime immigration visas would have to be obtained for Cynthia and the Mouttés, and American sponsors recruited for them.

There was also the question of a visa for Koestler himself. On her way back to London from Verte Rive, Mamaine called on the American consul in Paris, R. Clyde Larkin. She explained the situation: the bill had been passed unanimously in the Senate and there seemed no doubt that the House of Representatives would do likewise.

Larkin's reaction to this was odd. It was quite probable, he said, that the President would not sign the bill because this might encourage other ex-Communists to follow Koestler's lead. The President, he explained, might well wish to avoid 'a flood of ex-Communists entering the United States'. Larkin, it was clear, was not disposed to go out of his way to be helpful, but Mamaine, wishing to spare Koestler anxiety and worry that might in the end turn out to be groundless, did not report the conversation to him.

When Koestler, shortly after, got in touch with the Consulate, Larkin told him that it was legally quite impossible for him to accept his application either for a visitor's or a returning resident's visa while the bill was still pending. Koestler wrote off at once to his lawyer in New York, urging him to find out from Walter M. Besterman, Legislative Assistant to the House of Representatives' Judiciary Committee, if anything could be done to enable him to leave for New

York on 7th September even if the bill had not yet been passed. He recalled that Besterman had told him in Washington that means had been found of getting the Czech violinist and composer, Jan Kubelik, back into the United States while his bill was still pending.

A week later his lawyer reported that Besterman had assured him that the bill would pass the House on 7th August and be before the President on the following day.

> 'In preparation for its passage and being signed by the President,' he wrote a few days later, 'it is necessary that I know at which Consul's office you will apply to return to the United States. As soon as the Bill has been signed by the President I will see that the State Department notifies the Consul General's office at which you intend to apply of this fact in order to obviate any trouble for you.'

Thus reassured, Koestler busied himself with the necessary arrangements for Cynthia and the Mouttés. The Macmillan Company in New York agreed to sponsor the former (so long as 'any expense which should be incurred by us on Miss [Cynthia] Jefferies' account may become a first charge against your royalties'), and Budd and Vicki Schulberg did likewise for the latter. A passage was booked for the Mouttés on the *Ile de France*, sailing from Cherbourg on 25th September.

Koestler was in good spirits. The book was going well and he had Cynthia to help him with his copious correspondence. The French translation of *The Age of Longing* had been well received:

> 'The *Figaro Littéraire*,' he wrote to Mamaine on 30th July, 'had a rave-review about the book (will send it when I get the clipping), and according to the *Saturday Review of Literature* of July 7th, "The Age of Longing" is top of the list of "books being read throughout the country" (with "From Here to Eternity" in fifth place) . . . (I just see that the SRL list is based on "a comprehensive poll conducted among discriminating readers throughout the country" – I wish it were the undiscriminating readers).'

He was anxious to get back to the United States to hasten the law-suit he had brought against Sidney Kingsley (to prevent the latter's arranging the European production of the unrevised dramatisation of *Darkness at Noon*), 'as I cannot go on postponing the . . . arbitration date without spoiling my case.' The news that Kingsley was fighting back vigorously was an irritant:

> '[Kingsley] has counter-sued, expressly demanding that I should be deprived of any control of the play, on the grounds, believe it or not, that I have tried to sell the play on my own without his consent. This seems so absurd that according to commonsense I ought to win hands down. But what do we suckers know about American lawyers?'

He asked Mamaine to get in touch with his London agent A. D. Peters and insist that he, in consultation with his New York agent, Harold Matson, and his lawyer 'should take this thing off my mind. Insist on a clear answer whether Peters is willing to handle the matter as it has to be handled and take the burden off my shoulders or not.'

Matson, he complained, had sent on to him two letters addressed to him by Kingsley's lawyer

'without a word of comment or indication what they have answered or what I am supposed to answer . . .

'For the last 3 nights I couldn't go to sleep until 3 and 4 a.m. because of this matter. You know that this is a very rare occurrence with me.'

That apart, all was well. His letters to Mamaine – full of news, instructions, and injunctions – were buoyant and affectionate.

But during the second week of August everything had changed and all plans were cancelled. Mamaine had at last decided that it would be better for them both if they were to part. On 20th August Koestler wrote to her:

'Darling,

'. . . I have decided, regardless whether I go to the States or not, not to take Anna and Maxime. The responsibility and the burden of nursing them along is too great. To compensate them for the disappointment . . . I am building them a little house in Le Châtelet. It will cost me about 600,000 francs and it is the only thing to compensate them for their lost hope for a *retrait* for old age. I am signing the contract today at Maître Guitar's.

'My explanation to them was that as you can't stand the climate here on the river, it is doubtful whether you would be able to stand it on an island, which is also on the water. I said that it depends on what your doctor says after a week's observation. I explained to them that in view of this uncertainty we have to postpone departure at any rate; and that in order to take the uncertainty off their minds I am building their house whether we go to America or not; so they are just getting dressed to go to the notary.

'The purpose of this letter is to ask you to make things easier for me by immediately writing a nice letter to Anna and Maxime saying how sorry you are that your state of health "*met tout nos projets en doute*"; that you don't know yet what the doctor will decide; that Monsieur will keep them informed of all developments, and that you think of them with affection. This will simplify matters for me a great deal.

'We are starting to build the house immediately. This will occupy their minds and then I shall be able gradually to make them forget America and their hopes connected with it . . .

'My own plans are still in the air; I hope to get a cable today from Martin Richmond, and shall let you know.

'About Cynthia's plans she will write herself.

'If I go to the States I shall go by air. I have accordingly wired you today asking you to cancel all five passages. Enclosed the tickets, in case the French line needs them. Please have the refund paid into my account with Peters.

'About your bed, sofa and other furniture which you don't want to take over to England: the simplest way is that whenever you pick up an "occasion" to replace what is yours, buy it and have it refunded by Peter.'

This crossed a long letter from Mamaine to which he replied on 22nd August:

'Your letter of Monday.

'Don't worry about the divorce. Plenty of time. At present I still don't know where I am going to live.

'. . . The President has definitely not signed the Bill. I know this because the International News Service made sure on Paul Winkler's request. Whether the not-signing means implicit approval or not, I still don't know. Martin Richmond didn't answer my cable. Cy [Sulzberger] asked the Embassy to cable the State Department for information. No reply yet.

'Thanks for the photograph. "The Age of Longing" prints are in America. I don't feel like going through photographs just now. One day I will sort them out and send you what you want.

'I'll let you know about the visa business and about my plans when I have made up my mind . . .'

The bill 'for the relief of Arthur Koestler' had in fact become law at midnight on the 22nd. It had been passed by the House on 10th August and presented to the President. Consul Larkin's forecast had been correct. Truman declined to sign the bill, which, nevertheless, in the words of the note appended to the printed act by the Federal Register Division, 'not having been returned by him to the House of Congress in which it originated within the time prescribed by the Constitution of the United States, has become a law without his approval.'

Koestler's lawyer sent him a copy of the act (Private Law 221) which read in part that

'for the purposes of the immigration and naturalization laws, Arthur Koestler shall be held and considered to have been lawfully admitted to the United States for permanent residence as of the date of the enactment of this Act, upon payment of the required visa fee and head tax . . .'

That seemed straightforward enough. What obstacles could now remain in the way of Koestler's return to America? The lawyer's covering letter suggested that the bureaucracy might have a few in mind:

'. . . I am presently involved in endless red tape in trying to wrap up this project.

'The President did not sign your Bill and it became law automatically on Wednesday, August 22, 1951. Since that time I have been on the long distance telephone continually trying to both have the New York Office of Immigration and Naturalization receive instructions of this new law so that they would accept from me the head tax and visa payments and secondly, to have the State Department wire its Paris Consul of the fact of the new law and the payment of the head and visa tax and to issue to you a returning resident's visa. The first few days were wasted in awaiting the printed copy of the law which I have enclosed herewith. After I had this distributed to the various offices in Washington, I have been sitting in New York awaiting the time that they would accept my payments. Many phone calls, etc. As of this moment, notification still has not been received here and I am still with it, without interruption.

'I have been rushing this matter knowing full well that you desire to return on September 7 and have left no stones unturned. I hope you make it.'

Koestler, of course, now had no intention of leaving on 7th September, the passages having been cancelled. In any case he would (although he did not yet know it) have been unable to do so, the US bureaucracy in general and Consul Larkin's department in particular having prepared an ordeal for him.

On 25th August he had recovered sufficiently from the shock of Mamaine's decision to write to her about the future:

'Darling, I think I ought to tell you about my plans, which are gradually beginning to crystallise. The Maxime-Anna problem is settled, as I wrote to you; they are going to stay at Verte Rive, with the Americans [two officers to whom he was going to let the house, which he had decided not to sell after all], and going to build their house. Incidentally, they insist on repaying me at the rate of francs 5000 per month* – I am going to try to let the Island for 3–5 years, instead of selling it, for various practical reasons. – I am going to fly over in the second half of September; stay on the Island, by myself, until the letting is arranged; then live for a while in a hotel or boarding house – eg, there is one on Martha's Vineyard. Books and files I am going to leave for the time being here.

'Then I shall decide whether I really want to live in the States; but probably I won't. As I have to live in an English-speaking country, probably the only solution is to return to England. In this case I would have a furnished flat in London – no responsibilities – for the winter; and spend the summer here. I shall discuss all this with Peter [A. D. Peters, his agent] on Monday.

'About the bill . . . Harry didn't sign it; but I won't do any quixotic demonstrations about that.

'I am gradually returning to work; correcting the German proofs of the novel. Am also doing regular one-hour sculling daily.

'Keagy (the American officer who took this house) was during the Palestine war there as a volunteer army doctor in Tel Lenitsky; he is non-Jewish, became a political Zionist, but left in October '48 in disappointment because of racism and chauvinism in Israel. Isn't that a funny coincidence?

'He and the other officer are mid-westerners of the best type – the type you hardly know – And yet, America is less and less attractive to me – mainly because I feel it is the wrong country to live in as a writer . . .'

A. D. Peters arrived at Verte Rive just after a letter from Mamaine in which she told Koestler that she intended to buy a house in Hasker Street, behind

* But Koestler refused any repayment.

the Brompton Road, at the cost of £6,000. Koestler replied on 29th August to say that Peters' visit had proved a real boon. He had discussed all his main problems with him, and also the question of Mamaine's house. Although a house was a solid investment, he wrote, and a hedge against inflation, it would be a worrying matter if Mamaine were to reduce her interest-earning capital by £6,000. Peters and he had agreed that it would be a good idea for him to provide half of the purchase price in the form of a mortgage at a nominal interest.

> 'As I . . . have got £3,000 with Peter which bears no interest at all, I wouldn't lose anything and would have on the contrary an inflation-proof investment. You, on the other hand would not diminish your capital income and would save the 4½% interest which you would have to pay if you take a mortgage or money from a building society. The idea seems to me sound from every point of view; Peter will discuss the details with you . . .
>
> 'I don't want to argue now about your curtains, lamps, things, etc., but it stands to reason that if you furnish a house, every stitch and odd item will be a help and it would be just crazy not to take all that belongs to you or to buy the equivalent objects in London.
>
> 'I shall probably leave around the 15th to get matters in the States settled as soon as possible. I shall stop in London for a day; then we can discuss these details . . .'

Two days later he wrote again:

> 'I have received a letter from a furniture remover . . . saying that he has got orders . . . to transport piano, tables, etc. He says that he can only do it after September 5th and he sent a list of various complicated formalities necessary for the French export permit.
>
> 'I don't know how soon you want your furniture; it obviously depends on when you get the house. At any rate, it is inevitable that you should come over because a number of the formalities, for instance clearance from the French income tax, and about half a dozen legalised signatures, etc., can only be done by yourself. I hope that your tax situation is independent from mine. I have a date next week with the income tax people to clarify my situation, and I shall then find out. But you would anyway have to come to collect your silver and to choose all of the objects which you want to take – curtains, cushions, bed linen, etc. The best thing would be if you came after I left, that is, after September 15th. Otherwise it would have to be the week between the 9th and 15th, because before that the tax situation won't be clarified.
>
> 'All this is a hellish nuisance, but there we are.'

* *

He next turned his attention to another 'hellish nuisance' – Clyde Larkin's apparent determination to emulate the frustrating tactic of the eponymous villain in Gian-Carlo Menotti's opera, *The Consul*, the chilling Kafkaesque *verismo* of which was holding audiences spellbound in America and Europe.

By 24th August the American Consulate in Paris received notification from Washington that Koestler's bill had become law. So on that day Vice-Consul Imogene E. Ellis wrote to him as follows:

> 'Reference is made to your desire to obtain a visa permitting your return to the United States.
>
> 'From the information concerning your case available to the Embassy, it appears that you are eligible for a Section 4 (b) non-quota visa as an alien lawfully admitted to the United States for permanent residence returning from a temporary trip abroad. A memorandum concerning this type of visa is herewith enclosed for your information, together with two questionnaires which should be completed by you and returned to the Embassy at your early convenience.
>
> 'Please be assured that your application for a Section 4 (b) visa will receive every consideration consistent with the Immigration Laws and Regulations of the United States.'

Koestler completed the questionnaires as requested, returned them at his earliest convenience, and on 4th September went to the embassy to collect his returning-resident's visa. It was not forthcoming.

Instead, he was informed by Vice-Consul Imogene E. Ellis that it was withheld because 'he had been a member of the Communist Party'.

Koestler, exercising a degree of self-control which in the circumstances can only be described as miraculous, referred her to the Private Law 221 of the 82nd Congress, a copy of which was before her.

The vice-consul was not impressed. The text of the law, she pointed out, contained no reference to Koestler's Communist past. The fact that Report No. 407 of the Senate's Committee on the Judiciary, also before her, abounded in references to his Communist past she seemed to regard as an irrelevance.

Putting her attitude down to simple stupidity, Koestler insisted on seeing the Consul, R. Clyde Larkin, who quickly disabused him. It was he who had overruled the decision to grant a returning-resident's visa implicit in the Vice-Consul's letter of 24th August. He then went on to explain that he had requested further instructions from Washington; that in the meantime he would not issue Koestler with a visa; that he was determined to apply the same procedure to any other beneficiaries of similar laws that might be passed by the US Congress; and – a final stroke – that private laws of this type did not invalidate the ineligibility of former Communists for visas to the United States.

But it was the obvious purpose of the law passed for his relief, Koestler pointed out to the Consul, to overcome such obstacles. The act, in other words, was the expression of the considered and unanimous opinion of both Houses of the American legislature that his Communist past should be no hindrance to his residence in the United States.

Larkin's rejoinder to this was that he had no assurance that Koestler had not rejoined the Communist Party during his two months' absence from the United States.

During the heated conversation which followed he qualified the insinuation (as Koestler saw it) by observing that he had used it only to illustrate the difficulties confronting a US Consul in such a situation.

That was not good enough for Koestler, who left Larkin and went straight to Philip Bonsal, the US Chargé d'Affaires, who heard him out and promised to do what he could.

By the following morning Koestler, recalling all the stories he had heard of the torments inflicted by American consular officials, and in particular the absurdities to which Michael Polanyi had recently been subjected,* had decided to take a tough attitude.

> 'Since our talk yesterday,' he wrote to Bonsal, 'I have after careful deliberation, decided to make a test-case of this issue by insisting on your Consul's apology. Many thanks for your very kind efforts to intervene on my behalf, but, as I told you repeatedly, that was not the point of my visit to you. I feel that if people with the benefit of a special Act of Congress and so on accept the proceedings of this kind without protest there is no chance of redress for less privileged applicants.'

And so he wrote to Consul Larkin:

> 'I wish you to understand that this letter is not motivated by personal reasons. I have decided to make this a test-case for people in similar positions. While I shall always remain a friend and admirer of your country, I shall not enter your office unless a formal apology is offered . . .
>
> 'Allow me a general remark which will perhaps explain my attitude. Twice in the past your country has saved Europe; today the security and survival of Europe again depend on the United States. We Europeans have every reason to side with and to be grateful to your country; yet millions of Europeans are unreasonably and emotionally hostile to it. There are many reasons for this; not the least important are certain aspects of the treatment which applicants for visas encounter in some American consulates. I know of cases of people who committed suicide during the German occupation of France because, though your country was willing to give them a haven, they could not obtain the rubber stamp which meant survival. If applicants who are in a relatively privileged position accept unfair treatment without protest, there can be no hope for redress for the anonymous thousands whose life and death often depends on these technicalities.
>
> 'I have informed Mr Bonsal of our conversation and am sending him a copy of this letter.'

Larkin's request for 'further information' from Washington was manifestly unnecessary in view of the cable he had received from Washington on 24th August. Its wording, however, seems to have conjured up a bureaucratic obstacle which not even Bonsal could summarily demolish.

Koestler wrote to Mamaine on 7th September to tell her of developments and to ask whether, should it prove impossible for him to return to America, she

* See Notes page 365.

would be willing to go for a couple of weeks to see to the letting of Island Farm and retrieve their belongings. Bonsal, he told her, had hinted obliquely that it might be a good idea for Koestler to go to London for his visa 'and thus by-pass Mr Larkin's den . . . I am chewing that over and shall let you know.' He had finished chewing it over by the end of the letter, to which he added a postscript:

'After the usual changings of mind, I have, as usual, decided not to compromise – i.e. to wait for the visa in Paris and refuse it if not accompanied by the Consul's apology.'

'How absolutely extraordinary about Larkin,' Mamaine replied. 'It is hardly believable. Such things only happen to you. He must be either a Party member, or a maniac; no doubt the latter.'

She then told Koestler of the odd conversation she had had with Larkin some weeks before. This confirmed his suspicion that Larkin's action was maliciously arbitrary.

'I think,' Mamaine continued, 'you are absolutely right to insist on an apology from him before doing anything else at all. Your letter to him is very good. I can hardly wait to hear what happens next. Do please wire me if you're not going to turn up yourself. I do awfully hope that everything will go all right, as I am sure it can't fail to do, that he will grovel and that you will be able to come to London for a couple of days before going to the States. I can't help looking forward terrifically to seeing you, and shall be awfully disappointed if you don't come. I would like to show you my house, now bought all but for signing the contract . . . Also, I have caught a whale for the F.I.F. [Fund for Intellectual Freedom] I think, and very much want to introduce this whale to you so that you can complete the process of roping him in. He is an old friend of mine called Nicholas Monsarrat, who has written a book about the Navy during the war (a novel) called The Cruel Sea, which is a Book of the Month choice in the States, Book Society here, Evening Standard Book of the Month, sold to Readers' Digest, and the film rights sold. It has already sold 130,000 copies in England. Nick is a serious and conscientious man, likely to fulfil any obligations he may undertake; he spoke of giving a percentage of his film royaltics which will trickle in continuously over a longish period. I am awfully proud about this catch, if it works.

'Do wire me your moves. Of course if you can't go to the States I'll go over and do le nécessaire . . .'

Koestler had followed up a cable to his lawyer in New York with an explanatory letter which ended:

'It should be understood that, apart from the personal inconveniences (caused by the necessity of cancelling my reservation, postponing my departure to the United States, where I have urgent business to attend to), my motive in raising this issue is not a personal one. The context of the law passed on my behalf makes it clear that the law was primarily motivated by political reasons, namely, to make use of the experience which I have gained through my Communist affiliation in the 1930's and through the political fight which I have waged during the subsequent thirteen years. There are thousands of men and women in Western Europe whose experience is equally and frequently even more valuable because of a more recent nature. Clear-minded men in the United States realise the great value of such people and are fighting a hard battle against bureaucratic obstacles to make their experience available. My case is typical of this battle between political necessity and bureaucratic obstruction; that is why I am raising the whole issue. If even people who benefit from a special law and so on, encounter such arbitrary treatment and endorse it without protest, there can be no hope for others less privileged.'

The lawyer cabled in reply:

'Your problem requires Washington intercession cable instructions.'

By 8th September, however, there seemed no need for Koestler to take further action, for on that day the Chargé d'Affaires informed Koestler officially that, following a telephone call to the State Department, all obstacles to the issue of a visa had been demolished.

But that was not yet the view of the resourceful Consul Larkin who had no intention of taking the Minister's word for it and was obviously determined to spin the matter out and inflict the maximum annoyance and inconvenience on Koestler, to whom he wrote on 10th September:

'I have received your letter of September 5, 1951, concerning your application for a Section 4 (b) non-quota immigration visa to enable you to return to the United States as a permanent resident. You also refer to the recent bill passed by Senator Owen Brewster, and enacted by the Congress, namely Public Law No. 221, which became effective on August 23, 1951. Further reference is made to your interpretation of certain remarks I made to you and to your demand for a formal apology.

'In the course of our conversation regarding your application for a visa, I orally advised that the legal questions raised in your case have been referred to the Department of State in accordance with the regulations controlling the issuance of visas. Consequently, I have no alternative but to await the Department's response before issuing a visa to you.

'You further state in your letter that "while I shall always remain a friend and admirer of your country, I shall not enter your office unless a formal apology is offered" for certain "insinuations"....

'I did not state that I had no assurance that you had not rejoined the Communist Party during your last two months' absence from the United States. In our lengthy conversation of last Wednesday, you may recall that I immediately pointed out to you that you were incorrect in your assumption, in the course of my explanation of the difficulties regarding your case, that I made the insinuation that you had rejoined the Communist Party.

'In view of the above facts, there appears to be no basis for the statements ascribed to me and, consequently, no justification for your demand for an apology from me. I think that upon further reflection, you will agree with me.

'I assure you that your application for a visa will continue to receive every consideration consistent with the Laws and Regulations of the United States governing the issuance of visas.'

On the following day, formal instructions presumably having arrived, Larkin gave a little ground in a letter, signed this time on behalf of the Consul-General:

'. . . You are hereby informed that to establish your lawful entry into the United States in accordance with the provisions of Public Law No. 221, the following formalities are required:

'1. Payment to the Embassy of a visa fee in the amount of $10;

'2. Delivery to the Embassy for transmission to the Immigration and Naturalization Service, Department of Justice, of an international money order to the Commissioner of Immigration and Naturalization in amount of $8.00, United States currency.

'Upon compliance with the aforementioned formalities necessary to establish your status as a permanent resident of the United States, you should then execute your formal application at the Embassy for a Section 4 (b) non-quota immigration visa, as an immigrant who is returning to the United States from a temporary residence abroad. The fees established by the Immigration Act of 1924 for such a visa are $1.00 for the execution of such application and $9.00 for the issuance of the visa to you, if qualified. No final decision may be made regarding your eligibility to receive such a visa until after you have executed your formal visa application.

'Please be assured that your application shall receive every consideration consistent with the Immigration Laws and Regulations.'

Larkin still had a few cards up his sleeve. On 12th September the Chargé d'Affaires telephoned Koestler and advised him to go to the Consulate immediately to collect his visa.

'I thereupon,' Koestler wrote to Larkin later in the day, 'called around 11 a.m. your Vice Consul, Miss Ellis, and made with her a date for tomorrow morning, 9 a.m., to complete the remaining formalities. Miss Ellis called my attention to the necessity of paying the head tax of $8.00 in U.S. currency and suggested that this should be done in the form of an international money order. For the acquisition of a money order payable in dollars for however small a sum it is necessary to obtain permission of the French Government's Exchange Control Office – a procedure which, as the Post Office informed me, normally takes two weeks and sometimes a month. I therefore suggested to Miss Ellis that I pay the $8.00 by cheque on my New York Bank, which she said would of course be all right.

'At 4 p.m on the same day, Miss Ellis called me and informed me that on your instruction she had to refuse payment of the $8.00 (eight dollars) in question by cheque on New York, by traveller's cheque or by cash, and could only accept payment in the form of an international money order.

'I thereupon asked Miss Ellis to transfer my file to your Embassy in London, where I have made previous arrangements to go on Friday, September 14th. Miss Ellis assured me that my file will be transferred to London immediately.

'I feel that these facts ought to be on record . . .'

Having abandoned hope of extracting an apology from the Consul, he wrote to the Chargé d'Affaires on the 13th:

'I am leaving for London tomorrow, Friday the 14th. Following a previous suggestion of yours, I have asked Vice Consul Ellis to transfer my file to your Embassy in London. Miss Ellis has promised to do so immediately.

'In view of the fact that Mr Larkin has on several occasions reversed his Vice-Consul's decisions, it seems to me not unreasonable to expect that further hitches will occur in the transmission of the file to London. I have, for instance, passed the prescribed medical examinations, blood tests, etc., as on record in my file; so that only transfer of the complete file can prevent my having to start the whole procedure again in London.

'As you have been so very kind as to take an interest in this matter up to now, I should be very grateful if you could make sure that the complete file, including communications received from Washington, is indeed transferred without delay to the U.S. Consulate in London.

'My London address will be as from Friday night, September 14th: c/o Mr Hamish Hamilton, 43, Hamilton Terrace, London NW8.'

Koestler found a letter from Bonsal waiting for him at Hamish Hamilton's. The complete file, he wrote, was being transferred to London and would certainly be available at the consulate there on the morning of the 17th.

'I am sorry that this simple matter should have developed such complications, but I hope that it will now be worked out satisfactorily.'

It was, but not without a small parting shot from Larkin. Koestler's premonition that there might be further hitches in the transfer of his file to London proved to be correct.

'You may be interested in the temporary dénouement of the affair', he wrote to Bonsal on the day before he left for New York.

'1. My file arrived at the U.S. Consulate, London, on Tuesday morning. The medical documents were missing – see my enclosed letter to Mr. R. C. Larkin. This made it necessary to repeat the whole procedure of medical examinations and blood tests all over again.

'2. I do not doubt that the French Office de Change is willing to issue an international money order within two days on request of a member of the U.S. Diplomatic Corps; the delay given to me by the Post Office was, as I mentioned before, "at least a fortnight".

'3. However, the question of the international money order did not arise any more, as the Visa Section of the U.S. Embassy in London accepted without hesitation payment of the $8.00 in question in local currency.

> 'I would like to add that the Visa Section here handled the whole matter with exemplary speed and courtesy.
>
> 'I am leaving for New York tomorrow and shall, as I told you before, report in full my experiences with the U.S. Consul in Paris to the proper authorities in Washington – in the interests of other applicants.'

Bonsal replied to Koestler in America. He was delighted, he wrote, that the matter had been cleared up, and

> 'I hope that you will be coming back here one of these days and that we will have a chance to discuss other matters.'

But other matters would have to wait as far as Koestler was concerned. Having seen to it that the Larkin affair had an airing in the American press, he assembled complete dossiers for the State Department, the Senate, and the House Judiciary Committee's sub-committee for immigration. In his covering letter to the last he wrote:

> 'Needless to say that I am not taking this action for personal reasons, but because this case seems to me typical of what is going on in some American consulates in Europe. If this can happen to a person in a relatively privileged position, it is not difficult to imagine what treatment less privileged applicants receive. A good deal of the irrational hostility of Europeans against this country is due to such treatment. I believe that the setting up of a Congressional Committee to investigate the practices of U.S. consulates in Europe would unearth facts that would shake American public opinion. There would be no difficulty in obtaining hundreds of testimonials from witnesses who had experiences much worse than mine.'

Thanking him on behalf of the sub-committee, Walter Besterman remarked that his story was 'certainly most enlightening', although not new. 'Didn't we have operas written about consuls?'

But Koestler's efforts were not wasted. The members of the sub-committee were leaving shortly for Europe to investigate the administrative operations of US consular offices, and Besterman saw to it that Koestler's dossier would 'be well used'. Some time was to pass before the notorious attitudes of the consulates were effectively humanised, but Koestler eventually had the satisfaction of knowing that his reputation ensured that his own experience played a part in the process.

## CHAPTER XXVII

# *1951–1952*

As Mamaine had foreseen, she and Koestler missed each other very much, although both realised that they would eventually be happier living apart. No doubt the parting had been rather easier for Mamaine, for it was she who had made the decision, and because it was one she had come close to making on a number of occasions long before.

Still, she was depressed for a time and grateful for the affectionate letters which kept arriving from Koestler in America. Eventually she took an editorial job with the publishing firm recently founded by Derek Verschoyle, a former literary editor of *The Spectator*. Together with Celia she continued her piano lessons with their old friend Joseph Cooper, with whom they had studied years earlier, and practised without fail for two hours a day. She also realised a long-held ambition by learning classical Greek, travelling regularly to Acton to have lessons with a retired schoolmaster. She and Celia had a host of friends and acquaintances in London; like her work and her music and all her other interests, they kept at bay the sense of insecurity and anxiety to which she had always been prone. She succeeded in making a new life for herself, but it was one in which the husband she had left was always to have a place.

As for Koestler, he too had to remake his life. Before the break with Mamaine he had been acutely aware that in his career as a writer he was approaching a crossroads, the signposts of which, however, he could not see. Her departure jolted him into the shocked realisation of all that he had left undone, of those early ambitions unfulfilled, of the sad fact that, despite all the fame (and notoriety) that his political activities had brought him, he had for many years been travelling along a road that was not entirely congenial and would become even less so the more freely he spent his energies.

Hadn't he done enough? Hadn't he said it all? He wasn't, after all, a politician. What was he, then? No doubt it was to find the answer to that question that he had started to write his autobiography, the first volume of which he had almost completed in draft by the time of his return to Island Farm.

Before he could finish and correct the draft, however, there were other chores to do. The proofs of the German translation of *The Age of Longing* had to be corrected, and the garden – which had been neglected by the people to whom he had let the place during his absence – had to be put in order.

> '. . . shall write when I have a little time', he scribbled in a brief note to Mamaine soon after his arrival. 'At present haven't. Found Island in a deplorable state.'

The garden was a jungle. Half his tools were missing. The car had broken down. He hadn't been able to find a part-time secretary. And, to complicate matters, he had developed a kidney stone and was in consequence in some pain, often severe enough to keep him in bed. Since Sidney Kingsley and the approaching arbitration were much in his mind, and because he and Mamaine had taken to referring to the playwright as 'kidney', he was half-convinced that the cause of his affliction was psychosomatic. In spite of this, his letters were cheerful enough.

* *

Earlier in the year *The Humanist*, the journal of the American Humanist Association, had classified the many current meanings attributed to the term 'Humanism', from the collective philosophies of the ancient Greeks through the theistic concept of Christian existentialists and the atheistic version of Sartre and his disciples to the eclecticism of 'naturalistic humanism' – the product of the scientific age and centred upon a faith in the supreme value and self-perfectibility of human personality, rejecting both supernaturalism and totalitarianism.

Letters were sent to a wide variety of authors asking them what kind of 'humanist' they considered themselves. The extract from Koestler's reply, published in the October issue of *The Humanist*, shows how firmly he had rejected materialism:

> 'The term "supernaturalistic" begs the definition of nature. I believe this is not a problem of philosophy, but of semantics. If, however, your question refers to the nineteenth century materialism – that, of course, is dead as mutton. What will come after I do not know. We live in an earthquake and the new pattern of things has not yet crystallised.'

In the years to come he was to devote very close attention to that process of crystallisation, engaging himself in many a controversy with the diehards who deplored the crumbling of nineteenth-century certainties and seldom failed to denounce as 'unscientific' his various attempts to synthesise 'the new pattern of things'.

* *

But such excitements lay in the future. *The Humanist*'s inquiry was of interest to few. It was otherwise with Koestler's contribution to a special issue of *Collier's Magazine*, entitled *Preview of the War We Do Not Want* and published in October*. A large number of authors and journalists and politicians, including strategic and economic experts, had been commissioned to visualise and describe

* Edited by Cornelius Ryan, author of *The Longest Day*.

the state of the world in 1960 following a third world war. During the ten months it took to put the issue together the editors kept all the contributors informed of one another's suggestions and ideas, so that the finished product should have a planned and co-ordinated character.

Koestler's contribution was an imaginary description of social reconstruction and rehabilitation in a Russia devastated by atomic bombs and attempting to create representative political institutions after Western models. Much of the material for his descriptions of deprivation on a huge scale came straight from his own memory of the famine, the effects of which he had seen at close quarters in the Ukraine. His account of the creation of a 'convicts' republic' in the Kolyma peninsula was carefully based on his knowledge of what later came to be known as the Gulag Archipelago and its twenty million slave labourers.

The details of his sketch seemed wildly exaggerated to many of his readers at the time, but in the light of the subsequent revelations of Solzhenitsyn and others, they appear mild enough now.

> 'One question that people always ask [in the West] is never asked here [in Russia]: "What happened to Communism in Russia?" Everybody yawns when a visitor brings it up, because the answer is so obvious to every Russian. The answer is that there never was Communism in Russian; there were only Communists. When the Communists disappeared, Communism disappeared.
>
> 'Why is this so self-evident to every Russian, and so difficult to understand for people abroad? Because people outside Russia thought of Soviet Communism as a political system in the Western sense; or as some miscarried attempt to establish social justice; or as a kind of secular religion. It was, of course, nothing of the sort – except for a short period in the beginning, long since forgotten. For the last decades – as far back as the memories of the present generation can reach – it had ceased to be a political movement, for it had no opponents in Russia against which it could measure itself in terms of ideas or power. It could not teach the masses any programme or philosophy, for the line changed incessantly in a dizzy zigzag; yesterday's truth became today's heresy, and the very foundations of faith and belief were destroyed in the process.
>
> 'In a primitive community you can sometimes replace political thinking by a kind of simple loyalty to the government. But that loyalty too was destroyed when again and again men who were one day members of the Government confessed the next that they had always been traitors, spies and enemies of the people.
>
> 'When in the early years of the Revolution the priest vanished from the Russian scene, religion did not vanish with them; it remained alive with the people. But when the Communists vanished from the scene, Communism vanished with them because as a faith it had never existed among the Russian people.'

The issue raised a storm of protest, a fact which caused Koestler little surprise. He had learned from bitter experience how seductive was the policy of appeasement.

* *

Koestler's health continued to bother him, although he tried to conceal this from Mamaine.

> 'Darling,' he wrote to Mamaine on 5th November, 'I wish I hadn't told you so much about my silly kidney stone if it worries you so much. It's all over . . . It was probably psychosomatic; but whereas a psychosm. migraine is something anybody can have, a psychosomatic kidney stone is a sure sign of genius.'

But this was only to set her mind at rest. The stone was still there and still giving him pain.

> 'All goes well', he wrote, 'except for being overworked.'

He was writing the last chapter of the first draft of *Arrow in the Blue* and hoped to be able to get to London during January. So far he had found nobody who wanted to rent the island and was thinking of putting it up for sale.

> 'But I am no longer in a hurry,' he wrote on the 7th, 'as I can hold the fortress . . . until Christmas easily, and am for the time being quite enjoying it.'

Having found someone to look after the garden, he no longer had to bother with outdoor work,

> 'and the house I can easily cope with by eating out, and vacuum-cleaning once a week.'

His letters – chatty and reassuring – were like those of a husband left temporarily on his own. Yes: everything was under control; he was managing to look after himself; how was she getting on? Only once did he refer to their parting and the cause of it:

> 'As I live now rather like a hermit and have plenty of time to think and contemplate, I got a little distance [from] the whole thing and found, in retrospect, that I must really have made life rather insupportable for you; and feel sorry and guilty about it.'

In the middle of November the kidney stone gave him a bad bout of pain, but when the trouble was over he wrote:

> 'Darling, middle-age is setting in in earnest: I had a ten-day attack of kidney stone; most of the time either in mad pain or under morphia. The stone passed last Thursday – 24 hours before the time limit I had set with [the surgeon] for operating . . . it was quite an experience.
>
> 'Now I am still under the morphia-hangover, which makes one feel very depressed for three to four days. But the book is getting on and I hope that the depression will lift soon.'

* *

For some time it had looked as if Koestler's agent and lawyer would succeed in reaching a compromise with Sidney Kingsley, but early in December the playwright broke off negotiations. The case was scheduled to go before the arbitration tribunal in New York during the latter half of January. On 10th December Koestler wrote to Mamaine to ask for her help in preparing for the hearing.

'It seems that legally,' he explained, 'my case is very wobbly with a good chance of losing it because I gave him a free hand with the American version, and it will be extremely difficult to convince the tribunal that what politically is good enough for this country isn't good enough for Europe. The whole matter hinges on that point, that is on my contention that although the play received the critics' award and was highly acclaimed by American critics, its inaccuracies when dealing with the language and atmosphere of Communist parties in Europe would lead to a débâcle, and that a failure of the play in France and Italy would mean not only a personal loss of prestige for both authors, but would also be a political defeat in the propaganda war against Communists and fellow-travellers.'

The tribunal announced early in March that it had found in favour of Kingsley. On the 8th Koestler broke the news to Mamaine.

'Darling, the Island is liquidated, the law suit is lost, the book is finished, and I am washed out. I am staying with Jim Putnam until to-morrow, then I go for a week lecturing to Yale; then, from March 24 I shall be in a hotel in New York until I have wound up a few things; and come to England in the first half of April – probably nearer the 1st than the 15th.

'I would have to write about the law suit for hours, so I won't write at all. It has surpassed in squalor and grotesqueness everything you could imagine. For precisely that reason, it left me cold. The verdict is, that I have to contrasign any European contract that Kingsley puts under my nose within seven days; if I don't, he has the right to sign alone. A compromise verdict would have been bad; this verdict clearly disengages my responsibility and I can wash my hands of the thing with a clean conscience. They also awarded Kingsley damages of 5000 dollars, which are being paid by the Fund for Intellectual Freedom (who so far got 40,000 out of the play, so it doesn't hurt them too much). It was a first-rate lesson and experience; I shall tell you about it for hours . . .

'God, I am looking forward to staying in a hotel where the room-service will bring me breakfast and the valet will blow my nose for me!'

* *

On 15th April, having spent two weeks of hard work in the St Moritz Hotel on Central Park South correcting the galley-proofs of *Arrow in the Blue*, he left for France.

The American experiment was over.

# CHAPTER XXVIII

# *1952–1954*

AFTER A WEEK OR two in Paris Koestler moved back into Verte Rive and started work on the second volume of his autobiography. He was determined to be distracted no longer by the affairs of the Congress for Cultural Freedom, whose artistic jamboree, *Masterpieces of the Twentieth Century*, was then engaging the enthusiastic attention of the critics in Paris.

Some months earlier, before the decision to organise the festival had been taken, he had been busy promoting the idea of holding a congress, similar to the Berlin demonstration, in Vienna. He had discussed this at length in New York with a friend in the American service attached to the US High Commission in Austria.

The idea had been well received, and now his friend wrote to say:

> 'Sometime this week I will write you again on the subject that we discussed in New York. I am sure that your idea to meet on the periphery would be much more effective than such an effete gathering in Paris. In any event, I shall send you a letter and shall look forward with great personal pleasure to seeing you in Vienna. With my very best wishes and looking forward to a longer meeting with you in the near future . . .'

Koestler had had enough. His reply was brief:

> 'Regarding the Congress for Cultural Freedom: as you may have seen in the papers, they are holding a Festival in Paris which is now in full swing. I regard this as a waste of money and energy and have therefore resigned from the Executive Committee. I shall, however, forward your informal suggestion, with my full support, to the people who are in charge.'

He continued to correspond with Mamaine, giving her much valuable advice about her editorial work with Derek Verschoyle and enjoying her gossipy letters. By June he had decided to sell Verte Rive and look for a house in London. On the 30th, just before she left for a holiday in Majorca, with Mark and Irene Sontag, who had been neighbours in North Wales, Mamaine wrote:

'This is just a chatty letter, no more. I am sorry you do not seem to have sold the house yet. Are people not biting? . . . Haven't done anything much of interest except the usual parties with always the same people; one nice dinner at the Spenders with T. S. Eliot, Osbert Sitwell, John Hayward and Rosamond Lehmann. I am dining with them for the Hamiltons' ball. Will write and tell you about it, and about the Sontags. Address in Majorca: c/o Sontag, Cala Ratjada, Mallorca. Do write there. I wish you were coming.'

Her asthma, she assured him, was under control at last and he was to stop worrying:

'I really do feel FINE,' she wrote to Celia from Majorca, 'and consequently live in a state of mild euphoria.'

Koestler, by this time, had found a place in London, a tall corner house in Montpelier Square in Knightsbridge village, not far from Mamaine's little house in Hasker Street. On 20th July he wrote to her in Majorca:

'Am very fit. Didn't drink for 3 weeks just for the fun of it, and by that alone without any other diet lost 5 kilos – from 66½ down to 61½! I am falling out of all my suits. Did not succeed in selling the house, but shall probably let it for a year at Frcs. 60,000 per month, with a clause saying that if I can sell the tenants have to clear out within 60 days. Shall stay on till August 15th, as I don't want to interrupt the book. Hope this still reaches you in Mallorca; give Mark and Irene my longing love; ditto to you. A.K.'

But his work on the book had to be interrupted after all, as he told Mamaine a week or so later in what he described as a 'blitz-letter':

'House sold on good terms but have to vacate it by Friday – day after to-morrow. So you can imagine what state I am in. Got a reservation for bringing over the car for the end of next week – date not yet definitely fixed because of holiday rush – so shall arrive in London next Thursday or Friday and shall ring you. Don't know yet where I am going to stay first day or two but as I arrive per car that's no problem, so don't bother about reservations; shall possibly move straight into new house.

'Leaving here Friday, staying weekend at Winklers, then shall probably spend a few days in Normandy en route for Boulogne. So mail won't reach me in between . . .

'Gad, I am glad to be rid of house . . .'

* *

He had decided, as he told Jill Craigie (Michael Foot's wife) when he arrived in London, to become an Englishman; and to celebrate they had a memorable pub-crawl together in Hampstead.

Life in London soothed away his restlessness and he settled down to work. Cynthia came every morning to type and re-type the draft of *The Invisible Writing*, the second volume of his autobiography.

He saw Mamaine frequently. She 'would often look in', a friend recalled, 'and cook a meal for him or help him in one way or another, and they were happier during this period, living apart, than they had been for years living together'.

In August *Arrow in the Blue* was published to the acclaim of the critics. A year later, the draft of *The Invisible Writing* having been all but completed, Cynthia left for the United States to work for Ely Culbertson.

When the autobiography had been finally polished and delivered to his publishers, Koestler – not yet ready to embark on the scientific work for which he had been amassing notes – began to draft a novel, but found it hard going. He became restless again and, following the final dissolution of his marriage early in 1954, felt the need to get out of London. January and February he spent travelling with a girl-friend, first in the West Country and then in Austria.

On his return he found to his dismay that Mamaine had fallen ill again and was in University College Hospital. She seemed to be recovering well, however, and the prognosis was favourable, so Koestler, who had taken a house in Ischia for the summer, left London with an easy mind early in April to drive to Naples. A few days after his arrival on the island, he wrote to Mamaine:

> 'After a very enjoyable journey of 2000 miles, all alone in the old Citroën, and not even a tire-puncture all the way, I have at last arrived here – only to find that the house won't be ready for another fortnight. For the time being I am staying in a cottage belonging to a painter . . .
>
> 'I do hope to God you have left the Clinic long ago . . . I didn't ask for your news, while I was on the way, as I had no settled route and no forwarding address; and wanted just to put everything out of my mind.
>
> 'Do you remember Jack Newsom, and Chris, one-time neighbours from Island Farm? They embarked on April 23 on the "Roma" for Naples, on their first visit to Europe in ten years; they were madly looking forward to it, and intended to settle in Italy. Yesterday I got a cable: "Jack died of heart-attack on board – am continuing to Naples – love Chris." Have you heard of anything more cruel and senseless to happen? Somehow one can never escape *la vie tragique*.
>
> 'I am working away on the new novel, and in between basking in the sea and the sun. In Paris I bought three pictures for the house, which will épater you. Do give me your news in a long, long letter and all the gossip. Love, my sweetie.'

In the meantime Mamaine had been discharged (too early, as it soon turned out) from University College Hospital and had gone to stay with Celia in Fulham. Once again she fell ill and had to return to hospital – St Pancras this time. Once again she was discharged too soon, had a relapse and early in May was admitted to University College Hospital once more.

She had in fact been desperately ill but since she seemed to be on the mend by the time she felt well enough to reply to Koestler, she took care not to worry him.

> 'Sweetie,' he wrote on 19th May, in reply to a cheerful letter, 'What an absolutely ghastly disappointment that you had to go back to the Clinic. And

yet somehow I feel that perhaps this whole misery will nevertheless serve a purpose if something radical can be done to achieve a lasting cure. I see in the paper that there is going to be an International Asthma Congress shortly, though it doesn't say when and where. Ask one of your doctors about it. There is sure to be some new treatment cropping up, something new and effective as penicillin was for infections . . . I wish we could hold a Kriegsrat together. From this distance one feels helpless . . .

'Sweetie, how silly to ask *me* about *birds*. You know I am bird-blind. But I do love this Island. I haven't picked a tree frog yet, but I shall ask Auden (who lives a few miles away) whether there are any. He is very warm and cozy to get on with just now. Robin Maugham too was here, I took him sailing in the canoe, he promised to look you up; he is an amusing companion but . . . more full of complexes than most people.

'Do keep me posted, Darling, about your progress, plans, and general gossip. Funny how gossip-hungry one gets when abroad, even about people one doesn't care about. Much love, get well quick, sweetheart.'

But he was to hear no more from Mamaine. ('Somehow one can never escape *la vie tragique*.') On 2nd June she died and on the following day Koestler, distraught with grief, was back in London. A few days after the funeral he returned to Ischia, tormented now by remorse as well as sorrow.

Cynthia did her best to console him in a letter from New York dated 18th June, in which she urged him not to blame and torture himself. Mamaine herself, she wrote, would have been the last person in the world to wish him to do so.

But many months were to pass before Koestler was to feel at peace with himself.

# PART FIVE

# *1954–1956*

# CHAPTER XXIX

# *1954*

THE PLEASURES OF THE Bay of Naples offered little solace. Wystan Auden, Robin Maugham and the other lotus-eaters looking out at the world from Ischia (when not contemplating their own or one another's navels) were understanding and sympathetic. But their manner of life was far removed from his, and their company and conversation could neither fill the void left by the death of Mamaine nor exorcise the devils of remorse crowding into it. It was a bad time for him and he took little interest in the reception of *The Invisible Writing* (the second volume of his autobiography), which was published two weeks after Mamaine's funeral.

The reviewers on the whole were well disposed, although some were inclined to be patronising.

But in *The Spectator*, Emanuel Litvinoff took him very seriously indeed:

> '. . . Lying in a Franco jail for ninety-six days under imminent threat of the firing squad, Koestler sloughed the dead skin of his Communist faith. The shock of the daily mass executions, the strain of arrest and solitary confinement, induced in him a condition of self-estrangement during which he experienced a feeble Nirvana like "a quiver of the arrow in the blue". It left him with a certainty that a higher order of reality existed. "It was a text written in invisible ink . . . And although one could not read it, the knowledge that it existed was sufficient to alter the texture of one's own existence . . ."'

And yet, Litvinoff went on:

> '. . . in the fifteen years that have elapsed since his release from prison this recognition of a higher order of reality has produced no positive philosophy. Koestler has remained a Cassandra with an intractable conviction of the validity of his own pessimism . . . The intellectual leadership of the ideological war against Communism comes from a gifted group of European ex-Communists such as Malraux, Sperber, Koestler, Silone and Weissberg. For the most part, the religion of these men is a politically inarticulated

humanism. They face a cruel dilemma; they cannot endorse the professed values of their own side, nor its often shabby compromises with the problems of power. Yet they know from experience that the evils of Communism must be stopped . . .'

'*The Invisible Writing* . . . poses an irresistible question: Are the Koestlers, the Malraux, the Weissbergs and the Silones the right people to lead Western Europe into sanity? . . . One of the most formidable ex-Communists of them all, Manès Sperber, has written: "Mark this carefully: we stormed heaven not that we might live there but to show all mankind, *ad oculis*, that heaven is empty."

'In Sperber's empty heaven, Koestler discerns fragments of an invisible writing, but all he can spell out is an enormous Mene, Mene, Tekel. It is not a message that men can afford to accept with resignation.'

This came close to the heart of the matter. So did Michael Polanyi's review some time later in the *New Leader* which suggested that what Koestler had experienced in Seville jail was 'divine grace', and that the experience had left him tongue-tied.

'We close the book with Mr Koestler's two conflicting consciences, the scientific and spiritual, still locked in uncertain combat, leaving the scene together, swaying forward towards an unknown consummation.'

* *

In the autumn of 1954 Koestler was back in London, determined now to give up political writing for good and return to his early loves, the history and philosophy of science. But first, two essays had to be written for his second collection (and also by way of clearing his mind for the intellectual adventures ahead).

In the first of these, *Judah at the Crossroads*, he clarified and amplified the arguments set out in the concluding chapter of *Promise and Fulfilment*, his account of Palestine and the Zionist movement and the nature of the new State of Israel which in 1948 had successfully defied the Arabs' first attempt to destroy it.

He had once, of course, been a committed and active Zionist, but he was one no longer when he and Mamaine flew to Israel a week or so after the proclamation of the State and the Arab attack; and although he upheld the right of the Jews to defend at least part of the historic tribal homeland which had been recolonised, he had become increasingly critical both of the reality into which the idealism of Zionism had been led and, even more so, of the continuing life of Zionism outside Israel.

The message of *Promise and Fulfilment* had given great offence at the time both to Israelis and to the 'exiled' Jews who supported them morally and with money. His arguments were summarily dismissed or misrepresented (or simply misunderstood); and had it not been for his prestige, not to say his earlier support for the gunmen of Irgun Zvai Leumi, his Jewish critics would no doubt have joined the Communist Party of France in labelling him 'anti-Semitic'.

Now, six years later, he determined to put the record straight and spell out unequivocally his attitude towards Israel and the Zionism which had brought it into existence.

> 'To put it bluntly, it is the choice between either becoming a citizen of Israel or ceasing to be a Jew in the national, religious or any other meaning of the word.'

Judaism, he wrote, is unique among religions in that it is inseparably tied to the idea of a separate nation – and one singled out by God – a nation with a land of its own which had been promised by God to the children of Israel and from which, after some uneasy centuries of occupation and enjoyment, it had been exiled for two millennia. For those two thousand years Jews throughout the world had raised their glasses of wine at the end of the Passover meal and drunk a sacred toast to 'Next year in Jerusalem!' They had learned to refer to those twenty centuries as the Diaspora, the Age of Dispersion; and to the non-Jew as a Goy – a word roughly equivalent to the Greek 'barbaros' with the derogatory connotations of its derivative 'barbarian'.

> 'In the centuries that have passed . . . the concept of the Goy has lost some of its tribal emotionalism, but it has never entirely lost its derogatory echo. In the ghettos of Poland, the young men sang mocking songs about the drunken Goy, which were no nobler in spirit than the anti-semitic jingles about Kikes and Yids. A persecuted minority certainly has good excuses for repaying hostility and contempt in the same coin, but the point I wish to make is that we are faced with a vicious circle: that a religion with the secular claim of racial exclusiveness must needs create secular repercussions. The Jew's religion sets him apart and invites his being set apart. The archaic, tribal element in it engenders anti-semitism on the same archaic level. No amount of enlightenment and tolerance, of indignant protests and pious exhortations, can break this vicious circle.'

* *

The other essay which he wrote towards the end of 1954 (*The Trail of the Dinosaur*) summed up his thoughts about the perils threatening civilisation. It begins with an invitation to the reader to envisage a number of charts on which the progress of *homo sapiens* has been plotted. The first, illustrating man's power over his environment, would show an almost horizontal line from the point of origin to, say, 5000 BC, when the invention of a few simple mechanical devices amplified man's muscular strength. Here the graph would show an upturn. Thereafter, for the next five or six thousand years, the line would remain almost horizontal.

> 'But in the course of the last three hundred years, the curve would, for the first time in the history of the species, rise steeply in leaps and bounds, until it pointed almost vertically upward . . . like a cobra stabbing upward.'

A dramatic illustration.

And the second more specific graph, showing the destructive potential of this power, would be more dramatic still. On the other hand, the chart illustrating improvements in the means of human communication might lift the spirits with its almost vertical ascent? Not so. The shrinking of the terrestrial surface in terms of communication had not led to a proportionate increase in its 'intellectual cohesion'. The nations had not been brought 'nearer' to one another. Nor had the extension of the range of sense organs through radio and television increased, as might have been expected, the intellectual range of the human mind. The uniquely human mental powers of abstraction and synthesis have not, he asserted, been strengthened. On the contrary: the extraordinary amplifications of man's sensory powers had brought about a rapidly increasing deterioration of the intellectual and moral content of communication –

> '. . . not only the habit of reading, but the faculty of thinking in the abstract, conceptual terms seem to be weakened by the child's conditioning to easier and more primitive forms of visual perception. The dangers of this repression from the conceptual to the perceptual, from abstract language to picture-strip language, are less obvious and immediate, but in the long run no less grave, than the spectacular increase in destructive power.'

This seemed unduly pessimistic – not to say downright 'reactionary' in its implications – to 'progressives' in the fifties unable or unwilling to consider the proposition that in certain fields 'more might mean worse' (as Kingsley Amis was the first to suggest of the helter-skelter expansion of higher education). To most educationists and psychologists in 1954 such views were obscurantist and alarmist. But to an increasing number today the facts are self-evident and the cause of gravest concern.

Koestler would no doubt have been able, if pressed, to support all those imaginary demonstrations with data. He would have been hard-pressed to do so if challenged about the most important of his imaginary charts,

> '. . . on which we plot the progress of the species Man in moral philosophy, in cosmic awareness and spiritual clarity. This curve will show a slow rise during the prehistoric miles of nearly-flat stretch; then, when the power-curve . . . starts rising, the spiritual-curve . . . will begin to undulate with indecisive ups and downs; finally, on the last, dramatic one-millionth part of the chart, where the power-curve shoots skyward with insane acceleration, the spiritual-curve goes into a steep decline.'

'Cosmic awareness.' 'Spiritual clarity.' These were curiously vague and mystical terms to be coming so easily off the pen of one educated in the exact sciences, even when allowance was made for the fact that he was a notorious defector from the ranks of 'scientific Socialism'. They had little resonance in the optimistic fifties (and, besides, any bright undergraduate with the slightest knowledge of the works of Gilbert Ryle, say, or A. J. Ayer, would have no difficulty whatsoever in analysing them into non-sense. They have rather more in 1980.)

> 'To sum-up, our diagrams show an unprecedented increase in the range and power of the species' sensory and motory organs, coincident with a marked

deterioration of the integrative functions which determine spiritual maturity and social ethics. There are frequent instances in history of moral slumps followed by a new upward trend; the alarming thing is the coincidence of a period of unprecedented spiritual decline with an equally unprecedented increase of power. The Promethean myth seems to be coming true with a horrible twist: the giant reaching out to steal the lightning from the gods is morally insane.'

* *

Turning from the general to the particular – that is, to the menace to the Western democracies – Koestler dismissed Russell's advocacy of unilateral nuclear disarmament, just as he had dismissed the latter's earlier advocacy of a preventive strike against the Soviet Union. As for the abolition of nuclear weapons under effective international control, that was entirely desirable – but in the nature of things just as impossible to achieve.

'Unfortunately, the premises that we reject are not rejected by the philosophy of dialectical materialism which is the *credo* of our opponents; and our scepticism regarding the limits of man's ability as a computing machine is not shared by them . . . I would like to make this point clearer . . . their philosophical approach to, and their terms of reference regarding, the problem of war are different from ours.'

Not that Koestler thought it likely that the Soviet Union would launch an all-out nuclear attack on the West. The danger lay rather in its support of revolution in cockpits distant from its own territory or that of Western Europe and the United States, in subversion, veiled aggression and camouflaged political crimes.

'The possibilities of veiled aggression are inexhaustible; and it is unrealistic to believe that we can stop it by the threat of "massive retaliation" – which, if taken seriously, would mean that we ought to have reacted to the defenestration of Masaryk, or ought to react to the next People's Rising in Afghanistan, by unleashing the nuclear nightmare.'

What then should be done?

'To put it in a nutshell: *atomic weapons are necessary as a deterrent against atomic aggression, but ineffective as a deterrent against local and camouflaged aggression*. The security of our streets cannot be guaranteed by tanks, only by police officers in sufficient numbers, armed with conventional weapons to cope with conventional crimes. The practical conclusions are distressingly simple. The most conventional of all weapons, and the one which no nation can dispense with, is a people determined to fight on the beaches and to fight in the streets in defence of their freedom. However brave they are, they will never be able to stand up against an aggressor using the methods of total war. The oft-heard argument: "What is the good of arming a few more divisions when we know that in the case of a showdown Europe cannot be defended anyway?" is both cowardly and false. Any European Defence Community can never aim at more than to make Europe unconquerable *short of total war*. But it can never aim at less than this. If, in the early post-war period, Czechoslovakia and Poland had been equipped with the number of divisions and the unbroken spirit of Finland in 1939, the Russians could not have deposed the Polish Government, nor pulled their Prague *coup*. They would have been forced to show their hand and engage in open warfare – and the odds are that they would not have dared to take the risk.* It is indeed distressingly simple: free men must be prepared to defend their freedom or lose it.'

So much for the short-term political aspect of the crisis as Koestler saw it towards the end of 1954. His analysis and conclusion are even more cogent now than they were a quarter of a century ago. The many successes of 'veiled aggression' have raised many doubts about the democracies' ability, and will, to defend their interests against Soviet expansionism. That such doubts should exist at all may well be ascribed no less to the failure of the European Economic Community to become much more than an over-bureaucratised *Zollverein* than to America's Asian humiliation, the weakening of Executive authority, and the subsequent failure of nerve (with all its hideous consequences from Indo-China to Iran, and in Africa). But whatever the causes, the doubts exist; and their existence indicates the sad reality of the progressive demoralisation which Koestler foresaw all too clearly twenty-five years ago.

But he had said as much even earlier in one form or another. What of the long-term aspects of the deeper crisis of Western civilisation?

To get this into focus, Koestler looked back to an historic turning point – the emergence in the sixteenth and seventeenth centuries, following the Renaissance and the Reformation, of two apparently unrelated factors:

'. . . the rise of national consciousness, and the rise of a new philosophy. The latter, based on the discoveries of Copernicus, Galileo and Kepler, was gradually penetrating wider and wider strata of the public mind. If the earth no longer stood firmly planted by God in the centre of His universe, and was merely a small planet hurtling through space, then, though religious belief did survive, it could no longer command the exclusive interest of man . . . It was an historic turning point – the point where religion and science, religion and art, logic and ethics, began to part company and go their separate ways. From the beginnings of civilised life, man's fate had been determined, and his conscience guided, by some super-human agency; from now on this function was taken over by sub-human agencies. The deities of the past may have been coarse or sublime, scandalous Olympians or a pure God of love; yet they were wiser, more powerful and on a higher plane of existence than man himself. The new determinants of man's fate – mechanical laws, atoms, glands, genes – which gradually took over, were of a lower order than man himself; they defined his condition but could provide no guidance whatsoever for his conscience.'

So Koestler identified the source of the disease crippling civilised mankind – the split and widening gulf between religious faith and the 'rationality' of exact science.

* They took the risk readily enough in Hungary in 1956 when it had become clear to them that the West lacked the will to intervene; and later in Czechoslovakia; and most recently in Afghanistan. (And in Poland. . . ?)

> 'For a while the words *Liberté, Egalité, Fraternité*, produced a new magic, a seemingly apt substitute for the Holy Trinity. There were breathtaking attempts to create a Humanist creed, and attempts to worship the Goddess of Reason; political movements and secular religions succeeded each other, exerting their immensely dynamic, but short-lived appeal . . . Each of them promised a secular millennium, born out of a revolutionary apocalypse. Yet all the time, throughout these toxic excesses and spurious illuminations, there was a muffled feeling of uneasiness, of growing frustration, of spiritual desiccation . . .'

But with the beginning of the twentieth century came signs of an impending change. The scientific descendants of Galileo and Newton had discovered that the reduction of the universe to a mechanical model was not so easy after all. The great physicists of modernity were discovering the presence of entities and quantities and processes which eluded measurement by the most precise of the new instruments which technology had brought close to perfection – and, more startling still, which by their very nature would always elude it. Here was clearly a teleological crisis of enormous significance. And it was not confined to physics. In other sciences – biology, genetics, cosmology, psychology – similar crises were arising. What was happening, Koestler wrote, was that 'the living whole' was asserting its primacy over 'the measurable aspects of the parts'.

Koestler here was edging close to the heart of the matter with which he was obsessed (and which had obsessed the minds of the geniuses – Einstein above all – whose discoveries had created the crisis). But any reader who at this point expected to find Koestler attempting to discover some sort of answer to the overwhelming questions within the orthodoxy of any institutional religion was soon either relieved or disappointed. He poured scorn equally on the perfervid Roman Catholicism of Graham Greene and the cool Anglo-Catholicism of T. S. Eliot. He showed no intention of coming to grips with the idea of divinity. His intellect and imagination (although now jointly engaged in contemplations and speculations that can only be properly described as essentially religious in nature) wore a philosophical dress. And they were still rather uneasily orientated towards the future, as they had been when constricted by the framework of Marxist-Leninist orthodoxy.

> 'Is it really too much to ask and hope for a religion whose content is perennial but not archaic, which provides ethical guidance, teaches the lost art of contemplation, and restores contact with the supernatural without requiring reason to abdicate?'

And so this most interesting essay of Koestler's middle age, which contains the seeds of all the works that followed, ends rather lamely:

> 'We shall either destroy ourselves or take off to the stars. Perhaps the conquest of interplanetary space will cause a Copernican revolution in reverse, the emergence of a new kind of cosmic consciousness . . . Perhaps some unexpected discovery in the field of extra-sensory perception will provide us with a new spiritual insight, a new basis for our metaphysical

beliefs, a new intuition of our ultimate responsibilities . . . Once we hoped for Utopia, now, in a chastened mood, we can at best hope for a reprieve: pray for time and play for time; for had the dinosaur learnt the art of prayer, the only sensible petition for him would have been to go down on his scaly knees and beg "Lord, give me another chance".'

On that uncertain and disconsolate note he ended.

* *

There is an entry in his diary dated Sunday 19th December 1954:

'Decided to embark on Kepler biography – after toying with the idea for some 20 years. Wanted to write Kepler biography before the war. Had tentative contact with French publisher.'

But first he had to complete the collection and the editing of the essays, to which he gave the title of the last he had written, *The Trail of the Dinosaur*. By the middle of February 1955 the job was finished, and he wrote the preface:

'. . . In the ten years that have passed since *The Yogi and the Commissar* was published, all its pessimistic and seemingly absurd predictions have come true, but none of its optimistic and seemingly plausible ones – few and cautious enough though the latter were . . . "The typical career of the French politician," I wrote some years ago, "reads like a book, from left to right." Though I am not a French politician, the evolution reflected in these essays could be regarded as a confirmation of that rule – if the words "left" and "right" still possessed any concrete political meaning. One of the submissions of the present volume is that they have lost that meaning, and that man, if he is to survive, must shift the focus of his eyes to more vital questions.

'This book, then, is a farewell to arms. The last essays and speeches in it that deal directly with political questions date from 1950, and are now five years old. Since then I felt that I have said all I had to say on these questions which had obsessed me in various ways for the best part of a quarter-century. Now the errors are atoned for, the bitter passion has burnt itself out; Cassandra has gone hoarse, and is due for a vocational change.'

# CHAPTER XXX

# *1954–1956*

CYNTHIA, STILL WORKING IN America for Ely Culbertson, was painfully attempting to make up her mind to extricate herself from an unhappy love-affair. Koestler, who had kept in touch with her, was aware of the situation. Soon after he had sent the text of *The Trail of the Dinosaur* to his publishers, he wrote her a sympathetic letter of advice, ending on a humorous note. He was embarking, he announced, on a long, scholarly work on Kepler which would take him two years to write, and he was looking for a rich Brazilian.

In her reply Cynthia told Koestler that she had made arrangements to come to England towards the end of June to see her family and would not be returning to New York until early in September. He was not, she instructed him, to look for 'an elderly Brazilian widow' to support him for the next two years. She would tell him what to look for when next they met.

Cynthia had first come across the name of Kepler while typing Koestler's novel *The Age of Longing*:

> '. . . at Monsieur Anatole's party the French "novelist knight-errant" (affectionately modelled on Malraux) mentions in passing that "Kepler's search for the planetary laws was more an aesthetic than a pragmatic pursuit" and that the law governing planetary motion is "a particularly elegant gesture of God." '*

And then, having listened to Koestler's explanation, she recalled that passage in *Darkness at Noon* when Rubashov, the Old Bolshevik, and the aristocratic prisoner number 402 tap out an exchange on the wall between their cells:

> '. . . WHAT WOULD YOU DO IF YOU WERE PARDONED?
> 'Rubashov thought it over. Then he tapped: STUDY ASTRONOMY.'

Remembering this, Cynthia wrote that his proposed book about Kepler sounded 'simply wonderful'. She wished she were helping him with it.

By July 1955 a hundred-odd pages of Koestler's draft were in typescript.

* 'Twenty-five Writing Years' in *Astride the Two Cultures*, London, 1975.

And during that month Cynthia arrived in London to find that a new obsession had forced him to put it aside.

* *

During 1954 the long-running argument about capital punishment had become more vehement than ever before. Public opinion, according to the polls, favoured its retention, but it is probably true to say that the greater part of the intellectual community had come to regard it with abhorrence as a barbarous anachronism – and, furthermore, as one which innumerable statistical studies had seemed to deprive of any deterrent value.

England was one of the very few countries of the Western world not merely to have retained the ultimate punishment for the crime of murder but also to have gone on executing more than half of those found guilty. (In Scotland – where juridical procedure was, and remains, a great deal fairer to the accused than in England – the death sentence might still be pronounced but for many years the prerogative of mercy had invariably been exercised.)

Early in 1953 a dim-witted youth of nineteen, Derek Bentley, had been tried as the accomplice of his sixteen-year-old friend, Craig, who had shot and killed a policeman during an attempted robbery. Although it seemed likely that Bentley had tried to prevent his companion from firing the fatal shot, he was sentenced to death. This aroused widespread concern, but the Home Secretary declined to recommend a reprieve and Bentley was in due course executed. (Craig, who committed the murder, was too young for the hangman's attention, and is now living as a free man under another name.)

There was also growing concern about the execution of another dim-wit, Timothy Evans, who had been convicted of the murder of his child, and executed, on the evidence of a ghoulish pervert, Christie, whose pastime, it was later discovered, was murdering young women and keeping their corpses in cupboards or under the floorboards of his house, Number 10 Rillington Place, where Evans was a lodger.

But it was during the early part of 1955, with the trial and execution of Ruth Ellis, that the abolitionists were aroused to the greatest effort. Mrs Ellis, the mother of two young children, was an alcoholic. She shot and killed her brutal and unfaithful lover, Blakely, thirteen days after a miscarriage caused by Blakely's punching her in the belly during a quarrel and a day or two after he had left her for another woman.

During the trial the chief prosecuting counsel told the jury: 'There is evidence here of extreme emotional tension of the accused woman as a result of which she did what she did.' During his summing-up the judge said: 'You may think [this] young woman [was] badly treated by the deceased man.' A more appropriate adverb would have been 'atrociously', for the evidence had shown that Blakely frequently beat her, had lived off her, and had constantly deceived her – and that it was in a fit of wild and despairing jealousy that Ruth Ellis, still in love with the man who had so unspeakably maltreated her, killed him.

The case for a reprieve was overwhelming as *The Spectator* – then co-edited by the present writer with its then proprietor Ian Gilmour (now the Rt Hon Sir

Ian Gilmour, Bt MP) and a leading advocate of abolition – pointed out. But neither *The Spectator*'s pleading, nor the *Observer*'s, nor the *Economist*'s could budge the Home Secretary.

Ruth Ellis had undoubtably committed the crime. In law she was 'sane' and so responsible for her actions. The jury had arrived at the only verdict open to it. The judge had pronounced the only sentence open to him. And Ruth Ellis, the hapless woman at the centre of an unusually thick cloud of the morbid interest which customarily gathered around such cases, was put to death.

And her execution was to be the beginning of the end of capital punishment in Britain.

Following her hanging, Ian Gilmour wrote a closely argued and devastating condemnation of the Home Secretary's failure to recommend a reprieve. It ended:

> 'Many people think that the power of life and death which is vested in the Home Secretary is so onerous that his discharge of it should not be criticised. This view would be irrefutable if the man who exercised this power were in each particular case chosen by lot. But the Home Secretary is not an ordinary citizen chosen by chance. He is an ordinary politician who, if he thinks the duty intolerable, can refuse to undertake it. He is an ordinary politician who expects his other activities to be scrutinised and criticised, and there seems small reason for putting a taboo on criticism of one of the most important of his functions.
>
> 'The case of Ruth Ellis is another of those instances where the prerogative of mercy has broken down. Those who still approve of capital punishment have just as great a cause for concern about this as those of us who oppose it as a preposterous and revolting atrocity. The obvious remedy is to abolish hanging. Even those who do not agree cannot be content with the present position.'

* *

Capital punishment had been abhorrent to Koestler ever since, as he wrote later,

> 'In 1937, during the Civil War in Spain, I spent three months [in prison] . . . as a suspected spy, witnessing the executions of my fellow prisoners and awaiting my own. These three months left me with a vested interest in capital punishment – rather like "half-hanged Smith", who was cut down after fifteen minutes and lived on. Each time a man's or a woman's neck is broken in this peaceful country, memory starts to fester like a badly healed wound. I shall never achieve real peace of mind until hanging is abolished.'

Although Koestler had said goodbye to political activism, his crusading spirit was ready to be roused. The execution of Ruth Ellis and the controversy which preceded it and followed it galvanised him into action. When Cynthia arrived late in July at Montpelier Square (where she was to spend her vacation helping Koestler with his work), she discovered that he had

> '. . . found this new obsession, and a pretty overwhelming one it was too. He was like somebody possessed; the subject was never far from his mind. If he

went to a pub for a drink, he would start up a discussion with the publican. All publicans were hangers in those days, which, of course, was just what Arthur was hoping, and he would present a diabolically reasoned and objective case for abolition. Although he never managed to persuade a single die-hard publican, he never gave up hope. At the end of a working day, the obsession would continue to buzz maddeningly round his head, and he would spend the evening dictating notes to me for the following morning's work . . .'

The work in question, thoroughly researched and written, re-written, revised at top speed, was *Reflections on Hanging*, by far the most influential polemic against the advocates of capital punishment.

He finished it and wrote the preface on the 3rd October.

* *

But to write his reflections on the subject was not enough for Koestler. During July he went to see Victor Gollancz (who had published his *Spanish Testament* in 1937 and with whom he had worked for the Zionist cause) and suggested that they should collaborate in founding a National Campaign for the Abolition of Capital Punishment. Gollancz agreed. A few other leading abolitionists were approached, and on 11th August, at a meeting in Gollancz's office in Henrietta Street, they constituted themselves the executive committee of the national campaign. Present at that first meeting, in addition to Gollancz (who acted as chairman) and Koestler, were Canon John Collins, Gerald Gardiner QC (now Lord Gardiner), Christopher Hollis, Reginald Paget QC, MP (now Lord Paget), and Mrs Peggy Duff, who was appointed secretary and treasurer. Hugh Klare, the secretary of the Howard League for Penal Reform, was also present but only in an advisory capacity since it was considered that it might be damaging to the League if he were to be directly associated with a propaganda campaign in which no punches were to be pulled.

Within a fortnight several hundred pounds had been raised and a Committee of Honour was being formed, among the first members of which were Benjamin Britten, Frank Byers (now Lord Byers), Professor C. Day-Lewis, Jacquetta Hawkes, the Earl of Listowel, Henry Moore, Lord Pakenham (now the Earl of Longford), J. B. Priestley, Canon Raven, Moira Shearer (Mrs Ludovic Kennedy), the Rev. Dr Donald Soper (now Lord Soper), and R. R. Stokes, MP. The executive committee had been strengthened by the addition of the journalist Frank Owen, and Gollancz's wife, Ruth.

On 24th August a statement was issued announcing the launching of the campaign, appealing for funds, and setting out the methods to be employed by the campaign:

'The first of these will be educational. Books, pamphlets and shorter statements will be issued: public meetings will be organised: personal contact will be established with all who wish for information on the issues involved, with a view to forming a considered opinion.

'But the campaign will also be concerned to give those members of the public who are already opposed to capital punishment an opportunity for expressing their conscience in this matter. We shall suggest, for instance, that abolitionists may think fit to abstain from attending any place of entertainment, or party, on the evening preceding an execution, and may further think fit to attend, during the night preceding an execution, a place of worship or assembly (and we shall arrange for such places to be open for the purpose). Shopkeepers and owners of businesses who are opposed to the death penalty may wish to shut their premises for an hour or so during the day preceding an execution (where no public inconvenience would be caused) and to display a notice explaining their reason for doing so . . . We believe that a whole-hearted effort will put an end in a very short time to this blot on our national life . . .'

On 6th September the committee had its second meeting at which tactics for the months ahead were exhaustively discussed. Koestler, Gollancz and Owen were to act as a sub-committee responsible for putting pressure on the press, television, and radio. Circulars were to be sent to all members of the Howard League, Christian Action, the clerks of Friends' Meetings, constituency Labour parties and Cooperative Guilds. All Labour MPs had already received a circular with a covering letter signed by Paget. Christopher Hollis and Montgomery Hyde were deputed to think up the best means of enlisting support among Conservatives. A public meeting was to be held in the Central Hall, Westminster, on Thursday 10th November. Similar meetings were to be arranged in Glasgow and Edinburgh during December and in Liverpool and Manchester during January. At the end of the meeting Koestler reported that the final draft of his book, *Reflections on Hanging*, would be ready in a month's time.

* *

By which time Cynthia had returned, reluctantly, to New York, determined to try to make the best of a bad (or at any rate difficult) job so far as her private life was concerned, but longing at the same time to be in London, working with Koestler. During the voyage in the *Nieuw Amsterdam* she wrote to thank him for a wonderful summer which would be 'terribly hard to recover from'. If he needed her again soon, she would be 'back in a flash!' In any case, she would be coming to England on holiday during 1956 – and she intended to come back permanently in the not too distant future.

As soon as Koestler had finished *Reflections on Hanging*, the greater part of which had been typed and re-typed by Cynthia, he cabled her to tell her so and to announce he had started work again on Kepler. She replied at once on 5th October, giving him the latest news of her painful love-affair out of which the love was draining fast. Her friend was in the midst of a course of Freudian analysis and had announced soon after her arrival that during his treatment he should not make any emotional decisions. A day or two later, after a session with his analyst, he had announced that he was not fit to make her happy. The analyst had told him that someone undergoing treatment invariably chose another neurotic with the result that their marriage would end in chaos; and that in perhaps three years' time she would probably realise that she too ought to have treatment.

Cynthia was in a dead end and desperate to get out of it.

Koestler's response to this was immediate and simple. He wanted her back; and back she came; and a new life began for both of them.

* *

Koestler had hoped to finish his work on Kepler in six months or so. But when Cynthia returned to London she found that he had felt obliged to put it aside yet again in order to concentrate on the Campaign and its rapidly growing range of activities. She helped him with the compilation of the case-histories of the murderers who had been tried, found guilty, and executed between 1949 and 1953. This was eventually published in the *Observer* (whose proprietor-editor, David Astor, was one of Koestler's greatest admirers and supporters) above the pseudonym 'Vigil'.

As John Grigg (Lord Altrincham before renouncing his peerage and an active supporter of the campaign) was to write many years later in his essay *The Do-Gooder from Seville Gaol*:*

'The case-histories show convincingly that most murderers are not the calculating villains of crime fiction, but are either psychopaths or people caught in tragic personal circumstances, acting under the stress of sudden violent emotion.'

A week or two before the public meeting in the Central Hall, Koestler thought of a journalistic variation on this theme and discussed it with David Astor who took it up enthusiastically and agreed that J. B. Priestley would be the person best able to take the initiative. Astor wrote to Priestley and explained:

'The idea is that one should first try to contact a small number of writers who are known to take a keen interest in this subject . . . Each writer would in turn attend a murder trial and write a study of the murderer, intended to bring out his mental capacity, social and family background etc. These studies would be intended to form chapters of a book to be produced at the end of some six or twelve months, but each study would also be offered to a newspaper or periodical known to be sympathetic to the cause of abolition.

'If a number of suitable writers were willing to engage themselves in this project, we would then invite them to meet the editors or proprietors of those newspapers or periodicals known to be sympathetic. The purpose of this meeting would be to seek the agreement of all concerned and to arrange how the writers should be directed to the appropriate trials, how their writings should be divided amongst interested newspapers, and how a sufficient variety in their reporting could be obtained to make a book with a wide popular appeal . . .

'The reason why Koestler and I have turned to you is we think you are much the most appropriate person to act as ring-leader among the writers . . .'

* Included in the *Festschrift* entitled *Astride the Two Cultures: Arthur Koestler at 70*, ed. Harold Harris, London, 1975.

Priestley was not greatly impressed:

> 'While it would be a good idea for writers and editors and publishers (and possibly some people from T.V. and radio) to collaborate in a concerted attack on capital punishment, I must confess I don't really see the point of the plan you and Koestler are putting forward. It seems to me to be narrowing the attack instead of broadening it. I doubt if a careful study of the characters and background of murders would convert believers in capital punishment to our view. What I think it is much more likely to do is to show such people that there are aspects they have completely overlooked.
>
> 'It would be unreasonable of me not to be ready to defend this view or to make myself understand exactly what you and Koestler have in mind, so I shall be glad to join in any discussion . . .'

Astor, having consulted Koestler, decided to give a little ground and replied by return:

> 'I perfectly understand your hesitance about the idea I proposed in the particular form in which I put it. It seems to me, on reflection, that I made a mistake in narrowing the definition of what the writers might write about. This was also Koestler's view when I phoned him to communicate your reaction.
>
> 'We would like to take you at your word and invite your wife and yourself to have supper with us after the meeting at the Central Hall, Westminster to-morrow night, Thursday . . .'

The Central Hall, Westminster, was filled to its legal capacity on Thursday 10th November, and there was overwhelming support for the resolution that – because all available evidence in other countries showed that capital punishment was no deterrent and that its abolition had not led to any increase in the murder rate – its retention in Britain was unnecessary and so 'morally unjustifiable, and inconsistent with the self-respect of a civilised and supposedly Christian country'.

It was certainly an impressive demonstration, and so was the other held simultaneously by Christian Action in the nearby Church House. But news editors judged neither worth much space in the morning newspapers – a fact pointed out by Priestley to Koestler a few days later, adding that 'I feel that this campaign very badly needs a first-class press agent.'

During the discussion over supper that followed the meeting, Priestley was won round – or so it seemed – to the idea that had been put to him by Astor, and agreed to consider taking charge of its realisation.

However, relations between Priestley and Astor cooled, and, after a series of misunderstandings and bickerings, the project died.

* *

That was that. One bright idea had fizzled out, but there were plenty of others. At the second meeting of the executive committee on 22nd November it was reported that 10,383 supporters had already signed up and that the sum of £1,795 4s 0d was in hand; that Gerald Gardiner was writing a book to be entitled *Capital Punishment as a Deterrent and the Alternative*; that the pamphlets

*Capital Punishment: The Facts* and *Capital Punishment: The Heart of the Matter* were being sent to every Member of Parliament; that definite dates had been fixed for meetings in a dozen provincial cities at which Sir Beverley Baxter, Lord Hinchingbrooke, the Hon. J. J. Astor, Joan Vickers, Angus Maude, Kenneth Younger, Jean Mann and Anthony Greenwood would be among the speakers; and that Arthur Koestler had succeeded in enlisting the support of Edward Hulton, the proprietor of *Picture Post*.

Koestler, the main driving force behind the campaign, was up to his eyes in work, but with Cynthia to help him now. His chief preoccupation, of course, was the correction and revision of the text of *Reflections on Hanging*. It was indeed fantastic, as Cynthia had written, that he could have succeeded in writing such a fact-filled polemic in two months. During that short time he had read and digested a vast quantity of historical material and up-to-date statistics; he had sought and obtained the advice of British criminologists and, through his friend Arthur J. Schlesinger, Jr, such American authorities as Professor Wechler of the Law School of Columbia University, Professor Thorston Sellin of the University of Pennsylvania, John Bartlow Martin and Marcel Frym, Director of Criminological Research at the Hacker Foundation in Beverly Hills, California. He had also gone through the European literature on the subject recommended to him by Leon Radzinowicz of the Department of Criminal Science in the University of Cambridge.

As soon as he had completed the text he sent it to Gerald Gardiner who returned it two or three days later with several pages of notes typed laboriously by himself over a weekend, and with a covering letter which said that

> 'I thought that I knew pretty well everything that there was to be known about the subject but I find that I have learned a lot from it . . .'

Gardiner's notes on various points of detail had been most useful to Koestler during his final revision of the typescript; and he had accepted the eminent lawyer's advice on the dangers of libel, except in two or three points which he considered trivial. He then sent the revised typescript to Gollancz together with Gardiner's letter and notes. Gollancz returned the typescript on 1st November with a note to say that

> 'I am afraid I agree with Gerald Gardiner that all his points must really be met . . .'

In 1954 the publishers of books as well as of newspapers were, and with reason, even more fearful of libel actions brought against them than they are today.

> 'Sometimes,' Gollancz went on, 'one thinks a risk very small – and then things turn out badly . . . Will you let me have the manuscript back, amended, by return, as we now have a printer anxiously waiting for it.'

Koestler was irritated by this. He had already made it clear to Gollancz that he had erred quite far enough on the side of caution. After some discussion, however, he returned the typescript to Gollancz, amended as required.

David Astor and his staff condensed the text and serialised it in the *Observer* during February, under the pseudonym of 'Vigil'. The *Observer*'s readership responded immediately with a torrent of letters pro and con, mainly the former.

Koestler had expected Gollancz to rush the book through the press and get it into the bookstores while the controversy stirred up by its *Observer* serialisation was at its height. He was disappointed in this, however, and his disappointment was eventually to lead to a breach with Gollancz. When Koestler's text was in galley-proof, Gollancz sent it to be 'read for libel' by the solicitors, Rubinstein, Nash and Company. Stanley Rubinstein read the text and sought counsel's opinion – that of none other than Gerald Gardiner.

On 23rd January Hilary Rubinstein, Stanley's nephew, then working for Gollancz, wrote to Koestler about Gardiner's reply to certain queries raised by Uncle Stanley. Koestler's observation about certain remarks of Lord Chief Justice Goddard were at the root of the trouble.

A sentence considered particularly dangerous ran:

> '. . . But while some Judges are humane, others adhere strictly to the stone age of law.'

Hilary Rubinstein suggested that Koestler might tone this down to:

> 'Some judges adhere more strictly to the letter of the law than others.'

In this, Rubinstein was simply following the advice of Gerald Gardiner that while it was perfectly safe for Koestler to attack Lord Goddard for any opinions expressed by the latter in the House of Lords, it would be most imprudent to print anything which implied that Lord Goddard was a bad judge. Since this point had not been raised by Gardiner in his private, and extremely detailed, advice to Koestler, the latter was infuriated.

He reached for the telephone. Gollancz being out of town, he spoke to one of his chief assistants, and followed with a letter on 25th January:

> '. . . further to our telephone conversation of yesterday I confirm my oral statement that concerning the alleged legal risks pointed out in Mr Rubinstein's letter to me of January 23rd., I take full moral and financial responsibility for the consequences. If you want this statement formulated in more precise legal terms please have it drawn up by your legal advisors and I shall be delighted to sign it.'

On the very day Koestler had received Hilary Rubinstein's letter, Monday 23rd January, a man named Clarence William Ward, due to be executed on 26th January, was reprieved.

On Sunday 22nd January, Koestler had published in the *Observer*, under the pseudonym 'Vigil', an outspoken article about the trial judge's instructions to the jury who had tried Ward and the dismissal of Ward's appeal on 11th January. Until the publication of that article, the case – a humdrum tragedy – had attracted no public attention. Ward, a coalheaver of sub-normal intelligence, suffered from gastric ulcers. One night he came home tired and ill to find the eighteen-month-old illegitimate daughter of his mistress crying in her cot, which needed some repairs. The child herself was backward, and at eighteen months could neither stand, crawl, nor walk. Ward began to repair the cot and the child kept on crying uncontrollably. Ward's temper suddenly snapped and he shook the child violently. When he came to his senses and realised that he had killed her, he persuaded his mistress to help him bury the small corpse in a slagheap, where it was discovered nearly twenty months later, in September 1955. On 11th December of that year Ward was sentenced to death at Leeds Assizes.

A 'humdrum tragedy' – not to be compared in public interest with the case of Ruth Ellis, say – but Koestler was determined that Ward's execution would not pass unnoticed. Thanks to his success in interesting Edward Hulton, the proprietor of *Picture Post*, in the campaign, he had come to know the senior members of the magazine's editorial staff, who were now mounting their own campaign with Koestler's help against capital punishment.

Koestler, in his *Observer* article, did his formidable best.

Ward's appeal had been based on the grounds that the trial judge had misdirected the jury regarding the test they should apply to decide whether Ward was guilty of murder or manslaughter. That test, he told them, would be what a 'reasonable man would have thought or contemplated' while committing the crime. Ward's counsel argued before the appeal court that the test should be rather 'what went on in that particular man's head at that particular moment'.

> 'The Court of Criminal Appeal dismissed the appeal on January 11. Lord Goddard giving the judgement of the Court, endorsed the judge's direction to the jury that the only test which could be applied in these cases was "what would a reasonable man contemplate? If the act was one which any reasonable man must have known would cause death or grievous bodily harm, then it did amount to murder."'

Precedent being the basis of Common Law from time immemorial, Koestler wrote, it was to be expected that the Court's ruling against Ward would frequently be quoted in future in cases where the vital distinction between murder and manslaughter is involved. And so the law of the realm, put into everyday lay language, would be on the following lines:

> 'If A kills B in a frenzy of jealousy, or as a result of anger or nervous stress, the Judge will be justified in directing the jury to find the culprit guilty of murder and not manslaughter, because (cf. *Regina v. Ward*, January 11, 1956) "the test must be applied to all alike and the only test which could be applied in these cases was – what would a reasonable man contemplate?"'

The 'test of the reasonable man', Koestler went on, had long served to assess the gravity of *provocation* in the case of those not actually and clinically insane – ie, those who could in the eyes of the law be held to know the nature of their actions and also that they were wrong.

> 'The law on this point as it presently stands says that provocation can be regarded as a mitigating circumstance, reducing murder to manslaughter,

only if it is shown that the provocation not only deprived the accused person of his self-control, but was also sufficient *to deprive a "reasonable man" of his self-control.* This means that if the accused is mentally abnormal or for some other reason abnormally susceptible to provocation, he must still be judged *as if* he were an ordinary, reasonable, average Englishman.'

Ward, as we have seen, was reprieved on the day after the publication of that article, which had attracted a great deal of attention. Would the Home Secretary have recommended the prerogative of mercy if the article had never been published? Perhaps he should be given the benefit of the doubt? There were many at the time who thought otherwise.

* *

Victor Gollancz had now returned from holiday and joined in the battle over the alleged libel risk. He allowed the passages in question to stand, but the delay in publication meant that the original intention to publish the book immediately after the *Observer*'s serialisation of a considerable part of it (already going ahead) had to be abandoned. It did not appear until April, much to Koestler's annoyance. By that time he and Gollancz had crossed swords on another matter, which led to Koestler's resignation from the executive committee of the campaign, but not by any means from his active support of it.

* *

Public interest in the issue of abolition, aroused by the execution of Ruth Ellis in 1955, and sustained by the Campaign (the membership of which had reached almost 33,000 by February of the following year) and by the support of such publications as *The Spectator*, *Picture Post* and the *Observer*, was intensified by the serialisation of *Reflections on Hanging*. This was clearly reflected not only in the response of *Observer* readers but also in the correspondence and editorial columns of other newspapers and in radio and television programmes.

'Beyond question,' as John Grigg wrote years after it had done its work, *Reflections on Hanging* 'is a polemic of extraordinary power.'

No writer of such eminence had ever taken on such hanghard judges as Lord Goddard so directly and demolished their prejudices (disguised as arguments) so thoroughly. In his preface Koestler recalled that some of his 'learned friends' who had helped him with material for the book had warned him against offending 'certain venerable prejudices and traditional susceptibilities' concerning the law and its administration.

'I have disregarded their warnings,' he wrote, 'because appeasement never pays, and because I believe that the case for abolition has been weakened by lack of outspokenness.'

In the first page of his first chapter he went for the jugular of Lord Chief Justice Goddard, who had once delighted a Royal Academy banquet with the story of a judge who, after passing sentence of death on three men, was welcomed by a band playing a modified refrain of the Eton Boating Song: 'We'll all swing together'. He had found that story in an amiable 'profile' of Lord

Goddard published in the *Observer* four years before, which went on to tell another jolly story to illustrate the 'Goddard legend':

> 'When he first went to Marlborough, it was apparently a school custom to make every new boy sing or recite in his dormitory. Called upon to sing, the future Lord Chief Justice is said to have surprised the other boys by chanting in a piping voice: "You will be taken from here to a place of execution and hanged by the neck until you are dead. And may the Lord have mercy on your soul." '

The English, it seemed, found such stories highly humorous, just as the Scots in the early nineteenth century relished the pleasantries delivered by the more gruesome 'characters' in their Supreme Court at the expense of the wretches whom they were sending to their death.

Koestler had collected many such stories, with the object of illustrating the curious and paradoxical fact that in England, in so many ways the most civilised of countries,

> '. . . Hanging has a kind of macabre cosiness, like a slightly off-colour family joke, which only foreigners, abolitionists and other humourless creatures are unable to share.'

But there was nothing cosy or jokey about the items he culled from the reports of Royal Commissions on the subject of capital punishment. Among those who testified before the Royal Commission in 1950 were Mr Albert Pierrepoint, the public executioner (who, while not engaged on public duty, ran a public house called 'Help the Poor Struggler'); the acting Under-Sheriff for the County of London, Mr H. N. Gedge; and Lord Chief Justice Goddard.

Pierrepoint was asked whether he had had any awkward moments.

> '*Answer*: No, I have only seen one in all my career.'
> '*Query*: What happened?'
> '*A*: He was rough. It was unfortunate; he was not an Englishman, he was a spy, and he kicked up rough.'

Mr Gedge, asked about this particular incident, confirmed Mr Pierrepoint's description:

> 'Yes,' he said, 'he was a foreigner, and I personally have noticed that English people take their punishment better than foreigners . . . He just dived at the Executioner with his head, and then he fought with everything he had . . .'

Hanging, Koestler commented, seemed quite all right for Englishmen, who actually seemed to like it. It was only the foreigner, the outsider, who caused trouble, failing to appreciate the good clean fun, the solemn and ritualistic aspect of the occasion, and the venerable tradition which upheld it.

*Dura lex, sed lex*, most of the English judges said in chorus when the most barbarous aspect of England's penology was called in question. Koestler quoted Lord Chief Justice Goddard's summing-up to the jury in the case of Bentley and Craig.

The latter, who had shot the policeman, was sixteen years of age and was quite illiterate; his accomplice, Bentley (who went to the gallows), was nineteen, a Grade Four mental defective. Counsel for their defence had pointed out that their education had been provided mainly by gangster films and horror comics. Lord Goddard would have none of this nonsense:

> 'Now let us put out of our minds in this case any question of films, or comics, or literature of that kind. These things are prayed in aid nowadays when young prisoners are in the dock, and they have very little to do with the case. These two young men – boys or whatever you like to call them – are both of an age which makes them responsible to the law. They are over fourteen, and it is surely idle to pretend these days that a boy of sixteen doesn't know the wickedness of taking out a revolver of that description and a pocketful of ammunition, and firing when he is on an unlawful expedition . . .'

Was there much to choose, Koestler implied, between the Law Lords of 1748 and the Lord Chief Justice two centuries later?

He took his readers through the reform movement initiated by Sir Samuel Romilly in 1808 and fought every inch of the way by the judges. Romilly, defeated and dispirited, did not live to see the repeal of the Bloody Code in 1837 (he committed suicide in 1818) and the reduction of capital statutes from over two hundred and twenty to fifteen. The reformers did not rest content with that victory, of course, and their struggle continued throughout the century, always in the face of the Law Lords' implacable opposition. Koestler frequently in his quotations juxtaposed past and present to demonstrate that, whatever humanitarian reforms they had been obliged to accept, the belief in the death penalty as an effective deterrent had lost none of its magic for the judiciary.

During the debate in the House of Lords a century and a half later on the motion that capital punishment should be suspended for a trial period of five years, Lord Simon declared that their lordships had no right

> '. . . to risk an experiment which may put in jeopardy innocent human lives . . . women who at this hour fear, as they never feared before, the knock on the door after it was dark.'

Lord Goddard concurred, and found occasion during his speech to praise one of his predecessors, Lord Ellenborough; and the Lord Chancellor, Lord Jowitt, gave it as his considered opinion that Lord Goddard had shown in his speech that judges were not the inhuman creatures they are sometimes supposed to be. For example, he went on,

> 'When I think of some of the great Judges since Ellenborough's time, I think . . . of Lord Romilly – and who has done more to restrict and limit the death penalty than Romilly? – and of many other names which will occur to any educated person . . .'

Koestler's comment on the Lord Chancellor's rhetoric implied that the latter's own education could be brushed up to advantage: Romilly had never been a judge but a ferocious enemy of judges; he had never been a Lord; and he was not 'since Ellenborough's time', having killed himself in the very year that Ellenborough died. Nobody during the debate remarked on Lord Jowitt's confusion. Translated into political terms, Koestler wrote, the passage might read as follows:

> 'It is untrue that the Conservative party was opposed to nationalisation. When I think of some of the great Tories, Sir Nye Bevan, for instance, who favoured nationalisation, and of many other names which will occur to any educated person . . .'

He promised his readers further examples of

> '. . . the amazing ignorance of social history among the learned oracles; it is a characteristic feature of their mentally inbred world.'

And he was as good as his word. Small wonder that most of the Law Lords, and many of the leading Queen's Counsels at the Bar who had hopes of translation to the Bench felt a deep sense of outrage. Rude and disrespectful things had often enough been said before, and even written, about the Judiciary, but never quite so stingingly, so woundingly, with such a disgraceful lack of respect for a sacred 'tradition'. As instalment followed instalment in the *Observer*, and controversy flourished, it seemed all too likely that some powerful person would jump on him whenever he put a foot wrong.

At last he did just that, or so it seemed. On Thursday 8th March, in the House of Lords, Lord Waverley drew the Government's attention to an article written by Koestler which had been published in the *Observer* of 4th March. In this, following a reference to a certain disgusting incident alleged to have occurred during the execution of Edith Thompson, Koestler had 'purported to quote a confidential Home Office instruction to prison governors'.

The quotation, from a document dated 10th January 1925, ran as follows:

> 'Any reference to the manner in which an execution has been carried out should be confined to as few words as possible, e.g., "it was carried out expeditiously and without a hitch". No record should be taken as to the number of seconds and, if pressed for details of this kind, the Governor should say he cannot give them, and he did not time the proceedings, but "a very short interval elapsed", or some general expression of opinion to the same effect.'

This Home Office instruction to prison governors had been deprived of its confidentiality long before 1956. It had come to light thirty years earlier during the trial of a former governor of Pentonville Jail, one Major Blake, accused of publishing Official Secrets. It had frequently been quoted thereafter in literature on the subject. Its authenticity had never been called in question by anyone in or out of authority.

In reply to Lord Waverley, Lord Mancroft, Under-Secretary of State for Home Affairs, put the record straight in a manner which reflected badly on Koestler's integrity as a polemicist. The quotation, he said, 'suggests that Governors are instructed that they should invariably say in reference to a manner in which an execution is carried out that "it was carried out expeditiously and there was no hitch".'

Here, according to Lord Mancroft, Koestler had omitted important parts of the original Home Office instruction and given an entirely misleading impression of its sense and intention. The passage as a whole should read, he explained:

'No details of any execution should be given to anyone but the Coroner. The reply to any inquiry at the inquest as to the manner in which an execution has been carried out should be confined to as few words as possible, e.g., "It was carried out expeditiously and there was no hitch", or as the case may be. If there has been any hitch or unusual event the fact must of course be stated and an explanation given.'

Koestler, it was clear, had been quoting all too selectively. When Lord Mancroft sat down, Lord Hailsham rose to say that

'Having regard to the fact that, as appears from my noble friend's answer, the author of the article there referred to fell far short of the standards of integrity expected of a responsible author, and that the newspaper appears to have fallen far short of the degree of care which is required on the publication of a responsible newspaper, is it not clearly in the public interest that this should be made known? Might it not possibly be a suitable case for the Press Council?'

Lord Mancroft agreed that there

'. . . is much strength in what my noble and learned friend Lord Hailsham says'.

It did indeed turn out to be a suitable case for the Press Council, but not quite the case the Lords Mancroft and Hailsham had in mind.

Their words were quoted prominently in the following Sunday's *Observer*. But in the same issue Koestler published an article vigorously rebutting the implied accusation that he had deliberately omitted the missing passages, and pointing out that Lord Mancroft had neglected to mention the important fact that the passages in question had never been divulged or published before his speech in the Lords. This had been omitted by a Home Office spokesman in reply to an inquiry by the *Observer* on the day after Lord Mancroft had spoken. (It seems that the passages had been added to the instructions after they had been circulated, but at a date which the Home Office declined to disclose.) For good measure, the *Observer* published on the same page a statement by the Howard League for Penal Reform, pointing out that

'The wording of the Home Office instruction to Prison Governors, as given by Mr Koestler in the *Observer*, first appeared in a pamphlet issued by the National Council for the Abolition of the Death Penalty in June, 1928. It had then been incorporated into the Howard League's literature in good faith as the only available version.'

Which indeed it had been until Lord Waverley had elicited a fuller version from Mancroft. Koestler, therefore, declined to apologise to the noble lords but demanded instead that they should apologise to him. And so they did, after a fashion, on 15th March. Koestler was not satisfied and, taking Lord Hailsham at his word, decided that it was a suitable case for the Press Council; and on May Day the Press Council duly vindicated Koestler and the *Observer*, and mildly rebuked Lords Hailsham and Mancroft.

* *

A small victory, perhaps, but not negligible, and in the circumstances well worth fighting for. Koestler would have enjoyed the taste of it more, however, had the Campaign kept up its momentum and if his relations with Gollancz, cool enough already because the publication of *Reflections on Hanging* had been delayed until April, had not become something more than chilly.

Thanks largely, if not quite entirely, to the intensity aroused by the activities of the Campaign in general and Koestler's writings in particular, the House of Commons had decided to debate yet again, on 16th February, the question of capital punishment. The Government's proposition was that the death penalty should be retained, but the whips, as on earlier occasions, would be off and each member would be free to vote according to the dictates of his conscience.

On the Sunday before the debate an editorial in the *Sunday Times* asked whether there could be any possible reconciliation or compromise between the fervent abolitionists and the diehard retentionists, and went on to answer its rhetorical question plainly enough:

'In principle, none. Either the social order asserts the right to take life in its own defence or it does not. There is no compromise about death. A *via media* has been sought in a suspension of the death penalty for a period of five or ten years and the House of Commons may be tempted to so vote next Thursday. In our view this is not a compromise but an evasion.'

In the event, there was neither compromise nor evasion. Two hundred and ninety-three MPs (241 Labour members, 47 Conservatives, and 5 Liberals) voted for the abolition of capital punishment, as against two hundred and sixty-two (255 Tories and 7 Socialists) who voted for its retention. A famous victory? Koestler's keenest supporter, David Astor, thought so and sent him a congratulatory telegram as soon as he had heard the result of the division:

'Many congratulations on triumph of your cause. Success more yours than anyone else's.'

Gollancz too believed that victory had been achieved. He and Koestler had attended the debate, and as they left the Palace of Westminster together after the vote, the latter (who suspected – rightly, as it turned out – that the House of Lords would not accept the slender majority verdict of the Commons) was angered to hear the exuberant Gollancz tell one of the organisers of the Campaign that now there would be no need for public meetings.

Sharp words were exchanged. Koestler insisted that an executive committee meeting should be called as soon as possible. Gollancz, sensing that it would be a stormy one, agreed with reluctance, and a meeting was arranged for Tuesday 21st February.

The meeting was as stormy as Gollancz had feared, and it was clear to the others who attended* that the rift between him and Koestler had widened to the point where their incompatible personalities were exacerbating their acute differences of opinion.

Gollancz's many virtues as an activist and 'do-gooder' were somewhat vitiated, as even his many admirers would concede, by the fact that he was by nature impulsive, imperious, dictatorial and vain enough to expect his associates to respect his rightful position as cock of the walk. He was certainly unaccustomed to blunt criticism. His disagreement with Koestler was clearly coming to a head. Something would have to be done.

In the meantime, however, such disagreements did not impede the personal campaign which Koestler was running in the columns of the *Observer* and elsewhere. It moved David Astor, always the most generous of men in his appreciation of the talents of others, to dash off the following to Koestler on 10th March:

> 'I don't want to sound sententious, but want to say all the same that I believe your "hanging" journalism – the book extracts, the Vigil pieces and your handling of the attacks – have contributed something of real value to this country and to this newspaper. It is the episode that most deserves to be recorded in the history of this paper since I've been here. I'm very proud of being associated with what you have done and thank you very much . . . Hope you'll regard yourself as an honorary member of the *Observer* henceforth, as far as membership has positive attractions. (Don't reply.)'

It soon became clear that the Commons vote was not going to lead automatically and speedily (as Gollancz in his exuberance had imagined) to the end of the hangman's job. At best it could be regarded as the beginning of a long-drawn out struggle in which the retentionists would fight for some sort of compromise which would almost certainly be unsatisfactory.†

But Gollancz was adamant that the regional activities of the Campaign should be suspended and the greater part of its effort devoted to a 'spectacular' in the Royal Festival Hall. Koestler was not opposed to the Festival Hall project but he

* Ruth Gollancz, Gerald Gardiner, Frank Owen, Lord Pakenham and Peggy Duff.

† They did, and it was. The Abolition Bill got through the Commons only to be thrown out by the House of Lords. The unsatisfactory compromise was the Homicide Act of 1957 which attempted to distinguish between capital and non-capital murder – murder by gunfire, for example, being a suitable case for the hangman, while murder by poisoning, an offence always considered peculiarly abhorrent, was not. It was not until 1965 that the death penalty was suspended, and five more years were to pass before Parliament plucked up the courage to abolish it.

saw no reason why demonstrations in the provinces should be cancelled. Harsh words passed between them at a meeting of the committee on 13th March, and on the following morning Koestler wrote a lengthy letter to Gollancz offering to resign from the Executive Committee.

* *

Early in April his *Reflections on Hanging* was published in book form. The hanghards were even more appalled when they read the full text than the abolitionists were delighted, and even some of the more fair-minded opponents of abolitionism took exception to the less than respectful way in which Koestler had dealt with Lord Goddard (whose name rings like a death-knell through most of the chapters). Reviewing the book in the *Listener*, for example, Professor A. L. Goodhart wrote:

> 'His bitter attack on the judiciary is reminiscent of that made a century and a half ago by Bentham. But Bentham waited until his chief adversary had died before publishing his invective.'

The next issue of the *Listener* contained a letter from Koestler:

> 'Professor Goodhart seems to imply that I should have followed Bentham's example; but the precept that one should wait until one's opponent is dead before attacking him appears to me ethically questionable and liable to have a somewhat frustrating effect on public controversy. I take it that by "bitter attack on the judiciary", he means my long quotations from and short comments on the Lord Chief Justice's utterances on flogging, hanging and related topics. In contrast to the sentiments imputed to Jeremy Bentham, I wish Lord Goddard a long and happy life, but a speedy end to the principles advocated by him.'

Other reviewers, while acknowledging the masterly skill with which Koestler had condensed and presented a wealth of factual material hitherto known only to scholars specialising in the subject, either felt squeamish themselves, or considered that the 'ordinary reader' might feel squeamish, when faced with the gruesome details of execution; and there were some who considered that he might have been fairer, not so much to the 'hanghards' as to the many undogmatic people who were troubled about the possible consequences of abolition.

Ian Gilmour, reviewing the book in *The Spectator*, acknowledged this but went on to say that

> 'As he was oncc himself under sentence of death, his attitude is perfectly understandable, and if there are any disadvantages in his emotionalism they are outweighed by the power it brings to his writing. Indeed his moral fervour combined with his usual literary grace and distinction may conceivably penetrate the cocoon of complacency which protects many retentionists from the realities of the case . . .'

In retrospect one can see that *Reflections on Hanging* was largely instrumental, although it took time, in doing exactly that.

* *

Koestler did not rest on his oars after the publication of the book and his defence of his arguments against hostile critics. He continued to expend his energy on articles for the *Observer* and *Picture Post*, and he kept in touch with the committee after Lord Gardiner had succeeded Gollancz as chairman.

# PART SIX

# *1956–*

# CHAPTER XXXI

# *1956–1959*

THE TIME HAD COME, Koestler decided, to return to the work on Kepler. Feeling the need to escape from London and its distractions, he and Cynthia spent part of the summer working in a Wiltshire cottage which Wayland Young (now Lord Kennet) had lent him. In the autumn they looked for a country retreat of their own, and in October Koestler bought an old farmhouse, Long Barn, in the Weald of Kent, near Sevenoaks and a mile or two from the great house Knole. In the twenties Long Barn had been the home of Harold Nicolson and Vita Sackville-West, who kept it on when in 1930 they acquired Sissinghurst Castle and began to plan the gardens which are now one of the show-pieces of south-east England. Virginia Woolf and many more of the Nicolsons' literary friends were put up from time to time at Long Barn. The house, Cynthia recalls, was

'haunted by the Bloomsbury set'.*

If any ghosts less benign than those of Bloomsbury haunted the 'primeval barn' (as Virginia Woolf had described the old house), they did not distract Koestler from the ambitious task to which he had returned.

What had begun as a biography of Kepler was rapidly growing into something very much wider in its historical span, and extremely intricate in its interweaving of many complex strands of narrative, interpretation, argument, and speculation. He was now working towards a demonstration in historical detail of the irrational factor in the psychology of scientific discovery, the source of which he believed to be identical with that of those impulses which we describe as religious (or mystical) and aesthetic.

Kepler had been one of the heroes of his boyhood together with Newton, Darwin, Mach and the other great explorers of our own time whose discoveries have shaped the modern view of the universe and in the process crucially influenced philosophic thought in many of its aspects. In *Arrow in the Blue*, the first of his two autobiographical volumes, he has described how once, lying on a hillside near Vienna and looking up into the cloudless sky, he gave himself up

* *Op. cit.*

to a mood of mystic elation which was suddenly intensified into 'spontaneous illumination'. But this did not last:

> 'In the midst of this beatitude, the paradox of spatial infinity suddenly pierced my brain as if it had been stung by a wasp. You could shoot a super-arrow into the blue with a super force which could carry it beyond the pull of the earth's gravity, past the moon, past the sun's attraction – and what then? It would traverse interstellar space, past other suns, other galaxies, Milky Ways, Honeyed Ways, Acid Ways – and what then? It would go on and on, past the spiral nebulae, and more galaxies, and more spiral nebulae, and there would be nothing to stop it, no limit and no end, in space or in time . . .'

Until that moment he had been, he says, a true child of the nineteenth century – 'the century of crude philosophies and arrogant simplifications'. But the vision of the arrow soaring into the blue and beyond it on its straight Newtonian track into the blackness of space, on a flight without limit in space or end in time, forced upon him an obsession with the paradox of infinity and eternity which destroyed once and for all the certitude of his scientific text books.

> 'The idea that infinity would remain an unsolved riddle was unbearable. The more so as I had learned that a finite quality like the earth – or like myself reclining on it – shrank to zero when divided by an infinite quantity. So, mathematically, if space was infinity the earth was zero, and a year and a century were zero. It made no sense, there was a miscalculation somewhere . . .'

* *

But many great physicists, of whose activities Koestler as a schoolboy could hardly be aware, were also deeply concerned with that 'miscalculation'; and foremost among them was the finest and noblest of Newton's successors, Albert Einstein.

In 1905, which happened to be the year of Koestler's birth, Einstein published the first four of a series of papers which were (in conjunction with the discoveries and speculations of his contemporaries) to alter radically the concepts of space and time on which the Newtonian view of the universe had been so solidly based. One of these set out his 'special theory' of relativity. And eleven years later, while Koestler was grappling with the rudiments of physics, Einstein published his 'general theory'. The 'miscalculations' had been identified and corrected, theoretically, and one of the consequences of this modification of Newton's majestic synthesis was the undermining of the mechanistic philosophies derived from it during the Enlightenment and the resultant harsh determinism of nineteenth-century thought.

If Koestler, lying on that Austrian hillside and gazing up into the blue, had known of this, he would have had to contemplate the notion not only of the arrow flying on forever through infinite space but also, and simultaneously, of its flight across a universe which was spatially finite and infinite at one and the same time. The paradox of infinity and eternity was even more paradoxical than he realised. The flight to infinity – to put it simplistically – would return to its point of origin.

From Einstein's insights and the theories he drew from them; from the work of those who built theoretically and empirically upon his discoveries; and from the accelerating technological application of the multiplying discoveries – from these are derived the greatest material achievements of modernity: some beneficial, others threatening scarcely imaginable catastrophe.

The mind of a genius whose flashes of inspiration have led to the multiplication of human power to an extent that would have been inconceivable a century ago – even to the most ardent believer in 'science' as a sort of unquestionably 'progressive' and desirable substitute for 'religion' – can scarcely be described as simple. On the other hand, Einstein the man was almost saintly in his simplicity, his humility, and his preoccupation (after he had freed himself from Mach's influence) with problems which positivistic philosophy would dismiss as nonsensical. For him, as for all the truly original philosophers, the universe was in essence simple, harmonious, beautiful – and no less mysterious than it seemed to even the most 'primitive' of societies.

* *

It would be no great exaggeration to say that by 1955 Koestler was dogmatic only in his anti-dogmatism. He had been thoroughly inoculated by painful experience against infection by the absolute – although once in a mood of depression and puzzlement, as Cynthia recalls, he was to contemplate submission to the Roman Catholic Church (a conversion which would have given his instructor, one imagines, a few anxious moments).

Einstein's theories, like those of his great predecessors and contemporaries in the physical sciences (and rather more, perhaps, in the life sciences), were familiar enough to Koestler. His education, wide reading, and hard practical experience as Science Editor of the Ullstein chain of newspapers had made them accessible to him – in outline only in some cases, but in considerable detail in a surprising number. He also knew a great deal about the empirical verification of many of those theories – more than enough to realise that man's concepts of the universe 'out there', the macrocosm (and also, no less of the microcosm), were undergoing at an accelerating rate changes more radical than any that had occurred since the pre-Socratic philosophers of Ionia (if not quite, to put it figuratively in terms of the creation myth that remains one of the tap-roots of Western civilisation, since the expulsion of our progenitors from the 'garden eastward in Eden').

For many years he had been preoccupied by the implications for philosophy and psychology of the astonishing and increasingly numerous 'acts of creation' by the intuitive imagination of genius in many fields of science. It was, in fact, the nature of the creative mind which obsessed him above all.

Recalling the dominant passion of his youth which had returned to him in middle age, once he had put political activism behind him, he wrote:

> 'Broadly speaking, it had to do with psychological processes underlying, on the one hand, scientific discovery and artistic creation – the glory of man – and, on the other hand, his apparent blindness and insane urge for self-destruction – the predicament of Man. History reflects them both; but

their clearest reflection is to be found in the history of man's changing vision of the universe . . . The vision was to a large extent created, or transformed, by a small number of visionaries, and these are the individuals in whom the complex psychological processes of creation and destruction are exemplified – sometimes on a heroic scale, sometimes as a pathetic caricature.'

It had been Koestler's original intention to illustrate and analyse the 'act of creation' through the medium of a biography of Johannes Kepler – an intellectual and imaginative expedition into the interior of the mind of one of those outstanding (and eccentric, not to say cranky) men of genius whose lightning-flashes of intuitive understanding had illumined, enlarged and changed our view of the universe – and by so doing had also multiplied many times the perceived area of our ignorance.

There were many good reasons for this choice, quite apart from his long-standing interest in the extraordinary personality of the man. Einstein and his great contemporaries were far too close to be seen in perspective, and the revolutionary effects of their discoveries on the cultures of the civilised world would obviously take many decades to work themselves out. Innumerable books had been written about Newton and Galileo. But there existed no serious biography in English of Kepler; nor were his works, diaries, and voluminous correspondence accessible to the English reader:

'Yet Kepler is one of the few geniuses who enables one to follow, step by step, the tortuous path that led him to his discoveries, and to get a really intimate glimpse, as in a slow-motion film, of the creative act.'

It was not long, however, before he recognised that he would not realise his ambition by the portrayal of Kepler in isolation from his predecessors, contemporaries, and successors. Nothing is made (by man) out of nothing, and even the very greatest and most original innovators build on the past, the view of which is modified by their innovations just as the picture which they present will be modified by genius in the future.

Kepler's complicated edifice had been erected on the foundations of his predecessors, and especially on those laid by Canon Nicolaus Copernicus – that strange and melancholy Pole who, by the age of thirty, having studied at the universities of Cracow, Bologna, Padua and Ferrara, was – so it has been said – the only man in the world who knew everything that could be known about mathematics, astronomy, astrology, theology, medicine, the theory of money and much else besides.

So Koestler put aside for the moment his notes on Kepler to study Copernicus, a task which involved reading his great and almost unreadable work, *De Revolutionibus Orbium Coelestium*.

By the time he was distracted by the campaign for the abolition of capital punishment, he had in draft form a hundred-odd pages of manuscript.

* *

Koestler had already made a bold attempt to synthesise a theory of scientific discovery and artistic creativity, and explain the nature of the 'quantum jump', so to speak, which characterises the process by which scientists and artists arrive at their discoveries and creations. The result was *Insight and Outlook*, drafted during several years of intensive but frequently interrupted study, and revised under conditions of great discomfort and difficulty during the terrible winter of 1946/47 – a time when he was also plagued by a variety of personal and political distractions.

For the Anglo-Saxon reader it was an odd book – some 450 pages packed full of ideas on an immense variety of subjects (the inter-relationship of which was not always immediately apparent). Its subtitle was *An Inquiry into the Common Foundations of Science, Art, and Social Ethics*.

The great mass of intellectual and speculative matter was organised in four parts. The first was entitled *The Comic*, in the middle of which Koestler introduced his key concept of 'bisociation' which he defined provisionally as merely a convenient term referring to

> '. . . any mental occurrence simultaneously associated with two habitually incompatible contexts.'

The second part, entitled *Self-Assertion and Self-Transcendence*, began with a discussion of the physiology and psychology of weeping and ended with a chapter on 'The Regenerative Equilibrium of Civilizations'. In the middle of this part is to be found his key concept of the 'integrative tendency' in the evolutionary process in which he sketches his view of the relationship of the 'part' to the 'whole' in any mature organism:

> 'The part has to maintain its individuality, otherwise the organism would lose its articulation and revert to amorphous homogeneity; at the same time, it has to behave as a *part* in the whole, that is, in functional subordination. Now the individuality of the part consists in its being itself an integrated whole of a lower order – a sub-whole composed of sub-parts, which in themselves are sub-wholes, and so on. In this organic hierarchy the functional units of each level are all Janus-faced, as it were: they are wholes when facing downwards, parts when facing upwards. On the upper limit of the hierarchy, the same double aspect holds; the individual animal and man are organic wholes relative to their body, but parts of the higher integrative unit of the herd, insect state, family or society. Downwards the hierarchy extends through the colloidal and crystalline to the atomic and sub-atomic levels. The so-called "elementary particles" – electrons, photons, neutrons, mesotrons, and so forth – may probably be regarded as different patterns of energy concentrations, as differentiated wholes in the lowest structural level.
>
> 'The concept of the "functional whole" is defined as the pattern of relations between its parts, and not as the mere sum of its parts. Mere summational aggregation of parts does not lead to the formation of functional wholes. A heap of coal dust does not behave as a functional whole, and whatever its size, its integrative hierarchy reaches its upper limit on the crystalline level.
>
> 'In the evolutionary hierarchy, each level has its own set of integrative laws,

> or "organising relations"; on each level these are more complex than on the previous one. They imply the laws of the next lower level (as, for example, biology implies the laws of chemistry, which in turn imply those of physics), but they cannot be reduced to, or predicted from the lower level. Hence a thing or part will enter into different relations and behave in a different way according to the integrative laws to which it is submitted: an atom of carbon will behave differently in a heap of coal dust, in an inorganic compound, or in a protein molecule. In short, "the organism in its totality is as essential to an explanation of its elements, as its elements are to an explanation of the organism".
>
> 'This emphasis on the integrative power of the whole over its parts is a result of converging trends in biology, embryology, tissue culture, neurology and psychology. It has almost entirely replaced that last century's mechanistic and atomistic conceptions; it is variously called the holistic or organismic or Gestalt approach. It seems, however, that its implications have not yet been fully explored, and this section is meant as a step in that direction.'

In the third part, entitled *The Neutral Arts – Invention and Discovery*, he applies his theory of 'bisociation' to the process of scientific discovery – another of his key concepts. He illustrates it with the familiar story of how Archimedes discovered how to measure the volume of the allegedly pure gold crown about which his patron, Hiero, the ruler of Syracuse, had his doubts. He got into his bath which, being full, overflowed:

> 'Now Archimedes was in the habit of taking a daily bath but the experiences usually aroused by it were related to the sensations of heat and cold, fatigue and relaxation, sex and beauty, and so on. Neither to Archimedes, nor to anybody else before him, had it ever occurred to connect the sensuous and trivial associative contexts of taking a hot bath with the scholarly pursuit of the measurement of solids. No doubt he must have observed many times that if the bath were too full it would overflow to the extent to which he immersed his body in it. But this trivial experience was so intimately related to the context "bath" that it required the exceptional stress under which he laboured, and a particular constellation of circumstances, to break loose from its ties of associative habit and to perceive the overflow as a measurable liquid equivalent of the volume of the immersed solid.'

Archimedes, so the story goes, was so delighted with his discovery that he left his house and ran dripping through Syracuse, calling out *Eureka* ('I've found it').

Accordingly, Koestler wrote, following a technical discussion which I shall not attempt to condense,

> '. . . we shall henceforth call the mental process which produces an original and relevant bisociation the "eureka process". Apart from its picturesqueness, the term has the advantage of producing rage effects in behaviourists.'

The fourth part, entitled *The Emotive Arts*, has for epigraph two lines from *The Family Reunion* by T. S. Eliot:

*They don't understand what it is to be awake,*
*To be living on several planes at once.*

Here he discusses, in terms of his key concepts and hypotheses, various aspects of inspiration and creation in the arts, and ends with the development of his ideas about life's Trivial and Tragic Planes.

Most of us, happily, spend most of our lives on the Trivial Plane, only very rarely 'in moments of elation or anger' experiencing the Tragic Plane and its 'un-commonsense, cosmic perspective'. There are, however, times when ordinary people, facing imminent death or enduring protracted physical danger, live on the borderline, or intersection of the two planes. Many airmen during the war, Koestler noted, had eased the intolerable strain by

> '. . . projecting a trivial structure onto the Tragic Plane, in conventionalizing and banalizing Death itself by means of that curious schoolboy slang in which mortal crashes were referred to as "cheese" or "prang", and a friend's death or mutilation as "He's had it". By this process of trivialization and smug understatement, the universe becomes a silly thought, eternity embarrassing, and infinity bad form.
>
> 'The creative mind reverses this process. The mystic, artist, and philosopher are also condemned to walk the tight-rope on the intersection line of the two planes. While the conventional soldier or adventurer eases the strain by projecting his trivial attitude onto the Tragic Plane, the artist proceeds the opposite way: he experiences the trivial in the perspective of the tragic, in the light of "eternity looking through time". And therein can probably be found the essence of the artist's approach. This interlacing of the Tragic and the Trivial planes is implicit in all great works of art; it is the ultimate quality of the creative mind by means of which it is able to transcend the narrow limits of the self. And thus is man:
>
> '"*That great and true amphibium, whose nature is disposed to live, not only like other creatures in divers elements, but in divided and distinguished worlds.*"'

This ends the main text, which is followed by two appendices – *A Note on Nature and the Visual Arts* and *Other Theories of the Cosmic: Bergson and Freud*, and a select bibliography of formidable variety and scope.

* *

The book was not well received, as we have already noted, on its publication in 1949. Perhaps this is because it is a very 'Middle European' kind of book, covering a wide field of ideas with copious allusions to the work of authorities in a multiplicity of apparently disparate fields, abounding in analogy and rich in digressions, the point of which is sometimes not immediately apparent. It could be said, not unjustly, either that some of the material had not been fully digested or that the author had not taken sufficient trouble to make many of his analytical and expository passages sufficiently lucid. Nor does it often succeed in weaving together into a seamless whole its bewildering variety of strands.

Most lay reviewers did not know what on earth to make of it; and many academic critics – irritated after their occasionally petty-minded fashion by the incursion of an outsider (and one with no academic degree of any sort) into their closely guarded reservations – treated it with disdain. They were given a gratuitous opening by Koestler's postscript to his preface (dated Tel Aviv, July 1948):

> 'At the time of correcting the proofs, the author was acting as a war correspondent in Palestine. Cut off from his library, and deprived of normal means of communication with the outside world, it was in some cases impossible for him to insert page reference numbers into the footnotes relating to works quoted in the text. He wishes to apologise to the reader for any inconvenience caused by this unavoidable omission.'

Unavoidable? One can hear some of the more ungenerous of the learned clerks sniffing as they asked themselves why the fellow hadn't waited until he had returned from Palestine before passing the proofs and rushing into print like any damned journalist.

Koestler's preface begins with a bold flourish:

> 'Artists treat facts as stimuli for imagination, whereas scientists use imagination to coordinate facts. The aim of this book is, first, to show that such distinctions are not fundamental, that all the creative activities of man are based on a common pattern, and to present a unifying theory of humour, art and discovery, in which these are shown to differ merely in degree and not in kind. Secondly, the attempt is made to show the possibility of a system of ethics which is neither utilitarian nor dogmatic, but derived from the same integrative tendency in the evolutionary process to which the creative activities of art and discovery are traced.'

But a somewhat apologetic note dominates the concluding paragraphs in which he informs the reader that an attempt to synthesise the various trends he covers would be found in 'Volume Two, which is in preparation and will, it is hoped, appear twelve months after the first.'* This would elaborate his theory and coordinate it 'with biology, neuro-physiology, animal and child psychology, and so forth'. It was only in Volume Two that a number of objections arising from the matter in Volume One could be met, satisfying in particular the psychologist's need 'for a more detailed treatment of the theoretical aspects of the operative field, of the integration of lower into more complex fields, of the relation of bisociative to associative processes, and so on'.

> 'Thus the present volume follows in broad outline the original process of the working-out of the theory, while Volume Two is an attempt to put it on a more scholarly foundation.
>
> 'Accordingly, the terminology of this Volume is rather loose, and falls considerably short of the requirements of semantic purism. This is as inevitable in the first tentative stages of formulating a new theory, as it is necessary that in its final shape it should stand the acid test of semantic analysis . . .

* Fifteen years, as it turned out.

'Like many others before him, the author has tried to strike a precarious balance between the claims of the general reader and of the specialist, between intelligibility and precision. The result, as usual, is that verbose passages boring to the scholar alternate with others over which the general reader may stumble . . .'

All this was engagingly honest (and accurate) but not exactly inviting either to the specialist or the general reader. If the author himself was disappointed in the work he was offering, why should they bother to take it seriously?

But for all its structural oddities, its many more superficial deficiencies, and the general impression which it conveyed that it had been put together in too much of a hurry, it is a brilliant, and in large part, an original work. This was recognised by certain broad-minded and imaginative scholars with unimpeachable academic qualifications – Dennis Gabor, for example, who was awarded the Nobel Prize for physics in 1971 (and who praised it unstintingly in conversation with me as the product of 'the introspective analysis of his own creative mind'), Michael Polanyi, and a number of distinguished American academics with whom he had for some time been corresponding.

Among the heroes of Koestler's youth was Goethe. In an extremely interesting essay on *The Intelligentsia* (first published in *Horizon* in March 1944), he remarked:

'The first modern intellectuals were the Encyclopaedists, and they enter the historical stage as the great debunkers and iconoclasts. Goethe resurrected is unimaginable in our time, but Voltaire would be within a fortnight acclimatised in Bloomsbury, winning all week-end competitions of the *New Statesman*. For Goethe was the last Renaissance genius, a direct descendant of Leonardo . . .'

Koestler had done, and was still to do, more than his share of debunking, but most of his targets were those who regarded themselves as the intellectual descendants of the Encyclopaedists. No work by Goethe appears in the bibliography of *Insight and Outlook*, but hovering over many of the pages is the spirit of that genius who was poet, playwright, novelist, lawyer, courtier, administrator, critic, educationalist, womaniser, painter, theatre manager, philosopher, and also (to cut this catalogue short) the author of more than a dozen works on various scientific subjects.

I do not propose to discuss the ideas embedded in *Insight and Outlook*, because they are all incorporated in refined form in certain of his later works. The book was a failure, but a valuable one from which he learned a great deal.

* *

When Koestler returned to his Kepler manuscript during the summer of 1956, he realised that to begin his narrative with an account of Copernicus, and the philosophical time-bomb ticking in *De Revolutionibus Orbium Coelestium* and the heliocentric hypothesis which displaced the planet Earth from the centre of the universe, would be inadequate.

Behind the learned and eccentric canon was the giant figure of Claudius Ptolemaeus, the Greek astronomer, mathematician, and geographer who worked in Alexandria during the second century AD. Ptolemy's thirteen books, written in Greek, were first entitled *The Mathematical Collection*, and later, *The Great Astronomer*. In the ninth century they were translated into Arabic for the Caliph al Ma'mun under the title of *al Megiste* (meaning, roughly, *The Greatest*). The *Almagest*, as the work is now known, was familiar to Arab scholars during the years of Islam's temporal power which extended from the Atlantic, north and south of the Strait of Gibraltar, to the Indonesian Archipelago. Some knowledge of it gradually seeped through into the Christian world through the Hebrew translations made in Spain by the learned cousins of the Children of Ishmael. But it was not until the twelfth century that it was translated from one of the Arabic versions into Latin and so, in due course, like the scientific works of Aristotle (the original Greek of which had to pass through Syrian, Arabic, and Hebrew before the text became available to the West in Latin), into the intellect and imagination of Saint Thomas Aquinas, whence they issued in the form of the Christian cosmology which survived the challenge implicit in Copernicus's revolutionary *Concerning the Revolutions of the Heavenly Bodies*, and only began to crumble after Galileo's undiplomatic attitude towards the Holy Office's guardians of orthodoxy resulted in quarrel and scandal.

But Koestler's studies were to take him beyond Ptolemy to Aristotle and Plato; and beyond them to Aristarchus and Pythagoras of Samos, who had brought to Magna Graecia the ideas of the pre-Socratic philosophers of the Greek colonies of Ionia – Thales, Anaximander, Anaximenes, Xenophanes, Heraclitus, and the other stars in that distant galaxy where distinctive and systematic Western thought was born.

Cynthia has an amusing story which illustrated Koestler's obsession with the 'twin stars', Aristotle and Plato, when he was drafting his Part One of *The Sleepwalkers*, an account of the earliest cosmologies.

> 'I remember one bleak night . . . when his obsession . . . became unbearable. He had to talk to somebody about it. Henry Green lived around the corner and had studied Classics, so we went to see him. Arthur, alas, got little out of the visit, except perhaps letting off steam. But Henry did: he had nothing to say about Plato and Aristotle, but he looked on and listened, obviously bemused by the sight of a man with a burning obsession. Sebastian, Henry's son, plied Arthur with vodkas, but even they did not help. When at last we left he was as tormented as ever by the twin stars; somewhat the worse for wear and staggering slightly, he wondered if his mind would give him any peace to sleep.'*

Once at Long Barn, however, he succeeded in getting the 'twin stars' into focus and plotting the twists and turns of philosophical thought and religious speculation which had put an infinite space between them and the bright stars, soon to be dimmed, of Ionia.

* *

* *Op. cit.*

Deeply immersed though he was in his research into the origins of the New Science (and increasingly obsessed by the philosophies and ideologies which were its by-products), Koestler still found time to help the Abolition Campaign as best he could. He kept in touch with the committee, and in a friendly letter of advice to Gerald Gardiner, who had succeeded Gollancz as chairman, he clearly expressed both his passionate conviction and his skill as a propagandist:

> 'I share your view that public meetings and Press campaigns against capital punishment *per se* are basic and essential, but I believe that this must be complemented by laying stress on the individual man and woman being hanged. This for two reasons: (a) we reject hanging because of the live individuals who are being hanged, and (b) public emotion can only be crystallised on concrete people – Bentley, Evans, Ruth Ellis, etc.
>
> 'The objection against this is that one does not want to make capital out of a person facing death. But that depends for what purpose you want to "make capital". To increase the circulation of a paper – no. To make capital out of death against death – yes. *Sub specie aeternitatis*, the only point in the senseless deaths of Bentley or Ellis seems to be that they are hastening the abolition of the death penalty. Not to "utilise" with reverence and utmost efficiency the lesson derived from these pointless killings would mean, it seems to me, denying our purpose . . .'

There were also innumerable letters to be read and (many of them) answered, for *Reflections on Hanging* was now arousing interest and controversy in many countries other than the United Kingdom where the death penalty was still in force.

But most of his activities on behalf of the Campaign had to be given up.

Without Koestler's active participation and dynamism, the Campaign soon lost its momentum. Early in July 1957 Peggy Duff wrote to Cynthia to say that the headquarters of the Campaign had moved from Gollancz's offices in Henrietta Street to that other stronghold of causes good, bad, indifferent and dotty – Number 10, Great Turnstile, the home of the *New Statesman*. The letter-heading of the paper on which she wrote, announcing that she turned up at the office only twice a week, was not that of the Campaign (which for several months had lacked the wherewithal to pay her) but of the National Council for the Abolition of Nuclear Weapon Tests. The sponsors of this organisation were a mixed bunch: E. M. Forster; Earl Russell; the Rev. Dr Donald (now Lord) Soper; Professor Barbara (now Lady) Wootton; Sir Compton Mackenzie; Sir Herbert Read; Ben Nicolson; Michael (now Sir Michael) Tippett; Rose (later Dame Rose) Macaulay; Professor C. H. Waddington; James Campbell of the National Union of Railwaymen; and the Rev. Sir George MacLeod (now the Very Rev. Lord MacLeod of Fuinary). Peggy Duff asked Koestler if he would like to join them. She enclosed a pamphlet with the letter. Koestler read it, and replied:

> 'Beloved Peggy, I'll do anything you ask, but your pamphlet is disturbingly ambiguous. Does your campaign demand that nuclear tests should be

unconditionally stopped by the United Kingdom regardless of whatever other nations are doing? Or does it demand that the tests should be stopped by international agreement? Forgive me if the question sounds idiotic, but the pamphlet isn't a model of clarity either.'

Koestler liked and admired Peggy Duff's enthusiasm and capacity for hard work. His view of her political judgement was another matter. Peggy Duff knew this, of course, and in her reply to his questions about the National Council for the Abolition of Nuclear Weapon Tests (out of which grew that great left-wing cause of the later fifties and sixties, the Campaign for Nuclear Disarmament, and the annual march of the stage-army of the good – and not so good – from Aldermaston), she agreed that the pamphlet was no model of clarity, being a rehash of an earlier effort. She repeated her invitation and added:

'. . . we spend a lot of time brushing off the C.P. [Communist Party of Great Britain] and fellow-travellers, but if the Council ever gets taken over by them I will warn you and we can resign together. Yours till the crack of doom or the next H Bomb war.'

But Koestler, guessing (rightly) how this particular venture would develop, still declined to be associated with it:

'I am sorry to say,' he wrote, 'that I am not convinced. I am simply unable to decide the rights and wrongs of the issue. There are too many variables in the equation; but, at any rate, this is a purely political issue, and, as you know, I have retired from that kind of thing. Sorry to disappoint you.'

With that Koestler returned to *The Sleepwalkers* and his latest hobby, chicken farming: '. . . he has seventy-eight,' Cynthia told Peggy Duff '(he ate two) and 150 more are arriving next month in tiny cardboard boxes. All the eggs at Long Barn are "hand laid"!'

During the summer of 1957, Koestler was invited by Fritz Molden to give the opening lecture at his Summer School in Alpbach, an attractive village in the Austrian Tyrol. Welcoming a break in his intensive work on *The Sleepwalkers* (in which the biography of Kepler was now embedded), he accepted the invitation, fell in love with the place, and decided to return in 1958 and find a site on which to build a house that would take the place of Long Barn as a retreat from London.

At last, in the spring of 1958, he wrote the last page of *The Sleepwalkers*. When copies of the revised typescript (a bulky one) had been safely lodged with his publishers, he and Cynthia went off to spend the summer in Alpbach. They found a site, then an architect, and arranged for the construction of the *Schreiberhäusel* (the 'writer's cottage') as they were to call it, to begin during June 1959.

Koestler, as always in the interval between completing a book, correcting the proofs, and starting a new work, was depressed and restless. Cynthia knew the signs and helped him through the difficult period by her calm acceptance of his changing moods. But what she found (and still finds) puzzling

'. . . is this: if he is so unhappy when he is not writing, why is he always in such a tormented hurry to finish the book he is working on? It almost seems as if the agony of writing were the more unbearable. Then follows the misery of the after-book depression.'

He had an idea that might be worked up into a novel, began to draft it, and abandoned it. (Fourteen years were to pass before he turned again to the medium of fiction.)

There was something else on his mind. In the concluding section of *The Sleepwalkers* - the Epilogue in which he jumps from the publication of Isaac Newton's *Principia* in 1687 to a consideration of its implications for scientific and philosophical thought, and so for the fate of mankind, during the three subsequent centuries - he had written:

'Our hypnotic enslavement to the numerical aspects of reality has dulled our perception of non-quantitative moral values; the resultant end-justifies-the-means ethic may be a major factor in our undoing.'

Brooding on this in Alpbach, he asked himself whether the religions and philosophies of the East had anything to offer to the West in its crisis of modernity. Aldous Huxley and other refugees from Europe in California seemed to think they had. So did many of the younger generation who found comfort and inspiration in popular expositions of Yoga and Zen. Before them, Schopenhauer had discovered a source of consolation in the Upanishads. And long before Schopenhauer, during the Dark Ages of the West, Saint Augustine had drawn inspiration from the works of Plotinus, who had in his turn been influenced by Indian mysticism. Perhaps there was some antidote in the East to the poisons that seemed to be coursing through the veins of the West and impelling it towards either the eventual acceptance of a robot-like existence under totalitarian tyranny or to self-destruction?

One day he told Cynthia that a

'. . . visit to India and Japan was on the cards, and spent the autumn reading up and preparing for the journey. His main purpose was to visit holy men and psychiatrists.'*

In December he left for the East and spent almost four months travelling in India and Japan, visiting institutions of one kind and another, interviewing 'saints' and savants, and amassing hundreds of pages of carefully detailed notes. He travelled, as he wrote later,

'. . . in the mood of a pilgrim. Like countless others before, I wondered whether the East had any answers to our perplexities and dead-locked problems. I chose [India and Japan] because they are at opposite ends of the spectrum: one the most tradition-bound, the other the most "modern" of the great countries of Asia. I did not hope for any ready-made answer, but was anxious to look at the predicament of the West from a different perspective, a different spiritual latitude.'

* *Op. cit.*

His inquiries yielded no answer, ready-made or otherwise, but in the end there was a revelation of sorts which encouraged him to return to the struggle from which his journey had been in some sense an escape:

> 'I started my journey in sackcloth and ashes,' he was to write in the final paragraph of *The Lotus and the Robot*, the book in which he described his pilgrimage, 'and came back rather proud of being a European. It may be a somewhat parochial pride, but it is not smug, for, as a Hungarian-born, French-loving English writer with some experience of prisons and concentration-camps, one cannot help being aware of Europe's past sins and present deadly peril. And yet a detached comparison with other countries of the way Europe stood up to its past trials, and of its contribution to man's history, leaves one with a new confidence and affection for that small figure riding on the back of the Asian bull.'

* *

On his return to England from the Far East during April 1959 he began to work up his notes into a book, but found it heavy going. During the summer in Alpbach, while the *Schreibershäusel* was being built, he did more work on it, drafting a chapter or two, but without much enthusiasm. Supervising the building of the house, according to Cynthia,

> '. . . prevented him from finding the peace he needed. Besides, that burning obsession which accompanies the writing of all his books, was lacking. It had all been wastefully channelled into the building and the usual frustrating dealings with elusive builders.'*

* *

An invitation came from Manchester University to deliver a course of three lectures on human creativity. With some relief he set aside the draft of his book about the East; and his preparation of the three lengthy lectures revived his ambition to write a truly scholarly sequel to *Insight and Outlook*. But he had scarcely started to arrange his already voluminous notes and organise a research programme when the arrival of a guest from India, Jayaprakash Narayan, directed his mind back to the East and the book.

On the whole, Narayan's visit to London was a disappointment for Koestler; but at least it stimulated him to pick up the bits and pieces of his draft, and the diary he had kept during his travels in the East, and to write *The Lotus and the Robot*. The typescript was complete by the end of April 1960. Before its issue in book form, two lengthy extracts - 'Yoga Unexpurgated' and 'A Stink of Zen' - were published in *Encounter*.

When the book was published later in the year and Koestler's descriptions of Yoga and Zen were seen in their full context, there was little controversy. With the exception of a critic in the *Hibbert Journal* who remained 'unshaken in his belief that the wisdom of the East is a great, though subterranean, force which enables many men and women even at the present time to live fairly fruitful

* *Op. cit.*

lives', and that of an anonymous reviewer in *The Times Literary Supplement* who complained that

> 'Time and time again he threw the baby out with the bath water - it is as if an Oriental, disgusted with Stratford commercialism, were to write off "Shakespeare and all that lot" as bunk,'

it was generally agreed that Koestler's account was authentic; justified in its dismissive treatment of the more extreme aspects of Yoga and Zen; by no means unsympathetic in its depiction of the sages whom he had interviewed (one or two of them extremely curious by any standards, occidental or oriental); and immensely enjoyable, on a different level, as a travel book.

The poet D. J. Enright, who knows the East well, summed up his reactions thus:

> 'The only general criticism that can be made of this book is that Mr Koestler concerns himself too exclusively with the very old and the very new – in fact with the Lotus and the Robot – and doesn't allow enough weight to what lies between. The territory, of course, that a visiting VIP doesn't see much of: that is, lots and lots of human beings, very different from us, and very similar to us. Their problems are essentially the same as ours, though manifested in different forms. They cannot provide us with *the* answer – is there one? – nor we them. We can offer possible solutions to some specific problems; they can offer possible solutions to other specific problems. East and West are meeting – and must go on meeting, but not only at their lunatic fringes. Unfortunately that is where they do chiefly meet these days. Hence the special deflatory value of Mr Koestler's sharp book [which Enright thought superior in its observations of Japanese society and culture to Fosco Maraini's *Meeting with Japan* – high praise indeed].'

But it was not only the occidental critics, with or without personal knowledge of the East and some acquaintance with its religions who joined in the general chorus of praise. That brilliant journalist Ved Mehta, for example, although he had certain reservations, acknowledged that *The Lotus and the Robot* was

> '. . . redeemed by the gentle and humane spirit of the author which pervades the book, softening the brutal effects of his discoveries,'

although his analysis of the springs and effects of Zen Buddhism would

> 'infuriate Dr Suzuki, the Hollywood Yogis, the North Beach Beats, *New Yorker* intellectuals, and chi-chi groups in London and Paris, not to mention the smug Japanese who think Zen to be their main contribution to modern thought.'

Koestler had returned from his pilgrimage to India and Japan somewhat disillusioned,

> '. . . in a sense . . . impoverished rather than enriched. I felt that I had been put in my place – and that my place was Europe. But at the same time, looking at

the tiny Continent from the vastness of Asia, I gained a fresh impression of its compactness and coherence, and a more intense awareness of its unique history – its unity-in-variety in Space, and continuity-through-change in Time . . . Continuity-through-change and unity-in-diversity seem to be the preconditions of a living culture . . .'

So he wrote in his epilogue to *The Lotus and the Robot* – ten pages or so of reflection in which one can hear the echoes of a hundred generations of the wisest men of the West, including many whose wisdom was expressed in forms which led them to be denounced by the intellectual heirs of the nineteenth century's pseudo-science (and especially that determinism derived from Plato, Hegel, and Marx) as obscurantist, reactionary 'fascists'.

# CHAPTER XXXII

# *1959*

WHEN KOESTLER WAS STILL on his Eastern travels, *The Sleepwalkers: A History of Man's Changing Vision of the Universe* was published.

It would be impossible to summarise the contents of this many-faceted work accurately within a reasonable space (as critics better qualified than I discovered), and I shall not attempt to do so. The brief account that follows singles out simply those aspects which, I think, illustrate most vividly the essence of Koestler's thought and indicate the direction in which it was moving.

The history begins with a description of the phenomenal universe shaped by the religious myths and astronomical observations of the ancient Babylonians. It ends with the publication in 1687 of Sir Isaac Newton's *Principia*, after which cosmology became a disciplined science and

> 'All mysteries seemed to have been banished from the universe and divinity reduced to the part of a constitutional monarch who is kept in existence for reasons of decorum, but without real necessity and without influence on the course of affairs.'

In an epilogue of some thirty pages Koestler discusses the discoveries he had himself made in his study of the great discoverers, and then goes on to examine the implications of these within the context of the orthodox idea of 'science' as established in the nineteenth century – that is, a purely rational, empirical activity which results in a steadily increasing body of verified factual *knowledge* the soundness of which is beyond dispute, as opposed to the subjective and so uncertain nature of *wisdom* acquired by minds working intuitively and imaginatively outside what has come to be known as 'scientific method'.

The 'Sleepwalkers' were those whose discoveries had led men to view the world not as the solid centre of a finite cosmos but rather as an infinitesimal part of an infinite universe which could be adequately described and understood only in the symbolic language of mathematics. The odd thing that Koestler had discovered during his psychological probings into the minds of some of those geniuses, whose discoveries were eventually to underpin the supreme rationality of the Enlightenment, was not merely that they were in themselves as often as not extremely irrational. There was no particular surprise in that, of course: the absent-minded or otherwise eccentric professor had been a figure of fun since the beginnings of scholarship.

More surprising was the fact that they tended to stumble on their seminal discoveries like sleepwalkers, or find them without looking for them while they were in that trance-like state more usually associated with the revelations of mystics or the inspiration of artists. The key insights of science, in short, seemed to arise not from the painstaking effort of ratiocination but from flashes of intuition which came unbidden when the conscious mind was scarcely active – like Wordsworth in vacant or pensive mood; like Coleridge in his drugged sleep; like Picasso finding without seeking –

> 'A picture comes to me a long time beforehand,' Picasso said to Christian Zevros in 1934;* 'who knows how long a time beforehand, I sensed, saw, and painted it and yet the next day even I do not understand what I have done. How can anyone penetrate my dreams, my instincts, my desires, my thoughts, which have taken a long time to fashion themselves and come to the surface, above all to grasp what I put there, perhaps involuntarily?'

Such were the questions Koestler attempted to answer in his inquiry 'into the obscure workings of the creative mind' of the scientific genius; and

> '. . . I shall not be sorry,' he wrote in his preface, 'if, as an accidental by-product, the inquiry helps to counteract the legend that Science is a purely rational pursuit, that the "scientist" is a more "level-headed" and "dispassionate" type than others (and should therefore be given a leading part in world affairs); or that he is able to provide for himself and his contemporaries a rational substitute for insights derived from other sources.'

In one of its aspects *The Sleepwalkers* can be likened to a portrait gallery in which one approaches a great triptych along a corridor the walls of which are crowded with pictures, a few fairly large, most no more than sketchy miniatures, of the prominent figures of antiquity and of the Dark and Middle Ages. The corridor then opens out into a hall dominated by the triptych. The central and largest panel is a full-scale portrait, which obviously reflects the painter's sympathy with his subject, of Johannes Kepler, who was born in 1571 and died in 1630. This is flanked on the one side by a rather smaller panel out of which looks the dimmer, timid, and somewhat sour face of Copernicus, who died twenty-eight years before Kepler was born, at the age of seventy; and on the other by a panel, painted in brighter and harsher colours, which displays the aggressive features of Galileo, who was born seven years before Kepler and lived twelve years longer. On the wall behind the triptych there is a sketch of Isaac Newton who came into the world in the year when Galileo left it.

Thus the major portion of Koestler's exhibition spans the sixteenth and seventeenth centuries, the years when Renaissance and Reformation bore their fruits: the division of Christendom and the death of its old scholasticism.

* 'Conversations avec Picasso' in *Cahiers d'Art*, Vol X, Paris, 1935. Quoted in *Letters of the Great Artists*, Vol II, Ed. Richard Friedenthal, London, 1963.

'In the index to the six hundred-odd pages of Arnold Toynbee's *A Study of History*, abridged version, the names of Copernicus, Galileo, Descartes, and Newton do not occur. This one example among many should be sufficient to indicate the gulf that still separates the Humanities from the Philosophy of Nature. I use this outmoded expression because the term "Science", which has come to replace it in more recent times, does not carry the same rich and universal associations which Natural Philosophy carried in the seventeenth century, in the days when Kepler wrote his *Harmony of the World* and Galileo his *Message from the Stars*.'

Such were the geniuses who created the upheaval of what we call the Scientific Revolution but which was known in their day as the New Philosophy.

'The revolution in technology which their discoveries triggered off was an unexpected by-product; their aim was not the conquest of Nature, but the understanding of Nature. Yet their cosmic quest destroyed the mediaeval vision . . . and transformed the European landscape, society, culture, habits, and general outlook as thoroughly as if a new species had arisen on this planet.

'This mutation of the European mind in the seventeenth century is merely the latest example of the impact of the "Sciences" on the "Humanities" – of the inquiry into the nature of Nature on the inquiry into the nature of Man. It also illustrates the wrong-headedness of erecting academic and social barriers between the two; a fact which is at last beginning to gain recognition . . .'

But while there existed histories of science which contained such information as the dates on which the mechanical clock and the law of inertia made their first appearance, and histories of astronomy which informed one that the precession of the equinoxes was discovered by Hipparchus of Alexandria,

'. . . surprisingly, there exists to my knowledge no modern History of Cosmology, no comprehensive survey of man's changing vision of the universe which encloses him.'

This, Koestler explained to the reader, was what the book was aiming at. He also made it clear what the book was not. It was not, for example, a history of astronomy, although there were of necessity a great many references to that whenever it was necessary to bring into sharper focus the 'vision of the universe'. Nor was it a work of 'popular science', although he had described his intellectual expedition, and his discoveries, and the conclusions in language that could be understood by the general reader. He had begun it at the earliest known period when there was a systematic study of the skies; and if he had ended it with the publication of Newton's *Principia*, that was not only because he had to confine his vast subject within manageable limits, and because for all practical purposes our view of the universe was still basically Newtonian, but also because, although Einstein's discoveries had clearly revived and revolutionised the study of cosmology, the emerging form of the new cosmology was still uncertain

'. . . and it is too early to assess its influence on culture . . .'

Here I should like to invite the reader to note in passing (for reasons which will soon be apparent) that, although he had earlier indicated and was soon to demonstrate in detail the gulf between the 'Humanities' on the one hand and 'Science' or the 'Philosophy of Nature' on the other, Koestler employs the word 'culture' simply and without definition or qualification. The point has its importance. I am mindful of the admonition of that prince of wide-ranging philosophers, defender of the free spirit, and implacable enemy of nihilism and totalitarianism, Sir Karl Popper, that one should never let oneself

> '. . . be goaded into taking seriously problems about words and their meanings. What must be taken seriously are questions of fact, and assertions about facts . . .'

But it is difficult not to be so goaded by the way in which many social scientists who happen to be a great deal more socialist than scientific have mauled the word 'culture', and the concept. Some of their sophistries and casuistries are enough to induce a certain fleeting understanding of the sentiment Hanns Johst put into the mouth of one of his characters (but not – I must add for the benefit of today's equivalents of Johst on the 'fascist left' – for the same reasons): '*Wenn ich Kultur höre . . . entsichere ich meinen Browning.*'

When Koestler writes 'culture' he does not mean 'literary culture' or 'scientific culture' (far less 'bourgeois culture' or 'working-class culture', or any other such misplaced metaphor drawn from sociology or 'scientific socialism' or pretentious dilettantism), or culture in the narrow sense employed correctly by anthropologists. It is quite clear that he means something akin to Matthew Arnold's

> '. . . culture, the acquainting ourselves with the best that has been known and said in the world, and thus with the history of the human spirit,'

which is not unrelated to Goethe's observation that

> 'In my profession as a writer I have never asked myself how I may be of service to the whole. But always I have only sought to make *myself* better and more full of insight, and then only to express what I had recognised as good and true.'

Although 'Science' in the sense of the pursuit of exact, finally determined and objective knowledge had been increasingly separated from 'Philosophy' in the sense of the pursuit of approximate truth and wisdom, and although both activities had been fragmented and scattered and confused by ever-increasing specialisation (and an obscurantist neo-scholastic positivism), Koestler's recurring use of the word 'culture' implies a concept which embraces both pursuits, suggests the possibility of a revived 'Philosophy of Nature' – and reflects his convictions that it is only within the context of such a concept that the split mind of modern man can be made whole.

This impression is strengthened by his explanation of why the book is sketchy in some parts and detailed in others. His selection and emphasis of the material, he wrote, had been guided by his interest in certain specific questions – and these questions were the *Leitmotif* of *The Sleepwalkers*.

First came the twin threads of Science and Religion,

'. . . starting with the undistinguishable unity of the mystic and savant in the Pythagorean Brotherhood . . . and ending in the polite and deadly "divided house of faith and reason" of our day, where, on both sides, symbols have hardened into dogmas, and the common source of inspiration is lost from view.'

That common source of inspiration was the second *Leitmotif*: the

'psychological process of discovery as the most concise manifestation of man's creative faculty;'

and also the

'. . . converse process that blinds him towards truths which, once perceived by a seer, become so heartbreakingly obvious.'

Such blindness was not to be found, however, only in the minds of the 'ignorant and superstitious masses', as Galileo had described them. It was even more strikingly evident in Galileo's own mind, and in the minds of other geniuses like Aristotle, Ptolemy, or Kepler. The systematic study of the history of science, Koestler pointed out, was a relatively new discipline, little concerned as yet with psychology.

In his biographical and psychological studies of the sleepwalkers portrayed in the triptych which dominates the book – and especially his account of the life and work of Kepler, who had himself written so frankly and without reserve about his thoughts, his feelings, his obsessions – he demonstrates and defends his thesis in no cold and detached manner but rather with that intellectual passion which had informed his political and philosophical essays, as it had informed his novels.

He does not observe his subjects as if they were thinking-machines on marble pedestals. Far from it. Nor does he look at them from the lofty standpoint of the present as if they were historical curiosities. His approach is rather that of one who has succeeded in both thinking and imagining himself into their own time (as he had thought and imagined himself in *The Gladiators* into the dying days of republican Rome, and in *Darkness at Noon* into the nightmare of Stalin's purges) without sacrifice of his analytical capacity. It is as if he were personally involved and detached at one and the same time. He does not conceal his own bias, which makes Kepler a more sympathetic character than the shadowy Copernicus on the one hand or the quarrelsome Galileo on the other.

Whether or not he does either or both of these an injustice, and to what extent, are questions for scholars who have devoted their entire attention to them. More important is the fact that Koestler employed his many skills to dislodge them from their pedestals, bring them down to earth, display them as men among men, and dispel many of the myths by which the enthusiasts of 'progress' have all but deified them. More important, too, is his demonstration of the way in which they were often right for the wrong reasons, fitting their true insights and accurate observations into hypotheses which they knew to be demonstrably false, to 'save appearances'. And most important of all is his assault on the widely held notion that 'scientific progress' is an orderly and entirely rational process. It is, rather, something that evolves

> '. . . by occasional leaps and bounds alternating with delusional pursuits, culs-de-sac, regressions, periods of blindness and amnesia. The great discoveries that determined its course were sometimes the unexpected by-products of a chase after quite different hares.'

Koestler's great array of descriptions, illustrations, analyses, hypotheses, and arguments in support of them, is like a huge and at times apparently disorderly army advancing on a broad front, giving a little ground here, gaining rather more ground there, but always advancing until the crucial battleground is reached where its heaviest armour is concentrated for the *Schwerpunkt* that will punch a hole in the enemy's defences and allow free passage to the mobile forces which will, with luck, bring about his defeat.

The enemy goes in many guises under many names, but for present purposes it may be identified simply as the cocksure, arrogant, and intolerant 'scientism' of the nineteenth century still surviving in the rationalistic-mechanistic philosophies of the twentieth; in neo-Darwinian orthodoxy; in behaviourism and reductionism transformed from useful methodologies into dogma – 'the nihilism of today' as Professor Viktor E. Frankl, the neurologist, has described it.

There are those who contend that Koestler's assault in *The Sleepwalkers* (and subsequent campaigns) was launched against the ghosts of old soldiers who had long since faded away. But it would be all too easy to give innumerable examples to prove the contrary. Here is a simple one, from the closing pages of a short illustrated book* on Charles Darwin by a biologist and a geneticist, both vigorous proponents of neo-Darwinian orthodoxy. It follows an account of Darwin's burial in Westminster Abbey.

> 'And so the two greatest scientists that England has produced came to lie side by side in the Abbey – Newton, who banished miracles from the physical world and reduced God to the role of a cosmic designer who on the day of creation had brought the clockwork mechanism of the universe into being to tick away according to the inevitable laws of its nature; and Darwin, who banished not only miracles but also creation and design from the world of life, robbed God of his role of creator of man, and man of his divine origin.'

But neither of these men performed the feats attributed to them here. Neither Newton nor Darwin believed that their theories provided ultimate explanations. Of course, they believed in the truth of their theories, as theories, but in neither case that it was the Truth, The Whole Truth, And Nothing But The Truth. Such triumphalism was the characteristic not of these great and modest men but of the arrogant dogmatists who followed them.

The introduction to *The Sleepwalkers* had been contributed, appropriately, by Herbert Butterfield, Master of Peterhouse and Professor of Modern History in the University of Cambridge, whose own foray into the field had yielded

* *Charles Darwin and his World*, by Julian Huxley and H. B. D. Kettlewell, London, 1965, 1974.

the *Origins of Modern Science*, first published ten years earlier.* With the open-minded generosity characteristic of this scholar, he acknowledged in effect that history was too important a matter to be left entirely to professional historians – especially to those who considered that they could lay out a field of thought properly by merely measuring with a ruler.

> 'Sections of history are liable to be transformed – or, even where not transformed, greatly vivified – by an imagination that comes, sweeping like a searchlight, from outside the historical profession itself. Old hunches are then confirmed by fresh applications of the evidence or by unexpected correlations between sources. New matter emerges because things are joined together which it had not occurred to one to see in juxtaposition. New details are elicited, different details become relevant, because of a fresh turn that the argument has taken.'

This was the process, he wrote, which Koestler had carried further, thus giving the subject a number of unexpected ramifications. By looking at the scientific achievements in isolation, but also at the working-methods behind them and a good deal of private correspondence, Koestler had employed his historical imagination to put the great thinkers back into their age (instead of reading too much modernity into them or plucking anachronistically out of their context certain aspects of their work which seemed to have a modern ring) – and he had succeeded in doing so without making them meaningless.

> 'History,' he concluded, 'is not to be judged by negatives; and those of us who differ from Mr Koestler in respect of some of the outer framework of his ideas or do not follow him in certain details, can hardly fail to catch the light which not only modifies and enlivens the picture but brings out new facts, or makes dead ones dance before our eyes.
>
> 'It will be surprising if even those who are familiar with this subject do not often feel that here is a shower of rain where every drop has caught a gleam.'

* *

Literary editors had reserved ample space for reviews, and the book was subjected to close scrutiny by an imposing array of professional historians, philosophers, astronomers, and non-academic writers with a particular interest in one, or some, or all of the subjects touched on. Most of them, however stringent their adverse criticisms of one aspect or another, or of the author's method and general approach, agreed with Butterfield, if not so elegantly (though there were some, it is true, who thought it more of a torrential downpour than a shower, and were concerned to take shelter rather than look for unlikely gleams). However surprised some of them were at this bold entry into a closed shop by a worker without a union card, so to speak, they took the work seriously. (One may ignore its anathematising by 'committed' Marxists – those whose 'overall outlook in science history', as Professor Mark Graubard, zoologist, biochemist, and historian, wrote later in his assessment of the book, 'was that of Brecht's play *Galileo*!') Even those who found most to disagree with

* In 1949, when Koestler's *Insight and Outlook* had also been published.

(mainly in Koestler's unsympathetic treatment of Galileo, or his summary handling of pre-Renaissance thought, or his disproportionately brief discussion of Newton and his synthesis, or his meagre references to Descartes, or the pessimism implicit in the epilogue, or the anti-progressivist attitude – this last pounced upon in *Tribune* by Koestler's erstwhile collaborator, Michael Foot) – even they conceded that the author had done a solid job of research, and they found much to praise in the use he had made of his discoveries.

Shortly before the publication of *The Sleepwalkers*, the eminent astronomer Bernard (now Sir Bernard) Lovell had delivered the annual BBC Reith Lectures on much the same subject as that of the book. Koestler wrote a long letter to *The Listener*, refuting Lovell's conclusion that 'the story is mainly one of the persecution of astronomers on religious grounds', correcting Lovell at some considerable length on a number of points, and ending with the assertion that the story was rather one of

> '. . . the struggles of men like Kepler and Galileo against the academic backwoodsmen in their university chairs, aggravated towards the end by a fortuitous conflict with equally doctrinaire theologians.'

The relevance of the story in the circumstances of the twentieth century, Koestler concluded

> 'is the fact that while the Churches have moved to a more liberal attitude towards science, some contemporary scientists (and Professor Lovell is not one of them) are eager to force upon us as gospel truth certain controversial working hypotheses concerning causality, chance and the nature of reality which may in the end prove to be as rash and ill-informed as some of Galileo's assertions were, and which, if accepted at face value, would reduce our concept of the world into that of "an abstract heaven over a naked rock".'

A month after the publication of Koestler's rather magisterial letter, Lovell reviewed *The Sleepwalkers* amiably in the *Sunday Times*, praising Koestler's initiative and describing his narrative as one which 'covers important ground and will stand in its own right as a valuable document'. Undeterred, however, by the arguments advanced by Koestler in his letter to *The Listener*, Lovell was most critical of the treatment of Galileo:

> 'This section of the book displays a protracted feat of mental agility in which Mr Koestler refuses to recognise the true nature of the conflict.'

Having listed his objections in a firm and civil manner, Lovell ended his review thus:

> 'From his investigations of the processes of thought of these early scientists Mr Koestler wants us to believe that science as it subsequently developed is not a purely rational pursuit. No doubt scientists are as capable of "double-think" as their neighbours, but if Mr Koestler really believes that the individual personality determines the main stream of scientific advance then he should inquire into the processes through which any scientific paper has

to go before it sees the light of day in the journal of a learned society – or he should study the life and work of Max Planck, whose quantum theory ushered in a revolution in physics and philosophy as great as Galileo's work in cosmology.

'"The Sleepwalkers" is a valuable and provocative book. It is a work with a noble aim undermined by the author's own process of double-think, which he attributes to his subjects and by implication to all their successors.'

The various stings urbanely implanted by the tail of Lovell's review, which Koestler read in India, stimulated a reply which appeared in the *Sunday Times* a fortnight later. The rights and wrongs of the particular and technical points at issue in the Galilean controversy need not concern us here (and, in any case, I am academically unqualified to offer an opinion on the merits or demerits of the arguments on these by either side); but Koestler's final paragraph is an illustration of the passion engendered by what he obviously regarded as the latter-day *trahison des clercs*:

'The cavalier fashion in which Professor Lovell dismisses the argument by which Galileo tried and failed to prove the motion of the earth as an "inconsequential minor issue", while describing his failure as a success, seems to me an illustration of the modern scientist's ignorance of the past history of his own science, and of that arrogant contempt for the humanities, against which the book under discussion was partly directed.'

Strong words. Fighting talk. But Koestler's rejoinder did not prevent Professor Lovell from reviewing *The Sleepwalkers* no less amiably (though equally critically) in the *Saturday Review* when the American edition was published a few months later. The sting in the tail this time was not quite so sharp:

'The author's anxiety springs from a desire to preserve all the help that the unification of faith and reason can give to a world which is now equipped with the means of committing racial suicide. "The Sleepwalkers" is a brilliant and provocative book, one which would certainly have been placed on the Index with the "Dialogue" had the author lived in another age.'

* *

Certainly that part of *The Sleepwalkers* which most critics on both sides of the Atlantic were at one in considering the most controversial was the lengthy section entitled 'The Parting of the Ways' in which Koestler recounts in detail the quarrel between Galileo and the Church (in which he had many influential supporters) which eventually resulted in the decision of Urban VIII (who had formerly been, together with Cardinal Bellarmine, among his greatest admirers) to have Galileo tried by the Holy Office on the charge of heresy.

Koestler had no great difficulty in demolishing the simplistic legend of Galileo, the hero, the embodiment of enlightenment, persecuted by the

Church, the embodiment of obscurantist bigotry. The affair was a great deal more complicated than that; and neither during the proceedings nor after their conclusion was Galileo in any way ill-treated. What was controversial about Koestler's handling of the subject was neither his destruction of the legend, nor his admission that he found the personality of Galileo singularly unattractive, but rather his argument that the trial need never have taken place; that no real issue of principle was in fact involved; and that on balance the greater part of the blame for 'the greatest scandal in Christendom' was not Urban's but Galileo's – and this because of his vehemence, shiftiness, vanity, and pig-headed refusal to heed the friendly political advice of Cardinal Bellarmine, the General of the Society of Jesus, that to preach the Copernican system *as if it were an established truth rather than a working hypothesis* would arouse the fury of the Aristotelian scholastics (to whose ossified conservatism Bellarmine and many other leading theologians of the time were no less opposed than Galileo).

Professor Lovell's strictures in this connection had been severe. But they were as honey compared with the acid of the review which appeared in *Isis*, the journal of the American History of Science Society. The joint authors were the eminent specialists in Galilean studies, Giorgio de Santillana (whose works Koestler had consulted and drawn upon) and the younger Stillman Drake.

These two scholars certainly did not incline to Professor Butterfield's view that 'here is a shower of rain where every drop has caught a gleam'. For them it was obviously much more like a Vesuvian downpour of cinders and ashes threatening to bury the idealised image of their hero. Having noted with prescience that Koestler's ambitious attempt to outline a history of cosmology had been carried through with such verve, brilliance and lavish display of scholarship that 'it bids fair to become a standard book for the lay public, including many philosophers and historians of ideas', they then distorted Koestler's questioning of the notion that the scientists (being allegedly more 'level-headed' and 'dispassionate') were especially qualified for a leading role in the world affairs into the assertion that 'scientists should be denied a share in cultural and social leadership'.

With that distortion as sufficient justification, they went on to denounce Koestler's account of their hero with a hail of accusations of 'imposture', 'insolence'; 'perverse', 'dishonest' and 'insolent' misrepresentations; not to mention 'serious and deliberate misstatements' and 'deliberate distortions'. Even when all allowances are made for the reflex action of specialists when somebody – especially when that somebody is a weighty non-specialist – stands on their toes, their review was far more vehement and vituperative than could possibly be justified by the nature of the particular points on which they joined issue with Koestler.

The following issue of *Isis* carried a lengthy reply by Koestler in which he patiently answered their points *seriatim* and ended with an expression of regret that some historians of science considered his inquiry into 'the obscure workings of the creative mind' as sacrilege,

'. . . and seem to regard it as their duty to act as self-appointed Vigilantes – thereby inviting the obvious comparison with Caccini's resounding denunciation of *Ye Men of Galilee*'.

This was a reference to the sermon – against mathematicians in general and Copernicus in particular – preached in Florence by a fanatical Dominican, Thomasso Caccini, who chose as his text:

'Ye men of Galilee, why stand ye gazing up into the heavens?'

Santillana and Drake picked up the allusion at the end of their long and unrepentant footnote to Koestler's reply, and gave no hint that they had been stung by it.

Koestler, they insisted, had succeeded, by suppressing the full views of various scholars and quoting only whatever supported his thesis, in whitewashing a judicial crime and denigrating its victim.

'Of the trial, a witness of undoubted piety, Father Castelli, wrote in Galileo's day: "It is among such judges that we must live, must die, and what is worst, must keep silent." It grieves us to think that Mr Koestler, who has so often stood up for justice, who in this very work undertook to do eloquent justice to Kepler, should have read those words and chosen to ignore them. For our part, witnessing such an iniquitous rewriting of history, we could not keep silent. But now we shall resume our gazing into the heavens.'

Koestler let it go at that and resumed his gazing into the recesses of the creative mind.

* *

This was not to be the end of the story, however. Many years later the Franklin Institute of Philadelphia, one of the oldest such institutions in the United States, at which lectures on science and technology have been given since 1824, intended to invite Koestler to deliver a paper on Kepler.

But an article in *The New York Times* suggested that he had been 'barred'. Koestler wrote a letter for publication by the *Times*, and the editor of the correspondence page passed it to the author of the article, Robert Reinhold, who wrote to Koestler as follows from Cambridge, Massachusetts, on 4th March 1972:

'The editor of our correspondence page has asked me to write to you to convey some clarifying information in connection with your recent letter about the Kepler article. As author of the story, I can say on very good authority that this is what happened:

'The sponsors of the Philadelphia meeting (the Franklin Institute) had planned to invite you, to deliver a paper, I believe. Before the invitation was sent, however, certain historians intervened to eliminate your name. Since the invitation was never sent, you obviously had no direct way of knowing you were so excluded. In retrospect, the use of the term "barred" was perhaps not the best choice. But the facts remain.

'Since this additonal information would appear to have a significant bearing on your comments, we are passing it along to you in case you should wish to recast your letter and resubmit it for publication.

'P.S. To judge from my correspondence, the incident has stirred considerable indignation in this country.'

*Odium academicum* is a strong corrosive, and resistant to the solvent of time.

# CHAPTER XXXIII

# *1959*

THERE WAS LITTLE SENSE of crisis, if any, in the English air during 1959. Far from it.

The British, as Mr Macmillan observed a little later, 'had never had it so good'. For all that, there were many stirrings in the intellectual community which indicated a deep-seated malaise. The Suez debacle of 1956 had brought home unequivocally to intellectuals the fact of Britain's loss of power. Much of the discusson was couched in cultural terms, and much of it was confused and bitter – evidence of an idealism frustrated by the accelerating speed of political and technological change, and the underlying fear that the general realisation of Britain's loss of power would be followed quickly by a decline into decadence.

The feeling had been articulated most vividly in dramatic terms by the principal character, Jimmy Porter, in John Osborne's *Look Back in Anger*. It would be difficult to exaggerate the impact which this play had in 1956, and the sympathy which many intellectuals felt for the frustrations of Jimmy who, in despair because of the absence of any cause worthy of his support, cries out:

> 'There is murder in my brain, and I carry a knife in my heart for every one of you. Macmillan, and you, Gaitskell, you particularly.'

It is that sensational moment which one may arbitrarily, but not unreasonably, select as the beginning of the cultural debate which accompanied the process of coming to terms with Britain's diminished stature among the powers of the world.

That was still the question being asked with increasing urgency two years later, when Koestler was opening his long campaign against the Moloch of materialism sired by the first Industrial Revolution upon the Enlightenment. The initial impact of that campaign was muffled by a fog of intellectual uncertainty and confusion which can best be illustrated by an account of a controversy about the central theme of *The Sleepwalkers* which was aroused, however, not by that thoughtful book but rather by a lecture delivered in Cambridge in 1959 – a lecture eventually seen by some as in effect a sermon in praise of 'the new Baal'.

Sir Charles Snow's Rede Lecture, which he entitled *The Two Cultures and the Scientific Revolution*, was delivered in Cambridge University at the very time when it was certain to receive the widest attention. Its impact was immediate, being published in full in the June and July issues of *Encounter* and later issued in book form on both sides of the Atlantic.

Snow's education had been scientific and it was as an academic physicist at Cambridge that he began his professional life. Later, however, he became a civil servant, combining his duties as a senior bureaucrat with the planning and writing of eleven books – an immense *roman fleuve* under the general title of *Strangers and Brothers* – in which the struggles for power among the bureaucrats of Whitehall and the dons of Cambridge were depicted with a wealth of intertwining details, though in no psychological depth whatsoever. The plots were so involved and thriller-like (Snow's first effort as a novelist had in fact been a thriller) that the books were compulsive reading in spite of their dull and plodding narrative style and stilted dialogue. Their immense commercial success ensured the maximum publicity for his lecture. The phrase, 'The Two Cultures' – which he distinguished not altogether clearly as, on the one hand, the 'Traditional' or 'Literary', and, on the other, the 'Scientific' – passed immediately into common usage. Snow, almost overnight, added to his reputation as a celebrated novelist that of a sage. His views were discussed at length, and for the most part with approval, in the press, and expounded in schools and colleges. He was in demand as a lecturer. He found himself on the crest of a wave which his lecture, phrased as it was and coming when it did, had both heightened and accelerated. The exposition of his thesis was, in fact, one of the key effects of 1959.

If he had confined himself in his lecture to a discussion of that bias towards classical (or 'traditional' or 'literary') education in most of Britain's better junior and senior institutions of learning widely held to have been largely responsible for depriving society of the technologists which it badly needed to see our industrial and economic structures through the changes which were obviously going to be forced upon them by events (and so on society as a whole), the result would undoubtedly have been interesting. But its effect would hardly have been sensational. In the event, of course, he went much further than that, in urging the overriding importance of what he described in a somewhat vague and shallow manner as the 'Scientific Culture'. And in the process he touched a public nerve which the probes and scalpels employed by Koestler in *The Sleepwalkers* had not yet reached.

* *

It was a research scientist, the biochemist Michael Yudkin, who offered the first significant and closely reasoned criticism of Snow's windy and ill-argued lecture. It was published in the *Cambridge Review* and at the time attracted little attention, although Yudkin demonstrated clearly enough that Snow was much more concerned with power, politics, ideology and technology than with 'Science' or 'Culture', however defined.

But it was not until February 1962 that the great 'Two Cultures' balloon was well and truly pricked. The deed was done by F. R. Leavis during that month in his Richmond Lecture delivered in Cambridge. His theme was 'Two Cultures? – The significance of C. P. Snow'.

The full text of Leavis' devastatingly ruthless analysis and destruction of Snow's thesis was published in *The Spectator*. It was brutal, cruel and defamatory, and it should be recorded that Snow, having been shown the transcript by a member of my staff (I was editing *The Spectator* at the time), generously agreed to its publication in full, although it must have wounded him sorely.

The normal print-order of the paper was doubled for the occasion, but that was insufficient. The issue was sold out within hours. The debate became a controversy which raged in the paper's correspondence columns for a few weeks, and spread to other periodicals on both sides of the Atlantic and in Europe, which had not hitherto paid any attention to it.

*The Spectator* offered its own opinion when I closed the correspondence, in an editorial written by my deputy, Anthony Hartley. Its concluding paragraphs should be quoted here:

> '. . . there is one word lacking in the Rede Lecture, the only word which can give significance to an attempt to bring science and literature together, or to unite the efforts of politician and technocrat. The word is "philosophy", and in its secular significance it takes the form of that effort to impart moral direction which is to be found in the best nineteenth-century English writers. After being told that scientists have the future in their bones it is salutary to read the opinion of William James: "Of all the insufficient authorities as to the total nature of reality, give me the 'scientists' . . . Their interests are most incomplete and their professional conceit and bigotry immense. I know of no narrower sect or club, in spite of their excellent authority in the lines of fact they have explored, and their splendid achievements there." And, it must also be said, the claim of scientists to play a part in government cannot easily be reconciled with the facility which they have shown in shrugging off the consequences of their work. If a writer had worked for the Nazis as the scientists who developed the V2 worked for them, he would have been condemned by an Allied tribunal or, at least, suffered grave inconvenience. He would not have been transported to a position of affluence and authority in the U.S. or the U.S.S.R. Scientists cannot have it both ways.'

In plain fact, Hartley continued, the cult of science and technology without an adequate sense of moral direction, as exemplified by Snow's celebrated lecture, was no more than the 'scientism' of the nineteenth century dressed up in the fashionably emotive garments of aid to underdeveloped countries, higher standards of living, et cetera.

> 'Knowledge is power, but it is not the knowledge of how that power should be used. That is the affair of the conscience and consciousness. To admire a tyrannical political regime for its technological achievements [as Sir Charles

had publicly, indeed ostentatiously, admired the technological achievements of the Soviet Union; see the transcript of the televised conversation between Sir Charles and Malcolm Muggeridge published in the February, 1962, issue of *Encounter*] is on the same level as to admire it for having a large army . . . It is the business of writers, philosophers, and moralists to represent those values which can alone give life to culture or the vast human achievements of science. They can and should learn from science and scientists, but the essential role they themselves have to play is not to be thrust aside with talk of "natural Luddites". If we think to some purpose, then we shall be able to make the future instead of being carried along by it like children in the arms of an automaton.'

And so, having delivered with a certain delicate accuracy the *coup de grâce* to Snow's thesis, which had been battered so ferociously by Dr Leavis, Hartley's editorial ended:

'The questions begged by *The Two Cultures* are precisely those we must answer.'

* *

And they were precisely the questions which Koestler had begun to answer three years before in *The Sleepwalkers*.

It was, above all, *philosophy* which imparted moral direction to all the historical, biographical, psychological, cosmological and other studies brought together between the covers of that substantial work, and which most of its reviewers had unaccountably overlooked.

This in part may be ascribed to the fact that, thanks to the overwhelming impact of *Darkness at Noon*, Koestler had been type-cast as a 'political novelist', and by many as a militant reactionary. Some years were to pass before the implications of his thought could be seen in clear focus by members of the intellectual community, whatever their views on the nature of 'culture'. This reflected badly on the general health of the community.

As John Wain put it in *The Hudson Review**, referring to the letters in support of Snow published by *The Spectator*:

'It is these pages that deserve serious attention as a barometer of the present state of intellectual England. I have no space to quote: the entire document will be consulted, not once but repeatedly, by anyone (now or in the future) who wants the flavour of 1962 in England. In a word, the quality of the support offered by the Snow faction was such as to prove beyond doubt one of Leavis's main points: that the elevation of Sir Charles to his present position of Tribal Sage is the work of forces which exist independently of him and of which he has become the focus: that he has been "created" by the "cultural conditions manifested in his acceptance". Most of the correspondents who rushed to pull out Leavis's darts, and apply balm of one kind and another,

* Summer, 1962.

offered such perfect illustrations of the *naïveté* and emptiness that Leavis was attacking that they left nothing for a pro-Leavis party to do.'

A harsh judgement, but justified. And it was to the counter-attack on the '*naïveté* and emptiness' implicit in the nihilistic determinism which still permeated so many and such wide areas of the 'Scientific Culture' – ie, scientism – that Koestler was already devoting his attention.

# CHAPTER XXXIV

# *1959–1968*

WITH THE PUBLICATION OF *The Sleepwalkers* – the first fruit of the 'vocational change' he had announced in 1955 – the pattern of Koestler's activities changed dramatically. He became increasingly involved in the exploration, in width as in depth, both alone and in collaboration with others, of the ideas first sketched a decade earlier in *Insight and Outlook* and developed to some extent in the historical and biographical contexts of *The Sleepwalkers*.

During the following decade he was to be engaged in intensive research in many fields, and in conversation and correspondence with an astonishingly wide range of natural scientists and technologists, psychologists and philosophers and other scholars whose interests were not wholly centred on their own inevitably narrow specialisations and who shared Koestler's anxiety about the *hubris* of certain philosophical outlooks based on a narrow concept of scientific method. He was to travel widely throughout the East, Europe, and America, researching, lecturing, taking part in conferences, some of which he chaired and one of which he organised. As he put it himself at the end of the decade:

> 'For the last ten years, my main interest has been the history and the present state of science, and its impact on our view of the world. The books that were the result of this interest brought in a number of invitations to scientific symposia – interdisciplinary or technical – and provided the opportunity for informal discussions with representatives of some of the main branches of contemporary research. They made me aware of a certain discontent with the prevailing philosophical bias which – whether explicitly formulated or tacitly implied – seems to linger on as a heritage from the nineteenth century, although the new insights gained by contemporary research have reduced it to an anachronism . . .'

His studies were eventually to lead him to the controversial conclusion that one of the major dilemmas facing modern man – the control of intraspecific aggressiveness, unique to *homo sapiens* in all the animal creation, in an age when his power of destruction was multiplying almost beyond belief – was something to be solved neither by philosophy (religious or otherwise in its nature) nor by psychology and political action, but rather by neurophysiology and psychopharmacology.

From time to time he felt impelled to renounce his farewell to arms as a political writer, and renewed his warnings to the West of dangers which on the whole it preferred to ignore; and he also expended energy and money on civilising projects in the social field.

* *

On 18th January 1909 in Juno, Alaska, one Robert F. Stroud was tried on a charge of manslaughter, found guilty, and sentenced to a lengthy spell of imprisonment. Seven years later he killed a prison guard during a fracas, claiming at the subsequent trial that he had done so in self-defence. His plea was not accepted and he spent the next forty-one years in solitary confinement in a variety of federal prisons, ending up in Alcatraz.

In 1957 Warden Madigen of Alcatraz considered it safe to allow Stroud, now aged sixty-nine, the 'privileges of the yard'. Whether Stroud needed the company of his fellow-humans by this time is a question that cannot be answered with any certainty. Many years earlier, he had been allowed to keep canaries in his solitary cell. Tolerant wardens in one jail after another had allowed him to enlarge his aviary. At one point, in an unusually spacious cell in a jail which offered rather more than the average amenities, he was caring for and observing no fewer than three hundred live birds in his cell. He became, in fact, an ornithologist of some note.

By the time he landed up in the (now abandoned) jail on the bleak rock in the middle of the icy tide-race of San Francisco Bay, and the Robert F. Stroud Committee had publicised his extraordinary story, he was known to newspaper-readers round the world as The Birdman of Alcatraz.

During the spring of 1958 Koestler was approached by Stanley Firman of Beverly Hills and invited to join the honorary committee agitating for the release of Stroud.

He was happy to accept. In August 1959, he learned from Stanley Firman that Stroud, frail and unwell, had been quietly and without fuss transferred from 'The Rock' during July to the federal prison hospital in Springfield, Missouri. Stroud had written to Firman to tell him that he was happy there. Firman passed the news on to all members of the honorary committee, including Koestler. Whereupon Koestler wrote to Stroud:

> 'As you probably know, I have the privilege of serving on the committee for your release. Stanley Firman sent me a copy of your letter of July 18th to him, containing the wonderful news of your transfer to Springfield Hospital, and your glowing description of it. I was delighted to read it, both for your sake and for the sake of your fellow-inmates, who enjoy the physical and mental comforts of the place. Judging by what you say, we have nothing as advanced in England. I do hope that this apparent first step towards your complete release will be quickly followed by others. And don't bother to answer this . . .'

The example of Stroud, who had taught himself Latin, Italian and French during his half-century of incarceration, as well as making himself no mean ornithologist, was to inspire Koestler to one of his most imaginative ventures.

* *

In the fall of 1960, during a break in the drafting of the book that was to become *The Act of Creation*, Koestler found himself reflecting on his own various prison experiences. He dwelt especially on those weeks in the Seville jail when he had kept himself sane by drawing on the resources of his well-stocked mind – recalling his favourite books and reading from the screen projected in his mind, reciting poems that he had learnt by heart, working out intricate mathematical problems. He recalled his hunger for paper and pencil, and how during his first few weeks in jail he had tried to scrawl his diary on the wall with a piece of wire broken off from his bedstead.

But he had been lucky. His spells of imprisonment had been brief. He had been treated well, on the whole (except by the French in Le Vernet). In Seville he had eventually been provided with books, paper, and pencil. And from the jottings which he managed to smuggle out of jail on his release he had made a most moving book.

It must be very different, he thought, for the majority of those sentenced to long periods of utter boredom, their minds atrophying, their personalities changing usually for the worse. For most of them, their incarceration could hardly be a 'creative experience'. But some at least might have untapped resources of which they were unaware – resources which they might be able to discover and put to creative use if they had some positive encouragement and incentive to make the effort. And so an idea began to form in Koestler's mind: a trust fund to finance an annual competition for prisoners who had some urge to express themselves in creative forms, as poets, novelists, short-story writers, painters, composers, scientists. Having talked the idea over with C. R. Hewitt, David Astor, and A. D. Peters (who responded at once with an offer to put up £100 a year to cover administrative expenses), he began to put his plans into shape. He proposed to:

> '. . . provide an annual prize of, say, £500 with a few modest consolation awards of £5 or £10 to anyone serving a sentence in one of H.M. Prisons or Borstal Institutions for a creative work in the fields of literature, the arts and sciences. The object of the scheme would be (1) to provide a spiritual or mental release to those physically confined; (2) to find one man each year of proven ability in one of these spheres and provide a sum of money available on his discharge (with no strings attached) to spend (or not) at his discretion on pursuing his bent, for a reasonable period, free from the financial and other worries which normally beset a discharged prisoner on his release.'

Four or five trustees would be nominated by Koestler and it would be their duty to see that the objects of the scheme should be properly pursued,

> '. . . or if the scheme proved unworkable, the annual income should be used

> for a purpose as near akin as possible to the original, and, in particular, in an imaginative and exciting way, to stimulate as far as possible and in as many cases as possible the mind and spirit of the prisoner. It should at all times remain a "special purpose" trust, with the obvious loophole to make such changes as possible in practical detail as may be necessary. But at no time should its funds be used for general prison welfare or aftercare, where they would in any case be a drop in the ocean.'

It was also his intention to arrange for the transfer to the trustees, in the event of his death, the sum of £20,000, to provide a gross income of, say, £800 to £1,200 per annum.

In the middle of January 1961 Koestler spelled out his idea in a letter to the chairman of the Prison Commission, A. W. (later Sir Arthur) Peterson, who sent a representative, Charles Cape, Head of Prison Education and Welfare, to a meeting with Koestler and his friends. Cape seemed most favourably impressed by this imaginative (not to say, in the miserable context of English penology, revolutionary) plan. But weeks passed and nothing was heard from the Prison Commission.

At last, more anxious than ever to see the scheme 'set in motion forthwith', he wrote to Cape and reminded him of their meeting. Was there any news? The Commissioners, Cape replied, were still weighing up the pros and cons before reporting to the Home Secretary. The delay must have irked Koestler; but judged by normal bureaucratic standards, a decision in principle was arrived at with commendable speed. A month later he had a letter from Peterson to say that:

> 'I have now heard that the Home Secretary [R. A. Butler] approves in principle your generous proposal for the institution of an annual award for creative work by prisoners subject to the conditions . . . that the subject-matter of the work must not be concerned with the prisoner's conviction or sentence, prison life or prisoners, and that income or sale-money derived from a prize-winning entry (as distinct from prize money) must be paid not to the prisoner but into the Trust on the understanding that the Trustees should be empowered in their discretion to make a donation to, or to apply money for, the benefit of the prizewinner or his dependants after his discharge.
>
> 'As regards the scale of the prizes, there would be no objection to prizes up to a limit of £25 . . . but it would be preferable that this limit should not be exceeded. Perhaps you would be good enough to let me have your views on this point.'

Koestler's view was that £25 was much too little. He suggested as a compromise one annual award of £100, four of £50, four of £25, and ten of £10. This, after much deliberation, was accepted by the Commissioners and the Home Secretary, and Koestler went off to Alpbach for the summer, leaving Peters in charge.

Astor and Koestler had originally envisaged the *Observer*'s being officially associated with the Trust, and the former intended to contribute substantially to its funds. But on reflection, and having discussed the matter with senior members of his staff, Astor decided that this would be likely to present difficulties. He was right in this. Hewitt had a meeting with the Prison Commissioners about various details and learned that they were opposed to any member of the Newspaper Proprietors' Association being involved, in that capacity, in the scheme. They considered, however, that Astor's membership of the Trust in his private capacity would be valuable. They saw no harm in the fact that Astor, by getting a preview of the winning entries would have the first pick of whatever might be worth publishing.

Towards the end of May, however, Astor had some misgivings about the degree of editorial support his fellow-trustees might expect from the *Observer* itself. It was one thing for the paper to associate itself editorially with Koestler and his crusade against capital punishment; but this latest venture did not lend itself to an equal expenditure of energy and space.

However, he agreed to remain a trustee.

In the meantime, the Prison Commissioners had consulted the prison governers about the scheme, asking them for criticisms and suggestions; and on 21st August, Duncan Fairn, who had now taken over from Cape, wrote to Peters to suggest that some sort of handicap ought to be introduced for those prisoners who could be described as professionals in the field of the arts, and also, to ensure that the inmates of Borstals would have a fair chance, that there should be separate categories for those over and those under twenty-one years of age. Koestler agreed.

Towards the end of the year things began to move quickly. On 1st December he opened an account at Westminster Bank in favour of the Arthur Koestler Award and signed a banker's order authorising payment of £400 into this account on the last day of December and on the same day for the seven subsequent years.

Later in the month the Commission sent out a circular to governors about the scheme:

> 'Annual awards may be made to inmates of both sexes in Borstals and prisons, other than closed local prisons, for original work in the fields of literature, arts and crafts, and in musical composition. A first prize of £100, two prizes of £50, four prizes of £25, and ten prizes of £10 will be available for distribution annually on August 31st according to the recommendations of a panel of experts . . .'

Among those who had already agreed to judge the entries were Henry Green, J. B. Priestley, V. S. Pritchett, Philip Toynbee, Sir Kenneth Clark, Eric Newton, Robert Powe and Sir Arthur Bliss.

Peters was not altogether happy about the facilities likely to be granted to prisoners who wished to compete. Would this, he asked Koestler, depend on the whim of each governor? Would there be facilities available over and above the normal prison routine?

'You remember that I told you about a writer friend of mine who was in jail some years ago? He said that there was only one pen on each floor with a very bad nib, and that when a friend sent him some nibs they were held back until the day of his release.'

Although no public statement about the Award had been issued, news of it was leaked and small items were published in the *Daily Express*, *The Times*, and the *Daily Sketch*. The 28th December issue of *Time* magazine announced:

'Pushing ahead with his campaign to humanise Britain's dismal prisons, Home Secretary Richard Austen Butler announced his newest device for rehabilitating jailbirds: a $280 prize for the best original literary, artistic or musical composition produced behind bars. Unmentioned, at his own request, was the instigator and donor of the Award: Arthur (*Darkness at Noon*) Koestler, 56, whose *Dialogue with Death* and *Scum of the Earth* grew out of his own imprisonment by the Fascists during the Spanish Civil War and by Vichy France during World War Two.'

During the next few weeks discussions went on among the trustees and between them and the Prison Commissioners. Early in April Koestler told Peters that he had

'just had a bright idea. I would suggest, if the idea appeals to you, to tell Fairn when you talk to him on the telephone, that if, say, thirty to fifty pictures, drawings, et cetera, come up to the general standard of works one sees around in galleries, one might rent a small gallery and make an exhibition of prisoners' art. Personally I am convinced that we will have sufficient good entries.'

Peters agreed. He thought that with luck they might even sell some of the paintings on behalf of the prisoners. But, he added, there had been complaints from instructors at Wandsworth and Wormwood Scrubs, that prisoners there were not being allowed to enter their works. Peters had taken this up with Fairn who had told him that there should be no misunderstanding here, because it had been clear from the beginning that the competition was not open to those in closed local prisons. On 24th April, Koestler wrote to Fairn about this:

'It is quite correct that we agreed to exclude local prisons, but it is also true that the Trustees were not aware at the time that some prisoners served long sentences in local prisons. It would, of course, be nice if such cases could be allowed to participate in the competition, but if for technical reasons this should be impossible, then it just can't be helped.'

There were 164 entries by the closing date: 70 in the arts and craft section, 80 in the literary, and 14 in the musical. Peters reported to Koestler that the literary entries were not up to much:

'I have reduced the field to about 12 entries. Nothing good enough to excite the *Observer* or any other paper, I'm afraid. Music: Sidney Torch has chosen three, but only one is possible, a waltz. Arthur Bliss accepts Torch's verdict . . . I suppose we must award £400 in prizes, and it is now obvious that the bulk of the money must go to arts and crafts. Music is not worth more than one prize of £10, but we could, if you think we should, give two more of £5 each. Literature on merit doesn't deserve more than £50 at most as a first prize (too much, really), two of £10, and three of £5 . . .The danger lies in encouraging incompetents to believe they are budding geniuses.'

An exhibition of the winning entries was opened at the Home Office by Peterson.

'There were about a dozen journalists present,' Peters reported to Koestler, 'but the Press coverage was poor. Perhaps they expected more exciting pictures. I must admit that the quality of the art was very poor, but there were some fine entries in the crafts.'

The first prize in literature went to a prisoner who had submitted a short novel and a poem. Koestler was much taken by the latter and sent it to Melvin J. Lasky. He and Stephen Spender looked on it more favourably than Peters and judged it suitable for publication in *Encounter.* It compared (and compares) favourably with the average run of effusions subsidised by the Arts Council.

DRUMMA

I had a dream of a Versailles marquise
– Petite and svelte, six inches small,
her hair whitepowdered, built up high –
Confronting on a kettledrum a Chinese mandarin
– Seven inches of stately decorum
topped by a tortoiseshell comb –

White shoulders, blue brocade strewn with pearls,
Faced yellow silk embroidered with dragons,
Lusty green dragons lolling large red tongues,
Quite unlike St. George's victim on the pendant
which hangs from her necklace.

Curtsies from her
And courtesy from him;
Bows; she the head,
He from the waist;
Smiles, repetitive routine of smiles,
Useless words, sounds:
No understanding.

Pauses get longer,
Tempers get shorter,

She taps her heels,
He stamps his foot.
Miniature thunder comes from the drum,
The sound ripples the skin;
Courtly marquise, imperial mandarin
Fall on their backs, feet in the air,
Unmannerly end to a mannered affair.

Moral:

There's danger for people of all nations
In a lack of basic communications
And it's possible to go under
To the roar of self-made thunder.

It was, on the whole, a not too bad beginning.

* *

There were more entries in 1963, the Scottish Office having decided to allow prisoners in jails north of the border to take part. The standard of the arts and crafts entries was high and the *Daily Mirror* undertook to organise an exhibition of the entries.

By the middle of November the final selections had been made and the prize money divided among 36 prisoners from 18 prisons and Borstals. A working model of a Ferris wheel brought its constructor £30. In the music section, the first prize, of £20, was awarded to a prisoner serving his sentence in Broadmoor for three choral preludes. Don Robson, serving his sentence in Dartmoor, won the first prize in the literary section (£25) with his novel, *Young and Sensitive* (later called *Young and Tender*). Peters reported to Koestler that Hutchinson (Koestler's British publishers) had agreed to issue Robson's novel; and that Macmillan had taken another prizewinning entry for inclusion in their annual *Anthology of English Short Stories.*

Don Robson in particular seemed to be a real find:

'You already know,' Robert Lusty, chairman of the Hutchinson Publishing Group, wrote to Koestler on 16th January 1964, 'how impressed I have been by Don Robson's *Young and Tender*, and I am delighted to hear from Peters this morning that . . . he is well on the way to completing a second novel.

'You, I gather, are to be kind enough to write an introduction to *Young and Tender*, and it would be very helpful – for we do not want to delay for long – if you could do this pretty rapidly . . .

'It is a most moving piece of writing, and because of the circumstances surrounding it it is pretty certain, I think, to attract a good deal of notice, although I find it very hard to prophesy what sort of sale it will achieve.'

Mr Don Robson had demonstrated a truly egalitarian spirit of enterprise when he submitted his novel *Young and Sensitive.* Lusty had observed to Koestler that this moving piece of writing was pretty certain, 'because of the circumstance surrounding it', to attract a good deal of notice. It did, and not only at the time of publication, when it was proudly announced that American rights had been sold, that translation rights had been acquired by French and German publishers, and that Penguin Books would in due course be issuing it in paperback.

In September 1965 Koestler's solicitors put out a statement on behalf of the Trustees to say that

> '. . . it has been ascertained that the novel did not in fact represent the unaided work of its author but derived largely from a paperback novel previously published in the United States (and at the time available in Dartmoor's Prison library).'

*Young and Tender* was none other than *Fires of Youth*, the original author of which, Charles Williams, had been denied in his native America the admiration and praise heaped upon Mr Robson in England for his plagiarised version. As one reviewer struck by its 'primitive drive' had observed, more truly than he realised, it possessed 'a crude, jagged sort of veracity'.

Mr Robson's industry as a copyist had resulted in some embarrassment and vexation all round, but at least it had brought an extra bonus of publicity for the scheme.

Although the scheme has not yet led to the discovery of another O. Henry, quite a few of the prisoners who submitted short stories or novels have found themselves in print. Perhaps the most notable success in this field was *Cauldron*, published by Macmillan – a novel about the battle of Arnhem by an ex-officer who had taken part in it. He wrote it in Wormwood Scrubs where he was serving a life sentence for the murder of his mistress's lover.

As the years passed, the number of entries grew. By 1968 the value of the scheme was beyond question. In that year, shortly before Koestler renewed his covenant, Lord Stonham, Minister of State at the Home Office, suggested to Sir Hugh Casson – who had succeeded A. D. Peters as chairman of the trustees – that the scheme should be widened in scope to include vocational and industrial work in prisons. An appeal was launched and the response was generous. Now that so many others had put up money, Koestler thought that his name should be removed from the awards, but the Home Office and the trustees would not hear of it.

Some of the most gifted award-winners – well on the way to becoming old lags when they decided to try for a prize – have succeeded on their release in earning a living by their art or craft which they would probably never have developed had it not been for the scheme. By this time a creditable list of success stories has been built up in the Home Office files. But it is not by these, as John Grigg has commented, that the success of the scheme is to be judged.

'The chief benefit of it to prisoners,' as he wrote in his contribution to Koestler's *Festschrift*, 'is that it gives those with very slight talent, but with some desire for self-expression and self-improvement, a motive for work in prison and – if they win a prize, however small – a sense of achievement.'

Even the unlucky Mr Robson must have felt some sense of achievement when he had finished copying out Mr Williams' paperback novel. Besides, if it had not been for his achievement, few if any people on this side of the Atlantic would ever have heard of the original book.

# CHAPTER XXXV

# *1961–1964*

DURING THE LONG YEARS of preparation for the sequel to *Insight and Outlook* (intended, as he had written in the preface to that work, to place 'on a more scholarly foundation' his general theory of creativity and discovery), Koestler had been in correspondence with several psychologists, biologists and neurologists, some of whom he had met during his visits to the United States.

Among them was Dr Timothy Leary, then working at the Center for Research in Personality of Harvard University's Department of Social Relations. On 4th January 1961, Leary wrote enthusiastically to Koestler about the 'mind-expanding' potential of certain hallucinogenic drugs:

'Things are happening here which I think will interest you. The big, new, hot issue these days in many American circles is DRUGS. Have you tuned in on the noise?

'I stumbled on the scene in the most holy manner. Spent last summer in Mexico. Anthropologist friend arrived one weekend with a bag of mushrooms brought from a witch. Magic mushrooms. I had never heard of them, but being a good host joined the crowd who ate them. Wow! Learned more in six hours than in past sixteen years. Visual transformations. Gone the perceptual machinery which clutters up our view of reality. Intuitive transformations. Gone the mental machinery which slices the world up into abstractions and concepts. Emotional transformations. Gone the emotional machinery that causes us to load life with our own role-ambitions and petty desires.

'Came back to USA and have spent last six months pursuing these matters. Working with Aldous Huxley, Alan Watts, Allen Ginsberg, the poet. We believe that the synthetics of peyote (mescalin) and the mushrooms (psilocybin) offer possibilities for expanding consciousness, changing perceptions, removing abstractions.

'For the person who is prepared, they provide a soul-wrenching mystical experience. Remember your enlightenments in the Franco prison? Very similar to what we are producing. We have had cases of housewives understanding, experiencing *satori* and describing it – who have never heard of Zen.

'There are the inevitable political-sociological complications. The expected groups are competing to see who should control the new drugs. Medicine and psychiatry are in the forefront. Psychiatric investigators (hung up as they are on their own abstractions) interpret the experience as PSYCHOTIC – and think they are producing model-psychosis. Then too, the cops and robbers game has started. Organized bohemia (and don't tell me it ain't organized, with rituals as rigid as those of the Masonic order) is moving in. There is the danger that mescalin and psilocybin will go the way of marijuana (a perfectly mild, harmless, slightly mind-opening substance, as you know). And of course the narcotics bureau hopes that it will go the same way – so they can play out their side of the control game.

'We (mainly Allen Ginsberg and I) hope to keep these drugs free and uncontrolled. Two tactics. We are offering the experience to distinguished creative people. Artists, poets, writers, scholars. We've learnt a tremendous amount by listening to them tell us what they have learnt from the experience.

'We are also trying to build this experience in a holy and serious way into university curricula. I've got approval to run a seminar here – graduate students will take the mushroom regularly and spend a semester working through, organizing and systematizing the results. It's hard for me to see how anyone can consider himself a theologian, psychologist, behavioral scientist if he has not had this experience.

'So. How does it sound? If you are interested I'll send some mushrooms over to you. Or if you've already been involved, I'd like to hear about your reaction. I'll be in London around June 8th and would like to tell you more about the cosmic crusade . . .'

By a curious coincidence this letter arrived in London shortly before Koestler left for San Francisco to take part in a symposium on 'Control of the Mind' organised by the Medical Center of the University of California, in which the influence of drugs on the individual was one of the main subjects of discussion.

It was a distinguished interdisciplinary occasion. Here Koestler met for the first time, or renewed acquaintance with, various eminent neuro-physiologists and psychologists. He struck up a lasting friendship with Holger Hyden, the cytologist, head of the Institute of Neurobiology and Histology of Gothenburg University. The theologian Martin D'Arcy, SJ, was present. So was Aldous Huxley, who had been invited, like Koestler, in his capacity as 'creative writer'. Huxley had been for many years a leading proselytiser of the use of hallucinogenic – so-called 'psychedelic' – drugs for the procurement of enjoyable quasi-mystical states of ecstasy. (Timothy Leary had been late in discovering their properties. *The Doors of Perception* and *Heaven and Hell* had long been established as the principal gospels of the drug cult.)

Koestler was interested in the psychiatric use of the hallucinogens, and in the possibility of employing them experimentally in the investigation of extra-sensory perception: but he disagreed profoundly with Huxley's notion of 'pressure-cooked mysticism' in which the innermost recesses of the mind were unconditionally surrendered to external chemical agencies. In this, if in nothing else, Huxley seemed to Koestler to be in league with the behavioural psychologists and monistic philosophers for whom Man is merely a conditioned-reflex automaton, and the concept of 'mind' an empty nonsense.

But Huxley was in a very small minority at this occasion. Most of the participants arrived by their own routes and in their own terms at the same conclusion as that succinctly expressed by Father D'Arcy:

> 'There is a last mysterious layer in the self that can never really be touched, an ultimate self which enables priests to withstand torture, madmen to retain a vestige of sanity, and brave soldiers to resist brain-washing.'

Koestler, in short, found no lack of expert scientific support for his hostility to the mechanistic determinism of many behavioural scientists and their allies among reductionist (and ultimately nihilistic) philosophers.

But he had other investigations to make, and lectures to give, in America, and so his return journey from San Francisco took him by way of three universities where interesting research was in progress – the University of Michigan at Ann Arbor, Harvard in Massachusetts, and Duke University in North Carolina.

* *

At Ann Arbor he studied the experiments conducted with *planaria* by Professor James V. McConnell, of the Department of Psychology. These small flatworms occupy an important place on the evolutionary ladder, being the lowest animals to possess a brain and a central nervous system and the highest to multiply first by fission and then, in maturity, sexually. They are hermaphroditic, possessing both sets of reproductive organs. Among their many peculiarities is their habit in summer of shedding their tails and growing new ones, while the discarded tails develop new heads. During the mating season they become cannibals, devouring any organisms which they can capture – including their discarded tails. If a flatworm in the laboratory is sliced into half a dozen segments, each segment will then develop all the missing organs and grow into a complete hermaphroditic individual.

More interesting than these oddities, however, was the question which McConnell's experiments were designed to ask. It was known that flatworms were capable of learning and possessed a memory. But did a sixth of a flatworm which had regenerated itself physically, regenerate also the memory possessed by the whole of which it had once been a part? The experiments showed that it did. Not only that: they showed that if an individual flatworm, trained to respond in a certain way to a given stimulus, were sliced into segments, the regenerated individuals retained as much of their acquired learning as did their unsliced siblings trained in the same manner.

The cells responsible for the regeneration of the six parts into six new wholes must carry chemical 'blueprints' of the complete mature individual creature just as the germ cells do in sexual development, and McConnell's experiments demonstrated that those 'blueprints' also carried forward traces of learning acquired by the ancestral animal.

And so did those lowly and bizarre creatures, in which the embryonic intelligence may be observed in action, call in question neo-Darwinian dogma, and, while not exactly confirming the Lamarckian theory that acquired experience can be transmitted genetically, tend to support the later suggestion of Darwin himself that:

> 'The birth both of the species and of the individual are equally parts of that grand sequence of events, which our minds refuse to accept as the result of blind chance.'

They suggested, in short, that the evolution of species was not 'blind chance', as neo-Darwinian orthodoxy has it, in the form of random mutations preserved and reinforced by natural selection – or not, at any rate, merely that alone. They offered support for the ideas of purpose and freedom and dignity.

Koestler was heartened by Professor McConnell's flatworms.

He was also heartened by his experience of psilocybin – the hallucinogenic drug derived from the 'magic mushroom'. Dr Pollard, the English psychiatrist in charge of the unit investigating this and other drugs, accepted him as a guinea-pig, administered eighteen milligrams of psilocybin, and switched on a tape-recorder to catch Koestler's responses to the beauties of that 'Other World' promised by Aldous Huxley. There were indeed some spectacular and enjoyable visual distortions to begin with, but gradually the transformations became horrific, the pleasant face of Dr Pollard, for instance, being transformed into such an evil phantasm as might be imaged forth by the brush of Francis Bacon.

Throughout the experiment, which lasted for two hours or so, Koestler's outward behaviour was normal and, although he had no control of his perception of the world, he *knew* that he had lost control of it and he *knew* that what he was experiencing were the symptoms of a chemically induced state of insanity. Time and again, while the action of the drug was strongest, he made an effort, without success, to switch off the phantasmagoria.

It is perfectly clear from the transcript of his recorded commentary that while his *brain* was affected by the drug, his *mind* remained autonomous and capable of rejecting the induced illusions and delusions.

Further encouraged by this experience, he left Ann Arbor for Harvard, where there were various scientists to be seen. At the Center for Research in Personality he studied the effusions of certain well-known writers and scholars written or dictated while in a state of 'gratuitous grace' (as Huxley would have described it) induced by psilocybin, mescalin, or lysergic acid (LSD).

They were drivel, entirely lacking in artistic merit and without any theoretical value, save in so far as they demonstrated the adverse effect of the drugs on the normal neural processes of the brain.

In spite of this, and no doubt persuaded by Leary's infectious enthusiasm, he swallowed twenty-two or twenty-four milligrams of psilocybin, together with a number of acquaintances, and listened to a recording of chamber music. It was, to begin with, a wholly agreeable experience and he felt that the harmony of the spheres was being revealed to him. But his mind, suspecting that he might just as well have been listening to Liberace, told him otherwise. The experience

'. . . had nothing to do with genuine appreciation of music: my soul was steeped in cosmic schmaltz. I sobered up, though, when a fellow mushroom-eater – an American writer whom I otherwise rather liked – began to declaim about Cosmic Awareness, Expanding Consciousness, Zen Enlightenment, and so forth. This struck me as downright obscene . . . This pressure-cooker mysticism seemed the ultimate profanation. But my exaggerated reaction was no doubt also mushroom-conditioned, so I went to bed.'

Koestler's next visit was to the Parapsychology Laboratory of Dr Joseph B. Rhine and his wife, Louisa, at Duke University in North Carolina, where for three decades the various alleged manifestations of extra-sensory perception – telepathy, clairvoyance, precognition and psychokinesis – had been systematically studied by statistical method, mechanised controls, and mathematical analysis.

Both Rhines had begun their professional careers as university lecturers in biology, but in 1926 they had boldly put their reputation at risk by their decision to apply 'scientific method' to psychical research – which most scientists at the time would have considered a contradiction in terms. Although their experiments had never succeeded in proving the hypothesis of ESP – and perhaps never could do so conclusively – the Rhines' strictly functional approach had yielded results which suggested that some people seemed to be capable of acquiring knowledge and of communicating with other people by some means wholly unknown to science and, indeed, contrary to scientific logic. Although most academic psychologists remained (and remain) hostile to the hypothesis, by the time Koestler first visited the Rhines (whose work he had long known and admired), several universities and other institutions – in the Communist world as well as in the West – had conceded that the systematic study of alleged paranormal phenomena was an activity that could be tolerated.

To that extent at least the Rhines had succeeded, and psychic researchers from many countries came to visit their 'laboratory'. Koestler, already well-disposed to their aims and activities, took to them at once, and was dismayed to discover that his admiration was not shared by members of the other faculties. The Rhines, he found, were living in the shadow of suspicion generated by the innumerable fraudulent 'mediums' and soothsayers who throughout the generations had preyed upon the credulous and unhappy searching for some substitute for religion.

Koestler told the Rhines that he had already suggested to Timothy Leary that he should collaborate with them in experiments designed to investigate the effect of hallucinogenic drugs on the subjects undergoing the card-guessing or dice-throwing tests in the Parapsychology Laboratory. Leary had welcomed the idea. So did the Rhines, who were grateful to Koestler – pathetically so – for bringing their laboratory and the Harvard Institute together. J. B. Rhine's sense of isolation was all too sadly apparent in a letter he wrote to Koestler thanking him for his

'generous gesture and effort . . . in bringing us into active acquaintance with Drs Leary and Barron [Dr Frank Barron, later Professor of Psychology at the

University of California, Santa Cruz]. You will see what I mean when I mention that Dr Leary was down here a few months ago, and remarked to someone that "This is where the famous Parapsychology Laboratory is." I was at Harvard about a year ago and gave a lecture to the graduate students in psychology, but I met no outstretched hand from the large staff of psychologists in the Harvard community.'

* *

On his return to London, Koestler wrote to Leary:

'As you realised, I got quite obsessed with the idea that the ESP possibilities of the mushroom should be thoroughly investigated. I found in Duke a mixed company of Chilean, Egyptian, Californian, etc., spirit-seekers of varying degree of seriousness. But the three people who run the show – Rhine, Mrs Rhine and Pratt – are really outstanding people, both with regard to devotion to a heretic brand of psychology, which they pioneered, and to intellectual integrity.'

His disagreement with Leary, however, about the 'mystical' or 'creative' properties of the hallucinogenic drugs he made abundantly clear in a dismissive article, including a graphic account of his own experiences at Ann Arbor and Harvard, which he published in the *Sunday Telegraph*. He sent a copy to Leary with a covering letter:

'Thinking matters over in the relaxed and pedestrian atmosphere of London, I feel even stronger that no creativity can be bought this way. People here who have worked with mescalin, Smythies for instance, think the same. But I also still feel that the ESP side is worth trying and might be more rewarding than the "creativity" angle . . . In the meantime, keep well; don't indulge too much in mushrooms,* and give a *signe de vie* from time to time . . .'

Having prepared a series of articles for the *Observer*, in which he used all that he had learned in America as ammunition against the orthodoxy of academic psychologists, he wrote to Rhine about an idea that had just occurred to him:

'. . . here it is for what it is worth. All expert gamblers at roulette who rightly or wrongly believe that they have Psi faculties, only make bets on those occasions when they feel a definite hunch. In between they let the throws pass, often for half an hour or so. But the subject in a card-guessing experiment must, under present procedure, make a guess at every card, hunch or no hunch. I would suggest trying an altered procedure. The subject is allowed and encouraged to say "Blank" whenever he feels like it – from a single card to an entire run. The drawback is obviously that since the guesses would now become more rare, the subject would attribute to them increased importance and this might increase his self-consciousness. But it need not necessarily be so. At any rate, it might be worth trying the same subject under as far

* Dr Leary, as his subsequent career spectacularly demonstrated, failed to take Koestler's sober advice.

as possible the same conditions by the traditonal method and by the guess, blank, blank, guess, blank, guess, guess, etc., method. Even the frequency and rhythm of the guess-blank sequences might turn out to be interesting. What do you think?

'Should anything positive come out of it, I have no objection to your mentioning that the experiment was suggested by me. On the contrary, I would be proud for having made some contribution, however small, to ESP . . .'

He and Cynthia then left for Alpbach, where he resumed work on *The Act of Creation*. From time to time he heard from Dr Leary, who wrote on 25th April about

'Big doings with Rhine. He came to Harvard for a panel discussion . . . Overflow audience. Much excitement and very favourable reaction. Rhine was delighted. I spent a day with him and tried to get him out of the old laboratory routine. Not much luck.'

This was followed in a week or so by a letter from Dr Rhine about the occasion:

'I had good treatment at Harvard when I gave a talk there . . . Dr Leary . . . came out forcefully and flat-footedly in his gratitude for "these ESP pioneers" . . . On the whole, there was no doubt that parapsychology was inching along . . . I was impressed by what Leary had to say and by the man himself. I do not really think that he will do anything himself, except encourage those who are ready and waiting to do it.'

A prophetic remark.

During April and May, Koestler's articles appeared in the *Observer* and succeeded in stirring up (as they were obviously intended to) a fierce controversy which continued well into June. Some of the heated exchanges were most revealing, and gave Koestler an indication of the kind of criticism likely to be levelled by some outraged specialists when the *magnum opus* on which he was engaged came to be published. The attack was led by N. S. Sutherland of Oxford University's Institute of Experimental Psychology.

'It is misleading to suggest,' he wrote, 'that anyone can understand the progress of a science without knowing the facts which that science has discovered and without hard intellectual work. Yet the idea is growing in this country that the opinions of any novelist or playwright on any cultural subject are worth hearing . . . and nothing ridiculous is seen in this.'

Following a number of technical criticisms (which were hotly refuted in a later issue of the paper by Professor James V. McConnell of Ann Arbor), Dr Sutherland dealt his final blow:

'One of Koestler's conclusions is as follows: "the reality is the individual, an elusive entity, with a blur of unpredictability at its core." He presents no evidence for this other than a bland assumption that because at the moment

> we cannot make accurate predictions about some kinds of behaviour, we never shall be able to. If Koestler wishes to be convinced of the predictability of human behaviour, including his own, I will undertake to make ten predictions about Koestler's behaviour over the next week and to send these in a sealed envelope to the *Observer*. I would be prepared to stake a large sum of money that Koestler's behaviour will conform to my predictions.'

Koestler, not the man to take this sort of thing lying down, put aside the draft of *The Act of Creation* and replied:

> 'If [Sutherland means] that artists have no right to talk about culture, no further comment is needed. If it is meant as a personal insinuation that as a "novelist or playwright" I know nothing about science, he is evidently unaware of the facts. As for his suggested bet of ten predictions in a sealed envelope "for a large sum of money", I shall be delighted to accept it, if Dr. Sutherland will define the terms of the bet and exclude trivial predictions of the type: "he will eat, sleep, exhale $CO_2$, respond to stimuli, and read Feiffer in the *Observer*", in which case I would prefer to stick to the predictions of my favourite palm-reader.'

Professor A. J. Ayer (now Sir Alfred) was (and is) known to his friends as Freddie. In one of his articles Koestler had re-christened him Frederick. The professor took lofty exception to this, and to the suggestion that he was a behaviourist:

> 'This is quite false, as Mr Koestler could have discovered by reading anything I had written on the subject.'

Koestler replied:

> 'I apologise to Professor A. J. Ayer for my faulty extrapolation from the sociable Freddie to Frederick. But he is too modest in assuming that I have not read his writings – of which I like best his reflections on the [professional soccer] Cup Final in last week's *New Statesman*! He also objects to my calling him a Behaviourist, which I did not. I was quoting Professor Wilder Penfield who "had some scathing things to say about those contemporary English philosophers, the Behaviourists of logic, who refuse to acknowledge the existence of a mind-body problem. He singled out Gilbert Ryle and . . . A. J. Ayer." Since Behaviourism is a school of psychology, the reference to "Behaviourists of logic" is obviously metaphorical, intended to convey a common element of aridity and pedantic irrelevance in both approaches to the problem of man.'

And so the controversy raged on, to the delight of the *Observer*'s more philosophically minded readers, until 4th June, when the editor, David Astor, closed the correspondence (regretfully, I suppose).

In many ways, indeed, the controversy was more illuminating than that over the 'Two Cultures', for it demonstrated the passion with which the inheritors of the nineteenth century's mechanistic materialism were still prepared to defend a position which had been rendered indefensible decades earlier by the greatest scientists, and philosophers of science, of the century.

* *

During the spring of 1962, irritated by having to leave his dogs in England, when he and Cynthia moved to their summer quarters in Alpbach, Koestler decided to launch a crusade for the amendment of Britain's stringent quarantine laws. He published a lengthy article in the *Observer* on the distress caused to dogs and their owners, and advocating

> 'the exemption from quarantine of dogs (and cats) born and bred in this country, returning from abroad in their owner's care, equipped with a British veterinary surgeon's certificate of having been inoculated against the hazards of rabies not less than one month before leaving the United Kingdom and not more than two years before the date of return.'

Over a thousand dog-owners wrote to the *Observer* and the Canine Defence League in support of the proposal. But the Government was not moved. Nor, for once, was David Astor moved to support the crusade whole-heartedly in the *Observer*'s editorial columns (as he had supported the campaign for the abolition of capital punishment). The farthest he was prepared to go in this direction was a note suggesting that the Government should invite some body like the Medical Research Council to hear expert witnesses on the question of

> '. . . whether the reforms proposed by Mr Koestler would increase or decrease the risk'.

Astor's judicious (or lukewarm) attitude towards the issue annoyed Koestler greatly, and a long time was to pass before the breach between them was healed.

* *

Nevertheless, early in 1963 he accepted an invitation from the *Observer* to write the concluding article in a series under the general heading of *What's Left for Patriotism?* Instead of discoursing on the subject of patriotism, Koestler wrote a mordant piece about the deplorable state of the economy, the irresponsibility of the trades unions, the Communist influence in the labour movement, and so on. It has worn well. With a few alterations, it could have been re-published with commendations from Mrs Margaret Thatcher and Sir Keith Joseph on the eve of the general elections of 1979.

The article, entitled 'When the Daydream has to Stop', caught the eye of Melvin Lasky, who then commissioned Koestler to act as guest editor of a special issue of *Encounter* devoted to the state of the nation. Koestler accepted willingly. Ever since he had returned to England in 1952 he had kept a file – labelled 'Suicide of a Nation' – of newspaper clippings about the gloomier, seedier, frequently alarming, and invariably depressing aspects of the British social, economic, political and intellectual scene.

Setting to work, he recruited a mixed bag of seventeen (for the most part) lively journalists, historians, economists, and Conservative and Labour politicians. Their contributions, with two exceptions, advocated more or less radical reforms of one sort or another, ranging from the abolition of the English class system, through the reform of Parliament and the trades unions, to the throughgoing re-organisation of the educational system – themes which are still all too dismally familiar today.

One of the exceptions was Malcolm Muggeridge who retreated from despair into a Swiftian mood of bitter satire and emerged at the end into a kind of appalled resignation:

> 'The New Towns rise, as do the television aerials, dreaming spires: the streams flow, pellucid, through the comprehensive schools: the BBC lifts up our hearts in the morning, and bids us good night in the evening. We wait for Godot, we shall have strip-tease wherever we go. Give us this day our *Daily Express*, each week Dimbleby. God is mathematics, crieth our preacher. In the name of Algebra, the Son, Trigonometry, the Father, and Thermodynamics, the Holy Ghost, *Amen*.'

The other exception was that somewhat mercurial journalist Henry Fairlie who (having at that time a fairly intimate connection with the Conservative Party's Central office) took a good old stout John Bullish Tory line and asserted – with much excellent argument – that the principal thing amiss in the 'State of England' was the proliferation of 'State of England' writers who would be better employed writing autobiographies, novels, or poems than pretending to be engaged in an objective concern for the 'State of England' by contributing to collections of 'State of England' essays.

Koestler in his introduction likened the average Englishman to an

> 'attractive hybrid between a lion and an ostrich. In times of emergency he rises magnificently to the occasion. In between emergencies he buries his head in the sand with the tranquil conviction that Reality is a nasty word invented by foreigners.'

And in his postscript, having concluded that the real villain was England's complex class system, he wrote that his personal inclination was to give priority to the reform of England's

> 'out-dated educational system, out-dated in almost every respect – 11-plus, streaming, curriculum, segregation by class and sex – which perpetuates the iniquities of the past. It tears the nation apart and provides, generation after generation, a new crop of unwilling combatants for the cold class war. Equal opportunities for equally gifted children regardless of the status of the parents seems to me the basic axiom of social justice on which a free society must be built.'

Eighteen years and innumerable reforms later, we are still at it, filling the newspapers and the remaining reviews with complaints about the 'State of England' – not least about the complex class system and the state of education.

The special issue of *Encounter* appeared in July 1963 and was a great success. (Later in the year it was issued in book form by Hutchinson.)

The enjoyable interlude over, Koestler returned to *The Act of Creation*. By the end of the year it had been completed. By March 1964 page-proofs had been sent to many of the authorities on whose work Koestler had drawn. And in May the book was published.

* *

*The Act of Creation* is by any standard an astonishing work of erudition, brilliance, originality, and – because of its author's refusal to be intimidated by the prevailing idea that any intellectual, especially in the field of science, who steps outside the small and special patch of expertise he has made his own, is *ipso facto* unworthy of serious attention at the highest level – daring to the point of foolhardiness.

In another century (I wrote of Koestler thirteen years ago) he

> '. . . would have been known as a "thinker" or "sage". . . Long before western "liberals" even began to try to understand the evil secreted by systems designed to make man and society conform to the procrustean abstractions of utopian ideologies, Koestler had not only in person experienced that evil at its most potent but had embodied it, for our enlightenment, in works of imagination. And then . . . he embarked on a survey of man the discoverer (or scientist) and man the maker (or artist) . . . The fragmentation of western culture, accelerating since the High Renaissance, has led to, among much else, a grotesque overvaluation of the "expert" or "specialist", which in turn helps to accelerate still more rapidly the process of fragmentation. But Koestler, like Goethe, knows the imperative need to connect, only connect.'

The comparison with Goethe is inescapable when considering *The Act of Creation*, in which Koestler ranges freely and with apparent ease over almost every province of knowledge of the material with which to construct both a general and a special theory of scientific discovery and artistic creation, with particular reference to the innovational faculty of genius.

The book consists of two complementary parts. The first part sets out his general theory and is rather more accessible to the average reader than the second, much more technical, part in which he places his theory in the context of a comprehensive hypothesis of a hierarchy extending from the simplest living organism to the most complex neural processes of the human brain (and the mind which co-exists with it in a mysterious symbiosis unique to man).

Since it is quite impossible to summarise this enormously rich and ambitious work adequately in limited space, I must drastically condense and simplify in a manner which will inevitably obscure the complexities and subtleties of Koestler's arguments. The reader unfamiliar with the book should bear this in mind. To the reader who knows it, my apologies.*

* In the 1969 Danube edition of *The Act of Creation*, Book Two is omitted because, Koestler writes in his preface, it 'did indeed turn out to be too technical for the general reader . . .' Its essentials are subsumed in *The Ghost in the Machine* and summarised in *Janus*.

In the first half of the book, then, Koestler sets out – with a wealth of illustration, analogy, and metaphor – his theory of human creativity and discovery. The key concept here is 'bisociation', which he explains as the sudden perception of something

'. . . in two habitually incompatible associative contexts. This causes an abrupt transfer of thought from one matrix to another governed by a different logic or "rule of the game".'

By 'matrix' is meant

'. . . any skill or ability . . . any pattern of activity governed by a set of rules – its "code". All ordered behaviour, from embryonic development to verbal thinking, is controlled by "rules of the game", which lend it coherence and stability, but leave it sufficient degrees of freedom for flexible strategies adapted to environmental conditions.'

Underlying comic inspiration, scientific discovery and artistic originality is the same bisociative pattern, the same mental jump from one plane to another. In the case of wit and humour, the energy generated by the bisociation is discharged in a response that can vary from an explosion of bawdy laughter to a slow smile of appreciation. It is for this reason, Koestler explains, that he begins with an analysis of humour:

'. . . it is the only domain of creative activity where a complex pattern of intellectual stimulation elicits a sharply defined response in the nature of a physiological reflex.'

Whatever the variety of humour, from the broadest of aggressive, sexual or scatological jokes to the higher and witty forms of irony, satire and comedy, the underlying pattern is invariably bisociative – 'perceiving a situation or event in two habitually incompatible associative contexts . . . [which perception] causes an abrupt transfer of the train of thought from one matrix to another governed by a different logic or "rule of the game".'

Koestler gives many examples of varying degrees of complexity. One of them must suffice here. Freud in his *Wit and its Relations to the Unconscious* quotes a story told by the eighteenth-century French wit (devoured for his pains, incidentally, by the revolution which he had at first supported) Sébastien Chamfort:

'. . . a Marquis at the court of Louis XIV . . . on entering his wife's boudoir and finding her in the arms of a Bishop, walked calmly to the window and went through the motions of blessing people in the street.

'"What are you doing?" cried the anguished wife.

'"Monseigneur is performing my functions," replied the Marquis, "so I am performing his."'

The Marquis obviously took a view of cuckoldry and adultery very different from, say, Othello's. But it is not merely the unexpectedness of his reaction to catching the Marchioness and her episcopal lover *in flagrante* that produces the comic effect:

> 'The crucial point about the Marquis's behaviour is that it is both unexpected and perfectly logical – but of a logic not usually applied to this type of situation. It is the logic of the division of labour, the *quid pro quo*, the give and take; but our expectation was that the Marquis's actions would be governed by a different logic or code of behaviour. It is the clash of the two mutually incompatible codes, or associative contexts, which explodes the tension.'

His study of comic inspiration merges into that of scientific discovery. Here he demonstrates, with copious examples from the history of science, that the great discoveries have usually been made, not in the sober light of routine and systematic research or consolidation, but in lightning-flashes of sudden insight generated by the (usually unsought) bisociation of two quite separate and normally incompatible matrices or planes of logic. Archimedes, Gutenberg, Kepler, Newton, Darwin, Einstein – their greatest discoveries all have in common the fact that they were made in the light of that creative act of imagination which owes as much to the unconscious as to the conscious activities of mind and brain. Furthermore, Koestler demonstrates, they were generally made when the conscious mind, frustrated or blocked by the inadequacy of customary techniques and habitual logic, was quiescent 'in vacant or in pensive mood'. Unable for one reason or another to move forward, the mind temporarily retreats from the point at which further ratiocination seems pointless, the better to be propelled over and beyond the obstacle by inspired bisociation. This may be called the principle of *reculer pour mieux sauter* (and Koestler makes powerful and persuasive use of it in the second, more technical, half of the book).

And so to innovation in the field of artistic creation. Here, too, Koestler successfully applies his theory to all the arts – or to their manifestations, at any rate, on the upper levels of value uneroded by the passage of time and changes in taste.

> 'The difficulty of analysing the aesthetic experience is not due to its irreducible quality, but to the wealth, the unconscious and non-verbal character of the matrices which interlace in it, along ascending gradients in various dimensions. Whether the gradient is as steep and dramatic as in a Grünewald or El Greco, or gently ascending through green pastures, it always points towards a peak – not of technical perfection, but of some archetypal form of experience . . . a work of art is always transparent to some dim outline of ultimate experience – even if it is no more than the indirect reflection of a reflection, the echo of an echo.'

Koestler is writing here about painting, but his words are equally applicable to the other arts.

The concept of bisociation, then, as the spontaneous and sudden convergence, collision, or intersection of different 'matrices', or associative contexts governed by different 'codes' or 'rules of the game', is central to Koestler's theory of human creativity which stretches in an unbroken spectrum from the 'Ha-ha!' of the bawdy joke, through the 'Aha!' of Archimedes discovering in his bath how to measure the volume of Hiero's crown, to the 'Ah!' of wonder as the artist realises that he has on the instant received – out of the blue, as it were – knowledge of how to get his poem, or his painting, or his string quartet right.

It may be objected, however, that we can quite often laugh at jokes which are obviously contrived and laboured; that much progress in science and technology is made by the dogged plod of researchers, not greatly blessed with imagination, along the straight path of induction; and that most of us often find it easy enough to enjoy, and sometimes even to admire, contemporary works of literature, music, or painting in which the element of 'inspiration' is not conspicuous. This is true, but it does not invalidate the general theory as it applies to the imaginative innovators of unquestionable genius – Einstein, for example, 'bisociating' energy and matter in his equation $E = mc^2$, and in the process of synthesis transforming both.

Koestler explains the second-rate in art as follows:

> 'If a work of art strikes one as hopelessly dated, it is not because its particular idiom dates from a remote period, but because it is spelt out in a too obvious, explicit manner. The Laocoon group is more dated than the archaic Apollo of Tenea in spite of the vastly superior representational skill of the Hellenistic period . . .'

Embodied in the archaic and apparently simple Apollo is the genius of inspiration, and this speaks to us across the ages more clearly and with deeper significance than the superb craftsmanship of the three Rhodian sculptors who, centuries later, created the complex group of Laocoon and his sons in their terrible death agony.

It is the genius of true inspiration, the light that mere reason alone cannot generate, that Koestler's general theory seeks to explain.

* *

Had Koestler left it at that, *The Act of Creation* would still have been a remarkable achievement: an aesthetically satisfying, well-founded and variously suggestive synthesis. Here, for example, are a few sentences which have more sense in them than all the angry pages of the 'Two Cultures' controversy:

> 'To derive pleasure from the art of discovery, as from the other arts, the consumer – in this case the student – must be made to re-live, to some extent, the creative process. In other words, he must be induced, with proper aid and guidance, to make some of the fundamental discoveries of science by himself, to experience in his own mind some of those flashes of insight which have lightened its path. This means that the history of science ought to be made an essential part of the curriculum, that science should be represented in its evolutionary context – and not as a Minerva born fully armed . . .
>
> 'The creative achievements of the scientist lack the "audience appeal" of the artist's for several reasons . . . – technical jargon, antiquated teaching methods, cultural prejudice. The boredom created by these factors has accentuated the artificial frontiers between continuous domains of creativity.'

But Koestler went far beyond the exposition of his general theory in the latter half of the book. Here, drawing upon his encyclopaedic knowledge of recent advances in biology, he plants his theory firmly in the rich humus of a hypothesis which extends the purposeful, or creative, faculty, in greater or lesser degree, to all living creatures from the single plant or animal cell to Mozart – all of which employ the tactic of *reculement pour mieux sauter*. Every living thing has its place in an ordered and orderly hierarchy. Everything is both a part and a whole, in some degree dependent, in some degree autonomous. In everything there is pattern, design, order, organisation – and purpose.

Having demonstrated this at various physiological levels, he turns back to man and society and the never-ending dialectic of self-assertion and self-transcendence. His challenge to the dogmatists of neo-Darwinian orthodoxy he now extends, at length and in detail, to their camp-followers of behaviourist psychology and positivist philosophy who offer the bleak view of man as a mere mindless stimulus-and-response, cause-and-effect mechanism of reflexes, brought to birth in a random manner by a series of unimportant accidents and doomed like the rest of creation to the absolute disintegration – the 'final solution', as it were – promised by the Second Law of Thermodynamics.

It would be a very dull dog indeed who failed to find this polymathic work exhilarating (or infuriating, or both).

* *

The book's reception in Britain and North America (and in due course elsewhere in various translations) more than made up for the disappointment Koestler had experienced years before on the publication of *Insight and Outlook*, which could now be recognised for what in truth it was – a first draft, rough in parts and far from complete, of *The Act of Creation*. There were very few dull dogs among its reviewers, and even they had the wit to recognise the extraordinary range of Koestler's scholarship and acknowledge the encyclopaedic value of the book as an incomparably rich assemblage of sources. (The bibliography lists something like 400 works of psychology, physiology, philosophy, history, biography, astronomy, cosmology, educational theory, poetry, aesthetics, epistemology, mathematics, chemistry, physics, pharmacology, zoology, ethology, etc., etc., all of them cited in the text.)

Much of Koestler's argument in both parts of the book was extremely controversial (rather less so now, I should imagine) and many of the reviews took issue with one point or another in varying degrees of critical rigour. That was to be expected, of course, no less than the fact that in a work of such scale and complexity there should be some errors of fact and interpretation. But what must have been particularly gratifying for Koestler, apart from the natural sense of achievement, was to see his work as a scientific thinker taken seriously by scientists over whose domains of specialisation he had freely ranged. Even many of those who found it most difficult to accept his theory in whole or in part, seemed to concur with the final paragraph of the review in *Nature*:

'The merit of Mr. Koestler's book lies in pointing the way towards a better understanding of science. If science creates new knowledge, we cannot forget the unconscious processes from which it springs. We must reject the view still widely held that science progresses through intellectual and logical thinking and, in consequence, revise the narrow, mechanistic criteria which are used for judging whether a theory is acceptable or not.'

There was one exception, however, and that was a formidable one: Dr P. B. (later Sir Peter) Medawar, the distinguished zoologist. In a lengthy article in the *New Statesman* he scrutinised Koestler's generalisations and dismissed them together with many of the particular arguments in support of them, and the style of the prose. It was undoubtedly what in less elevated circles is known as a 'hatchet job'.

He opened on a note of praise, reminiscent of Mark Antony's praise of Brutus:

'The author of *Darkness at Noon* must be listened to attentively, no matter what he may choose to write upon. Arthur Koestler is a very clever, knowledgeable and inventive man, and *The Act of Creation* is very clever too, and full of information, and quite wonderfully inventive in the use of words.'

After such an ominous introduction, Koestler (who read the review in Alpbach) must have been prepared for some less complimentary observations to follow, but scarcely, one imagines, for such lusty swings of the axe as the following:

'. . . as a serious and original work of learning I am sorry to say that, in my opinion, *The Act of Creation* simply won't do. This is not because of its amateurishness, which is more often than not endearing, nor even because of its blunders . . .

'There are passages . . . which convince me that he has no real grasp of how scientists go about their work . . .'

To Medawar's ears Koestler's analogies and metaphors

'sound silly, and I believe them to be as silly as they sound . . .

'*The Act of Creation* is so full of vitality that it creates around it an aura of good-to-be-alive, and though Koestler regards himself as the author of a new and important general psychological theory, I am delighted that, in writing a "popular" work, he has in a sense appealed to the general public over the heads of the profession. But certain rules of scientific manners must be observed no matter what form the account of a scientific theory may take . . . Koestler seems to have no adequate grasp of the importance of *criticism* in science . . .'

The general tone of the review was one of outrage suppressed with difficulty – rather like that of the attack by Santillana and Drake on *The Sleepwalkers*, but much less direct and abusive. In so far as I can judge, the specific and substantive points of adverse criticism do not seem to be of great significance. Without damaging Koestler's theory, however, they served to indicate the intensity of Medawar's hostility to the philosophy implicit in every chapter of the book. It must have conjured up in the mind of more than one reader the vision of an irate keeper confronting an intruder, almost speechless with rage and hammering his walking-stick against the board which announces that trespassers will be prosecuted.

In the next issue but one of the *New Statesman*, Koestler dealt easily and civilly with the specific points made by Medawar, and ended:

> 'The rest consists of ironic innuendo and *ex cathedra* pronouncements: "Certain rules of scientific manners must be observed," Professor Medawar informs us. I wish he had lived up to his precept.'

Medawar's subtended comments on Koestler's reply did little more than strengthen the impression that he was, perhaps, alarmed as well as outraged by this 'amateur's' act of trespass. Koestler, he concluded, must have had some doubts about the wisdom and taste of his final sentences,

> '. . . and I suppose it will only make matters worse if I say I forgive him. I will not, however, forgive him for hinting that I didn't read his book, nor for the fact that I had to spend hours and hours and hours in doing so.'

There were many learned doctors – dozens of them – in universities and other institutes of learning throughout Europe and North America whose unsolicited letters to Koestler showed that they took a view of the book very different from Professor Medawar's. It would be tedious to list all the eminent physicists, chemists, biologists, classicists, historians, psychologists, zoologists and educationists who showered praise and constructive criticism on him, but I must quote briefly from the letters of a few of them.

From the neurophysiologist, Professor Paul Weiss of the Rockefeller Institute, New York City:

> 'It is rare in these days to come across a book which at the same time has broad conceptual perspective and disciplined command and responsibility in matters of documentary detail: in other words, creative scholarship.'

From the radiotherapist, Professor D. W. (later Sir David) Smithers:

> 'I believe this to be a great book. There were moments when I thought that it was also a great craggy collection of things you could not bear to leave out, and that it would have been better with some drastic pruning, but on reflection I wouldn't have missed a word of it. It shows the most immense industry and covers a range of reading which produced in me both wonderment and envy. It also shows an extraordinary breadth of understanding. Half way through I discovered to my surprise and delight that . . . a layman understood things that I have been trying to say to doctors for 15 years, and which I have had such great difficulty in persuading them to accept.'

From C. P. Snow:

> 'May I tell you how deeply I admire *The Act of Creation*? I have just had a long and wearing trip in the deep South of the United States. I carried a proof copy

of the book round with me and talked about it a great deal . . . It is a most remarkable work, which only you could have written. I don't go all the way with you in your new constructs, but then you wouldn't expect any set of ideas as original as these to be totally accepted. They will, nevertheless, have an intensely powerful effect on Crick [Dr. F. H. Crick, the molecular biologist] and his friends, and I eagerly await the outcome.'

From Dr Konrad Lorenz:

'. . . you see very much the same problems as I do.'

From Professor F. A. Hayek:

'I am at the moment deriving much stimulation and enjoyment from *The Act of Creation*, since in more than one respect it closely touches on problems which have occupied me much in recent years.'

From Professor Dennis Gabor:

'I am now reading the second part . . . and I am full of admiration for the enormous material which you have put in comparatively good order . . . I have learnt no end from your book, which contains material which I would never have had patience to master on my own . . . I am very glad indeed . . . to learn that the fossil behaviourists are reeling under your blows. For my part I am more and more convinced that psychology is by far the most important science of our time, and it is heartbreaking to see we are not sending our best talents into it, as we ought to. Amateurs to the fore! I hope you will continue on the glorious though sometimes thorny path . . .'

Many of the scientists who wrote to Koestler confessed themselves puzzled and dismayed by the manifest hostility of Medawar, whom they all admired and respected. Gabor, for instance:

'I am sorry to hear that [*The Act of Creation*] did not get a good reception from Peter Medawar, for whom I have a great respect. Sometime . . . I should like to bring you together with [him] if you do not mind. I know (he told me himself) that he has the greatest respect for you . . .'

Another distinguished physicist (who must remain nameless here) worried away in a long letter at the problem of Medawar's hostility. Referring to certain adverse criticisms by two well-known psychologists, he wrote:

'These two are in a groove and intellectually mediocre. Not so Medawar. He writes with a sense of responsibility and must regard himself as the spokesman of scientists on his own high intellectual level. In his review he is defending something against a danger that is threatened in your book. He can write with the assurance that his defence will be approved by his fellow scientists. The review presents two riddles and one can find in the history of science innumerable examples of the same riddles . . . What is Medawar defending? . . . How can one account for Medawar's choice of weapons? The question is really puzzling. Contrast the character of the book and the character of the review. The book is richly documented with facts based on scientific discoveries that are well authenticated. The logical reasoning is acute and inescapable. The presentation is so clear that each point tells. Medawar does not like the argument and finds it necessary, in the interests of science, to counter it. But he does not employ facts and logic. Instead, he employs the method of discrediting . . . The purport of the review is that scientists will do their best to take no notice of the book . . . Why does Medawar make out a bad case for whatever he is defending while he and his colleagues are all convinced that he has a cast-iron case? The situation arises so frequently that an understanding of it is urgently called for.'

Koestler himself, who admired Medawar, offered no explanation. Replying to another correspondent who had raised the question, he wrote:

> 'If Medawar could be dismissed as an orthodox pedant, it would be understandable. The rub is that truly original minds can be that narrow – from Galileo and Newton onwards. But science is a passion as emotively coloured as art, so one need not wonder that scientists are passionate.'

The problem remains, however. Medawar's review conveyed to many that this brilliant and likeable man was engaged not so much in criticising the contents of *The Act of Creation* as in lashing out in an uncharacteristically inexact manner at some threat he discerned in it. How to explain this?

Professor Weiss, in a letter to Koestler, remarked that one of his findings concerning the dynamics of the central nervous system was

> 'as valid as ever – and equally obscure as at the time I conceived it. How could it be otherwise, if, during the past forty years, the people who have been brought face to face with facts, like scary rabbits, preferred to look the other way, where they did not have to face them.'

Sir Peter Medawar is no scary rabbit, but it is not, I think, unfair to suggest that he looked somewhat to the side of the facts paraded by Koestler.

# CHAPTER XXXVI

# *1964–1970*

BY THE SUMMER THE PAIN, such as it was, of the sting implanted by Professor Medawar had been effectively soothed by the invitations now arriving in large numbers from centres of learning. He had already been offered a year's fellowship at the Center for Advanced Study in the Behavioral Sciences at Stanford, California, but because of other commitments could accept only for the second semester – that is, for the first six months of 1965. A brief visit to Tokyo had to be fitted in, and a conference on the island of Delos organised by the Greek planner C. A. Doxiadis to discuss his concept of 'ekistics' – the international study, that is, of human settlements – by economists, psychologists, sociologists and experts in other disciplines. This was followed by a symposium on 'Brain Function and Learning' at the University College of Los Angeles, and a lecture at the Santa Barbara campus. Life was full and enjoyable.

> 'He was excited by this,' says Cynthia, 'because he enjoyed above all hard-headed – and hot-headed –discussions in overlapping fields of science . . .'*

The papers on creativity delivered by Koestler at the symposium in the University College of Los Angeles and to a student audience at Santa Barbara were well received. He made such a favourable impression at the latter that the chancellor of the campus, Vernon I. Cheadle, offered him a Regents' Lectureship for the remainder of the academic year. On his return to London, Koestler had a letter from Cheadle regretting that other commitments had

> '. . . made it impossible for you to accept my invitation . . . It may be possible to renew our invitation to you at a future time. We shall have to be satisfied for the present, at least, that we have had the privilege of having you for a visit, short as it was . . .'

But an even warmer compliment came from Professor Sidney Hook of the Department of Philosophy in New York University, who wrote on 1st November to say that

* *Op. cit.*

> 'An Albert Schweitzer chair in the Humanities is being established at New York University and I should like to nominate you for it if there is any chance you would accept the invitation were it offered.
>
> 'The Chair pays £10,000 approximately a year: housing and other perquisites are provided. You can take it for a period of years or for life.
>
> 'Your duties would be light: one course of lectures in a subject or theme which falls in the field of the humanities, three public lectures a year, and an occasional opportunity for a few advanced students and some of your colleagues to talk to you.
>
> 'It is a fabulous sort of thing and it ought to go to a fabulous person! There is no reason to believe that being a "Professor" will interfere with your writing plans. Many professors write, and besides you won't be an ordinary professor.
>
> 'If you are interested, will you let me know at once and I shall have the President send on details or better still cable me.'

Koestler was, naturally, flattered and moved by this, especially since Hook's letter implied clearly enough that the job was his for the taking. But his objections to permanent residence in America had not weakened.

> 'I felt really moved by your letter,' he replied. 'But as I said in my cable, I do not want to leave Europe. You spoke of the possibility – always assuming your nomination goes through – of a Chair for life or "a period of years". If it were for one year I would indeed gladly accept but I imagine that is out of the question . . . Thank you again for your trust.'

* *

Koestler's interest in the evolutionary process in general, and especially the inexplicably rapid development of the human brain, had grown more intense, and he was more preoccupied than ever with the mind-body problem. The idea of the brain as nothing but an especially complex computer was more than ever abhorrent to him. A new work was slowly taking shape, and he was constantly stimulated by the correspondence now pouring in from all quarters. I shall quote only a particularly suggestive (and unintentionally flattering) letter from Dr Irving D. Harris of the Department of Mental Health at Chicago's Institute for Juvenile Research:

> 'I have noted that what you call Bisociation is the hall-mark of the creative activity of first or only sons of the mother (Kepler, Newton, Shakespeare, Einstein, yourself). Later sons do not use this psychic process overly much. In fact, they often mistrust and oppose the speculative, combinatory leaps (e.g., Francis Bacon, Hume).'

Koestler was not without a proper pride in his achievement, but he must have been surprised to find himself bracketed with such giants.

What he was looking forward to most keenly during his six months at the 'think-tank' at Stanford, apart from daily contacts with experts in all the disciplines over which his mind had for years been ranging, was close collaboration with Professor Karl Pribram, the neurophysiologist attached to the School of

Medicine's Department of Psychology. His appetite was whetted by a letter from Pribram reminding him that

'. . . Your speech is all set . . . for January 21, 1965 at 7.45 p.m. at the Memorial Auditorium. You are going to be talking about "extra-conscious factors in creativity".'

He was well accustomed by this time to the exemplary administrative thoroughness of American academics.

At last, on 2nd January, Koestler and Cynthia left for America. They stayed for a few days in New York where Koestler had lengthy discussions with Michael Polanyi about a conference on the philosophic foundation of cultural unity which the latter was helping to arrange, with the backing of the Ford Foundation. *The Act of Creation* had given the idea a fresh impetus, and multiplied the problems. As Polyani put it a little later in a letter to Koestler:

'You have given a phenomenological framework which includes biological perspectives. This raises new questions for the nature and justification of knowledge and for the cosmic framework in which our mind forms part. The organisers of the conference hope that such contributions as you have made can also be found in the writings of other of our contemporaries and will lead the way to a renewal of our philosophic foundations.'

From New York City Koestler and Cynthia went to California by way of the University of Colorado, where Koestler took part in a symposium on the 'New Science', and on 15th January they arrived at the pleasant house in Palo Alto which was to be their home for six months. On that day *Time* magazine published the following item:

*Married.* Arthur Koestler, 59, Hungarian-born author, once a Communist, later a supreme critic (*Darkness at Noon*); and Cynthia Koestler, 37, his South African-born secretary, who changed her name from Paterson to Koestler a year ago in London; he for the third time, she for the second: by a city clerk in Manhattan.'

* *

There were forty-nine Fellows in the Palo Alto 'think-tank' that year. Forty-eight of them were academics with impressive letters of accreditation to put after their names – biologists, economists, historians, classicists, psychologists, anthropologists, sociologists, political scientists, physicists and educationists from all the great universities of North America and three or four Dutch, French, Italian and Rumanian institutions. In Koestler's *curriculum vitae*, against the entries 'formal training' and 'professional career' was the bleak word 'none'. But his 'catalogue of interests' was formidable:

'a. Learning, problem-solving, scientific and artistic creativity in their psychological and neurophysiological aspects.

'b. Psychology and neurophysiology of the emotions with particular reference to laughter, weeping and the role of the parasympathetic in emotion.

'c. The hierarchic principle in organisation and behaviour.
'd. History of science.'

So were his 'priorities for 1965':

'a. Inter-disciplinary seminars on b.
'b. Editing a book by various hands on c.
'c. Attempting an inquiry on the working methods of scientists (approximately based on Jacques Hadamard's *The Psychology of Invention*, Princeton University Press, 1949).'

Koestler's practice during the six months at Palo Alto fully lived up to his promise. He and Professor Karl Pribram jointly directed a seminar on 'self-regulating hierarchic organisations'. In addition to the many Fellows who attended the twenty sessions, covering every field in the behavioural sciences, there were participants from outside, among them Professors Frank Barron, Ernest Gellhorn, Ernest Hilgard, Roman Jakobson, Robert Rosenthal, and Paul Weiss. (This was the seed-bed out of which Koestler's next book, *The Ghost in the Machine*, was to grow – and also, at a later date, that 'book by various hands', *Beyond Reductionism*.)

For three months he also conducted a weekly seminar on 'Habit and Originality' for graduate students in psychology at Stanford University, and a weekly 'Colloquium on Partly-Baked Ideas'. The inspiration for the latter had come from a book entitled *The Scientist Speculates – an Anthology of Partly-Baked Ideas** which had as epigraph a quotation from *The Evolution of Physics* by Einstein and Infeld:

> 'The formulation of a problem is often more essential than its solution, which may be merely a matter of mathematical or experimental skill. To raise new questions, new possibilities, to regard old problems from a new angle, requires creative imagination and marks real advance in science.'

The preface to this book, to which almost a hundred leading authorities in various fields had contributed, consisted of a single sentence:

> 'The intention of this anthology is to raise more questions than it answers.'

And that, of course, was also the intention of the colloquium.

Nor was this all. The range of his activities, as well as his interests, at Palo Alto was astonishing. On the one hand, he and James J. Jenkins, a psychologist from the University of Minnesota who specialised in psycholinguistics and verbal behaviour, aphasia and higher mental processes, collaborated on a research programme which yielded a learned paper on 'Inversion Effects in the Tachistoscopic Perception of Number Sequences'. On the other hand, he wrote and directed for the diversion of the Fellows an Aristophanic satirical farce entitled *Cloudcuckoocamp* (or Nephelokokkuxia) in a mixture of prose and verse in the manner of *The Birds*. It was, not surprisingly, directed against the ratomorphic behaviourism of Skinner and his disciples. A few lines will give its rich flavour:

* Ed. I. J. Good, Heinemann, London and Toronto, 1962.

'*Chorus Leader:* We shall start with our worshipful liturgical chant:
Hocus, pocus, spiritus,
Stimulus, responsibus
'*Chorus:* Holy Pavlov, pray for us
'*Chor. Lead.:* Smite the heretic!
'*Chor.:* Block his synapses!
Extinguish his reflexes!
'*Chor. Lead.:* Put him into a Skinner Box!
'*Chor.:* Get Hebb and Hull into his skull!
Make him behave, behave, behave.
'*Chor. Lead.:* And now let us repeat our sacred vows.
'*Chor.:* I shall not cherish any ambition which is beyond the rat's condition
*Chor. Lead.:* I shall not boast of any skill
Which rats cannot be taught at will
'*Chor.:* I shall confine my dreams and visions
To lever-pressing competitions . . .'

It is not surprising that ten years later Dr Preston S. Cutler, Associate Director of the Center, could still reassure me that

'We have very lively and fond memories of Arthur Koestler.'

* *

Having declined still more of the flattering invitations that came flooding in from American universities – although prudently taking a 'rain-check' on the more tempting of them, such as one from Yale – Koestler and Cynthia returned to Europe. He got down to the lonely work of drafting the book, *The Ghost in the Machine*, which had been taking shape during his months at the 'think-tank'. It was not easy. This book, he told Cynthia,

'. . . was going to be as light as a soufflé. He was cheered by this thought, having spent so much time in recent years wading through heavy-handed scientific jargon and even having to resort to it himself . . . As I typed the first hundred pages I wondered what had happened to the soufflé; it had become as heavy and solid as a dumpling. It was only when he reached Part III that one began to see that this dumpling was the massive foundation on which the alarming theory (more of which later) propounded in this part was built. As he neared the end of the book, Arthur became more and more tormented with the thought that it was not one book but two . . . I was a bad listener, rubbing my eyes, nodding . . .'

There were breaks, of course, to relieve the strain, not least his correspondence with the zoologist Alister Hardy, who shared his interest in paranormal phenomena and mystical experience, and with Herbert Butterfield, a deeply religious man as well as a profoundly influential scholar. His admiration for these men, whose learning and achievements were unchallengeable, was fully reciprocated, and the warmth of their friendship, and of certain others, protected him from the chilly winds that sometimes blew from other quarters of Academe where rigid orthodoxy prevailed and 'Partly-Baked Ideas' would have been regarded as a very bad joke.

September was a particularly busy month for Koestler, and work on the manuscript was suspended for a time. On Thursday the 2nd, three days before his sixtieth birthday, he delivered a paper on 'Evolutions and Revolutions in Science' at the annual meeting of the British Association in Cambridge. And a week after his birthday he flew to Washington to deliver a paper on biological and mental evolution during the bicentennial celebrations of the Smithsonian Institution. In this he argued persuasively that the discoveries of the biologist Walter Garstang in the twenties strongly supported his contention that the tactic of *reculement pour mieux sauter* applied to mental as well as to biological evolution; fitted neatly into his theory of creativity; and confounded

> '. . . The old-fashioned behaviourist's view of the rat in the maze as a paradigm of human learning . . . a kind of blind man's buff – random mutations preserved by natural selection, or random tries preserved by re-inforcement.'

During his stay in Washington he met Paul D. Maclean, Chief of the Laboratory of Brain Evolution and Behavior at the National Institute of Mental Health in Bethesda, Maryland. This resulted not merely in a lasting friendship but, as we shall see, in Koestler's most controversial proposition.

* *

The occasion of his sixtieth birthday was marked by the *Jewish Observer and Middle East Review* in a sympathetic but shrewdly critical analysis of Koestler the novelist by Renée Winegarten. His earliest work in the field of fiction – *The Gladiators* and *Darkness at Noon*, both written in German – were also his best, she wrote (in a judgement from which few would now, I think, dissent).

> '. . . he is in everything, and consciously, the European *par excellence*.'

Miss Winegarten was particularly concerned – understandably if excessively – with the weaknesses of *Thieves in the Night* and she undoubtedly had a point when she declared that his ambivalent attitude to Zionism

> '. . . could not have been far from that of his protagonist, Joseph, who says: "The trouble is that the whole issue . . . has lost its reality for me. I no longer care a damn about Round Table Conferences, Arabs, Hebrews, and National Homes."'

His heart, she thought, was not in the novel as such:

> 'At the peak of his fame, he is reported to have told Sartre, of all people, that he considered himself a better philosopher than a novelist. This is a view which I think few will share, preferring to see in him a brilliant manipulator of ideas.'

Precisely where one draws the distinction between 'philosophy' and the 'manipulation of ideas' (or between either and 'ideology', perhaps) is no clearer today than when Miss Winegarten wrote these lines in 1965: but I think it not unfair to assert that in his development as a 'thinker' (to put it in a simpler, if old-fashioned, way) Koestler has been more successful than Sartre, who succeeded only in reducing to venomous rabble-rousing absurdity his synthesis of atheistic existentialism and neo-Marxism after the school of Frankfurt-am-Main.

But Miss Winegarten had more interesting things to say. Koestler's personal experiences, she pointed out, had left him haunted by the political and ethical questions of ends and means, and the corrupting effects of power. On the one hand, nothing could be achieved without ruthlessness: on the other, he could not tolerate the sacrifice of the individual to the Moloch of Utopia. Where, then, was the line to be drawn?

> 'He saw that the idealists end by creating a world that horrifies them, echoing with the screams of the crucified, peopled by narrow brutes like Gletkin who destroy them, or by "Hebrew peasants" who leave them scornful and dissatisfied.
>
> 'This is a problem inherent in the very nature of man, his aspirations and achievements, and one which might, for convenience, be placed under the theological heading of the consequences of original sin. But while Koestler, usually so self-aware, comes close to this theological position when he implies that all are guilty of some crime or betrayal, he never openly adheres to it.'

Miss Winegarten was not to know, of course, that Koestler was at that very time working towards a startling explanation of 'original sin', and a means of expiating it – neither, it is true, theological in nature.

Elsewhere in her essay (which is confined, as I have said, to Koestler as a novelist), she makes an observation which could be applied even more accurately to his other writings (especially since I am not inclined to argue with any vehemence against her opinion that *Darkness at Noon* is the only one of his novels likely to survive, because 'it is the epitome of a state of mind, even in its equivocation'):

> '. . . how far can his books be detached from what George Orwell called his "life style"? Surely V. S. Pritchett was right when, in an article in *Horizon* in 1947, he foresaw that Koestler's vestiges would one day be collected like the vestiges of Byronism. For if Koestler has not had Byron's influence and progeny, he is, I submit, a similar incarnation of the malaise of a generation.'

True enough: but it was the malaise not of his own but of numberless generations past and to come which now obsessed Koestler. And it was now, naturally enough, at the time of his greatest effort, that he had to deflect the ever-increasing demands on his time, often from people whom he liked no less than he admired.

In the middle of March 1966, Cynthia went down with a fairly severe attack of infective hepatitis. A month later, as Koestler wrote to Professor Hayek, explaining why he could not attend a conference at Bellagio, she was

'. . . still in a precarious state, and the doctor warned me of the danger of a relapse if she is prematurely placed under strain. As we are at the moment without any domestic help she tires easily. I cannot leave her alone to cope with this rather big house for a week or ten days.'

Koestler had also addressed an audience at the Foundation for Advanced Education in the Sciences. Here too his theories were well received. Dr Seymour S. Kety, then Chief of the Laboratory of Clinical Science, wrote on behalf of the Foundation to say that

'. . . the size of the audience was an indication of the interest which your lecture aroused. The scholarly and philosophical dissertation which we had the pleasure to hear was exactly what was needed in this hard-nosed environment. The Seminar the next day was again an example of the high-level scholarly dialogue which we need very much in addition to the rigorous research for which we are usually known.'

In the autumn he took time off from his work on *The Ghost in the Machine* to review Konrad Lorenz's *On Aggression*, a work which touched on his own preoccupations. He was critical of Lorenz's use of the behaviour of the greylag goose as a paradigm for the bonds which unite human communities:

'Lorenz believes that the evil in man originates in an evolutionary shortcoming: because he lacks the deadly natural weapons of other carnivores, he also lacks the built-in inhibitory mechanisms "preventing the killing of con-specifics until, all of a sudden, the invention of artificial weapons upsets the equilibrium of killing potential and social inhibitions". Selective pressure did the rest to produce a species of intra-specific killers.

'This is an arguable hypothesis, even if it can reflect only part of the truth; but there is no need to go into it because, as Lorenz himself points out, the holocausts of human history were not caused by murders committed for personal motives by aggressive individuals, but by "militant enthusiasm" *ad majorem gloriam* in the service of a cause. This is at the point at which a serious discussion of man's predicament could start: but unfortunately we are once more referred to the goose . . .

'Behaviourism started by rejecting the pathetic fallacy; it ended up by replacing the anthropomorphic view of the rat with a ratomorphic view of man. Now Professor Lorenz seems to offer us an anseromorphic view [*anser* = goose] . . .'

* *

On 24th February 1967, Paul Maclean wrote from Bethesda:

'I hope that this letter will arrive in time to be with you when you deliver the manuscript of your book . . . to your publishers on Wednesday, March 1st. I so wish not because you will need a midwife. I have no concern that the two faces of your Janus will present any obstetrical problem . . . I would like to have this letter there to congratulate you upon this your latest "Act of Creation", a really seminal book! I think you have accomplished a remarkable synthesis of a diversity of difficult subjects and in such a way that one might think of you as a bundle of authoritative holons operating according to the best Janus principle. Your book shows the brilliance of what happens when an author's irresistible ideas meet with formerly immovable objects . . .'

* *

In May Koestler and Cynthia left for Alpbach where he began to collect the essays and occasional pieces of the previous twelve years.* In the autumn he began to organise an interdisciplinary conference on the life sciences to be held in Alpbach during June of the following year. And in October *The Ghost in the Machine* was published.

* *

A month or two earlier Koestler had sent an advance copy to Ernest R. Hilgard, Professor of Psychology at Stanford University. He had met Hilgard during his semester at the Palo Alto 'think tank' and become friendly with him. On 19th September Hilgard wrote to thank him, adding:

'It is interesting how your intemperate attacks on Behaviourism make such anti-Behaviourists as George Miller and me tend to come to the defence of our colleagues. You do make a good case for some limitations in the approach, and I welcome the way in which you make us all re-examine our positions.

'The most unexpected part of your argument is that in favour of pharmacology to introduce the Brave New World. I see nothing in your description of that Utopia, by the way, which gives an attractive picture of life full of meaning and purpose. I can just see us all united in a stadium singing our national anthem entitled "A Hymn to Hierarchy" . . . Have fun!'

Hilgard was not the only reader to be surprised by Koestler's argument 'in favour of pharmacology to introduce the Brave New World'.

There are three parts to the book, entitled respectively *ORDER*, *BECOMING* and *DISORDER*. Much of the material in the first two parts, dealing for the most part with psychology and evolution, is a re-working, in language accessible to the layman, of the extremely technical Book Two of the original edition of *The Act of Creation*. It also refines his general and universally applicable theory of hierarchy – the Open Hierarchical Systems Theory – in which any organism, biological or social, is composed not of mere 'parts' but of 'holons', which are defined as:

'self-regulating open systems which display both the autonomous properties of wholes and the dependent properties of parts. This dichotomy is present on every level of every type of hierarchic organisation, and is referred to as the *Janus Effect* or Janus principle.'

* *Drinkers of Infinity*, London, 1968.

Once again, and more zestfully than ever before, he takes on the orthodox neo-Darwinian evolutionists and Behaviourist psychologists who elaborate the former's orthodoxy by 'proving' that mice and men are no more than mechanical assemblages of reflexes responding automatically, according to their genetic programming, to the random stimuli of an environment entirely lacking in meaning, value or purpose. His assault is frontal, ferocious, and often very funny. He allowed the Behaviourists to hold themselves up to ridicule, as in Professor Skinner's profound analysis of a common and usually enjoyable ('cultural' even) domestic event:

> 'The verbal stimulus "come to dinner" is an occasion upon which going to a table and sitting down is usually reinforced by food. The stimulus comes to be effective in increasing the probability of that behaviour and is produced by the speaker because it does so.'

And as in that of Skinner's predecessor, Professor Watson, concerning artistic creation:

> '. . . how do we ever get new verbal creations such as a poem or a brilliant essay? The answer is that we get them by manipulating words, shifting them about until a new pattern is hit upon . . . Not until the new creation aroused admiration and commendation, both his own and others, would manipulation be complete – the equivalent of the rat's finding food.'

Koestler set himself up, bravely and gaily, in opposition to those who would make stones of us. His courage was inspiriting. So was his critique of Darwinian orthodoxy in which he argues persuasively that 'purpose' or 'initiative' could always and everywhere be discerned in the process of trial and error by which a blob of protoplasm becomes man. He also argued that acquired characteristics *can* be inherited – a grave and encouraging Lamarckian heresy against the fanatical faith of neo-Darwinism. And he held all his arguments together in the hypothesis of a cosmic hierarchy in which everything is both a whole composed of constituent wholes composed of . . . and so ('downward' and 'inward') *ad infinitum*; and also a mere part of a whole which is a mere . . . and so ('upward' and 'outward') *ad infinitum*.

However, something, in the case of man, according to Koestler, has gone wrong with the evolutionary process. Why does man kill members of the same species, unlike innocent animals, which, in any case, kill only to eat? Why cannot man be like other creatures (save the suicidal lemmings) and limit his increase?

Because, Koestler explained, of an evolutionary error (of a sort well enough known but, in the case of man, with fearful implications). Our Cro-Magnon 'ancestor', a man of sorts, had a brain like ours; and our superiority to him is by no means strong enough to make our possession of this superb instrument any less nonsensical. We, like Cro-Magnon man, resemble the ignorant Arab who asked Allah for an abacus and was presented, as a result of a malicious djinn's intervention, with a skyscraper housing a huge computer and a book of instructions he couldn't read.

Reason and imagination are dissociated. Hence trouble. Our power of self-transcendence feeds tribal, social, national, ideological, etc., aggression. Hence still more trouble. And the outlook is now more troubled than ever it was, given (a) the population explosion and (b) our skill in making nuclear explosions that can make short work of populations.

Koestler explains the predicament of man, a unique species, by drawing heavily upon the work of Dr Paul Maclean (Chief of the Laboratory of Brain Evolution and Behavior in the American Institute of Mental Health). *Homo sapiens* is indeed a 'unique species' or 'special creation' – *but only in the sense that he is a biological freak, an evolutionary accident*, as a result of which the neo-cortex of his brain (the reasoning part, that is, which in its electro-chemical operation can be likened to an infinitely complex computer) grew enormously in size and, presumably, in an incredibly short space of geological time, at some unspecified period in prehistory. As a result of this freakish development, the 'tumorous overgrowth' of the human neo-cortex is imperfectly co-ordinated with the two other and older parts of the brain which we have inherited from primitive mammals and still more primitive reptiles.

From this appalling flaw in this fearsome biological freak, appearing suddenly on the scene (for it should be emphasised that the 'missing link' which so greatly intrigued the Victorians and Edwardians is still missing), comes man's aggressive-ness (unique in the animal creation) and the dreadful predicament of humanity today which is intensifying exponentially thanks to recent advances in science and technology and the huge engines of corruption and destruction spawned by them.

Having completed in some considerable detail his disturbing diagnosis and even more disturbing prognosis, Koestler writes out his prescription. Since a biological malfunction needs a biological corrective, the remedy must obviously be found in the biological laboratories in the form of some substance which will somehow reconcile our unique reasoning power with our primitive instincts. Molecular chemistry must come to the aid of humanity before Man destroys himself (and perhaps all other life on Earth). The psychopharmocologists must produce some sort of hormone pill which will promote cerebral co-ordination, harmonise thought and emotion, 'restore the integrity of the split hierarchy' – and, in short, put us back (although Koestler certainly does not say so, and certainly will not thank me for my interpretation) in that garden planted by the Lord God 'eastward in Eden'.

But might not the New Adam get for his pains (just like the Old Adam) rather more than he bargained for?

And is there not something odd (not to say 'materialistic, crankish, or naïve') to find the great defender of the free human spirit who attacked the devotees of the drug cult so trenchantly (and warned his friend, the unfortunate Timothy Leary, so wisely against the futility of looking for enlightenment in magic mushrooms, hallucinogenic cacti, and other substances synthesised in labora-tories) demanding a psychopharmacological pill for universal salvation?

How is this extraordinary aberration to be explained?

Writing to me on 31st May 1974 about Koestler's work, his old friend and fellow-Hungarian the late Professor Dennis Gabor said that Koestler

'. . . once told me: "I want to die a satisfied agnostic."'

On the evidence of the strain of distinct but unformulated religious sentiment that runs through all Koestler's best and boldest work, and of the arguments in the final part of *The Ghost in the Machine*, I interpret that remark of his to Gabor as indicative not of complacency but of an overwhelming desire to rationalise out of existence that sense of dread and awe which, on his own showing, haunted his childhood. In his advocacy of psychopharmacological salvation, he was in my opinion acting against his own true nature and shielding his eyes from the brightness of divinity (or the blackness of the void) with a shade of dubious composition.

Seven years ago Dennis Gabor ended that letter to me, from which I have already briefly quoted, as follows:

> 'There is no doubt that in the last decade a psychological change has happened in Arthur. He *did possess* a scientific-analytical mind. I not only knew this but *felt it* by the strong resonance every bit of his earlier writing evoked in my own mind, which I think can be described as simple scientific-technological. I know my own limitations and I know that I can be wrong – who knows, perhaps he has seen the light which I cannot see?'

Perhaps Koestler had. But it seemed to me as I read the book before its publication in London, and then as I wrote my review of it, that Koestler, having been almost blinded by the light which we can all see, most of us faintly, was attempting to dim it (if not to switch if off) by means of a 'scientism' no less dangerous – and in its potential probably much more so – than that of the cocksure scientists, technologists, psychologists, philosophers and totalitarian political scientists against whom he had struggled so bravely ever since the god of the great Marxist-Leninist heresy had failed him.

* *

*The Ghost in the Machine* was discussed in *The New York Review of Books* at great length, in close detail, and with his usual scrupulous care by Koestler's friend (and probably most sympathetic, though rigorous critic), Dr Stephen Toulmin, the philosopher of science. It was clear from his opening paragraph not merely that he had taken the book with all the seriousness it demanded, but also that he had penetrated to the core of it:

> 'What do we demand of Science? Vitamin-reinforced bread and astronautical circuses; *Genesis* according to Hoyle and the Revelations of Teilhard the Divine; piecemeal, tentative theories about those aspects of nature that we can now bring into focus; or a bit of all three? That question must not be answered in a hurry. For all three ambitions – technological, theological and philosophical – have been operative throughout the development of scientific thought, and its history could be written with an eye to the changing balance between them.'

It was true, he observed a little later that many

'. . . tough-minded scientists . . . dislike having science linked with theology even more than with technology, regarding their tender-minded colleagues' effusions about Creation, or design, or freewill, as a mark of soft-centeredness for which Science herself (Hagia Sophia) is in no way responsible. Still: from the time of Newton until barely a century ago, the theological aims of science were accepted as co-equal with its theoretical aims, so that "natural theology" was an institutionalised element in the scientific enterprise itself . . . Natural Theology has become wholly "disestablished" from the Kingdom of Science only in the twentieth century.'

One healthy effect of this, according to Toulmin, was that

'. . . it has made scientists intellectually responsive to one another's judgements, not only about the doctrines they are ready to assert, but – more important – also over the questions about which rational judgement must be for the moment suspended. In this respect they have gone beyond Socrates, for whom maturity lay in the personal acknowledgement of that he did not know, to the position of Cusanus. Wisdom lies, for them, in the institutionalisation of ignorance.'

Toulmin developed and illustrated this criticism in great detail. He had read, he said, the conclusion and climax of the book several times, and still could find no real connection between Koestler's prescription for a Pill to cure human folly and 'scientific evidence' (Toulmin's inverted commas) adduced in its support. The climax of an argument occupying three large books was only a demand for

'. . . a new, superior tranquilizer or "mental stabilizer" with which we are to control our own brains, rather than change our children's. But why do we need all the preceding argument to prove what a drink or phenobarb will demonstrate – that applied biochemistry can help to settle the nerves.'

Toulmin went on:

'I have good reasons for insisting that, in the last resort, Koestler's book must be considered not as science, but as theology. Scientifically, there is never sufficient reason for choosing one world-view rather than another; and there are usually good arguments for suspending judgement and declining the choice. If Koestler had written throughout in the spirit of Leibniz rather than Goethe – simply emphasizing the need to supplement "mechanicist" explanations of physiological structures by "organicist" analyses of the functions and activities of the systems concerned – things would then have been very different. The result might then have been to improve our understanding, but it would have led to no message.'

Having written his review, but before its publication, he received a letter from the publishers' publicity director, above whose signature was glued a red, heart-shaped pellet. In *The Ghost in the Machine*, it ran, Koestler

'. . . proposes a pharmaceutical solution to man's self-destructive urge:

a pill to correct the streak of paranoia inherent in man which, in this post-Hiroshima age, must inevitably lead to extermination.

'The birth control pill can save man from outbreeding himself. The pill which Arthur Koestler foresees can save man from genocide.

'If there were such a pill – a "peace" pill – would you take it?'

Toulmin reproduced this as a postscript to his review, adding three comments:

'. . . This sort of publicity speaks for itself, since it uses the language of quackery, not of science.

'The claims made for this imaginary pill are oddly like those Leary makes for LSD, and the arguments against them are the same – that a pharmaceutical millennium would only threaten our capacity for moral and intellectual judgement, and accelerate our return to the world of *Darkness at Noon*.

'Finally, if there were such a pill, would Arthur Koestler take it?'

For myself, in agreement with Toulmin but from a somewhat different point of view, I cannot think of any argument strong enough to support Koestler's Faustian plea for a cupful of transformation from some Mephistophelean alembic. It reminded me of a passage in *Arrow in the Blue* where he is describing himself and his romanticism at the age of twenty-five:

'It is all a matter of character alchemy. Mix in a mortar an acute sense of loneliness with an obsessive thirst for absolute values; add to this an aggressive temperament, sensuality, and a feeling of basic insecurity that needs constant reassurance through token victories; the result will be a fairly toxic potion.

"*A bellyful of this witches' brew*
*And every wench is Helena to you*,"

as Mephisto remarks . . .'

If Koestler had been wounded by Toulmin's adverse criticism of *The Ghost in the Machine* any more deeply than by Medawar's attack on *The Act of Creation*, he showed no signs of distress. On the contrary, he entered with zest into a phase of productivity which, as I write these lines, is very far from ended. And if he had been disturbed by the hostile attitude of certain academic scientists, psychologists, philosophers, sociologists and politicians, there were many consolations.

Sometime earlier he had been strongly tipped as a likely recipient of the Nobel Prize for Literature, largely, I gather (not from him), on the basis of *Darkness at Noon*. In the event, it was denied him, whether because of Sweden's delicate position as a tremulous 'bridge' between East and West, or for some other reason, I do not know. But in the middle of January 1968 he received a letter from the Rector of Copenhagen University to say that he was to follow Winston Churchill, Bertrand Russell, and Laurence Olivier as the fourth recipient of the Sonning Prize

'. . . in recognition of your contribution to literature and European culture in general, which in so many ways has stimulated the European debate . . .'

His acceptance address, conflated with a paper read in September of the following year at the fourteenth Nobel Symposium in Stockholm, *The Urge to Self-Destruction*, may be read in his collection, *The Heel of Achilles: Essays 1968–1973*.*

The spring of 1968 was spent in organising 'The Alpbach Symposium', a gathering of distinguished academics concerned in greater or lesser degree with the 'emancipation of the life sciences from the mechanistic concepts of nineteenth-century physics, and the resulting crudely reductionist philosophy.' Koestler was somewhat disappointed by its failure to produce a 'coherent alternative world-view', but in other respects it was successful.

In November, after completing – together with the academic psychiatrist J. R. Smythies – his editing of the transcript, he read a paper, 'Rebellion in a Vacuum', at a symposium in Queen's University, Kingston, Ontario, later receiving from the Chancellor, together with Pierre Trudeau and René Durbos, an honorary Doctorate of Law, his first academic distinction. He was awarded the degree *honoris causa* as one

> '. . . trained as a scientist, widely travelled journalist, author of novels and of many essays, incisive critic of a powerful ideology which he had the courage both to espouse and to renounce; who has concentrated his gift of imagination, scientific insight, and compassion to explore how in his inner ways a man may outface cynical violence and all assaults upon the body and the mind; who lived undefeated at the storm centres of the corrupt and disastrous years and came to a new home with his haunting sense of wonder unimpaired, and resolutely led his writing in a clear arc from *Darkness at Noon* to *The Act of Creation* . . .'

From North America he and Cynthia left for a tour of Australia (his impressions of which, according to the Australian High Commissioner in London, formed 'a picture . . . which no Australian, and few visitors who know my country, would recognise') and the South Pacific. They returned westward by way of Puerto Rico, where he took part in a symposium organised by the American College of Neuropsychopharmacology, arriving in Europe in time for Koestler to take the chair at another symposium on *Drugs and Addiction*, at the Duttweiler Foundation in Zurich.

* *

In September the edited transcript of the Alpbach Symposium was published in a volume of almost five hundred absorbing (though often densely technical) pages under the title *Beyond Reductionism: New Perspectives in the Life Sciences*. These pages amount to a sledgehammer attack on 'the four pillars of unwisdom', as Koestler in the final session described the doctrines that had come under close examination:

'1. That biological evolution is the result of nothing but random mutations preserved by natural selection;

* London, 1974.

'2. That mental evolution is the result of nothing but random tries preserved by reinforcements;
'3. That all organisms, including Man, are nothing but passive automata controlled by the environment, whose sole purpose in life is the reduction of tensions by adaptive responses;
'4. That the only scientific method worth that name is quantitative measurement; and, consequently, that complex phenomena must be reduced to simple elements accessible to such treatment without due worry whether the specific characteristics of a complex phenomenon, for instance, Man, may be lost in the process.'

In his organisation of the symposium, Koestler had obviously been at his persuasive best; and the transcript shows how impressively and fluently he could discourse and dispute with experts in various disciplines – and in their own technical languages. He did not push his notion of psychopharmaceutical salvation on this occasion. Indeed, he seemed to be backing away from it slightly.

Koestler started off the discussion:

> '. . . may I make a factual correction, or the whole discussion will be distorted. I never asked or wished for a drug to block aggression; on the contrary: what I asked for and wished for is a drug which blocks devotion, that fanatical loyalty to a leader, to a flag, to a creed, the hypnotic suggestibility of the mass-mind which caused all the major disasters of history.'

To which Professor Kety, slightly taken aback, it would seem, replied:

> 'Well, actually that is even harder. We may find a drug that might block aggression – but loyalty, that is an effect that is so subtle and so complex, I don't even begin to see that pharmacology . . .'

At this point he was interrupted. Perhaps he was grateful for the interruption. At any rate, there was little, if any, further attention paid to the theory of universal salvation by means of 'Peace Pills'.

*Beyond Reductionism* is, to my mind, an immensely stimulating and inspiriting work. As Gerald Leach concluded in his review in the *Observer*:

> 'if any reductionists are planning a public comeback they will be foolhardy if they launch it without first countering all the arguments and evidence collected here.'

In the final session at Alpbach, Paul Weiss observed that he and his fellow-participants owed Koestler 'a tremendous debt of gratitude.'

So, I think, do we all.

# CHAPTER XXXVII

# *1969–*

IT MAY BE EVIDENT to the reader that I am not entirely in sympathy with the sharp change of course taken by Koestler's mind in the latter half of the sixties. For that reason, and also – quite apart from the question of my competence – because I am myself indifferent to the so-called 'psi-factor' in all alleged paranormal phenomena such as telepathy, psychokinesis, precognition and the like, I hope that I may be forgiven if the last part of my biographical account is offered in summary form.

That there is a book to be written about Koestler's researches and speculations in this field (where, as I have suggested elsewhere, he seems to be attempting to escape from the Pentateuch and the Gospels), I have no doubt. But I am not the man to write it; and I say this not merely because of my prejudices (and ignorance, too, no doubt), but also because of my respect for, and admiration of this 'representative European intellectual's' achievements in those other fields in which I am rather more at home.

* *

Of the books begun and abandoned during 1969, one (to quote Cynthia)

> 'was to be about Semmelweiss, the doctor who abolished puerperal fever in his hospital in Vienna by insisting that all doctors and nurses wash their hands before tending to patients in childbirth. But this novel idea was not accepted by the medical profession and Semmelweiss came to a tragic end. As Semmelweiss was a Hungarian, Arthur had the advantage of being able to read material in Hungarian, a secret language to most people. Alas, the documentation was sparse. A biography of Mesmer against the background of the times was another still-born idea – the material, too, was scant, and Arthur was disappointed in Mesmer as a person.'*

Something, however, was to come of another idea he toyed with in London and Alpbach during that busy year – a satirical-tragical-farcical novel about the scholars travelling (like himself now) from symposium to symposium: academic 'call-girls', he nick-named them.

* *Op. cit.*

> 'During the summer . . . he wrote, among other things, two short stories ("The Chimaera" and "The Misunderstanding"), which later became the Prologue and Epilogue to *The Call Girls*. "The Misunderstanding" he sketched out entirely one evening after dinner over a bottle of wine. After-dinner ideas were frequently rejected the morning after. But "The Misunderstanding" was an inspiration which he dashed off in the heat of the moment the following day – a rare thing for a slow writer like Arthur. The idea that Christ had wanted to die to draw God's attention to the sad state of the world was one he had had at the back of his mind for several years. I heard him trying it out one evening on an old friend, a Jungian analyst, and had thought he would one day write an essay on the subject.'

During November he delivered a paper in London at a conference of the World Psychiatric Association – on the provocative question, 'Can Psychiatrists Be Trusted?' Next came a lecture at the Cheltenham Festival in which he spoke of

> 'a recurrent pattern in the history of science and art in which, broadly speaking, both seem to move through cycles of Revolution-Consolidation-Saturation-Crisis and New Departure.'

In literature as in science, he argued, the law of diminishing returns could be circumvented only by the application of the principle of *reculement pour mieux sauter*.

Coming to a stop in his draft of *The Call Girls*, he applied the principle to himself, put the manuscript on one side, and looked round for another subject. He had for some time been thinking of writing an essay on Paul Kammerer. This Austrian zoologist of distinctly Lamarckian leanings had committed suicide after being accused of faking the results of an experiment on a toad designed to prove that acquired characteristics could be genetically transmitted. Kammerer was also a supporter of Jung's theory of 'synchronicity' – i.e., a principle which purported to give purposive and a-causal meaning to a sequence of otherwise apparently meaningless coincidences. This made him an even more attractive subject for Koestler.

Cynthia may now take up the story. As she and Koestler were

> 'spending four weeks in January and February in Alpbach, he decided to ask a research student and translator at the University of Innsbruck, who had transcribed the tapes for *Beyond Reductionism*, to see what material she could dig up on Paul Kammerer, starting with the obituaries. The obituaries from the Viennese papers arrived a week later. The suicide note alone showed that Paul Kammerer was no ordinary person. The quest for Kammerer became an intriguing work of detection, and grew into a book – *The Case of the Midwife Toad*. His obsessive feelings were divided between the figure of Kammerer and the background – the birth of Neo-Darwinism. When he had told the story of the forgery of which Kammerer was accused, Arthur then turned to Kammerer's fat book, *The Law of the Series*. He had read it as a student and

always been intrigued by it. As he delved into "confluential events", he got more and more involved in ESP and in ESP and physics. He had not studied the progress of physics beyond the 1920s; when he brought that knowledge up to date, it made his mind boggle. The book began to grow, but it grew out of hand. It seemed to be turning into two books. Once more, Arthur could not make up his mind what to do. He thought he could solve the problem by having two parts: Part I – The Case of the Midwife Toad, and Part II – Psi. But still he was not happy. And where did the chapter on "The Law of the Series" go? He was reminded of his mistake in making one book out of Parts I and II of *The Act of Creation* (to solve a publishing difficulty) and of *The Ghost in the Machine*. And the same was the case with *Spanish Testament* (the first part political, the second – *Dialogue with Death* – introspective). In December, when he was well into the ESP bit, he at last cut the nerve between the two intended parts. He revised the first draft of *The Case of the Midwife Toad*, put "The Law of the Series" into an appendix, and finished the book by the end of the year.

'Part II – "Psi" – became *The Roots of Coincidence*. He now gave this a rest and went back to *The Call Girls*. It was not until March 1971 that he was to take up the threads again of *The Roots of Coincidence*, at a time when he got stuck with *The Call Girls*. *The Roots of Coincidence* was finished at the end of March.

'Since 1937, when he was in prison in Spain, Arthur has been interested in ESP. The chapter "Hours at the Window" bears witness to his long-standing belief in the power of mind over matter. In *The Sleepwalkers* he describes the mysticism of Kepler which led him to formulate his Three Laws. Trinity: "the sun represents the Father, the sphere of the fixed stars the Son, the invisible forces which, emanating from the Father, act through interstellar space, represent the Holy Ghost". And: "Thus a purely mystical inspiration was the root out of which the first rational theory of the dynamics of the universe developed". In the Epilogue he writes: "At the beginning of this long journey, I quoted Plutarch's comment on the Pythagoreans: 'The contemplation of the eternal is the aim of philosophy, as the contemplation of the mysteries is the aim of religion.' For Pythagoras as for Kepler, the two kinds of contemplation were twins; for them philosophy and religion were motivated by the same longing: to catch glimpses of eternity through the window of time."

'Tucked away in Appendix II of *The Act of Creation* is an essay on "Some Features of Genius" (both this Appendix and Appendix I were almost thrown out altogether, as they did not fit into the mainstream of the book). This part deals with the mystical or metaphysical quest of the scientist – from the Greeks to Pasteur. Arthur calls the Greek attitude to science "a quest transcending the mortal self". In Benjamin Franklin's case, like Kepler, "a mystical conviction gave birth, by analogy, to a scientific theory". And Maxwell: "In this case, too, religious belief became a spur to scientific activity . . . The connection between Maxwell's religious and scientific views is indeed just as intimate as in the case of Franklin or Kepler". Lastly, Pasteur: "In old age he would often browse in his earlier publications. Turning the pages of his writings, he would marvel at the lands that he had revealed by dispelling the fogs of ignorance and overcoming stubbornness. He would live again his exciting voyages, as he told Loir in a dreamy voice: 'How beautiful, how beautiful! And to think I did it all. I had forgotten it.'"

'During the time of Pope John, Arthur was attracted to Roman Catholicism. I remember one evening his brother-in-law, Arthur Goodman, who was a Catholic, expressing doubts about his religion. Arthur made such a moving dissertation about the beauty of symbolism in the Catholic faith that his brother-in-law, whose doubts were real, was quite overwhelmed. Arthur was equally vehement about not taking that symbolism literally.

'On the other hand, as he says, with his head in the clouds, he likes to keep his feet planted firmly on the ground. Mysticism *per se* is not enough for him; indeed it disgusts him. In a discussion with a Jungian friend, he once said that he believed in wading into the sea with one's feet in the sand as long as one could. Only when the water got too deep was it permissible to float. He divided people into waders and floaters.'*

* *

*The Case of the Midwife Toad* was published in 1971. It was favourably received, especially by those who were becoming known (in certain circles) as 'the Koestler clique'. Others, like Professor J. M. Thoday of the Department of Genetics in Cambridge University, were less enthusiastic. Thoday's review† was coldly dismissive. Following a lengthy, dispassionate, and close examination, he concluded:

> 'The author of this book is the same man who wrote that notable essay, "The God that Failed". Is he still unable to recognise that scientific truth is not to be judged by the motivations of scientists, nor by whether one likes what one thinks are its consequences, nor by its consonance with any faith, but is only to be approached by a painstaking attention to the factual evidence, to the logical justification of interpretations of that evidence, and, most essentially, to the design and execution of experiments that test these interpretations?
>
> 'It is certainly a good thing that old work that has been dismissed should be reviewed from time to time, but this is not the way to do it. It is to be hoped that Koestler will not now see fit to write an apologia for Lysenko.'

Undeterred by this magisterial rebuke, Koestler continued his researches into the 'Psi-Factor', and when they were completed and the book drafted (*The Roots of Coincidence*), he turned his attention once more to the neglected manuscript of *The Call Girls*.

In the autumn of 1971 he sold his house in Alpbach, the *Schreiberhäusel*, having decided to look once more for a country retreat in England. He and Cynthia found one during January 1972 in the depths of the Suffolk countryside, not long after he had appeared in the New Year's Honours List as having been made CBE, a Commander of the Order of the British Empire.

Paul Maclean wrote to congratulate him on *The Case of the Midwife Toad*, and

* *Op. cit.*

† In *Heredity*, Vol. 28, Part 2, 1972.

added a note about his pleasure on reading during New Year's Day that the Queen had decorated Koestler with the MBE. Koestler put him right amusingly:

> 'Thank you for your letter of January 6th with your misguided reference to an MBE. This is given to slimy bureaucrats with a reptilian brain. Next comes the OBE, which is a lower mammalian attribute. Then comes the CBE (Commander), given to people supposedly endowed with the rudiments of a neo-cortex. It is at the same time the lowest rung on the snob ladder. So I am consulting my lawyers whether to sue you for slander.'

In April he started work on the part of the book, *The Challenge of Chance*, which he was writing in collaboration with Sir Alister Hardy and Robert Harvie – a development of the attack on 'mere chance' he had launched in *The Roots of Coincidence.*

He also found time during that hectic year to go to Reykjavik and cover for the *Sunday Times* the farcical chess world championship match between the title-holder, Boris Spassky of Russia, and Robert Fischer of the United States. He seems to have enjoyed it.

Later in the year he took part in a symposium organised in Amsterdam by the Parapsychology Foundation, and in September delivered a paper on *Science and Para-Science* at the Foundation's convention in Edinburgh.

Later still he received, and accepted with pleasure, an invitation to write the article on *Wit and Humour* for the XVth edition of the *Encyclopaedia Britannica.*

* *

*The Roots of Coincidence* was published early in 1972.

'*NO HEADS IN THE SAND*' was the heading of Nigel Dennis's admiring review in the *Sunday Telegraph*, an oblique reference not to Koestler's well-known views on England's political ineptitude but to his Lamarckian observations of the curious callosities on the backside of the ostrich. '*EXTRA SENSORY BEE IN KOESTLER'S BONNET*' announced the favourable views of William Cooper as expressed in *The Times Higher Education Supplement.*

And so on . . .

The book was certainly no more, as Koestler's old friend Philip Toynbee wrote in the *Observer*, than

> 'a comparatively minor posting station on this particular pilgrim's progress'.

Of much less esoteric interest was his satirical *conte*, *The Call Girls*. It may be taken as the expression of his disappointment at the failure of the Alpbach Symposium to yield a new and generally acceptable *Weltanschauung*. But his disappointment did not weigh heavily upon him. It was also (to quote myself)

> '. . . a brief but comprehensive satire on those peripatetic academics who can never resist the temptation to air their well worn ideas at foundation-sponsored conferences.'

And it showed that he could, after all, laugh at himself (or smile at any rate).

* *

The following year, 1973, saw the completion and publication, with much more gratifying publicity of *The Challenge of Chance*. For some time interest in alleged 'paranormal' phenomena had been growing, and it was now not only merely respectable but positively fashionable to take an intelligent interest in telepathy, Unidentified Flying Objects, inexplicable coincidences, spoon-bending and the like. It was amusing to see how many of the reviewers, like Cyril Connolly in *The Sunday Times* and Philip Toynbee in the *Observer*, slipped in their own bits of anecdotal 'evidence' – although the latter, to be fair, took care to distance himself from those who

> '. . . use "paranormal" where "supernatural" would do just as well, if not better . . .'

Out of respect for Koestler and his colleagues in the exercise, I shall refrain from quoting Brigid Brophy's ferociously funny description of it in *The Listener* under the heading, 'A Classic Non-Contribution to Knowledge'.

In 1974 Koestler's latest collection of occasional pieces – a few papers delivered on the 'call-girls circuit', a great many brief book reviews, and some light travel-pieces – was published under the title of *The Heel of Achilles*.

It amounted to a somewhat insubstantial re-working of themes which by this time tended to droop like the psychokinesiologist Uri Geller's spoons and forks. A few reviewers took advantage of the invitation implicit in the title and aimed their barbs at Koestler's heel. A particularly sharp arrow flew from the little bow drawn in the *Evening Standard* by Patrick Cosgrave:

> 'The work of Arthur Koestler is, in the most literal sense of the word, soulless . . . What is, of course, causing the decline of the West at the moment is not the lack of any dully scientific desire for improvement of the kind Koestler advocates, but the decline of our spiritual, soul-based consciousness of values and rules beyond our rational comprehension, a decline to which such as Koestler have made a major contribution with the silly mechanism of their physiological arguments.'

That must have stung, but he had, after all, made himself an easy target for smart young archers like Mr Cosgrave, who ended with a quiverful:

> 'The pity of it is that, according to his credits, his bombastic addresses are invariably delivered to the highest councils of the medical and scientific professions, which leads us to suppose that all these solemn folk who created our modern scientific age are pretty shallow after all, and quite incapable of putting forward proposals worthy of consideration regarding the behaviour or the improvement of man.'

In July 1974 he was made a Companion of Literature, an honorific title invented in the first place for Churchill, I believe, by the Royal Society of Literature, of which body he had long been a Fellow.

The following year saw his seventieth birthday, marked by the publication of a *Festschrift*, *Astride the Two Cultures: Arthur Koestler at 70*, in which the best contributions by far were the simple, unaffected and vivid memoir by Cynthia (from which I have already quoted copiously) and a particularly acute appreciation of *Darkness at Noon* by the late Goronwy Rees. Koestler must have smiled wryly as he read Rees's essay, for, as his friend and editor, Harold Harris, remarked in his introduction,

> '. . . it has always seemed to me that recognition of his contribution to science has meant far more to him than the much wider international reputation he enjoys as the creator of one of the great novels of the twentieth century.'

In 1976, Koestler hastened to publish *The Thirteenth Tribe*, a speculative work of historiography which suggested that the greater part of modern Jewry – the Ashkenazim, that is – is ethnically Caucasian rather than Semitic, being descended from the Khazars, a Turkish-speaking people along the lower Volga who were converted to Judaism in the eighth century of the Christian era. It was a thesis greeted with less than universal enthusiasm.

Leon Wieseltier's sceptical review in *The New York Review of Books* ended with a flourish that can only be described as indubitably Jewish:

> '. . . Arthur Koestler is of course free to go his own way, but not because his grandfathers roamed the steppes. He is no Khazar. The evidence for his Jewishness rests not in the ratio of his blood cells, nor in his Hungarian birth – the Magyars emigrated from Khazaria in the ninth century – but in the much less controvertible fact that only a Jew would have taken so much trouble to come up with an alibi for his own self-effacement.'

* *

His next published work was *Janus: A Summing Up*, a systematic condensation of those speculations, hypotheses, theories and systems which he had developed over the years. It was indifferently received, largely, I think, because the effort of summarising and systematising such a plethora of ideas had given the result a distinctly dogmatic air; and also, no doubt, because of his curious explanation of the accidental genesis of man as an unfortunate mistake on the part of Evolution and his suggestion of correcting the error, by means of a 'Peace Pill' – not to mention his subsequent expeditions into the tangled scrub and boggy thickets of the 'paranormal'.

Mary Warnock (one of the most readable of the Oxford philosophers, and wife of another) reviewed the book critically – but not at all patronisingly, although she obviously considered the non-Platonic features in his theory (i.e., the bits about the 'tumorous overgrowth' of our neo-cortices and the notion of a Pill to put them in their proper place) rather odd.

She found the final and metaphysical (or 'theological', as Dr Toulmin would, a little less accurately, have described it) part of the book strangely moving – with its hints of some mysterious and occult world (? heaven) in terms of which the familiar worlds of perceptions and concepts might one day be reconciled and rendered intelligible. Mrs Warnock was not, unlike some fierce critics, unsympathetic. Far from it. But, she concluded,

'. . . how extremely un-English it all is. Descartes, Leibniz, Goethe, Teilhard de Chardin, Jacques Monod, George Steiner – one can list endless Europeans who have claimed to explain everything, to bring all science and all history into one enormous system. But only poor Coleridge, struggling with his vortices, has represented the UK in this sport, and he cannot be thought to have been very successful. No gold medals for him. As a spectator sport it may appeal to many. But to participate in it, one needs a head for heights and indifference to pitfalls which few of our countrymen seem to have . . . And the elevated view we are asked to take of the human scene, far higher than a mere Olympian view, since it takes in other galaxies, even other spaces, as well as our own, may seem in the end to lead to nothing but vertigo. For my part, like Hume, I would rather have a game of backgammon; or even Racing Demon.'

There is the voice – civil, cool, witty and clear as a bell – to be heard in the middle of that enviable Anglican (I do not use the word exclusively in its ecclesiastical sense) *via media* which Koestler, in his rather exasperated way, admired – but along which he could never walk straight for any length of time.

And with her good-humoured remarks, we may now take leave of the subject of this biography, wondering what next he will surprise us with when he returns from his latest forays into the thickets and bogs that seem to be crowding in more menacingly than ever on our *via media*.

# *Bibliography*

1934 *Von Weissen Nächten und Roten Tagen* (White Nights and Red Days). This account of Koestler's travels in the Soviet Union during 1932 and 1933 was to have been published in Russian, German, Ukrainian, Georgian, and Armenian editions. In the event, however, only a truncated version of his original German text was issued in Kharkov by the Ukrainian State Publishers for National Minorities.

1937 *Menschenopfer Unerhört* (Unprecedented Human Sacrifice). A propaganda work about the Spanish Civil War published by Willy Muenzenberg's Editions du Carrefour in Paris, which also issued a French version entitled *L'Espagne ensanglantée* (Bloodstained Spain). *Spanish Testament*, the English version published in London towards the end of the year, also contains Koestler's account of his imprisonment in Spain, *Dialogue with Death**, written shortly after his release. It is this latter part which has survived, the first and earlier propaganda section having been suppressed.

1939 *The Gladiators**

1941 *Darkness at Noon**

1941 *Scum of the Earth** (the first of his works to be written in English).

1943 *Arrival and Departure**

1945 *The Yogi and the Commissar** (a collection of essays and articles written between 1941 and 1944).

1945 *Twilight Bar: An Escapade in Four Acts* (a play first performed in Paris in 1946).

1949 *Insight and Outlook: An Inquiry into the Common Foundations of Science, Art, and Social Ethics*. (This book, long out of print, sets out most of the themes dealt with more systematically in later works.)

1949 *Promise and Fulfilment: Palestine 1917–1949.*

1950 (With others) *The God that Failed: Six Studies in Communism*, introduced by Richard Crossman

1951 *The Age of Longing**

1952 *Arrow in the Blue** (the first of two volumes of autobiography, ending

with his application in December 1931 to join the Communist Party of Germany).
1954 *The Invisible Writing** (the continuation of his autobiography, ending with his escape from France in 1940, via Casablanca and Lisbon, to England. His experiences in 1939 and 1940 are covered more fully in the earlier *Scum of the Earth*).
1955 *The Trail of the Dinosaur** (a collection of essays and articles written between 1946 and 1955).
1956 Reflections on Hanging* (bound up with *The Trail of the Dinosaur* in the Danube Edition).
1959 *The Sleepwalkers: A History of Man's Changing Vision of the Universe**
1961 *The Lotus and the Robot**
1961 (With C. H. Rolph) *Hanged by the Neck: An Exposure of Capital Punishment in England*
1963 (Editor) *Suicide of a Nation: An Enquiry into the State of Britain Today*
1964 *The Act of Creation**
1967 *The Ghost in the Machine*
1967 Article on *Johannes Kepler* in *The Encyclopaedia of Philosophy* (New York)
1968 *Drinkers of Infinity* (a collection of essays and articles written between 1956 and 1957).
1969 (Editor, with J. R. Smythies) *Beyond Reductionism: New Perspectives in the Life Sciences: The Alpbach Symposium*
1971 *The Case of the Midwife Toad*
1972 *The Roots of Coincidence*
1972 *The Call-Girls*
1973 (With Sir Alister Hardy and Robert Harvie) *The Challenge of Chance*
1974 *The Heel of Achilles* (a collection of essays and articles written between 1968 and 1973).
1974 Article on *Humour and Wit* in the 15th edition of the *Encyclopaedia Britannica*
1976 *The Thirteenth Tribe*
1978 *Janus: A Summing-Up*
1980 *Bricks to Babel: Selected Writings with Comments by the Author*
1981 *Kaleidoscope*

*Note: Titles marked with an asterisk are available in the uniform Danube Edition which Hutchinson began to issue in 1965.

## *A Note on Sources*

As I explain in the Preface, I have drawn heavily in the early part of my narrative on Koestler's four volumes of autobiography or chronicle. It would seem unduly pedantic to give chapter and verse for every excerpt from (the Danube Edition of) these works, to which the reader hitherto unfamiliar with Koestler's life will naturally wish to turn. It is enough here, therefore, to indicate that the indented passages between pp 4 and 16, and on pp 73, 74, and 280 are from *Arrow in the Blue*; those between pp 50 and 73, and on pp 127 and 128 are from *Scum of the Earth*; and those between pp 20 and 50, and on pp 115, 116, 174, and 175 are from *The Invisible Writing*.

Passages quoted *passim* from his other writings are as follows: on pp 17 and 18 from *The God That Failed*; on pp 80, 81, 82, and 83 from *The Yogi and the Commissar*; on p 84 from *Arrival and Departure*; on pp 121, 123, 141, 157, 166, 181, 187, 189, 190, 207, 251, 252, 253, 254, 255, 256, and 259 from *The Trail of The Dinosaur*; on pp 154 and 155 from *Promise and Fulfilment*; on pp 281, 282, 296, 297, 299, 300, and 301 from *The Sleepwalkers*; on pp 283, 284, 285, 286, and 287 from *Insight and Outlook*; on pp 291, 292, 293, and 294 from *The Lotus and the Robot*; and on pp 333, 334, 335, and 336 from *The Act of Creation*.

The greater part by far of my primary sources (including the seven-eighths invisible beneath the surface of my text) are Koestler's papers (and reminiscences, recorded or otherwise) and the late Mamaine Koestler's papers.

Other secondary and a few primary sources are identified either in the text or in footnotes. (It will be understood, I hope, that some of my primary sources have had, for reasons of tact and discretion, to be left unidentified.)

Excerpts from various writings of George Orwell are for the most part taken from *The Collected Essays, Journalism and Letters* . . . (London, Secker & Warburg, 1968), as follows:—*Volume II*: in *Koestler* p 81, *Orwell* p 384; K p 82, O p 256; K p 86, O p 235; K p 87, O pp 243 and 244. *Volume IV*: K p 105, O pp 17 and 18; K p 106, O p 76; K p 107, O pp 120 and 121.

There is no space available to list the books consulted in the preparation of this book. Even if there were, it would no doubt be pretentious to do so. To say as much may itself seem pretentious. So be it.

# Notes

*Page* xii *'Mamaine's letters to her twin . . .'* — I first learned of the existence of this collection, covering in much detail most of the years of Mamaine's life with Koestler, from Mrs Celia Goodman after she had read in *The Times Literary Supplement* that I was engaged on the work. Following a friendly and useful discussion, she had them all photocopied at my suggestion so that without mutilating the orginals she could delete such very private confidences which she would not wish me or Koestler or anyone else to read. That done, she sent the material to me *via* Koestler who had hitherto declined Mrs Goodman's invitations to read them. For him it must have been a most moving, and occasionally an extremely painful, experience. It would have been understandable had he objected to, or at any rate expressed some reservations about, Mrs Goodman's making available to me such intimate documentation. Whatever his feelings, however, he did neither at that time and passed on the entire collection to me without comment, except for a number of marginal notes identifying some of the *dramatis personae* and elucidating certain allusions which would otherwise have been obscure. Occasionally, while reading early drafts of chapters in which I made much more copious use of Mamaine's correspondence than appears in the version as published, Mrs Goodman would suggest that perhaps I should delete this or that passage as reflecting badly, and possibly unfairly, on Koestler. Whenever I told Koestler of this, he told me to let the passage stand. In the event I respected Mrs Goodman's wishes.

5 '*neither had the slightest vestige of the ghetto mentality.*' — And only a trace of it remained in Koestler's paternal grandfather who had fled from the Pale into Hungary for some unknown reason during the Crimean War. During his walks in the Budapest parks with his grandson, the old man sometimes bought the young Koestler a ham sandwich, a delicacy of which the child was especially fond. When Koestler asked him why he did not buy one for himself, his grandfather replied enigmatically that it was because he 'had been brought up in prejudice'.

6 '*New inspiration came with the emergence of Vladimir Jabotinsky . . .*' — 'Emergence' is hardly the *mot juste* for Jabotinsky's position at this period in his astonishing career as journalist, poet, orator, soldier (founder of the Jewish Legion during World War One, and organiser of the Haganah in Palestine after it), linguist, Ukrainian nationalist, anti-Bolshevik, anti-Nazi, and for a time supreme commander of the Irgun Zvai Leumi. As founder and head of the Jewish youth movement, Betar, he had for many years before Koestler met him been an inspiration to scores of thousands of young Jews throughout Eastern Europe. His copious writings under the pen-name of Altalena had given him a reputation far beyond orthodox Zionist circles, and his growing militancy in the early twenties strengthened his position immensely among those, like Koestler, whose consciousness of their ethnically Jewish identity was at odds with their distaste for Yiddish and the dogmas, rituals, and customs of Judaism, and who were increasingly impatient with the cautious policies and bureaucratic complexities of the official World Zionist Movement led by Chaim Weizmann.

Koestler's associates in the foundation and leadership of the Austrian branch of Jabotinsky's World Union of Zionist Revisionists were Paul Diamant, Benjamin Aksin, and J. Herrlinger (who later, on emigrating to Palestine, hebraicised his name to Mareni). Writing to me during March 1974, Dr Mareni expressed his surprise that Koestler had not written much more fully about his Zionist activities in Austria during his student days. 'I believe he underestimates the importance of those activities . . . Debates between the two groups, i.e. the followers of Weizmann and those of Jabotinsky, continued throughout the year in Vienna . . . they sometimes degenerated into brawls, as in the case of a threatened sabre duel between Dr Diamant and Dr Schabel, Koestler and myself having been chosen as seconds to Dr Diamant . . . Koestler was active in organising new groups. Among those the women's organisations in Wiener Neustadt and Kornenburg were particularly important since they became in later years, when both Koestler and I had left Austria, the centre of Jewish actitivities in those places . . . Professor Benjamin Aksin of the Hebrew University, Jerusalem, Koestler and myself are the only surviving members of the Action Committee which in turn created the ideological basis for the two groups of partisans leading the main battle against the British Administration in Palestine: the Irgun Zvai Leumi (National Military Organsation) and the Lechi (Fighters for the Liberation of Israel, and known to the British as the Stern Gang after its founder, who had broken away from the Irgun after Jabotinsky's death). The successor to these organisations is the Likud . . . which won a third of all seats at the last parliamentary elections (1974).'

7 '*In his inaugural speech to the Knesset in June 1977, Menachem Begin quoted Jabotinsky's saying . . .*' — The context is especially interesting when it is recalled that Jabotinsky had, in his own words, 'no inner contact with Judaism' and had 'never breathed the atmosphere of Jewish cultural tradition' in his youth. Begin quoted the whole passage:

'The true core of our national uniqueness is the pure fruit of the Land of Israel. Before we came to Israel we were not a nation and we had no existence.

On the soil of the Land of Israel, from the fragments of diverse tribes, was the Hebrew nation formed. On the soil of the Land of Israel did we grow up. Upon it we became citizens, we fortified the faith of the One God, we inhaled the breath of the land, and in our struggle for independence and rule we were enveloped by its atmosphere. The grain that flourished on its soil sustained us. It was in the Land of Israel that the concepts of our prophets developed, and in the Land of Israel the Song of Songs was first uttered. All that is Hebrew within us has been bestowed upon us by the Land of Israel. Everything else that is within us is not Hebrew. The People of Israel and the Land of Israel are one.'

That was and remains the chief inspiration of Jabotinsky's most famous disciple and successor, Menachem Begin, who more than any other transformed the Ukrainian's romantic nationalism – or 'racism' – into hard-headed determination to see that Eretz Israel would be coterminous with *all* Palestine. It was also, of course, Koestler's inspiration in the first flush of his Zionist enthusiasm after he had discovered that he was 'Jewish' and therefore 'different' from those in whose culture he had been reared. Even when he had renounced Zionism with a vehemence which led many of his former associates to think of him as anti-Semitic, he still had a soft spot for the militant heirs of Jabotinsky for whom the Land of Israel was Palestine undivided.

14 '*But even if Koestler had been emotionally much more mature than in fact he was, it is unlikely that his work would have allowed him to develop a lasting relationship with Bébé or any other woman.*' — In his recollections, Koestler is decently discreet about his sexual affairs. He is no kisser-and-teller, and it is quite obvious that in his relations with women he was motivated not by the mere love of conquest but rather, as in his philosophical and political preoccupations, by an immature and intensely romantic thirst for the absolute. *Das Ewig-Weibliche zieht uns hinan.* In *Arrow in the Blue* there is an unflattering self-portrait of the author at the age of twenty-five when he enjoyed, as Herr Redakteur at Ullstein Verlag, not merely an imposing desk, a secretary of his own, and two telephones, but three or four concurrent mistresses. But he still felt himself to be immature, spiritually empty, desperate to find the perfect cause – and the perfect love.

'The phantom that I was after is as old as man: victory over loneliness through the perfect physical and spiritual union. Surely a modest aim? And certainly not an original one . . . Mix in a mortar an acute sense of loneliness with an obsessive thirst for absolute values; add to this an aggressive temperament, sensuality, and a feeling of basic insecurity that needs reassurance through token victories: the result will be a fairly toxic potion.

*A belly full of this witches' brew*
*And every wench is Helena to you,*

as Mephisto remarks to Faust, and Mephisto after all is the most understanding and sympathetic character in Goethe.'

Time and again he thought he had found the real Helena (see pp 20 and 30 above). But Helena, once deprived of her magic and mystery, always depressingly resolved herself after an hour, a week, and in rare cases a month or two, into a sister figure – and so taboo!

18 *'My mind, for a moment, was blank. Then a name occurred to me, and I said "Ivan Steinberg . . ."'*, — What made him think of 'Steinberg' – 'stony mountain'? Suddenly he remembered a psychoanalyst in Palestine, Dr Har-Even, who had urged him to return to Vienna and resume his studies, warning him that if he failed to do so he would forever remain 'a runaway and a fugitive'. *Har* in Hebrew means 'mountain', and '*Even*', 'stone'. It was the 'language of destiny', Koestler recalled many years later, that had come unbidden to his tongue.

19 *'It was by such means that the innumerable Comintern* apparats *were at the time fishing for the hearts and minds of liberals . . .'* — With what success we are still being reminded as ostensibly respectable members of the 'Establishment' are revealed as traitors who have purchased immunity from prosecution by 'cooperating' with their interrogators. *Plus ça change* . . . however, and the latest Soviet-inspired and, to some extent, manipulated 'peace campaign' flourishes even more spectacularly than its predecessors before and after World War Two.

23 *'After three weeks in Baku, where he had an unhappy love-affair . . .'* — With a stunning 'Helena' with 'soft brown hair which shimmered in the light of the candle, and a profile of classic purity . . .' She was employed by the town Soviet as a clerk with the Water Board and was suspected by the local GPU officials and one of their narks, a weaselish German who befriended Koestler, of being a '*spionka*' – a spy, or at any rate, an unreconstructed *bourgeoise*. Koestler, jumping to the conclusion that the girl had abstracted a document from his pocket, denounced her to the GPU's German nark. Knowing nothing of this, the girl took leave of him on the quay as he embarked for Krasnovodsk on the Turkestan shore of the Caspian. As the ship drew away, he was crushed into a stupor of apathy by misery, remorse, and guilt. But before long he was stirred out of his apathy by the onset of acute physical discomfort. From this Helena's embraces he had contracted the clap – which he accepted 'without shock or surprise, with only an aching tenderness for the slim, lonely figure left behind on the quay . . .' He never saw her again. He wrote many letters to her, which were unanswered. He never learned what became of her. And he was never to forget her.

24 *'At Ashkhabad, the capital of Turkmenistan, where there was no hotel, the GPU found a cell-like room for him in the* dom sovietov *. . .'* — As he lay dejected on his bed he heard the strains of *My Yiddishe Momma*, sung by Sophie Tucker, coming from a gramophone in the adjacent cell. He got up to investigate and so made the acquaintance of Langston Hughes, the young black American poet whose work he had read and admired in Berlin. Hughes had come to the USSR to write the script for a propaganda film about the state of the blacks in the United States – a project quashed by the United States' diplomatic recognition of the USSR. Now, as a consolation prize, he was enjoying (or enduring) the

same itinerary as Koestler. In his 'autobiographical journey', *I Wonder as I Wander* (New York, Hill & Wang, 1944) Hughes gives a vivid and amusing account of his first encounter with Koestler in Ashkhabad and their subsequent pilgrimage to Merv, Bokhara and Tashkent.

27 *'I began to write the play then and there . . .'* — After three vodkas, as he explains, and inspired also by the German refrain of the popular song which the café orchestra was playing:

> '. . . If you love me you must steal for me,
> And tell me fairy tales of a happy land . . .'

Two creatures from outer space arrive and tell the world that only happy planets have the right to exist and that if mankind cannot abolish its misery within three days it will be painlessly liquidated. A Dictator of Happiness, a crazy poet, is given absolute power. 'And lo, it works . . . money is abolished, authority is abolished, all taboos are smashed, all curtains raised.' Alas, the spacemen are impostors without power to enforce their ultimatum. So mankind deposes the Dictator of Happiness and sinks back into its customary miseries.

*'Soon after his arrival in Budapest he gave the typescript of the play to a friend, Andor Németh.'* — Németh was an agreeable and exceedingly eccentric writer and editor who had given generous encouragement to Koestler in his juvenile attempts at authorship.

28 *'Early in September . . . he . . . started work at . . . the headquarters of Willy Muenzenberg, the Comintern propaganda chief in Western Europe.'* — Muenzenberg was a propagandist of genius, the equal of his adversary Goebbels. Born in Thuringia in 1889, he left school at an early age and laboured for six years in a shoe-factory. Later, working in a pharmacy in Zurich, he made the acquaintance of Lenin, Trotsky, and other Russian exiles who converted him. Expelled from Switzerland in 1917 he joined the *Spartakus-Bund.* When the Spartacist revolt had been crushed and Karl Liebknecht and Rosa Luxemburg executed, he rose effortlessly through the international Communist movement. By the time Koestler came under his wing, he was controlling from his headquarters in Paris an enormous propaganda empire known to all Communists and fellow-travellers as the 'Muenzenberg Trust'. His greatest achievement, probably, was the invention of the camouflaged 'front organisation' which netted (and still nets) scores of thousands of the ignorant, naïve, and well-meaning 'progressives'. On the executive committees of its various ostensibly philanthropic offshoots sat, as Koestler writes, 'highly respectable people, from English duchesses to American savants, who had never heard the name of Muenzenberg and thought that the Comintern was a bogey invented by Dr Goebbels'. He is still remembered with admiration and affection by ex-Communists who saw the light a little before him and were not important enough, perhaps, to pay for their defection with their life as he did.

29 *'His cousin Theodore from Budapest unexpectedly turned up in Paris where he had established a French publishing house.'* — This was in fact Francis Aldor. He and his brother traded in London under the name of Aldor Books. Koestler's books published under his cousins' imprint were hack works produced at top speed to keep the pot boiling – simmering, at any rate – but it should be said that they were respectfully and favourably reviewed by such eminent pundits as are accustomed to hold forth on such matters.

33 *'At this stage, Dorothy's brother, Ernie . . .'* — Ernie in due course vanished into the Gulag Archipelago, never to be heard of again. The Party had forbidden Koestler to have any dealings with Swiss Communists, but at the home of the German-Swiss novelist, Jakob Humm, they were able to keep in touch with the true faith. There Koestler met for the first time Ignazio Silone, whose first book, *Fontamara*, had been an immediate success. For some years Silone had been distancing himself from the Communist Party and so declined to join the *Fraktion* in the ostensibly literary 'Humm Circle' in Zurich – one of the innumerable *Fraktionen* in similar intellectual coteries throughout the Western World, working to create a climate of public opinion '. . . favourably or at least benevolently neutral, to the Great Social Experiment in Russia and its Western extension, the People's Front against War and Fascism'. Koestler, who had read and immensely admired *Fontamara*, had eagerly looked forward to meeting Silone at one of the Humms' soirées, but in the event '. . . found him a kind but very reserved person, wrapped up in himself, surrounded by a soft but impenetrable cloud of melancholy and depression. To my great disappointment I was unable to find any real personal contact with him.' And so it was to remain. Whatever Silone's view of Koestler, he could neither understand, or was bored by, his admirer's attempts to arrive at a warm personal relationship with him. But, of course, southern Italians are a realistic breed not at all given to romantic enthusiasms.

35 *'But . . . bohemian Budapest . . . could not for long provide adequate compensation for the strain of frenzied work by which Koestler was earning his living. He decided to return to Paris.'* — There he got a part-time job with a 'press agency' *L'Agence d'Information Inter-Continentale*, which had recently been opened by a fellow-Hungarian, Alexander Rado. It was, of course, a propaganda outfit, relying heavily for its material on the Comintern's political intelligence branch. The cobbling of two or three 'news-letters' a week seemed a fairly pointless exercise to Koestler at the time, since none of the newspapers to which the articles were sent ever seemed to pay. It was not until 1949, when Koestler read Alexander Foote's *Handbook for Spies* that he learned what an important figure Rado was in the Kremlin's spy network. In 1937 Rado moved to Geneva where under cover of a partnership in an old established firm of mapmakers, he became director of the Red Army intelligence station. Through one of his agents, Rudolf Pressler, he succeeded in establishing direct contact with the German High Command. In 1943 when both the *Abwehr* and the Swiss security service were closing in on the network, Rado suggested to Moscow that he should seek asylum in the

British Legation and continue operations behind the screen of diplomatic immunity. The British welcomed the idea but Moscow vetoed it and Rado had to go into hiding until the liberation of Paris. After a fortnight of interrogation at the Soviet Military Mission about the breakdown of the network, he and Alexander Foote, who had been his deputy, were instructed to leave for Moscow in the first Soviet aircraft to take off from Paris after the liberation. The aircraft touched down at Cairo to refuel and Rado disappeared. According to Foote, Russian agents succeeded in tracking him down and bringing him to Moscow where he was 'shot for negligence in allowing his cipher to fall into the hands of the Swiss police, for falsely reporting that the network in Switzerland was liquidated, and for embezzling some fifty thousand dollars'. His efforts to obtain British protection had come to nothing. He was, it seemed, just one of the hundreds of thousands whom the Allies allowed to be delivered to the Soviet firing-squads or to slave camps. In *The Invisible Writing* Koestler wrote a bitter epitaph for his old friend and benefactor: 'Alex Rado, the gentle, lovable, scholarly, master-spy, was one of the victims of the occident's guilty ignorance and homicidal illusions.' Rado, however, had not been shot. He survived to write an account of his activities, *Codename Dora* (translated from the German by J. A. Underwood and published in London by Abelard in 1977). In this there is no mention of being summoned to Moscow or going to ground in Cairo; but while he cites a number of authors who are critical of Foote's *Handbook for Spies*, he does not himself refute his deputy's story. In his epilogue he writes:

'I now live and work in Socialist Hungary, the goal for which I joined the Communist Party more than half a century ago. In 1955, after a series of protracted and difficult ordeals and after more than 36 years spent abroad I was at last able to return home.' He reveals nothing about those 'protracted and difficult ordeals' – in the Gulag Archipelago, no doubt.

37 '"*In the end Otto* [*Katz*] *suggested,* faute de mieux, *the London* News Chronicle . . . *Otto had friends on the paper's staff* . . ."' — Otto Katz, who later adopted the name André Simon, was Willy Muenzenberg's right-hand man. In 1952 he was hanged in Prague as 'a British spy and Zionist conspirator'.

53 '*Koestler, Leo Valiani, a member of the Italian anti-Fascist underground* . . .' — In *Scum of the Earth*, Valiani is called Mario.

61 '*But Father Piprot* . . .' — Father Piprot, who is called Darrault in *Scum of the Earth*, wrote to Koestler from Paris seven years after the débâcle:

'Dear Friend,

'This is Father Darrault (alias Piprot . . .) who is writing to you!

'The "metteur-en-scene raffiné" has made you a writer and me a reader . . . Your faithful recollections touched me deeply. But I must tell you that our meeting is also vivid in my memory. In my mind's eye I can see that little group of exhausted soldiers arriving at the barracks (and what barracks!) . . . You had two bottles of Bordeaux in your haversack and you called us over to have a drink.

Something I said caught your attention and you asked me point-blank, "Are you a priest?" Yes . . . "A Catholic priest?" Yes. You opened the second bottle "I can talk to you?" But of course. "Now?" Whenever you like. You left the uncorked bottle with your comrades, telling them to finish it, and we went out into the passage. "Can I talk to you in complete confidence?" You know very well that you can talk to a priest in total confidence. "Yes, I know. Excuse me. But, you know, in certain circumstances . . ." Don't worry; carry on frankly. "I must tell you something first . . . because then you may not wish to hear my confidences." That would really surprise me, but let us see. "I am a Jew." At first I was speechless so I simply embraced you. Then I told you that I had many Jewish friends. "Not all priests are like you." I'm trying to reassure you, I said, but you're sceptical. "That's not all . . . I've something else to say before talking to you and maybe this time you'll be shocked." You hesitated . . . I have come out of prison." I explained to you that I had been a chaplain to ex-prisoners, and it was then that we talked of the "Metteur-en-Scene". You were relieved and relaxed and able at last to speak freely . . .

'It will not surprise you if I tell you that every day since that first meeting I have prayed for you. After our separation I constantly asked the "Metteur-en-Scene" to look after you . . . My prayers are not for your "conversion", believe me, but simply those of a friend into whose heart you have entered and where you remain.'

62 '. . . *a friendly official directed them to Mr E. E. Bullen, the English chief accountant of the Société Shell du Maroc*' — Thirty-eight years later, Mr Bullen, living in retirement at Southend-on-Sea, happened to read the Danube edition of *Scum of the Earth*. He addressed a letter to the publishers, Hutchinson, and asked them to forward it to Koestler, 'because,' he wrote, 'I am sure he would be interested to know that one of Ellerman's pawns of 1940 is still alive and kicking.' In his reply Koestler wrote that he was 'delighted to hear from you again and I am glad to let you know that I am also still alive and kicking . . . As a test of my own memory, may I ask you a silly question: am I right in thinking you are or were ginger-haired . . .?' 'Yes,' Mr Bullen confirmed, 'I was ginger-haired, and still am, on my covered parts.'

Bullen had been put in touch with 'Ellerman', who had come to Casablanca from Lisbon after the fall of France to organise escape routes for British soldiers, by the general manager of Shell in Morocco, Monsieur A. Fanvelle, an ardent Anglophile. When the agent's position in Casablanca became too risky, he handed over to Bullen who was able to carry on for several months. But in April 1941 he was arrested by the Vichy Chief of Police and put in '*residence forcé*' at Ifrance in the Atlas mountains. A year later he escaped, made his way to Lisbon, and thence to England.

74 '*During their first meeting in 1941, Strachey asked Koestler . . .*' — In Strachey's book *The Strangled Cry* (London, The Bodley Head, 1962) he gives an amusing account of that first meeting: 'In the spring of 1941, I was serving as the Adjutant, or maid-of-all-work of No 87 Fighter Squadron of the Royal Air

Force at that time stationed near Bath. One day a pilot opened the door of the Mess and said, with disinterest, "Someone to see the Adjutant." There entered the rumpled battle-dressed figure of Arthur Koestler of the Pioneer Corps, surely one of the oddest men ever to dig a British latrine.' Discussing *Darkness at Noon*, he observes that 'When it was published . . . the book . . . broke friendships, split families . . .'

Hugh Thomas in his biography of Strachey (London, Eyre Methuen, 1973) describes the effect of the book on Strachey's wife, Celia. She 'had found D. at N. (sent to her by Strachey) unbearable, and nearly had a breakdown in the spring of 1941. She had, however, in consequence "slid out" of Communism, though she never became anti-Communist and never made a really sharp break. That meant a clash with some of Strachey's new friends. For example, Strachey had been in the habit of dropping in to see Arthur Koestler for a talk and a drink at his house in Tryon Street on his way back to St Leonard's Terrace from the Air Ministry. But one night he rang up Koestler and said, in his matter-of-fact voice: "Arthur, I'm afraid that my nightly visits to you will have to stop. Celia cannot stand you, and you see that I'm really in a position of having to choose between you and her. I'm sure you will understand that I shall have to choose her." Afterwards, however, Strachey and Koestler met surreptitiously. (Koestler was naturally distressed.)'

76 '*"Cyril," says Koestler, 'took me under his wing . . .'* — In a light-hearted moment he tried his hand at English verse, composing a metrically uncertain 'Blackout Ballade' which he dedicated to Cyril Connolly. The first verse gives the rather surrealistic flavour:

'Never were the stars so bright, so green the slits of traffic-lights
In Wadi Piccadilly.
The fog is merely alcoholic, the Yankees even are bucolic,
Each tart is like a lily
Of the valley of Piccadilly.

'*It was a busy time for Koestler . . .*' — Among his various activities was the writing of a light-hearted column for the *Evening Standard* at Michael Foot's suggestion. Lord Beaverbrook invited him for a weekend in the country. 'In the morning,' Koestler recalls, 'he was huddled under a bundle of rugs outdoors in the pale sunshine. We talked about the Soviet Union, and to my objections he said: "Arthur, I believe in Uncle Joe. Uncle Joe is a democrat."' So his first weekend with Beaverbrook was also his last.

94 '*He had no definite news of his mother . . . but assumed that she too had been deported to Auschwitz.*' — Mr Saul David of Beverly Hills, California, has a vivid memory of Koestler at the Jerusalem home of Gershon Agronsky. 'I was a young Stars and Stripes correspondent traveling (at that moment) with Edgar Ansel Mowrer. Heady company for me.

'Also present that afternoon and evening was a gentleman whom I remember as the head of the state radio under the Mandate – an Englishman of the English.

'We talked a lot and drank while we talked. The conversation was entirely one of those conversations – the Mandate, the Balfour Declaration, the Nazis, the Jews, the Arabs and illegal immigration . . . round and round and round.

'I recall two things Koestler said. At one point, predicting the eventual success of the Zionists, he said ruefully that such a success would destroy that nervous, homeless Jewish intellectual who had been the civilizing conscience of the Christian world – and replace him with a race of "Jewish Tarzans". I was struck with the image, apparently coined at the moment. Later I read it somewhere in his writings and I have wondered since how rehearsed it might have been. The reason for such wondering comes from the other memorable Koestler remark that day.

'He had gotten into a spirited argument with the English official whom he addressed familiarly as Ronnie. Ronnie had been making the reasoned points about fairness to the Arabs, a balanced British foreign policy and the long view – all in a cool on-the-one-hand-and-yet style favored by colonial administrators discussing the passions of lesser breeds. Koestler listened and got increasingly irritated. I remember wondering if it was the drinking when he burst out in an impassioned interruption. He denounced the callousness of the icy logic imposed on people who were at that moment desperate and dying for lack of a place to go. He thundered like an authentic Old Testament prophet, demolishing the other man's position if not his argument. Ronnie stuttered and stopped. Koestler stopped. Ronnie murmured something about the unfairness of Koestler's argument. Koestler apologized but said it was impossible to be cool about such matters "when your mother has been baked in an oven in Lublin". That did it. No more argument.

'Later, Koestler having left, I said something to either Mowrer or Agronsky about that explosive moment and that terrible rejoinder. Whoever it was laughed and said "Koestler was right – but his mother was not baked anywhere. She is alive and well . . ."

'It was a marvelous truth-in-theatre moment. I have never been able to make up my mind whether Koestler meant us to believe, whether he had phrased it so as to deceive without falsehood or whether his dramatic sense had simply carried him away.'

102 '*There were signs . . . that if partition were enforced, the leaders of the Arab League would confine themselves to vocal protests.*' — Koestler's analysis was countered by the Arab League's able spokesman in London, Edward Atiyah, who denied that the Arabs could ever be reconciled to any partition of Palestine. Nor would the Zionists, he added, except in the naïve optimism of the gullible, be satisfied with what they got. 'Already their ambitions extend beyond Palestine and the Arab states know this. To give them a national base from which to extend and promote these imperialist ambitions would have the most unfortunate and incalculable consequences in the Middle East.'

112 'Darkness at Noon [le Zéro et l'infini] *had become a phenomenal success in France.*' — General de Gaulle – *le solitaire de Marly* – had read it at a sitting and

let it be known how highly he thought of it. The French Communist Party played their part in getting it to the top of the best-seller list and keeping it there. Local branches all over the country were instructed to buy up all copies as they appeared in bookstores and destroy them. But for all their dedicated zeal, they could not keep up with the public demand and the publisher's ability to meet it. Within a few weeks 200,000 copies had been sold.

116 *'Early in September Koestler went up to London . . .'* — That was a few days after the first anniversary of their moving into Bwlch Ocyn, an occasion celebrated by Mamaine in verse:

Bwlch Ocyn, Manod, Blaenau Ffest-
Iniog, Merionethshire – you've guessed,
'Tis the abode of ARTHUR K.
One year ago this very day

K, who from sunnier climes had come,
To make in CAMBRIA his home,
Arrived with MERMAID to begin
With her a life of carefree sin . . .

118 *'He knew also . . . that he would never again feel entirely at home . . . among people like Sartre and Simone de Beauvoir . . .'* — A large part, perhaps the greater, of the intellectual community consisted of Communists and fellow-travellers, and those like Jean-Paul Sartre and Simone de Beauvoir who were nominally independent but also unwilling to confront the Communists directly. Sartre's system of atheistic existentialism, with a strong admixture of romantic nihilism, but leaning in practice towards Marxism, was becoming a popular cult among young people. The outlook was bleak.

The early pages of Madame de Beauvoir's autobiographical *Force of Circumstance* (*La Force des choses*) display her interest in Koestler. Before the war she had read with approval *Spanish Testament*. In 1945 Cyril Connolly had given her an account of Koestler's success in England. Albert Camus lent her *Darkness at Noon* which she read at a sitting. Her account, however, of how the tumultuous newcomer burst into the *Temps Modernes* group is a nice balance of admiration and condescension. In the Pont Royal, she writes, he accosted Sartre with 'Hallo. I'm Koestler.' At their next meeting: 'In a peremptory tone softened by an almost feminine smile, he told Sartre: "You are a better novelist than I am, but not such a good philosopher" . . . That day we were a bit embarrassed by his self-taught pedantry, by the doctrinaire self-assurance and the scientism he had retained from his rather mediocre Marxist training. This embarrassment persisted . . . Success had gone to his head; he was vain and full of self-importance. But he was also full of warmth, life and curiosity; the passion with which he argued was unflagging; he was always ready, at any hour of the day or night, to talk about any subject under the sun. He was generous with his time, with himself, and also with his money; he had no taste for ostentation, but when one went out with him he always wanted to pay for everything and never counted the cost.'

*Force of Circumstance* had been preceded by an equally lengthy novel, *The Mandarins*, which covers the same period and also deals in great detail with the intellectual élite of Paris. In spite of the customary disclaimer that all the characters and situations are fictitious, it is obviously inspired by, if not precisely based on, fact; and Koestler is clearly recognised in the character of Scriassine, with whom the narrator has a brief and unsatisfactory affair.

119 '*In the middle of October Mamaine announced that she was about to leave for Paris . . .*' — She did not enjoy the frantic social round and it was not long before she was noting that 'I am at the moment in a state of profound melancholia in which even to write this letter is an almost superhuman effort . . .' Her spirits revived sufficiently to enable her to write an amusing account of a dinner party with André and Madeleine Malraux. 'The dinner started with oysters, and the Malrauxs had the bizarre idea of drinking whiskey with them till I said that this would very likely cause the immediate death of all, whereupon they suggested gin fizz! . . . Particularly fascinating was the spectacle of K and Malraux together – K unusually humble and hardly able to get a word in edgeways, Malraux obviously very anxious to impress K . . . [Malraux] talked mostly about politics – he is *franchement Gaulliste* (as is K with certain reservations) . . . He gives the impression of being very inhuman and impersonal, and it is difficult to see how anyone ever establishes an intimate contact with him; this is also the opinion of K though he knows Malraux well and they get on with each other.'

This was true also of Koestler and Camus, but with Sartre and Beauvoir it was a different matter. According to the latter, 'touchy, tormented, greedy for human warmth, but cut off from others by his personal obsessions – "I have my Furies," he used to say – Koestler's relations with us were always fluctuating . . .'

Of the full-blooded, card-carrying Communist authors, none was more hostile to Koestler than Louis Aragon who succeeded in preventing Koestler from giving a press conference at the premises of the Writers' Association. The reason he gave for this was that Koestler had been interned in Le Vernet and should never have been allowed to return to France. Perhaps he considered that Koestler had earned under false pretences the distinction of having been incarcerated in the company of so many loyal Communist supporters of the Hitler–Stalin alliance?

125 '*They returned to Paris . . .*' — They dined again with Malraux who explained his support for General de Gaulle. Mamaine recorded: 'When K. said "What about the General's entourage?" Malraux replied "*L'entourage du Général, c'est moi.*"'

127 'In the last days of 1947 Koestler completed *Insight and Outlook* and handed it over to Cyril Connolly to read . . .' — On 19th September 1965 the

*Sunday Times* published the transcript of a conversation between Connolly and Koestler in which there was the following exchange:

*Connolly:* '. . . your present preoccupation with science, it is really with interpreting science to the layman, isn't it? You don't strictly write for the scientist?'
*Koestler:* 'I try to avoid jargon and write for a large public, but the research in it . . .'
*Connolly:* I mean in the sense in which Bertrand Russell's *History of Philosophy* was written for a large public?'
*Koestler:* 'No. That *is* a popularising book. That, I am afraid, you have never understood, Cyril. It was a misunderstanding when I gave you *Insight and Outlook* to read. You then said, I remember, "Why do you waste your talents writing popular science?" But *The Sleepwalkers* is not popular science, it is a reinterpretation of the history of the philosophy of science written with as little jargon as possible, and as little technicality as possible. And *The Act of Creation* is, on the one hand, a frontal attack on that school of psychology and philosophy which dehumanises man's behaviour and on the other on logical positivism. But on the positive side it is, for better or worse, an original theory.'

151 '*The ship, the* Altalena . . .' — This, it will be recalled, was Jabotinsky's pen-name.

154 '*As the work continued, Koestler became increasingly irritable . . .*' — His old friend Teddy Kollek had become hostile, and David Ben Gurion was even more forthright about what he regarded as Koestler's dislike of the country and the people. In his autobiography, *Growing Up on The Times* (London, 1978), Louis Heren, in Israel as *The Times*' special correspondent, writes that 'Koestler's respect for the Irgun was further enhanced by his dislike of Ben Gurion and what he saw as the ghetto heritage of the older generation of Israeli politicians whom he despised. For him, their intolerance and self-righteousness diminished their impressive early achievements as settlers. He had a poor opinion of the Hebrew language and believed that Jewish religious practices were an invitation to anti-Semitism. He seemed at times to argue that with the creation of Israel its citizens should cease to be Jewish.'

158 '*Those curious results . . .*' — André Malraux in his *Antimemoirs* (trans. Terence Kilmartin, London, Hamish Hamilton, 1968) writes that General de Gaulle 'knew after the euphoria of the Liberation, that for millions of men he was their alibi'.

'*Koestler and Mamaine had decided . . .*' — It was characteristic of Koestler, although he had his book on Palestine and the birth of the modern State of Israel to complete before starting work on the novel that for some time had been gestating, that he should choose to live near the 'centre in which the chronic stresses of Europe become acute'.

After the war Koestler, like all foreigners who had served in the British Army, became eligible for naturalisation. He refused to apply, however, as Ernest Bevin's policy on Palestine had put him in a state of split loyalties. He was eventually naturalised on 7th January 1949, after the State of Israel had been established. His four sponsors were Dick Crossman, Michael Foot, Sylvester Gates (his former chief at the Ministry of Information), and John Strachey.

165 '*Two or three days passed before the newspapers got hold of the story . . .*' — The *Voix Ouvrière* of Geneva elaborated it with a few nice flourishes: 'The individual known as Arthur Koestler, a feeble and talentless writer, forgotten today, but who was clever enough to sell his books a couple of years ago by reviving an anti-Communism slightly dampened since the victory of Stalingrad, is trying again, as best he can, to get himself into the news . . . defending "true socialism" against the "brutish Communists". This pure representative of the "Western conscience" and anti-Communism is to be charged with drunkenness and disorderly behaviour.'

'"*Here is weekly digest no 1. The Crossman anthology* [The God that Failed] *is just out . . .*"' — In his introduction Crossman explained that the book 'was conceived in the heat of argument. I was staying with Arthur Koestler in North Wales, and one evening we had reached an unusually barren deadlock in the political discussion of which our friendship seems to consist. "Either you can't or you won't understand," said Koestler. "It's the same with all you comfortable, insular, Anglo-Saxon anti-Communists. You hate our Cassandra cries and resent us as allies, but when all is said, we ex-Communists are the only people on your side who know what it's all about . . ."'

166 '*Most reviewers of* The God that Failed *singled out Koestler's contribution . . .*' — The other contributors were Ignazio Silone, André Gide, Richard Wright, Louis Fischer, and Stephen Spender.

177 '*Arrived in Berlin. . .*' — They had been surprised to find as they boarded the train at the Gare de l'Est that the French security service had provided them with a bodyguard. There was another surprise awaiting them on the train. In the next compartment was Jean-Paul Sartre en route to a gathering of playwrights in Frankfurt. 'There being no restaurant on the train,' Mamaine noted, 'the police commissaire at the station had ordered for us boxes containing food and wine from the station buffet, so we invited Sartre, the bodyguard, and two Poles (Czapski and the editor of the magazine *Kultura*), who like us were en route for Berlin, to join us in our compartment and share our meal. This was our first meeting with Sartre since diplomatic relations between him and K. were broken off about 18 months ago. Sartre now doesn't drink at all but lives on Corydrane [a benzedrine-type stimulant drug] and was looking rather ill. However, he was as gay as ever, though said he hardly ever goes out now in the evening as it's so difficult to find anybody he agrees with about politics.'

Berlin, which Koestler had not visited for eighteen years, impressed him immensely. 'Post-war Paris,' he noted in his diary, 'was dim and drab but the people had only become a shade more asocial and *débrouillard* and public life only a few degrees more corrupt and fratricidal. The great lie of the Resistance had eaten itself into everybody's mentality so that the atmosphere was and had remained unreal, charged with an aggressiveness rooted in impotence and guilt . . . The way Berlin reacted to its incomparably more tragic experiences of the last ten years is so different that one would be tempted to believe the Nazis about the superiority of the German race . . .'

195 '*Out of the intensive planning – most of it directed and much of it actually conducted by Koestler himself* . . .' — This is undoubtedly the only conclusion to be drawn from the documents in Koestler's archives which were my primary sources; and it is a conclusion which was not questioned by Koestler when he read the draft. Others, however, I should add here, take a different view, including the official who floated the idea of the Congress for Cultural Freedom long before Ruth Fischer had heard of it (possibly from Franz Borkenau and Melvin J. Lasky during her meeting with them in Frankfurt). I have also had the following comment from someone intimately concerned with CCF, but who had not been present at the Berlin gathering: 'I should say that I was astonished by Arthur's account of his activities. It was contrary to everything which I had heard from a number of active participants.'

199 '*Mamaine then left for England* . . .' — Shortly before, she had dashed off a jubilant letter to Celia: '. . . wonderful news: we have decided to go and live in England . . . Of course further changes of plan are always possible on K's part . . .' They were!

202 '*Most enjoyable journey via Iceland and Greenland ring Ma* . . .' — Mamaine went to see Koestler's mother in Hampstead. '. . . the poor old thing spent half the time saying you never wrote to her, and the other half saying she wished she saw more of me. I do feel sorry for her and am going to make more effort.'

'I hear of you through my dear Mamaine,' Mrs Koestler wrote to her son, 'I can't tell you how much I love this charming person . . . I am so glad that Mamaine is in London. It compensates a little for my longing for you.'

232 '*By the following morning Koestler, recalling . . . in particular the absurdities to which Michael Polanyi had recently been subjected* . . .' — At this time the US consular service was notorious for its inflexibility in denying visas to anyone who might even have come within smelling-distance of a Communist. The British press at the time was full of complaints and protests. There is no doubt that some of the loudest protesters were indeed 'crypto-Communists' or fellow-travellers who had been rumbled. But there were many who had been guilty of nothing more heinous than accepting a flattering invitation to become a patron or honorary committee member of what seemed to be an impeccably 'good cause' which was later exposed as a Communist 'front'. This had happened to

Professor Polanyi – than whom it would be difficult to imagine a more unlikely Soviet agent.

250 *'In the first of these . . .'* — In this essay Koestler reproduced the greater part of the transcript of a lengthy conversation between Maurice Carr and himself which had been published in the *Jewish Chronicle* in 1949. Mr Carr's final questions in that interview were: 'Do you still regard yourself as a Jew? Do you wish others to consider you as being no longer a Jew?' Koestler's reply began: 'In so far as religion is concerned, I consider the Ten Commandments and the Sermon on the Mount as inseparable as the root and the flower.' And it ended: 'I regard myself first as a member of the European community; secondly as a naturalised British citizen of uncertain and mixed racial origin, who accepts the ethical values and rejects the dogmas of our Heleno-Judaeo-Christian tradition. Into what pigeon-hole others put me is their affair.'

279 *'In the autumn . . . Koestler bought an old farmhouse, Long Barn . . .'* — It was an odd coincidence that led Koestler, with his preoccupations, to this particular house. Nicolson had let it to Charles and Anne Lindbergh when, following the trial of the man accused of the kidnapping and murder of their first child, they fled to England to escape the remorseless attention of reporters and photographers. It was here that they heard the news on the wireless of the convicted man's electrocution. It was here that Lindbergh wrote his glowing accounts of the National Socialist regime. And in 1939, when Lindbergh had returned to the United States to preach the invincibility of the Nordic master-race, Koestler was in Le Vernet, suspected of still being a Comintern agent (and so *ipso facto* an ally of the National Socialist regime so much admired by Lindbergh). There is an excellent account of Lindbergh's activities in England and Germany during this period in Leonard Mosley's biography (*Lindbergh*, London, Hodder & Stoughton, 1976).

292 *'But he had scarcely started . . . when the arrival of a guest from India, Jayaprakash Narayan, directed his mind back to the East . . .'* — During his travels in India Koestler had met the ascetic Vinoba Bhave, who founded the *Bhoodan Vajna* movement, by which the wealthy were persuaded to make free gifts of land to the Harijans ('God's Children', formerly and less euphemistically known as Untouchables). The land reform so badly needed could be brought about, Bhave reasoned, by a change of heart rather than by revolution. By April 1954, the third anniversary of the movement's foundation, some three or four million acres had been donated to the landless. *Bhoodan Vajna* and its associated *Gramdan* (village cooperative) movements had certainly done much to quench some of the revolutionary fires then being busily stoked by Communists. It was appropriate, therefore, that Prime Minister Nehru should attend the anniversary celebrations in Bodh Gaya (the birthplace of Prince Sidhartha Gautama who attained enlightenment under the sacred peepul tree and so became the Buddha). Much more surprising was the declaration of the fiery Marxist revolutionary, Jayaprakash Narayan, that he had renounced politics, become a

disciple of Bhave, and intended henceforth to devote his life to the *Bhoodan* movement. The friends of the Congress of Cultural Freedom in India were understandably most interested in this famous convert. In London Koestler introduced him to a number of his influential friends, some of whom formed a Friends of Bhoodan Committee under the joint chairmanship of Professor Arnold Toynbee and Narayan. The idea of an urban *Bhoodan* was explored. Nothing came of it. In later years Narayan modified his adherence to *ahimsa* (the doctrine of non-violence) during the violent opposition to Indira Gandhi which led to her (temporary) eclipse. It is worth noting here that the egregious Scots-Canadian economist and exemplar of 'radical chic', Professor John Kenneth Galbraith, during his appointment as United States Ambassador to India, took an instant dislike to 'the friends of the Congress of Cultural Freedom' in that country, and promptly with great self-satisfaction saw to it that American financial aid to them was cut off.

294 *'So he wrote in his epilogue to* The Lotus and the Robot...'—'No one with any pretensions to intelligence should miss it,' *The Statesman* of Calcutta wrote of the book. That view was not shared by the Home Minister, Mr Lal Bahadur Shastri, who banned its importation on the ground that it contained 'objectionable remarks' about some of the Mahatma Gandhi's odder ideas about sexuality.

# *Index*

# INDEX

# INDEX

# INDEX

# INDEX

# INDEX